In the World

In the World
Reading and Writing as a Christian

John H. Timmerman
Donald R. Hettinga

BAKER BOOK HOUSE
Grand Rapids, Michigan 49516

I have given them your word and the world has hated them, for they are not of the world any more than I am of the world. My prayer is not that you take them out of the world but that you protect them from the evil one. They are not of the world, even as I am not of it. Sanctify them by the truth; your word is truth. As you sent me into the world, I have sent them into the world.

—Jesus' prayer for his disciples
[John 17:14–18, NIV]

Contents

Acknowledgments   11

Introduction: *Reading and Writing as a Christian*   13

Part 1 **Writing**

 1. Good Writing: *An Introduction to Rhetoric*   23

 2. Invention   29

 3. Structuring the Thesis   32

 4. Coherence   38

 5. Revision   43

 6. From Working Outline to Outline   52

 7. Documentation   57

Part 2 **Reading**

 8. Defining a Worldview: *Religion*   71
   Matthew Arnold, *Dover Beach*   74
   Bertrand Russell, *Why I Am Not a Christian*   76
   C. S. Lewis, *What Christians Believe*   85
   James W. Fowler, *Stages of Faith and Human Becoming*   96
   M. Howard Rienstra, *Who Is in Control?*   109
   Emily Dickinson, *Two Ways of Looking at God*   114
   Stephen V. Monsma, *Why I Ran for Congress*   116
   Dorothy M. Johnson, *Scars of Honor*   121

 9. Living Morally: *Ethics*   136
   Saint Augustine, *On Good and Evil*   139
   Lewis B. Smedes, *Why Get Married?*   146
   Cathy Stentzel, *A Quiet Conversion*   154
   Allen Verhey, *The Death of Infant Doe: Jesus and the Neonates, Mark 10:13–16*   161

John Donne, *No Man Is an Island* 174
Henri J. M. Nouwen, *A Place to Stand* 177

10. Exercising Stewardship: *Environmental Issues* 189
    Lynn White, Jr., *The Historical Roots of Our Ecological Crisis* 192
    Jay Van Andel, *No Silent Spring* 200
    James C. Rettie, *But a Watch in the Night: A Scientific Fable* 205
    Aldo Leopold, *The Land Ethic* 211
    Hugh Cook, *Pisces* 218
    Annie Dillard, *The Fixed* 231

11. Responding to Science 239
    Albert Einstein, *Religion and Science* 242
    Charles Darwin, *Natural Selection* 246
    Virginia Stem Owens, *And the Trees Clap Their Hands* 252
    Emily Dickinson, *"Faith" Is a Fine Invention* 258
    Philip Yancey, *In Defense of Pain* 259

12. Reading Literature 269
    Plato, *Censorship and the Nature of Art* 272
    John Gardner, *Moral Fiction* 289
    Flannery O'Connor, *Novelist and Believer* 294
    Nancy M. Tischler, *The Christian Reader* 302
    Thomas Howard, *On Evil in Art* 309
    Elva McAllaster, *Frater Ave Atque Vale* 314
    H. R. Rookmaaker, *Letter to a Christian Artist* 316

13. Using Language 322
    The Living Word: The Bible in Translation 325
    Henry Zylstra, *A Vital Language* 333
    Kathryn Lindskoog, *Pure Poppycock* 339
    John Steinbeck, *Profanity and Realism* 344
    George Herbert, *Jordan [II]* 353
    George Lakoff and Mark Johnson, *Metaphors We Live By* 355
    D. G. Kehl, *Have You Committed Verbicide Today?* 367

14. Understanding Ourselves in Relation to Society, Education, and Psychology 375
    Walter Wangerin, Jr., *The Empty Manger: A Christmas Story* 378
    Aleksandr Solzhenitsyn, *The Templeton Address: Men Have Forgotten God* 388
    Arthur F. Holmes, *The Liberal Arts: What and Why?* 398
    I. M. Cross, *You're Still Failing* 410
    John J. Timmerman, *Mr. Chips Couldn't Make It Today* 417
    Sietze Buning, *Long-Distance Compliments (from Father to Son)* 421
    Lillian V. Grissen, *His Path Is in the Sea* 425
    Raymond Grissen, *Toward Understanding Depression* 430
    John C. Blattner, *Jesus Will Give You Joy* 434

Rhetorical Index 443

Acknowledgments

The authors gratefully acknowledge the following colleagues who have read the text as it developed and whose comments and insights have helped shape it:

Lewis Archer, Whitworth College; Zenas Bicket, Evangel College; Norman Carson, Geneva College; David Chapman, Arlington Baptist College; Robert G. Collmer, Baylor University; Richard Cornelius, Bryan College; Daniel W. Doerksen, University of New Brunswick; Edward E. Ericson, Calvin College; Susan Gallagher, Calvin College; Rich Gray, Montreat-Anderson College; Paul Hesselink, Covenant College; Janet L. Larson, Rutgers University; Larry R. Long, Harding University; Elva McAllaster, Greenville College; Janice Neuleib, Illinois State University; Ann Paton, Geneva College; James Schaap, Dordt College; John W. Sider, Westmont College; Donn E. Taylor, Wayland Baptist University; George W. VanDevender, Hardin-Simmons University; Gene Edward Vieth, Concordia College; Eugene Warren, University of Missouri-Rolla.

Introduction

Reading and Writing as a Christian

A Christian view of rhetoric?

The issue is puzzling because most of us see writing as a necessary human function, simply a means by which we record thoughts in a lasting way. Writing, many believe, begins with speech, with the delight or need to communicate, and in many ways it seems hardly different from speaking. Isn't writing simply speaking on paper? And that function seems as natural—as human—as growing hair and fingernails. According to Henry James, writing is part of the "conduct of life."

Like speech, writing does begin, to a certain extent, in delight and need. We can learn as much from infants, who can teach us many things, from patience to love to service. But they also teach us about language. When do those first random noises change to words, from cooing to communication?

When the infant is about six months old, she starts experimenting with sounds. This little six-month-old is already a pretty wise human. She knows that certain sounds—babyish gurgles—will bring a smile and a hug from her parents. She knows, too, that other sounds—good loud wails or plaintive cries—will bring a bottle or a diaper change. Sometimes she can run the household with her array of noises. Only one-half year old, she discovers a certain power in shaping sounds to communicate her wishes, feelings, needs. And, of course, her learning has only begun.

Imagine that one day this infant lies in her crib practicing the sounds that are easiest for her, a jumble of *b*, *d*, and *m* sounds. It so happens that as she practices her *d*—"da-da, da-da"—her own father enters the room and, hearing his name called, showers hugs and laughter upon his daughter. "Hmmm," she thinks, "if I can get that kind of a reaction with a simple 'da-da,' I'll try it more often."

A few weeks later, she may happen to mouth a "bye-bye" while flinging her arms around, and her mother goes into an ecstasy of delight. Her little girl knows how to say "bye-bye"!

Thus, she takes the first tottering steps toward language. In time she will learn the two other major progressions in language, vocabulary and grammar, but she is on the way. Sound conveys meaning. As linguist William Vande Kopple has put it, her language is changing from "da-da" to discourse.

But why? Why don't we understand her "da-da" as referring to her mother? Her "bye-bye" as referring to her wanting a bottle? Of course she will make up some sounds in her growing years, composing her own unique terms for a bottle, or a drink of water, or her grandparents. She has a mind of her own, after all, and if she insists upon calling her grandfather something like "Apa," he probably will not mind. His pleasure lies in being recognized and named.

Clearly, however, the foundations of her communication rest upon a certain order, a pattern in which sounds suggest certain meanings. On that very premise a Christian view of rhetoric begins, for her quest for meaning in speech parallels, to a certain degree, our quest for meaning in writing. An assumption of order undergirds both forms of communication. Our rhetoric, the art of writing to communicate our views to an audience and to persuade that audience of the correctness of our views, resembles God's revelation of divine order to us. This order, too, insists upon certain presuppositions for spiritual meaning.

We note, first of all, that, insofar as we know, the ability to speak and write is a uniquely human activity, species-specific and species-universal. Beyond a few severely limited signal systems used by animals to communicate, there is nothing in the animal world that approaches human language in complexity, range of meaning, and playfulness. Since humanity is created in the image of God, it is not far-fetched to conclude that the ability to "do" language is part of what it means to be created in God's image.

When God created an ordered world, one in harmony with his divine master plan, this creation was in a living, dynamic relationship with its Creator. God walked *and* talked with Adam and Eve, giving them directions and commandments for preserving his harmonious world. But this dynamic relationship did not last.

One effect of the fall, when humankind turned from God's order to its own order, was a disruption of communion that occurred at several levels. First, and most wrenching, that close compatibility which humankind had enjoyed with God, some of which was certainly the pleasure of speaking together, was severed. Sin cannot stand in the presence of God, and as a result Adam and Eve were exiled from Eden. But at a second level, language itself was marred by sin and the severance from order. Perhaps the clearest manifestation of this occurred at the Tower of Babel, where humankind once again chose its own way over God's way, where human pride rose like an ugly scar against God's creation. In punishment God confused human language, an act which again emphasized the distance which humankind had allowed between itself and God's divine order. In terms of language, we see, then, a separation from God's perfect order. As humanity wanders physically and spiritually further east from Eden, its very language, once used to commune with God, becomes disordered.

The full pattern of Scripture, however, is not simply a pattern of humanity's progress into disorder. Rather, the pattern is one of restoration. To mend the chasm between God's order and human disorder, to bridge the gulf between human sinfulness and God's holiness, Jesus acted as the bridge-builder, the savior and restorer. We notice particularly how John announces this restoration in the first chapter of his Gospel: "In the beginning was the Word, and the Word was with God, and the Word was God" (John 1:1). Jesus appears as the *Logos*, the Word, the divine given human shape *and* human words. By the Word, order can be restored, and the human words of Jesus give the way to such restoration. We notice, furthermore, that after Jesus paid the supreme sacrifice for restoration of humankind to God, the Holy Spirit healed the rupture that occurred at Babel. At Pentecost the disciples were given the gift of languages, the ability *to communicate* the meaning of the divine Word with others, thereby restoring others *to communion* with God. In spiritual terms, then, language is more than simply an accident for expressing our wishes, feelings, and needs. Language is also a means for restoring divine order on this earth.

We might ask, however, whether this is not a special use of language—for preaching, evangelism, and the like? The answer is no. The redemptive task, rather, is the work of all the redeemed. All who have been transformed by the Word bear alike the responsibility to articulate the meaning of the divine Word in the words they speak and write. The prophet Jeremiah makes this task clear. People about him were content to wait for the Lord, or someone appointed by the Lord, to speak the word of redemption and direction. In response, Jeremiah says, "But 'the burden of the Lord' you shall mention no more, for the burden is every man's own word . . ." (Jer. 23:36). Moreover, it is clear in Scripture that the Christian is to take great care in the words he or she uses. The divine *Logos* should be clothed only in the best of words; for, as Jesus said, "I tell you, on the day of judgment men will render account for every careless word they utter; for by your words you will be justified, and by your words you will be condemned" (Matt. 12:36–37).

How do such presuppositions come to bear upon rhetoric—the art of writing well?

All writing is also at once ordering. The writer is always making choices—what position to argue, which word to use, or how to arrange sentences and paragraphs. The writer exercises a certain control over language in order to communicate his or her belief of what is true. The Christian writer is always remaking the divine harmony of God's creation. Several implications follow. Care should be exercised, first of all, not to make a false order. For example, many contemporary rhetorics are premised on an existential world-and-life view which suggests that the writer finds a personal meaning through writing. No absolute body of truth, they argue, exists outside the writer's own perception. All values are relative to the individual. Therefore, the writer writes in order to clarify his or her own world-and-life view. By expressing opinions and arguments in essays, one comes to know what one believes. The writing clarifies the writer's values, but the values are of one's own making.

Certainly, one can clarify positions and determine values by writing. But a Christian believes that there is an absolute guide for living, that it is knowable, and that the knowledge which one pursues will ultimately lead to God himself. The task in a composition course is to apply this belief practically. If truth—these ethical, moral, spiritual guides for living—is accessible, is revealed by an absolute, unfailing source, the task of the Christian writer is to bring that understanding to bear convincingly upon arguments, analyses, and perceptions. Just as we may discover these directions for Christian living by research in the Bible, by discussion with others, by careful reflection upon and application of these directions to our own lives, so too that process may apply to our writing of essays. Research informs us of options; the writing process clarifies both our understanding of the options and our position in relation to them. The work of writing clarifies who we are in relation to both God and the world about us.

If we accept the premises that God has created an orderly world, that this order has been disrupted by sin, and that one task of the Christian is to discover God's order and to bring it to bear upon the world in which he or she lives, certain implications evolve from these premises for our writing. Good rhetoric is not simply an option for the Christian writer; it is a responsibility.

One modern Christian writer who clearly recognized this was the poet and dramatist T. S. Eliot, winner of the Nobel Prize for Literature in 1948. Eliot had been, for many years, an agnostic, but yet had been profoundly troubled by the glib lip service which both Christians and non-Christians paid to the presence of the divine. Even as an agnostic, Eliot believed that if there is such a thing as an absolute body of truth and such a being as a divine God, one ought to take that truth a great deal more seriously than the present age demonstrated. Before his conversion to Christianity, Eliot wrote often of characters in search of some sure meaning. Bereft of divine leading, they inevitably fall short of such meaning. Thus, one of his troubled characters, J. Alfred Prufrock, in the poem "The Love Song of J. Alfred Prufrock," exclaims pathetically that "it is impossible to say just what I mean."

Following his conversion to Christianity, Eliot continued to struggle with the idea of giving a clear voice to Christian conviction in a troubled age. In *Ash Wednesday*, he laments the fact that with all our noise and hurry we fail to be quiet, to sit still, and to let the voice of the eternal Word speak through our own carefully chosen words:

> If the lost word is lost, if the spent word is spent
> If the unheard, unspoken
> Word is unspoken, unheard;
> Still is the unspoken word, the Word unheard,
> The Word without a word, the Word within
> The world and for the world;
> And the light shone in darkness and
> Against the Word the unstilled world still whirled
> About the centre of the silent Word.

Each of us, too, may find it difficult to "say just what I mean," losing touch with the Word temporarily. But the Word is eternal, waiting for us to approach it again. Therefore one needs a careful approach to rhetoric, to find the right words to give articulate voice to the Word.

For Eliot, as for any Christian, each word counts. Each word is freighted with the ore of eternal significance. For Eliot, rhetoric was more than mere communication—animals can communicate, within a limited range. Rhetoric was communion with the divine—something ordained by God for his people.

In the second movement of Eliot's "Little Gidding," the narrator walks the predawn, smoky streets of London during the fire bombings of the early 1940s and has a vision of a deceased poet. The deceased poet tells the narrator that "last year's words belong to last year's language." Writers are responsible to write clearly in the language of their age to people of their age. Does this recognition mean that the modern writer uses the slang and colloquialism of the time? Eliot averts this misunderstanding. "Our concern was speech," writes Eliot, "and speech impelled us / To purify the dialect of the tribe." The lesson is to use the best of modern language.

This point is expanded and specified in the final section of the poem where Eliot envisions a rhetoric partaking of a divine harmony. It is a living dance of language in which every word and sentence "is at home." The words should be neither "diffident nor ostentatious" (yes, rhetoric can become an end in itself), but should be common, "without vulgarity"; precise but "not pedantic." Every phrase, every sentence, has purpose: to illumine the divine harmony.

Shakespeare said, "Give thy worst of thoughts the worst of words." The challenge of a Christian rhetoric lies in the inversion of his injunction: "Give thy best of thoughts the best of words." Clothe the Word in words of royalty; give the *Logos* healthy flesh, not the common trappings of the age.

Are Eliot's cautions to use language carefully and responsibly pointless for the modern writer? Many people would say so. Language, they argue, is nothing more than a human function, and some people simply "do" it differently than others. Stockbrokers do it differently than welders. Professors do it differently than students. Americans do it differently than Britons. Consider the fact, however, that the use of language is also an ethical issue, that it undeniably involves our relationships with other individuals, and that certain ethical guidelines govern that involvement as surely as they do in all ways of living. One never simply *does* language. The way an individual addresses another often bears as much significance as the thing said.

Suppose you watch a gymnast with whom you have been friends for years and who has just performed a particularly intricate and demanding routine. You give her a hug of congratulations and exclaim: "Wonderful! You're a regular monkey!" The gymnast, the audience for your remark, is likely to be pleased with your praise. Now, suppose your two-year-old brother drops a bowl of cereal. You stamp your foot in dismay, slap his hand, and shout, "Wonderful! You're a regular monkey!" The effect is quite different. Your words are intended to hurt, and they do.

Since language serves to communicate, it necessarily involves other people. We speak or write to communicate ideas and attitudes *to others*. Consequently, we need to be aware of how our words are received by others. According to Proverbs 25:11, "A word fitly spoken is like apples of gold in pictures of silver"; a word spoken with the sense of propriety and order that Eliot encourages can be like a gift. But often we speak, and write, with improper words. These are presents, too, albeit of a different luster; yet for these too we are held responsible.

James writes that our words can present "a restless evil, full of deadly poison" (3:8).

In the same way that our inflections of tone and manner affect a listener, our adoption of a "voice" in rhetoric affects the reader. For example, nearly all rhetoric courses will require a composition written from a first-person point of view, told with the "I" pronoun. That I-teller may narrate the essay in one of several ways.

Consider first the circumstances of the argumentative essay in which you as the I-teller set forth a position. Perhaps you are profoundly upset by a certain event and wish to argue against it. Perhaps a certain advertisement has led you to a bad purchase. The product cost too much or did not perform as advertised. In such a case, you might use the I-teller as a means to vent your anger: "I loathe this product! I was cheated by the advertisement! I was treated unfairly when I tried to return it!" Like the exclamation marks, your anger is hard and punctuated.

The rhetorical effect of such writing, however, is that the essay serves only to vent your anger. The words are like fists thrown up to the reader, and the reader, quite often, will back away from what you have to say. You serve only your own psychological ends and fail to communicate effectively with the audience.

On the other hand, the I-teller can become one with the audience by narrating and capturing an experience that the reader can believe in or be persuaded by. Great travel literature often uses the first-person point of view as a narrative technique. John Steinbeck's *Travels with Charley*, Peter Jenkins's *Walk Across America*, William Least Heat Moon's *Blue Highways* all use this technique. In these cases the I-teller becomes a kind of metaphor which invites the reader to participate in the experience. Even though you are writing as the first-person narrator in an essay, that first person can include the reader by thoughtfully providing him or her access to the experience. In a sense, the I of the writer becomes one with the I of the reader. Here lies the key to the ethics of rhetoric: we need to put ourselves in the position of the audience and treat the audience as we would be treated ourselves.

Words, however, may also be used to cheat, to mystify and confuse, to lie to the audience. On the one hand, we consider the *manner* in which we use words, as with the gymnast or a baby brother. But that manner may also be calculated to certain purposes which also bear ethical significance. Consider the example mentioned earlier, the case of advertising. In a sense, the art of advertising is the art of using rhetoric to package a product in such a way that the consumer's rational awareness is bypassed and the subconscious world of desires and wishes is stimulated. Shoemakers, for example, do not just sell shoes; they sell comfort and style. Cosmetic makers do not just sell cosmetics; they sell sensuality, adventure, and romance. Cereal makers do not just sell oats and corn and rice; they sell nutrition, slimmer waistlines, and bulging muscles.

The products are put into rhetorical packages which appeal to human vanity. And many of our dollars go over the counter for that reason alone. The packaging of advertising—on everything from cars to political candidates, from carpeting to homes—has developed into a psychological warfare whose primary weapon is human need, whose goal is the winning of many dollars, whose victory march is one to the bank.

The rhetorical packaging—the messages, slogans, and songs of the advertiser—makes some things appear better than they are. If the advertiser can produce a snappier package, a more clever commercial, people will buy that product. But what child has not had a toy which broke after one use, or a toy which, despite the "five simple steps of construction" advertised on the package, won't go together? And who has not had the cereal which, despite its promises for a slimmer, trimmer, happier you, tastes like recycled coffee grounds? The packaging is everything. The effort intensifies to a psychological wrestling match: make the customer feel delight, make the customer believe that it is good, make the customer desire and reach for it.

Does it sound familiar? We have witnessed the pattern before in Genesis 3:1–7. The serpent was the most subtle creature alive. He gave Adam and Eve a most remarkable rhetorical package, telling them that "the tree was good for food . . . a delight to the eyes . . . and to be desired." The seduction of the audience by clever rhetorical packaging is as old as Eden, and our wandering east of Eden has ever been in pursuit of the same thing: gratification of our own desires.

It may be fairly argued, as we see in the later section on ethics, that no area of life is free from ethical responsibility. Certainly this is true also for rhetoric. The biblical guidance in this particular ethical concern is manifestly clear: we are responsible for our words and for their effects upon others. The Christian view of rhetoric, then, may be understood first of all as an effort to discover an order and clarity which mirror that of God, and secondly as a mandate to use ordered, clear writing in an ethical spirit of the Bible—to reveal truth, to ennoble ideas and language, and to dignify the audience as we would have ourselves dignified.

PART 1

Writing

1

Good Writing

An Introduction to Rhetoric

Think about the writing you like to read. What are its qualities? Perhaps it attracts you with a fresh, clear style. Perhaps it shows you something new, opens a world you have not seen before, or reminds you of one that you might have forgotten. Perhaps it stimulates you, makes you want to argue or shout; or, perhaps, it gives you a quiet feeling and makes you ponder the ideas or images presented.

The writing that you do for classes and for your career should have the same qualities, those that make us say, "This is good!" Good writing, however, is not easy; it's hard work, a fact that might be overlooked in the hurry to finish writing projects. Yet with the work, good writing is possible. The belief that some people lack the gift of writing isn't true.

Writing well is not simply a gift, but a skill; and skills are acquired, not given. If you had never played the piano before, you would not expect to be able to sit down at a Steinway and execute Chopin's "Etudes." Whatever plunking and bonking would come out, it would not be great music. That masterful play, however, might come with instruction and practice.

Like playing the piano, writing is a skill, but it will not be as difficult a skill to refine because you already know the basics. You already are familiar with words; you think in sentences. Aristotle pointed out that people either approach writing "quite at random" or demonstrate "a knack which comes from the acquired habit." The "gifted" writers are probably those who have honed their writing skills through instruction, practice, and revision.

Hard work does pay off, but it pays the most to those who have an accurate picture of the writing process. Three primary elements direct the process: purpose, audience, persona. Forgetting any one of these can transform your writing from clear to confusing, from exciting to dull. Consider the role of each of these in the writing process.

Purpose

When we write, we are writing in order to say something. We want to explain, to cajole; we want to argue, to implore; we want to humor or admonish—we want to do something. Yet as obvious as this point seems, we often forget it when writing for an instructor's assignment. Sometimes the assignments we receive do not encourage clarity of purpose. Sometimes we lack the time to write the paper we want. Sometimes we are simply careless. Whatever the reason, the fact remains that all too often we hide the purpose of our discourse. Notice how the following paragraph hides its purpose:

> The real disasters in life come when you get what you want. For almost a century now, a great many intelligent and well-meaning people have argued against any form of censorship of art and entertainment. Within the past twenty years, courts and legislatures have found these arguments very persuasive so that censorship is now a relative rarity in most states.

Although this seems to introduce a paper that will argue against gratification of desire or that will detail the scarcity of censorship, that is not the case. The author of this paper was really attempting to argue for censorship of pornographic material. Unfortunately, his purpose never becomes clear.

At other times, the problem comes not from the lack of an apparent purpose but from trying to say too many things at once. Notice how this writer starts his essay moving in several directions at the same time:

> Central America is a hot spot for the United States right now. Much talk about whether or not the U.S. should follow the course of further involvement has been in the news lately. The United States already has large amounts of money invested in Central America and it would seem that President Reagan is attempting to allocate more. Understanding the problems in Central America is difficult. Most people agree that direct involvement like that of Vietnam leads in a blind path to nowhere. However, because of the complexity of the situation, the fact that much of the

information coming from Nicaragua is polemic, and the apathy toward foreign affairs felt throughout the United States, the majority of our citizens do not hold any deeper opinion.

While we know that the author is writing about Nicaragua, that is about all we know. His precise subject is not clear. Will he write about American attitudes toward Nicaragua? Will he discuss whether or not the United States should be involved? Will he write about the complexity of the situation? As readers, we are impatient; we want to know where an essay will be taking us.

Audience

If all writing should be saying something, it should be saying something to someone. Closely paired with purpose in writing is audience. Again, the point is obvious but often ignored. All the elements of style—diction, syntax, tone—can work for you in addressing your audience.

We talk to children differently than to adults; we address a teacher in a different manner than we address our parents. We make those adjustments in our language almost automatically. We need to do the same thing when we write. Consider the differences in the four following approaches to a paper on a biblical image.

The first takes the form of a letter to an unbelieving friend:

Dear Talmadge,

The point you make in your last letter is right. Christianity sounds crazy when you pay close attention to the images of the Bible. But you've got to remember that much of Christianity is a paradox. In part, the images help us understand that. Take the one you complain about— being washed in the blood. Yeah, it *is* gross if you take it literally, but let me try to explain it. Understanding what washing meant to the Hebrews will help you understand what we Christians mean when we talk about being redeemed or about being servants or about being in the world but not of the world.

The second addresses the readers of a popular religious magazine:

"Yuck, Papa!" exclaimed my four-year-old, "I don't want to be washed in Jesus' blood. I don't have to, do I? Where do they get the blood?" Theological concepts we take for granted often become puzzling when we try to explain them to children. Words we read in responsive readings or sing in hymns suddenly sound foreign to us. What *does* it mean to be washed in blood? The answer to this question is not found in any one place in the Bible, for although this important image has its roots in the tradition of the Old Testament, it is also important to an understanding of New Testament concepts like justification, sanctification, and discipleship.

The third addresses the readers of a tract:

We all know what it's like to be dirty. We've sweated on the line in the factory or while pushing the lawn mower on a humid August afternoon. We've all felt dirty from guilt, too. Maybe it was that time we saw our best friend right after we had been gossiping about his love life. What we said wasn't terrible, but it sure made us feel guilty later.

Maybe you think Christians don't get dirty. They do, but they are different in one way. They have a way to get clean. The Bible says that Jesus Christ can wash any sins away.

The fourth speaks to the readers of a special column in the religion section of a city newspaper:

"Soak your shirt in cold water, Adrianne," called her mother, "I'll get the Axion." Most of us are as skilled as Adrianne's mother at removing a blood stain from a new blouse. Blood is one of those nasty stains that detergent manufacturers warn us about, and we are well prepared to fight it. Consequently, we can hardly help thinking Christians are crazy when they proclaim that to be as white as snow, people must be washed in blood. Even as a metaphor this does not work. Or does it? The paradox it represents is at the heart of the Christian religion and, therefore, deserves our attention.

As we indicated in the introductory essay, the writer's attitude toward the audience bears ethical significance. Consider two examples that demonstrate ethical guidelines for consideration of the audience. First, in an argumentative essay you want to demonstrate that your point of view is correct and reasonable. But do you do this by ignoring the credibility of the other side's argument? There must be another point of view, after all, or your own point of view is not worth asserting. To argue that oak is wood or that cocker spaniels are dogs simply is not very important unless someone else is convinced that oak is an automobile or cocker spaniels are rabbits. If you want to argue that modern society has to learn to relax more, that must be because modern society works too hard. If you want to argue that students should attend worship services more frequently, that must be because they are not doing so now. To get the reader to take your argument seriously, you need to demonstrate that you know both sides of the issue. Your argument always gains more merit, clarity, and reasonableness if you grant certain concessions to the other point of view. Indicate why modern society works too hard and what the good values of such work might be. Point out why students do not worship frequently enough and what the context for that failure might be. By establishing a certain sympathy, you can communicate with a larger audience—not just those already in agreement with you—and your argument acquires greater influence.

A second example bears upon our consideration of the audience. As a Christian writer you will want to make biblical truth come to bear upon your argument. We must understand, however, that Christianity is not something we "tack on" to our daily living. Rather, it becomes an integral part of daily life. In the same way, your Christian view should not be "tacked on" to your essay in a didactic closing statement. It must be integrated into the very fabric of the essay itself. The general concluding Christian statement is often sentimental, and sometimes offensive to the audience. The audience must be aware of your point of view throughout the essay. If you close the essay with a comment such as "God doesn't want us involved in Nicaragua," the audience might be offended. Why? The appeal is stated defiantly, not reasonably. And defiance works to alienate, not to educate, the audience. A mature consideration of the audience would permit the audience to follow your argument step by step through the essay, rather than rely upon a parting shot in the final sentence.

You need to consider audience in order to write ethically. You will be writing essays for different purposes and for different audiences. But in each case it will also be profitable to think of yourself as the audience and to ask how you would want to be informed, argued with, or written to. Think of this as "the golden rule of writing."

Persona

The term *persona* refers to the person doing the writing, the identity you assume whenever you write. Like a real person, this persona has a voice that tries to convince the audience of the truth of your perspective on the subject. You might be writing as a close friend of the audience, or you might be writing as an impersonal expert; you might be writing as a victim, or you might be writing as an activist. To decide on an appropriate voice, you should consider your purpose and your audience as well, for all three things work together.

If, as you work on a first draft, you consider your intentions (purpose) and your reader (audience), you will recognize the importance of your writing voice (persona). You will realize that how you say what you say will affect what your audience thinks of your ideas and, consequently, will determine whether or not you achieve your purpose.

Consider the voice of this chapter. By addressing our audience as *you* and by using examples, we have tried to create an informal, helpful voice. We could alter that voice by changing our diction, our syntax, or our attitude toward the audience. Compare what we have already written with the following paragraph:

> All discourse entails the use of a persona, a fictive identity that communicates the rhetorical stance of the author. Integral to this strategy is voice, the personification of style. One needs to select an appropriate and authentic voice in order to enjoy success as a writer.

No doubt as you read this version of the opening of this section, you imagine a different persona, one more formal and academic.

As with purpose and audience, your use of a persona bears certain ethical implications. Recognizing that you adopt different personas for different purposes—an informed persona, a highly formal one, an authoritative one—you bear a responsibility to maintain a consistent persona within one essay. If you write timidly and questioningly at first, then shift to an energetic, argumentative voice, then to a skeptical, scornful voice, the audience will be thoroughly confused.

But consistency isn't the only important issue. As a Christian, you will want to pay close attention to the type of persona whom you create. You need to remember that the eyes of others are on your persona just as they are on your person. Consequently, you will want to shape a persona who will bear witness to your faith. Here the significance of paying attention to the other side of an issue becomes important once again. You may believe that abortion is murder, but to use a persona who shouts that belief at the reader, pointing an accusing or condescending finger at her, may not be the best witness.

You will want your persona to represent your beliefs honestly. While the secular writer may be content with any persona that works successfully with the audience, the Christian is not. Saint Paul considered this issue in his second letter to the church at Corinth. In writing to that church, he anticipates their complaint that he might be using a dishonest persona: "For they say, 'His letters are weighty and strong, but his bodily presence is weak, and his speech of no account.'" To such complaints, Paul responds, "Let such people understand that what we say by letter when absent, we do when present" (2 Cor. 10:10–11). For you as for Paul, clarity and honesty of persona should be an ethical issue to which you pay close attention.

2

Invention

Getting Started

Perhaps the specific assignment of your instructor will give you some help in imagining the constraints of audience, purpose, or persona. Even if it does give you some direction, you still may have a difficult time arriving at and exploring a topic. Several techniques may help you beyond this impasse.

Freewriting

The ideas for the paper may very well be in your mind already; however, you might not be able to focus them because you're trying too hard to imagine your *entire* paper as a finished product. To get at those ideas, you can use this simple procedure: take pen in hand (or sit down at the computer keyboard) and begin to write. Bear in mind three guidelines, however. First, write for a preselected period of time (ten minutes works well). Second, don't stop writing but write whatever comes to mind. You may even write things like, "I hate doing this" or "This is stupid; I'm never going to come up with an idea." The idea is to keep writing. Finally, as you write at this stage, you need not worry about grammar or mechanics. Your goal is to discover new ideas, to tap the stream of consciousness in your mind. All of the things you write down may not be worthwhile or even relevant to your purpose, but if they are not usable, you can delete them in revision. As you write, a pattern should emerge that will provide a cluster of ideas or an angle of approach that you can develop further.

Looping

This is a variation on freewriting. You begin as if you were freewriting. The difference lies in your treatment of the finished product. Very often, you will discover that as you wrote you began to focus on an idea. Locate this idea and use it as the starting point for your next period of writing. You can continue this for several "loops" until you have a solid sense of topic, purpose, audience, and persona.

Cubing

To discover what you might write about a given topic (like apartheid or political action committees) imagine the topic to be like a cube that you can hold in your hands. On each of the six faces of the cube is an operation. As you imagine yourself turning the cube in your hands, perform each of these operations:

describe it   analyze it

compare it   apply it

associate it   argue for or against it

Clustering

Another good way to develop a topic is through clustering, which attempts to discover all the ideas that are associated or clustered around your topic. After setting a time limit of five or ten minutes, write your topic or a key word from the topic on a piece of paper. Then write other words that you associate with that key word.

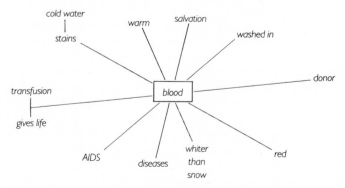

As you can see, you might create long branches forming subsets of associations. In the final step, you would analyze your drawing to determine the connections among the branches, connections that might well help you move toward a thesis statement.

Some General Advice

Carefully think through your purpose and audience as you consider these options, asking yourself what you want to tell your audience about this subject and what, then, you need to do to convince them of the truth of what you're saying. Think about whether something requires definition; whether an aspect could be compared to something else; whether a cause-and-effect relationship or a contradiction could be identified; whether the matter at hand is possible or impossible; and whether testimony of experts or statistics would support your case.

Ideas for essays can come from a variety of directions. Sometimes freewriting will help you discover a topic that you already know something about or will suggest a topic that you may wish to investigate. Sometimes consideration of your topic will lead you to books to read or people to interview. Whatever the source of the idea, you will usually need to do more research on the topic as you begin the process of writing. The best writing comes from writers who have immersed themselves in their topic.

As you read or interview or observe, record the questions and observations that occur to you. These will form stepping stones to a thesis. If, as you read his "Hills Like White Elephants," you wonder why Hemingway repeats the word *it* so often, write that question down. If, as you read about energy conservation, a question about the relationship between automotive style and fuel efficiency pops into your head, write it down. Questions like these and like "Why did the U.S. support the South Vietnamese government?" or "Why does Gabriel Garcia Marquez rearrange time in his fiction?" can lead to theses of interpretation.

Discovering a workable thesis is a key step in restricting your subject. For example, if your working thesis is that "the U.S. supported the South Vietnamese because of the Johnson administration's belief in the domino theory," you would have a narrower focus than you would if you were investigating "Vietnam" or even "U.S. involvement in Vietnam."

If your thesis changes as you gather evidence and jot down your ideas, don't worry. As the next chapter explains, you can shape it to reflect these shifts in meaning.

3

Structuring the Thesis

Imagine a first-grade art class in which the students are handed portions of clay by their enthusiastic teacher, Miss Sophia Grundy. When the clay is distributed, Miss Grundy returns to her desk, smiles at the puzzled students, and announces cheerfully, "Now make something!"

Depending upon their personalities, the first graders caress or bash the clay, smoothing, poking, or hacking as they please. Few if any "make" something.

In an analogous way, the subject matter, or topic, of your essay is the clay. The thesis is what you are going to "make of it." But in that making, two important guidelines direct the activity: first, a sure, funneling movement from topic to thesis; second, a clear claim, or thesis, for what you will assert in your essay. The word *thesis* comes from a Greek word meaning "to put down." The thesis clearly "puts down" or states what you intend to do in the essay. As such, the thesis makes a claim, but it also projects how this claim will be fulfilled in the essay.

Consider another hypothetical example. Zane Hastings, a student at R. U. Underhill University, has selected the general *subject* area of energy conservation. Because of the many concerns about energy conservation—use of alternate sources, dangers of different sources, depletion of sources, and so forth—Zane has narrowed the subject area to a *topic:* energy conservation in automobiles. Freewriting helped him formulate his topic even more precisely; so now Zane is ready to make a *thesis* about such conservation.

He wants to put that thesis in a rhetorical context that makes it relevant and compelling to the reader. In effect, he wants rhetorically to prepare the reader in advance to agree with his thesis. In this case, Zane constructs two introductory paragraphs in order to establish that context for his topic and then to funnel the description to the specific thesis claim and projection.

In the year 1933 the four-lane blacktop of Highway I-96 is little more than a dream. The roads between Grand Rapids and Kalamazoo ripple with potholes and ruts. Yet a small black sedan bounces along the muddy roads at the lively pace of twenty-five miles per hour. That sedan was the Ford Model A, widely acclaimed as the best car ever built. In fact, one sometimes sees one of those same Model As that made roads out of wasteland still moving sedately and unruffled along modern interchanges.

Compared to the graceful, trim Model A that traveled those roads in 1933, many contemporary vehicles seem awkward and clumsy. Like gluttons, these cars have accumulated all the excesses of luxury: fancy, bulky angles, huge amounts of useless chrome, and energy-wasting frills to appease the whims of pampered owners. By so doing, such automobiles have also developed into aggressive consumers of energy. Greater weight, fancier gadgetry, more powerful engines—all require more energy. The cost of getting someplace has escalated as drivers want to get to that place in the best of style; but the best of style is also at once the worst of energy conservation. Because of the acute need to conserve energy, I should like to argue that automotive styling and engineering must conform to the following guidelines: first, a reduction in vehicle weight to a maximum of thirty-five hundred pounds; second, a surcharge tax on luxury options of 25 percent; third, an improvement in fuel consumption to a minimum of forty miles per gallon.

Note the techniques Zane has used for his introduction.

Establishing context. Rather than beginning with a heated condemnation of automobile energy waste, one which might potentially alienate a reader who commutes to work, for example, Zane creates a positive tone toward cars in general. His point is not to argue against automobiles, but specifically to argue for a certain kind of automobile engineering which will responsibly consider energy conservation.

Imagery. Notice that the introductory paragraph provides a good beginning by its strong visual image. Immediately the reader is placed in a context or in a setting for the consideration of the topic. Furthermore, Zane focuses on a particular audience, one living in the geographical region of western Michigan. He has taken a bit of a risk by doing so, for anyone from outside that region might feel like an outsider to the essay topic. We assume that Zane is writing for a specific audience in that region.

Coherence. Notice also that the transition between paragraphs is such that the two are clearly linked. Paragraph 1 sets the scene, but it also immediately establishes automobiles as the subject. Paragraph 2 signals a change by the words *compared to.* The words imply that the tone of this paragraph will differ from paragraph 1.

Funneling. The introduction focuses nicely from the broad view of the opening portrait and the *subject* of automobiles, to the *topic* of energy conservation in paragraph 2, to the specific statement of *thesis,* or what Zane is going to argue about that topic. This movement from the general subject to the specific thesis shapes the funnel.

Thesis statement. The thesis statement in Zane's essay is called "polite statement," using the deferential "I should like to argue." Most instructors prefer more direct statements since such are far more forceful and energetic than the polite statement. A preferable revision would follow one of these models:

> Because of the acute need to conserve energy, I will argue that automotive styling and engineering must conform to the following guidelines. . . .
>
> Because of the acute need to conserve energy, automotive styling and engineering must conform to the following guidelines. . . .

Whatever the degree of directness the writer employs (and generally the more direct has more rhetorical force), he follows these particular steps in the thesis statement:

Transition to thesis:	Because of the acute need to conserve energy, auto-
Thesis claim:	motive styling and engineering must conform to the following guidelines:
Projection of argument:	first, a reduction in vehicle weight to a maximum of thirty-five hundred pounds; second, a surcharge tax on luxury options of 25 percent; third, an improvement in fuel consumption to a minimum of forty miles per gallon.

The model here provides a projection or forecast of the central points of the essay. Such a model provides an immediate and clear focus for the entire essay and greatly enhances both the writer's and the reader's sense of structure. When such a listing is used, it must employ the punctuation pattern used in the model. The colon introduces the points and semicolons separate the numerically listed points. If the numerical designations are not used, the points may be separated simply by commas.

The benefits of a thesis statement such as Zane uses here lie in the clear and direct *claim* and the *projection* of how the claim will be developed in the body of the essay. The structure of the thesis suggests the structure of the essay; each item in the thesis will generate a section of the essay. The thesis statement itself serves as an outline for the essay.

However, you should select a thesis pattern that fits the purpose, audience, and persona of the individual essay. The alternative patterns that follow provide models you can imitate in your writing.

Adverbial clauses. Such clauses answer why a claim is important or necessary. In the following statement, the author has decided to write about pornography and will supply reasons for taking her position in the projection. Note the very direct claim used here. Clearly this writer wishes to be more aggressive and assertive than Zane did in his essay on energy conservation. In this pattern the first adverbial clause of the projection is introduced by "because"; repeating this signal word in the second and third clauses is optional. Note, furthermore, that each of the clauses has an action verb.

Thesis claim: Pornography must be limited by legislation
Projection: because it contributes to a rise in crimes of sexual assault, because it demeans womanhood, and because it destroys the moral integrity of society.

The adverbial-clause pattern is particularly useful for essays of argumentation. The clauses establish reasons for your position and establish a context. When introduced by the word *although,* such clauses highlight the principle of concession discussed earlier. Such clauses indicate that there are two sides to the issue and thus something to argue about.

Noun clauses. The writer of this next essay is discussing a critical point in the history of Vietnam—the rule of Diem—and explains Diem's weaknesses as a national leader. The signal word *that* for the noun clauses may be omitted for the second and third clauses. In this model, the writer chose to keep it to strengthen the parallelism. But note that in the model using noun clauses the claim and projection merge with no clear division between them.

Thesis claim and Projection: I will argue that Diem participated in illegal activities, that he corrupted the morals of those about him, and that he ruled weakly and ineffectively.

This thesis does have good qualities. The argument is clear, and the three noun clauses are perfectly parallel with strong, active verbs. But compare it to the same thesis structured in adverbial clauses. Here each of the adverbial clauses of the projection gives clear reasons for the claim, and the entire structure is more direct.

Thesis claim:	Diem's government failed
Projection:	because he participated in illegal activities, because he corrupted the morals of those about him, and because he ruled weakly and ineffectively.

A two-sentence claim and projection. In the prior examples, we have stressed directness of statement, the need for parallelism, and action verbs in the thesis claim and projection. But a thesis statement should also be relatively brief. One of the worst errors you can fall into is to argue too long and too elaborately in the thesis statement. At the end of a very long sentence, the reader will emerge confused. List points; do not argue them. In the following example, the writer is preparing a paper stimulated by Aldous Huxley's novel *Brave New World*. Because of the very long thesis claim, the writer has decided to separate the claim from the projection. Notice that the projection in this case makes use of another kind of parallel structure, the prepositional phrase introduced with "by." Notice also the transition between claim and projection by repetition of the term *engineering*.

Thesis claim:	The prophetic voice of Aldous Huxley's *Brave New World* has been fulfilled in that contemporary man now engages in ge-
Projection:	netic engineering. The extent of this engineering may be seen by current experiments with DNA molecular structure, by continued work in producing "test-tube babies," and by inter-uterine surgery on the fetus to correct prebirth defects.

Periodic structure. By careful arrangement of syntax, even unbelievable topics can be made to seem quite believable, almost logical. Consider the following example, a variation of the first pattern; yet here the clauses precede the thesis claim which then appears as a conclusion. Because it saves the major point for the end of the sentence, this periodic structure gives the sense of logical persuasiveness even for highly unlikely claims.

Projection:	Because it efficiently opens skin pores, because it soothes irritated nerves and muscles, because it restores skin tone,
Thesis claim:	a one-hour daily mud bath should be required of all students at Zoo University.

Varied structures. Any of these patterns could lead to successful essays, but they are not your only options. You should always adapt your style to the rhetorical situation. Sometimes you may want to be less formal, ignoring these carefully structured patterns for ones less explicit. A confident writer might well develop new and lively techniques particularly suitable to a specific purpose, audience, or persona. Consider, for example, the following introduction from a first-person essay, "The Impending Energy Crisis," published by Allen E. Murray, president of the Mobil Corporation, in *Newsweek* (June 10, 1985):

> Whenever I warn people that another energy crisis is on the way, I draw raised eyebrows and skeptical sneers.
> "We thought we were through with those things," my friends hoot.
> "Don't we have oil and gas running out of our ears? And plenty of electricity?"
> My answer is, "Yes, for the moment," but I also add this warning: energy plenty is not going to last.

Studied carefully, the introduction reveals a clear thesis claim (first paragraph: an energy crisis is on the way), and a clear thesis projection (third paragraph: we are safe for the moment, but energy is not going to last). In this case, however, Murray has crafted short sentences and paragraphs to create the fast-paced style that you would expect in *Newsweek*.

4

Coherence

Most people know that paragraphs need to be unified in order to be understandable. Since a paragraph is a unit of thought, it should develop only one idea. When we read something like the paragraph that follows, we are troubled:

> Rock and roll has seen many changes over the past forty years. Many artists of the past have influenced the styles and techniques of some of today's music. Already in the 1950s and 1960s parents were objecting to Elvis Presley. Teen-agers then and now expect their parents not to understand what they like to listen to. Other totally new forms of rock and roll have developed in the past couple of years with not much influence from the past. New Wave music is a little bit of the past and a lot of fresh original ideas.

While all these sentences are roughly on the topic of rock music and are the product of one mind, we recognize that they do not form a unified paragraph, that the topic serves only as a stimulus, but not as an organizing principle. Reading a paragraph like this is a bit like stepping into a crowded room where each person is talking loudly to himself. Yet with the right cues, with some attempt at unity, the people in that room can join in flawlessly reciting a poem or singing a song.

Even when paragraphs are built around a unified topic, they still might not work the way we want them to if they are not coherent. *Coherence* is the term we use to describe the connections between ideas, to refer to relationships between sentences. Sometimes we also use the words *smooth* or *choppy* to identify coherent or incoherent prose. Consider this revision of the paragraph on rock and roll music:

Rock and roll has seen many changes over the past forty years. Many artists of the past have influenced the styles and techniques of some of today's music. New Wave music is one type of music that uses the techniques and styles of the past. New Wave uses more electronic instruments. New Wave music is a little bit of the past and a lot of fresh original ideas.

Although this paragraph now focuses on one topic—the relationship of New Wave music to rock and roll—it fails to move coherently from sentence to sentence. Small gaps prevent the reader from fully understanding the relationships among ideas.

By altering the structure, by using transitional devices, and by repeating key words, we can revise the paragraph into a more coherent—though far from elegant—piece of writing.

New Wave music enters the music scene as the latest variation on rock and roll. Although it uses the style of past rock stars, New Wave also introduces new techniques and instruments. For example, New Wave uses more electronic instruments than traditional rock and roll. In short, it combines a little bit of the past with a lot of fresh ideas.

As the next section will explain in more detail, simple changes like the ones made here can do much to clarify your writing.

The following exercise is taken from an actual class assignment, one which demonstrates the techniques that create paragraph unity and coherence, but also makes clear the use of different personas for different audiences. The first paragraph is taken from Matthew 14:22–27.

Then he made the disciples get into the boat and go before him to the other side, while he dismissed the crowds. And after he had dismissed the crowds, he went up on the mountain by himself to pray. When evening came, he was there alone, but the boat by this time was many furlongs distant from the land, beaten by the waves; for the wind was against them. And in the fourth watch of the night he came to them, walking on the sea. But when the disciples saw him walking on the sea, they were terrified, saying, "It is a ghost!" And they cried out for fear. But immediately he spoke to them, saying, "Take heart, it is I; have no fear."

The second example is from Marian M. Schoolland's well-known book of Bible teachings for children, *Leading Little Ones to God*, in which she retells the biblical passage for a different audience.

God takes care of *everything*. The whole big world is in His hands. The moon and the stars are in His hands. He takes care of the birds and the flowers. He takes care of little children. He takes care of you and of me.

Do you think God's children should ever be afraid? Oh, no! We should *trust* God. He has promised to take care of us *always*.

The Bible tells a story about Peter, how he did something wonderful one day when he *trusted* Jesus, and what happened when he stopped trusting Jesus.

Jesus' disciples were in a boat, on the lake. It was night. They had only the moonlight to show them the way to shore. And then a big storm came. The wind began to blow hard. It made the boat go the wrong way. And big waves began to splash into the boat. The disciples were afraid. And *Jesus* was not with them this time.

While they were trying hard to row the boat, suddenly they saw something on the water, something white and scary. It was moving. It was coming *toward* them. In the dark, they could not tell *what* it was. They became terribly frightened. That white thing was even worse than the *storm*!

Notice the techniques Schoolland uses to address the audience and to provide coherence. Consider also the character of her persona.

For an impromptu writing exercise, a class was given Schoolland's rendition with the following directions: "Without sacrificing Schoolland's clarity and teaching, rewrite the passage in adult-level prose, making use of techniques of coherence. Use as many *action* verbs as possible. Use no more than three paragraphs." One such response reads as follows:

When one reads Scripture, the feeling of God's provision for his people becomes clear. The message relays to us God's care and his watch over his children. One becomes assured that God will take care of his people because of his intimate concern for creation. God controls the moon, stars, birds, and flowers, and tends to them constantly. Consequently, he will tend to man, whom he made in his image. If he can keep track of, and care for, the world we live in, surely he takes care of you and me.

Knowing the intimate care God gives to all of his creation, one should trust him. He controls all things and watches over us. We should recognize his concern for us and trust him to do, through his creation, what is best for us.

The Scriptures give an example of the importance of trust in him, and the consequences of mistrust. Jesus' disciples were out on a lake when dusk set in, leaving only the glow of the moon to illuminate the way to shore. As the night got darker and thicker, the winds began to blow— slowly at first, but then gathering intensity. The waves began to roll and splash brutally against the boat. Storm clouds blotted out the light of the moon and the disciples, instead of trusting God, panicked. As they frantically rowed the boat toward shore, they saw something white and ominous out on the water in front of them, and it appeared to be coming toward them. The disciples shook in fear. Because of the darkness they could not distinguish the object which seemed to glow. Jesus' disciples stood paralyzed in utter fear of whatever was making its way toward the boat.

To take note of the techniques of coherence the writer uses, you might underline specific words that contribute to coherence and unity. Note the transitions between paragraphs, the repetition of key words, and the use of imagery as rhetorical techniques. Also, the persona and audience for these paragraphs clearly differ from those of the preceding paragraphs.

Structure

Since coherence has to do with connections and relationships, one way to achieve it is through the organization of your paragraph. As should the whole essay, the paragraph should develop naturally out of its purpose. A paragraph not only presents a unified parcel of information, but it does so for a purpose that is closely related to the thesis of the essay. Some paragraphs will raise questions; others will present arguments; yet others will refute objections; and, of course, many will simply provide evidence for one aspect of the thesis.

As you compose and revise, you need to consider whether the topic sentence of a given paragraph fits its development and purpose, for certain topic sentences suggest certain paths of development. Note how the following topic sentences might influence the shape of their paragraphs:

When Shelley entered the classroom, everyone reacted differently to her pink and green hair.

More than any other president, Nixon polarized the American people.

The events of the morning bore no clue of what would happen in the evening.

To proceed coherently, the first paragraph would record the various reactions to Shelley's coiffure. The second paragraph would cite examples of ways in which Nixon polarized the American people. The third paragraph would compare the events of the morning with the events of the evening. The most basic way to work toward coherence is to follow the dictates of your topic.

Transitional Devices

Since coherence is based on relationships, you can often enhance it by using words and phrases that move the reader from one idea to the next. When you revise your prose, keep in mind a list of these key words to include in your paragraphs. In reality, of course, coherence requires a sensitivity to language that results from something more than mechanical insertion of words. Yet this is a good place to begin.

on the other hand	nevertheless
up to this point	therefore
in addition	in order to
meanwhile	for example

Another good device is to repeat words within the paragraph. Nouns, pronouns, or synonyms that appear again and again remind the reader what the paragraph is about. Reconsider the second paragraph of chapter 1; the word *writing* appears in each sentence, and it appears in the subject position in almost every sentence. Remember that a coherent paragraph will not shift subjects.

The *writing* that you do for classes and for your career should have the same qualities, those that make us say, "This is good!" Good *writing*, however, is not easy; *it's* hard work, a fact that might be overlooked in the hurry to finish writing projects. Yet with the work, good *writing* is possible. The belief that some people don't have the gift of *writing* simply isn't true.

Like transitional phrases and like logical structure, repetition emphasizes the relationships between sentences, helping the ideas to cohere.

5

Revision

As you look over the first draft of your essay you may be surprised by what you find. Perhaps it proceeds from point to point as you thought it would. If so, you can fine-tune the draft. More probably, you'll find a differently shaped essay than you anticipated. New insights may appear in places where they don't fit. A paragraph in the middle may work better near the beginning. The conclusion of your draft may culminate in a different thesis from the one you began with. Any number of things could have happened while you were writing. Through writing you often discover new ideas and new ways of thinking; your draft doesn't always turn out exactly as planned.

The task of revision is to rethink your essay, reconsidering your purpose, audience, and voice in the light of the draft just written. Here again, coherence should rule. Each paragraph should lead to the next, and each should work toward achieving some aspect of the essay's purpose. Don't be afraid to cut out parts that don't work. The new thesis that appears in your conclusion may be the better one; don't be afraid to adopt it and to write another draft using it as your starting point.

Fine-tuning the Essay

Fine-tuning often makes the difference between a dull, plodding essay and one bursting with energy. But how do you achieve that energy? When drafting the paper, it's often difficult enough simply to get thoughts down coherently, to manage sentences and paragraphs into unified structures that say something.

43

Consider your draft as a slightly out-of-tune 1962 Chevy sedan. The car has a good, dependable motor—good for at least another hundred thousand miles—tucked under its rusty hood. It will get you to school and back home, but will do so in a plodding fashion. The car needs some revision to run right—a tune-up. Revising the essay is like pulling the Chevy into a garage—sometimes just for a tune-up, sometimes for a major overhaul. It will run better when the work is finished.

We need some special tools, obviously, to get the best results. Following are some of the proper tools of revision, ones which are quite easy to master and very effective when mastered.

Verb Revision

"Is-verbs"

Verbs form the heart of action in the essay, the muscle that pumps life into the writing. But how do you find flaws in verb structures?

Perhaps the weakest of all verb structures is the verb used in this sentence—*is*. The forms of the *to be* verb (is, are, was, were, will be, etc.) are commonly known as "is-verbs." Is-verbs perform much of the work of the English language since they supply the basis for simple declarative statements. But a sequence of simple declarative statements can become terribly simple—and tedious. Since these little verbs are the workhorses of language, you cannot possibly do away with them all; yet they can be limited or varied. To locate patterns of excessive is-verbs in your draft, spend a minute or two quickly circling the verbs with a colored pen. This will indicate clusters of three or four is-verbs. When you see such clusters you should revise for variety.

How to do this? First, change as many verbs as possible to action verbs. Consider the example of Zane's essay on energy conservation (see chap. 3). In its original draft, the first two sentences read like this:

The year is 1933. There is no I-96, and Highway 131 is little more than a dream.

The initial verb pattern is weak. Zane began with a "there is" structure, which uses an expletive and an is-verb—a word which means nothing and a verb which does nothing. Compare it with his revision:

In the year 1933 the four-lane blacktop of Highway I-96 is little more than a dream.

Guidelines: Avoid expletives or ambiguous pronouns with an is-verb (there is, there are, it is); change is-verbs to action verbs.

Passive verbs

A parallel difficulty is represented in this sentence by the passive verb. In a passive structure such as the sentence immediately preceding, a sentence gets twisted around and seems to flow backwards; the subject winds up at the end of the sentence or disappears and the reader is uncertain what the subject actually does. Yet you could clarify this easily. Simply put the actual subject in the lead position and make the verb active. The corrected sentence then might read like this: "The passive verb represents a parallel difficulty." The aim here is to provide clear, direct sentence structures.

Guideline: Make passive structures active by placing the subject in the lead position and using an active verb.

Sentence Variety

Short sentences are not inherently bad; nor are long sentences. Yet too many short ones can weaken coherence, and too many long sentences can produce confusion. As a general rule, the essay should strive for a variety of sentence patterns and lengths.

In this matter, style is like an aerobic dance class. The dance patterns run through a wide variety of movements, from simple stretching routines to unbelievably complex performances. In a novice class, the students are likely to master a few simple routines—knee-ups, kicks, pendulums—which they do over and over again. However dynamic the accompanying music, the class is an exercise in tedium by its simple repetition, something to be worked through and washed away in a warm shower. On the other hand, some classes have routines so intricate Houdini couldn't find his way through the maze. The best classes, of course, will have a happy blend of exciting and varied movements.

Guideline: Provide sentence variety.

But how do you achieve this variety? Start with an analysis of the prose in its rough draft. In the following example, note two things: the structure of each sentence in subject-verb pattern and the lengths of the sentences.

Last winter I went skiing at Aspen, Colorado. I stayed a week at the Hotel Jerome. The adventure in Aspen was both good and bad. The first morning, I skied from seven until noon. I could hardly stop for lunch. I skied all afternoon until it was nearly dark. It snowed that night as I have never seen it snow before. It was probably the heaviest snow I have ever seen. It was far too deep the next morning to walk outside. Avalanches were predicted on the mountains. As a result skiing was cancelled. To my dismay, I didn't ski again until our last day there. Then I didn't even stop for lunch.

Analyzing the paragraph, we would say that it has at least one good trait—unity of topic. But the defects are glaring. The sentence structures are a step above the Dick-and-Jane readers of first grade. If one were to underline the subjects and verbs of each sentence, one would note these specific weaknesses. Except for an occasional and very short introductory prepositional phrase, each simple, declarative sentence works with similar subject-verb-object patterns. Moreover, we note two expletive/is-verb structures—a word that means nothing and verb that does nothing—in sequence in the middle of the paragraph. The repetitive pattern cries for variety.

Furthermore, if we count the words in each sentence, we note a disturbing pattern in sentence lengths. The paragraph has a total of thirteen sentences in the following individual word lengths: 8, 8, 9, 9, 6, 9, 12, 10, 11, 6, 6, 12, 7. The average word length per sentence is 9, and all are within 3 digits of 9. This is like turning out hamburgers all day at a fast food chain. The patties are all basically the same, just garnished a bit differently. As the hamburgers are nutritious, so too the sentences get the job done. But reading thirteen sentences like these in a row is somewhat like eating even three hamburgers in a row—boring and upsetting.

Now observe how the writer revised the paragraph, combining sentences and varying structures. Although the writer would probably want to cut out some irrelevant information, this second draft shows the right direction in revision by giving variety:

> When I went skiing at Aspen, Colorado, last winter, I stayed a week at the Hotel Jerome for an adventure that might be described as both good and bad. The first morning, after having skied from seven until noon, I could hardly stop for lunch. I skied all afternoon until it was nearly dark. That night it snowed as I have never seen it snow before, probably the heaviest I have ever seen. The next morning the snow lay too deep to walk outside, and avalanches were predicted on the mountains. As a result, skiing was cancelled. To my dismay, I didn't ski again until our last day there. Then I didn't even stop for lunch.

The results of the revision should be readily evident, even though the essence of the paragraph remains the same. In the revision, the eight sentences average 15 words, but, more significantly, they present a range of word lengths: 29, 16, 9, 19, 18, 6, 12, 7.

This "quantitative analysis of rhetoric" provides a helpful guide for analyzing a series of essays in a writing course. You might compare an early essay of yours, for example, with a later essay to note progress or areas still needing work. Moreover, you can focus on other areas as well. Taken to its extreme, a quantitative analysis breaks down the essay to averages on the number of syllables per word, the number of words per sentence, the number of sentences per paragraph, and the number of paragraphs per essay.

However, this revision to gain sentence variety is not the end of the matter. Perhaps you can spot additional difficulties in the paragraph that the writer still has to correct.

Sentence Combining

The writer of that paragraph about the skiing trip had a problem of too many brief sentences in similar patterns. But how do you make little sentences grow? Or, on the other hand, how do you shed unwanted words that make the sentence slow and flabby? As aerobics makes muscles grow while you lose weight, so sentence combining puts muscled energy into your prose.

Note this important caution, however. Sentence combining is not an end in itself. Short sentences are not intrinsically bad—any more than short people are. All of us were babies once, and most people believe that babies are precious. But a whole roomful of babies can be quite nerve-wracking, just like a whole essay full of little sentences. In the same way, long sentences are not intrinsically good. If you walked into a room full of the Los Angeles Lakers basketball team, you might feel out of place. Yet those Lakers, like long sentences, have their perfectly appropriate place, in this case on the basketball court, where they perform as harmoniously as long sentences strategically placed in the essay.

Although necessary cautions accompany sentence combining, it does have useful purposes: to give variety in sentence length, to provide complex and compound structures rather than simple, declarative ones, to get rid of weak verbs. In the example of the paragraph about skiing, all three types of revision are used. See if you can spot them.

When and how do you use sentence combining? The following basic guidelines and methods present some good starting points.

Cumulative structures

Here, because several sentences describe one subject, the sentences can be combined. The cumulative structure is so called because it "accumulates," or adds information to the main clause.

Original sentences:	John played racquetball whenever he could. He played in the morning. He played in the evening. He even played in the middle of the night.
Combined sentence:	John played racquetball whenever he could, in the morning, in the evening, even in the middle of the night.

Periodic structures

In the periodic structure, the combined information leads up to or describes the subject in the main clause at the end of the sentence. The structure provides a certain suspense that enriches the prose.

Original sentences:	His clothes were tattered. His shoulders were stooped. He carried a trowel in his hand. His mortar board was heavily loaded. The brick mason bent to a new line of bricks.
Combined sentence:	His clothes tattered, his shoulders stooped, his trowel carried in his hand, his mortar board heavily loaded, the brick mason bent to a new line of bricks.

Note: In the original sequence, the sentences are not parallel in subject and verb. Ideally, the combination should keep all elements in perfect parallelism.

Compound structures

Sentence combining is a particularly useful tool for showing relationships between ideas. The compound sentence simply joins independent and relatively equal units of information. In this example from the sample paragraph on skiing, two sentences are joined by a conjunction.

Original sentences:	The next morning the snow lay too deep to walk outside. Avalanches were predicted on the mountains.
Combined sentence:	The next morning the snow lay too deep to walk outside and avalanches were predicted on the mountains.

Complex structures

The complex structure subordinates one unit of information to another. Such subordinate clauses give conditions, time frameworks, reasons, and so forth, for the main clause.

Original sentences:	Last winter I went skiing at Aspen, Colorado. I stayed a week at the Hotel Jerome. The adventure in Aspen was both good and bad.
Combined sentence:	When I went skiing at Aspen, Colorado, last winter, I stayed a week at the Hotel Jerome for an adventure that might be described as both good and bad.

The absolute phrase

The absolute phrase (or free sentence modifier) modifies no particular word, but the whole sentence generally. Unlike other modifying phrases, absolutes are not connected to the rest of the sentence by any joining words (a preposition, subordinating conjunction, or relative pronoun, for example). Instead, you transform the verb of one sentence to a participle.

Original sentences:	She ran to the store. Her purse jingled with change.
Combined sentence:	She ran to the store, her purse jingling with change.

Combining performs the task of building rhetorical energy and excising unnecessary words. One of the most powerful methods of revision, sentence combining helps you develop a smooth and forceful personal style. If you still wonder how it works, try to "decombine" a sentence. Break the original down into smaller sentences. For example, you could decombine the second sentence of this paragraph to look like this: "Sentence combining is one of the most popular current methods of rhetorical revision. Sentence combining helps the writer develop a smooth style and a forceful personal style." You can see the greater energy and coherence achieved by the combination.

Guideline: Where possible, consider sentence combining in one of the preceding patterns for sentence complexity and variety.

Diction

Almost always the diction, or word selection, of your essay can be improved by finding more nearly precise or powerful words. Even an occasional startling or unusual word can have a positive effect on the essay.

The following passage, from Stephen R. Donaldson's best-selling novel *Lord Foul's Bane* (New York: Ballantine, 1977), demonstrates the energy that careful diction provides in writing. At this point in the novel, a group of people led by Thomas Covenant, the book's hero, has

struggled to cross a barren wasteland and now appears suddenly on
the banks of the Soulsease River:

> Blue under the azure sky, it meandered broad, quiet and slow almost
> directly eastward across their path like a demarcation or boundary of
> achievement. As it turned and ran among the Hills, it had a glitter of
> youth, a sparkle of contained exuberance which could burst into laugh-
> ter the moment it was tickled by a shoals. And its water was as clean,
> clear and fresh as an offer of baptism (173).

Reading the passage, we sense the sudden delight of the travelers upon
discovering the river; we almost feel the excitement and freshness.
What makes this happen? Notice first of all Donaldson's diction. The
words themselves convey the spirit of surprise and wonder, words
like *achievement, glitter, sparkle, exuberance,* and *laughter.* Second, we
notice the lively use of figurative language with the river personified as
a living thing and with the striking simile of the last sentence.

While we all admire fresh and vigorous writing with effective diction, a strong caution is in order. Sometimes a writer can get so involved with using long or unusual words that the paper reads like a
thesaurus. For example, the radicals of the 1960s used this slogan:
"Power to the People!" Suppose they had consulted a thesaurus be-
forehand and had come up with something like this: "Prepotency to
the Populace!" Not quite as effective. The first guideline is to be precise. But feel free to use the uncommon or startling word on occasion.

A second guideline is to avoid colloquialisms, slang words, and
clichés. Although such expressions serve us perfectly well while we are
chatting in the coffee shop, they do poorly for most other audiences.
They simply aren't precise enough and, when removed from the gestures and vocal tones used in coffee-shop conversation, are often quite
meaningless. Consider the analogy of the out-of-tune Chevy used at the
beginning of this section. The Chevy is a bit like the way we casually
talk with friends. Sometimes the timing is off, a plug misfires; but the
car still runs. Our friends still understand us. But the situation is
different in the formal essay; there, because the audience is assumed
and can't ask questions, you need to make every word count. Obliter-
ate every cliché, slang expression, and colloquialism in the essay.

What is a cliché? A trite, commonplace expression. Often clichés
don't mean much of anything, like advertisements that have gone out
of use. One advertisement shouts that a certain soft drink "is it!" What
is "it"? No one knows. Later the company declares, "It's the real thing."
What is a real thing? And what *is* a real thing? Before you write, "He's
sadder but wiser," ask yourself how often that cliché has saddened you.

Clichés are thoroughly predictable—so much so that you can probably complete this list without hesitation:

He is greedy for filthy _____.

He is as strong as an _____.

They thank her from the _____ of their hearts.

He is as slow as a _____.

To be brutally _____.

A miss is as good as a _____.

I wrote this list by the sweat of my _____.

In the last _____, clichés are ridiculous.

Revision Checklist

Certain revisions are obvious, but also sometimes ignored. A routine checklist for your essay, for example, might include the following:

1. Does the beginning work to engage the reader?
2. Is the thesis clear?
3. Are the major points of the essay clearly indicated in topic sentences?
4. Are transitions between paragraphs and sections of the essay clear?
5. Does each paragraph develop a single topic? Is that topic in the subject position in all the sentences of the paragraph?
6. Is the body of the paper unified and free of irrelevant arguments?
7. Does the conclusion refer to the thesis? Does it refer to a central image or idea to provide unity? Does it make use of rhetorical techniques such as parallelism to provide paragraph unity? Does it introduce any new argument? It shouldn't. Does it end in a preachy, didactic fashion? It shouldn't.
8. Are all words spelled correctly?

6

From Working Outline to Outline

Many instructors will require an outline to be attached to an essay, but the greatest value of outlining to you as a writer lies in its function as an analytical and organizing device for the paper. The outline helps you gain an awareness of the essay as a whole, to cut out irrelevant arguments, to see the relation of the thesis to the whole, to plan the incorporation of research. Because of these benefits to you in writing, the emphasis in this section will be on the *working* outline, an overview or blueprint for the developing essay as a whole. The task of adapting a final outline from the working outline is fairly simple and is demonstrated at the end of this chapter.

The outline does, however, pose a problem for any writer. For example, we have already drawn attention to the value of freewriting. Freewriting recognizes the fact that you discover and channel your thoughts in the process of writing itself. Often a writer begins with a sense of what to say and confirms it by writing. It's a rare writer indeed who has a complete outline before actually writing the first draft.

On the other hand, you might write the entire essay and, when you then outline it, find sections and arguments wildly out of balance. Much better to discover that while writing rather than having to re-draft the entire essay.

It's an old problem: which comes first—the chicken or the egg, the essay or the outline?

The ideal seems to lie in a working outline, a rough plan for the essay that can be easily transformed into a final outline. The case which follows details one such working outline.

Joel Anker has received an assignment to write a paper on Aldous Huxley's *Brave New World*. While reading the novel, Joel marks passages that capture his attention. He begins to observe certain patterns of emphasis in the novel—a pattern of attitudes toward women, toward science, toward God. And then he notices a larger emphasis throughout the novel on how the Brave-New-World leaders engineer humanity. The novel opens with a portrait of test-tube babies being engineered to fill certain planned roles in society, as scientists, pilots, rulers, garbagemen, and so forth. From that opening portrait Joel observes a continuing effort by the Brave-New-World controllers to plan and control the lives of the citizens. Reflecting on the pattern, Joel sees links to genetic engineering in our own society. He has his subject for the essay, *Brave New World;* his topic, genetic engineering; and now a working thesis, the relation of genetic engineering in *Brave New World* to our own society.

That thesis will head the outline. The outline itself will detail how the thesis will be developed and concluded.

Joel faces two major challenges in his essay of literary analysis. The first is to analyze clearly and systematically the situation in *Brave New World*, called the primary text or source. Therefore, the first part of his essay will be devoted to such analysis, and he will be careful to relate subsequent sections to it. The second major challenge is to show the significance of the situation in *Brave New World* to contemporary life.

With a clearer idea of where he wants his essay to go, Joel begins organizing his research to support his argument. Note his specific steps on the working outline which follows.

I. Introduction

In the introduction Joel asks himself three key questions which help him start and focus the paper.

1. What is the *motivation* for genetic engineering in *Brave New World*? What is the guiding principle, the idea, or the philosophy behind it? The idea here is to supply a context for his argument.
2. What is the *actual process* of genetic engineering in *Brave New World*? Here the literary analysis of the primary text becomes more specific, and Joel has listed page references for key passages from *Brave New World* that he will either paraphrase, summarize, or quote directly in support of his analysis.
3. What are the *effects* of genetic engineering in *Brave New World*? This third question leads to implications which set up the transition to the body of his paper.

II. Body

1. Because the purpose of the working outline is to gain unity and focus, Joel has written some trial transition sentences between sections.
2. In the body of the essay, Joel will discuss the three major points of the thesis projection. On the outline he has listed references to

his notecards, numbered NC 1, 3, 8, and so forth, for quotations he wants to use in his discussion. His notecards will contain the full information he will need for his bibliography. The reference here merely identifies the source for later use.

3. Wherever possible Joel has tried to use one specific example for each thesis point. For instance, he has learned of a laboratory called the Jordan Laboratory which actually conducts genetic experiments. On the working outline (section II, A) he has written instructions to himself concerning what specific items to include about the laboratory.

4. Notice that Joel has reminded himself in II, A, 3 to include a transitional paragraph between section divisions.

5. Joel has also reminded himself to keep the essay focused on the primary work, *Brave New World*, by drawing parallels in the transition paragraphs.

The bracketed material represents editorial comment on Joel's procedure.

Working Outline

The prophetic voice of Aldous Huxley's *Brave New World* has been fulfilled in that contemporary society now engages in genetic engineering. The extent of this engineering may be seen by current experiments with DNA molecular structure, by efforts to construct a test-tube baby, and by interuterine manipulation of the fetus to correct prebirth defects.

[Thesis statement]

[Thesis projection]

I. Genetic engineering in *BNW*

[Introductory: supply the *why* or the background behind the *what* or the issue under examination. Provide a context for the reader.]

A. Philosophy of GE in *BNW*
    pp. 12, 16, 32

[Reference notes for discussion of book.]

B. Actual process of GE in *BNW*
    pp. 18, 107, 109

[The issue explained.]

C. Effects of GE in *BNW*

[Implications and tie to thesis.]

II. Transitional material into body
    Genetic engineering is being practiced in the United States today to an extent which makes Huxley's *Brave New World* appear to be a work of contemporary urgency.

[Trial transitional sentence]

[Include a general description of such engineering.]

A. Current experimentation with
   DNA molecular structure

    [First thesis point discussed]

  1. Practice and extent of
   experimentation
   Time (July 14, 1977),
   pp. 17–20, NC 1, 3, 8

  2. The Jordan Laboratory
   More evidence of this current
   experimentation may be seen
   by examining one laboratory
   in New State, Connecticut,
   the Jordan Laboratory, which
   has ties with York University
   but which is separately and
   heavily endowed by the
   Federal Department
   of Eugenics.

    [Trial transition sentence]

    [Provide statement of purpose
   of the laboratory, functions, work
   produced.]

  3. Reference to parallels with
   BNW, summary, and
   transition

B. Efforts to produce a test-tube
   baby
  1. The general medical
   procedure explained
   New Life Review (August
   1985), pp. 12–36, NC 12, 13,
   14, 15
  2. The Medical Origins Institute

    [Specific example]

  3. Parallels with *BNW*, etc.

C. Interuterine manipulation of the
   fetus
  1. Statistics on number of
   procedures and kinds of
   procedures
   *American Medical Association
   Journal* (Winter 1984), pp. 18–
   81, NC 21–25
  2. J. Fetal Memorial Hospital

    [Specific example]

  3. Parallels with *BNW*, etc.

III. Implications for the future

    [Remember techniques of
   parallelism, subordination,
   restatement.]

Final Outline

The prophetic voice of Aldous Huxley's *Brave New World* has been fulfilled in that contemporary society now engages in genetic engineering. The extent of this engineering may be seen by current experiments with DNA molecular structure, by efforts to construct a test-tube baby, and by interuterine manipulation of the fetus to correct prebirth defects.

I. Genetic Engineering in *Brave New World*
   A. The philosophy of genetic engineering
   B. The actual process of genetic engineering
   C. The effects of genetic engineering
II. Present State of Genetic Engineering
   A. Current experimentation with DNA molecular structure
      1. Practice and extent of experimentation
      2. The Jordan Laboratory
      3. Parallels with *Brave New World*
   B. Efforts to produce a test-tube baby
      1. The medical procedure
      2. The Medical Origins Institute
      3. Parallels with *Brave New World*
   C. Interuterine manipulation of the fetus
      1. Number and nature of procedures
      2. J. Fetal Memorial Hospital
      3. Parallels with *Brave New World*
III. Implications for the Future

7

Documentation

Much of the success of your research paper will depend upon its *authority*. Are the ideas expressed logically and convincingly? Can the assertions be supported by statistical data or by experts? Clear writing will establish a certain degree of authority. We all have had occasion to remark: "This person knows what he is talking about!" And to an extent we say that because of the way the ideas are expressed. But we also say that because of the careful research and documentation a person has done to support the ideas.

Much of that research depends upon hard and practical work in the library, locating and selecting accurate supporting information. Different instructors will employ different techniques to acquaint you with these resources. And to a large degree, you will adopt certain research patterns that work well for you.

For example, one person may feel comfortable taking notes on three-by-five-inch notecards and then arranging these for ready access while writing the essay. Others may feel more comfortable putting notes and quotations in a notebook and indexing them. This provides a broader context for consulting the research data. Still others may prefer working directly with the books and magazines related to their essay topic.

Regardless of the method of research adopted, certain fundamental principles govern good technique in quoting and footnoting research materials. But before examining those techniques, two cautions should be mentioned.

First, *authority*. Since the goal of research is to establish authority in your essay, you may be tempted to rely too much upon outside resources. If research gives the paper authority, you might think, then the more the better. Not so! In fact, large blocks of quoted material tend to distract a reader and to obscure the argument. You, the writer, must remain in control of the paper and use research *only to support your argument*. Because of this important rhetorical point, we will pay close attention to *subordinating* and *integrating* quoted material in the examples that follow.

Second, *plagiarism*. Whenever you begin to do research and to use quotations or statistics from that research, you confront the problem of plagiarism. The problem can arise in two ways. On the one hand, as you begin to do research, you may begin to wonder whether any ideas are your own. It may seem that every idea you have for your paper has already been expressed. Generally, the advice here is to relax. Certainly, others have grappled with similar ideas. That doesn't mean that you don't have the right to express your views on the subject. We have to understand that, to a large degree, certain ideas are of a general nature, and each of us works through them in his or her own way. On the other hand, however, you have to be careful about deliberately using, without acknowledgment, someone else's argument or words for expressing those ideas. This act is plagiarism.

A practical problem often arises here in taking notes. As a general guideline, notecards should have quotation marks around every word or unit of words copied from a source. Often, in the hurry to meet deadlines for essays, writers can become a bit sloppy taking notes, blurring the distinctions between quotation, paraphrase, and personal comments.

What is plagiarism? And how does a Christian writer deal with it? To understand fully the seriousness of plagiarism, you have to understand the moral nature of plagiarism, what exactly constitutes plagiarism, and what the academic consequences for plagiarism are.

The following document is adapted from a policy statement on plagiarism by one Christian college. Many colleges have similar documents, which provide both the moral context of plagiarism and specific definitions for what constitutes plagiarism.

English Department Policy on Plagiarism

PREAMBLE

The English Department considers plagiarism as a moral and not merely a legal matter on the assumption that the function of a college, particularly a Christian college, is not only to impart knowledge but also to nurture moral character. The department believes that plagiarism is not only legally but also morally wrong. First, it is a deception—of the instructor, obviously, but no less of the student himself. Cheating hides a person from the encounter with what he really is, what he really can do, or what he can be. Second, plagiarism is a theft—of the materials themselves, but no less of the right of the cheater's fellow students to equal consideration; for in effect the plagiarized paper throws all other papers into competition with work that likely has already been judged superior. Third, plagiarism breeds a moral atmosphere which denies all students the dignity and freedom due them as human beings. Inevitably, one cheater throws the taint of suspicion upon all, the entire climate is poisoned, and mutual respect is endangered. Furthermore, the values of humane education are perverted when the instructor is forced to give extraordinary attention to the integrity of the grade and can no longer assume the integrity of the student. To sum up, plagiarism is a sin, a violation of the Eighth Commandment. It is inimical to the values and ideals of a Christian educational institution.

The English Department, therefore, sets forth the following definition and policy:

Definition

Plagiarism means presenting as one's own the words, work, or opinions of someone else.

1. You plagiarize if you submit as your own work, without appropriate documentation or quotation marks,
   a. part or all of a written or spoken assignment copied from another person's manuscript;
   b. part or all of an assignment copied or paraphrased from a source, such as a book, magazine, or pamphlet;
   c. the sequence of ideas, arrangement of material, and pattern of thought of someone else, even though you express them in your own words.
2. You are an accomplice in plagiarism and are equally guilty if
   a. you allow your paper, in outline or finished form, to be copied and submitted as the work of another;
   b. you prepare a written assignment for another student and allow him to submit it as his work;
   c. you keep or contribute to a file of papers or speeches with the intent that these papers or speeches be copied and submitted as the work of someone other than the author.

This document also stipulates certain consequences for any act of plagiarism in that college. These consequences will vary from one institution to another, but generally they will require as a minimum penalty a failing grade on the plagiarized essay. It is expected, however, that any individual act should be treated in a spirit of correction rather than simply punishment.

Quotations

Remember that readability of your paper is the primary concern and that too many quotations can tend to blur your argument and slow the pace. You will have to be selective, then, in your quotations, using only those directly and significantly related to *your* argument. You do this, first of all, by working the quotations into the body of your paragraph. Integrate them. Avoid a lead-off quotation and then arguing from it. You are the authority in the paper, and you are using the quotation only to substantiate that authority.

The following examples demonstrate methods of smooth incorporation of the quotation.

Direct Quotations

If you quote directly, the material must, of course, be cited. The challenge here is to integrate the quoted material as smoothly as possible into your paragraph. Whenever possible, subordinate the quotation in your own sentence. For example:

Quotation incorporated into leading sentence:

Jones established that in the cases of these deaths the primary causes were "unsterile and unsanitary operating procedures, damage to the uterus resulting in massive hemorrhage and death, and improper operative and postoperative care leading to gross infection."

Quotation subordinated in a noun clause:

In his essay on veterinary medicine, Dr. Jonas Roberts advised that "the Cocker Spaniel should be given a weekly treat of egg and milk with one teaspoon of cooking oil."

Quotation introduced by a full sentence and a colon:

In his essay on veterinary medicine, Dr. Jonas Roberts advised the pampering of pets: "The Cocker Spaniel should be given a weekly treat of egg and milk with one teaspoon of cooking oil."

Quotation introduced by a phrase and a comma:

According to Dr. Jonas Roberts in his essay on veterinary medicine, "the Cocker Spaniel should be given a weekly treat of egg and milk with one teaspoon of cooking oil."

Block Quotations

As a general guideline, a quotation longer than five lines in your essay should be set off in a block format. It is set off by indenting the left margin five to seven spaces. Usually, block quotations are best set off by a colon. Following is an example. Notice that one way to sustain your authority in your writing is to follow up every block quotation with a sentence that analyzes its purpose or that points toward the next paragraph.

> In his study of fantasy literature, *Other Worlds*, John H. Timmerman writes of the importance of study in fantasy:
>
> > As a general premise we should agree that story seeks to free the imagination, to allow the imagination to live for a time in another world. This would be true of all great literature. In allegory the *author* deliberately patterns the fictional world in order to suggest specific meanings to the reader. To be successful, the allegorical *work* must be self-restrictive; that is to say, a figure who on page one represents death may not on page ten represent life.

Thus, if a fantasy story frees the imagination to explore other worlds, it also requires that the imagination be consistent in its structuring of those fantasy lands.

Ellipsis in Quotations

When do you use ellipsis, the series of three spaced periods that indicate material omitted from the original quotation? If possible, never at the beginning of a quotation. Almost always this can be avoided by subordinating the quotation to your lead clause (see the examples on p. 60).

If *extensive* or *intrusive* information should be excluded from the quotation in order to make your prose more readable, however, ellipsis can be inserted in place of that material.

Original quotation:	"Susan Waverly, a bright young scholar from Stanford University who has ably demonstrated her competence in genetic research, has argued before a Senate hearing that *in vitro* fertilization will one day enable all childless couples to enjoy the blessing of a family, perhaps as many children as they wish."
Elliptical quotations:	*In vitro* fertilization holds immense promise for childless couples. In fact, one recent article records the testimony of Stanford geneticist Susan Waverly, a testimony which can only be seen as encouraging to now childless couples:

[Three spaced
periods internally]
"Susan Waverly . . . has argued before a Senate hearing that *in vitro* fertilization will one day enable all childless couples to enjoy the blessing of a family, perhaps as many children as they wish."

[A final period
and three spaced
periods at the end]
"Susan Waverly, a bright young scholar from Stanford University who has ably demonstrated her competence in genetic research, has argued before a Senate hearing that *in vitro* fertilization will one day enable all childless couples to enjoy the blessing of a family. . . ."

Brackets

If you interject material into the quotation by way of explanation or indentification, use brackets to identify that material as yours.

John Little believes that "he [the Roman Emperor] had absolute authority in matters of life and death."

Notes and Footnotes

When you use information from other sources you need to document it. Most of the college writing you do will require you to use some form of documentation. In part, you need to do this to avoid plagiarism. Like stereos and real estate, ideas—at least certain kinds of ideas—are property, and they may not be used without permission. But there is a positive reason for using notes as well. When you write an academic paper, you participate in a long tradition of writing, a tradition that assumes that ideas build on other ideas. Thus, when you document your use of other sources, you are directing your readers to the information that shaped your ideas.

When should you provide documentation? The simplest answer is that you should refer to your source whenever you use someone else's ideas or whenever you make a controversial assertion. If the fact is common knowledge—that John F. Kennedy died in 1963 or that photosynthesis makes leaves green—you need not document your source. On the other hand, if you assert that Kennedy died as the victim of a conspiracy, you should document your source. The assertion is clearly controversial or the product of some historian's specialized research. The documentation in such cases makes the argument of your essay stronger because it establishes a scholarly context for your ideas.

When in doubt, document. At this stage of your career, you are wise to be careful. It is better to have a few too many footnotes than to be accused of plagiarism. Yet you should avoid peppering your essay with notes. Your instructor can provide more guidance on how to do this, but one way is to avoid the open-ended reference that simply directs the reader to some book on a library shelf. This practice can become both confusing and annoying to the reader. Such materials, which show works that supplied the general background of your research, should be included only in the bibliography.

Your teacher may ask that you use traditional footnotes; if so, you should consider the following example as a model. In it Gwen McNeill is writing an essay on C. S. Lewis's novel *The Lion, the Witch and the Wardrobe*. That work is referred to as her *primary resource*. The studies of Lewis and his novel that she researches are called *secondary resources*. Following is one paragraph from Gwen's essay, with the quotations that she must footnote labeled [**A**], [**B**], and [**C**]. The paragraph occurs midway in her essay when she is making a transition between discussing the novel simply as a children's novel and discussing the novel in terms of its symbolism.

One may see, then, that Lewis has achieved a remarkable success in *The Lion, the Witch and the Wardrobe* as a children's story. The novel has qualities of diction, adventure, pace, and excitement which captivate a young audience. Upon closer consideration, however, the careful reader also observes a work of intricate symbolism rooted in familiar biblical types and passages. The great lion Aslan, for example, clearly has symbolic significance. Upon first hearing the lion's name from Mr. Beaver, the children begin to experience a strange feeling:

> "They say Aslan is on the move—perhaps has already landed."
> And now a very curious thing happened. None of the children knew who Aslan was any more than you do; but the moment the Beaver had spoken these words everyone felt quite different. . . . At the name of Aslan each one of the children felt something jump in his inside.[1] [**A**]

Of this passage, Peter J. Schakel comments, "The reader, too, to some extent, shares the experience. He or she doesn't know who Aslan is, but some of the sense of excitement, of awe, and of expectation is conveyed to him or her as it is to the children."[2] [**B**] Later the children discover that their initial feelings of excitement are surpassed by a deeper feeling of love. Seeing the shorn face of Aslan as he is prepared for execution, Susan believes that "Aslan looked to her braver, and more beautiful and more patient than ever" (p. 151). [**C**] Clearly, Aslan has become to her someone most precious and meaningful.

Notice, first of all, that Gwen has provided an excellent transition by using summary and key words like *however* to change the focus of her essay. In the paragraph, she quotes three times, in each case nicely integrating the quotation into the context of her discourse. The quotations flow smoothly; the writer retains authority. Here is the footnoting technique for each quotation.

A. This is Gwen's first quotation from the primary source, set in block quotation form because of its length. Because she will quote from this primary source several times in the essay, she elects to use parenthetical page citation for future references. The first footnote must be a full entry; and, if the primary source will be used for future parenthetical reference, she will include an additional sentence stating that fact. Her full first footnote, then, will appear like this:

> [1]C. S. Lewis, *The Lion, the Witch and the Wardrobe* (New York: Collier Books, 1970), p. 64. Page references for quotations from *The Lion, the Witch and the Wardrobe* are hereafter cited parenthetically in the text.

When should you use parenthetical reference in this system? As a general guideline, use such reference when you quote from a primary source more than three times in a typical essay. Otherwise, and for secondary-source notations, use individual footnotes.

Notice also that Gwen has omitted a part of the original quotation, accurately indicated by the use of ellipsis.

B. Gwen's second quotation is from a secondary source, a critical analysis of Lewis's works. The proper footnote form is as follows:

> [2]Peter J. Schakel, *Reading with the Heart: The Way into Narnia* (Grand Rapids, MI: William B. Eerdmans Publishing Company, 1979), p. 22.

Note that the full title of the book, taken from the title page, is used. If Gwen were to quote from this book again she would use a shortened form:

> [2]Schakel, *Reading with the Heart*, p. 92.

C. The third quotation demonstrates the proper form for subsequent notation of the primary source. Since the initial footnote has indicated the procedure, the writer simply enters the page number in parenthesis *between* the quotation marks and the sentence period.

If parenthetical notation is used with a block quotation (which doesn't use quotation marks), the parenthesis falls outside the sentence period.

As you plan to type your final draft, your first question will be whether your instructor requires footnotes (at the bottom of the page) or endnotes (on a separate page at the end of the paper). In either case, each footnote is intended to be read as one sentence, and, con-sequently, each follows a careful pattern of internal punctuation.

A book with one author:

[1]Northrop Frye, *Anatomy of Criticism: Four Essays* (Princeton: Princeton Univer-sity Press, 1957), p. 52.

A book with two or three authors:

[2]Bob Woodward and Carl Bernstein, *The Final Days* (New York: Simon and Schuster, 1976), p. 107.

(**Note:** Place the authors' names in the order in which they appear on the title page. If there are more than three authors, use the first name and the Latin term *et al.,* which means "and others.")

An edited book:

[3]Rodney J. Mulder and John H. Timmerman, eds., *Markings on a Long Journey: Writings of John J. Timmerman* (Grand Rapids, MI: Baker Book House, 1982), p. 101.

An essay in an edited book:

[4]Steve J. Van Der Weele, "From Mt. Olympus to Glome: C. S. Lewis's Dislocation of Apuleius's 'Cupid and Psyche' in *Till We Have Faces,*" *The Longing for a Form: Essays on the Fiction of C. S. Lewis,* ed. Peter J. Schakel (Kent, OH: Kent State University Press, 1977), p. 183.

A translation:

[5]Giovanni Boccaccio, *The Decameron,* trans. Richard Aldington (New York: Dell Publishing Company, 1962), p. 18.

An article in a journal with pagination complete in each issue:

[6]Richard L. Harp, "The Christian Reader and the Christian Life," *Christianity and Literature,* 25, No. 3 (Spring 1976), p. 10.

(**Note:** The number 25 refers to the annual volume number; No. 3 refers to the number of the journal within that annual volume.)

An article from a journal with continuous pagination throughout the volume year:

⁷Paul F. Reichardt, "Gawain and the Image of the Wound," *PMLA*, 99 (March 1984), p. 155.

An article in a monthly magazine:

⁸William Broyles, Jr., "The Road to Hill 10," *The Atlantic* (April 1985), p. 90.

An article in a weekly magazine:

⁹Robert C. Christopher, "Let's Give Pearl Harbor a Rest," *Newsweek*, 14 October 1985, p. 24.

An unsigned article:

¹⁰"50 Protesters March Against Abortion," *The Grand Rapids Press*, 7 May 1985, sec. 1, p. 2, col. 4.

Your teacher, however, may wish you to use the method of parenthetical citation recommended by the Modern Language Association (MLA), an association of more than twenty-five thousand teachers of English and other languages. Each parenthetical citation in the text of the essay refers the reader to the more complete information about that source that can be found in the bibliography or list of works cited which should complete your essay. Additional examples of this style can be found in the second edition of *MLA Handbook for Writers of Research Papers* by Joseph Gibaldi and Walter S. Achtert (New York: Modern Language Association, 1984). What follows, however, is a brief introduction that will allow you to cite the most common kinds of sources; the citations are keyed to the bibliography that appears at the end of this section.

A reference without the author's name:

Perhaps most intriguing to young readers is the first book of the series in which the children wander into Narnia through a magic wardrobe (Lewis 25).

Notice that you provide only the author's last name and the page number of the reference and that the parentheses fall within the final punctuation of the sentence.

A reference that uses the author's name:

Of this passage, Peter J. Schakel comments, "The reader, too, to some extent, shares the experience" (22).

Since the text of your essay provides the reader with the author's name, the reference needs only to list the page number.

A reference to more than one work by an author:

In the final book of the series, the children encounter a form of the anti-Christ, the god Tash (Lewis, *The Last Battle* 87).

In this instance, your object is to provide just enough information so that your reader can find your reference in the bibliography; an abbreviated form of the title serves well.

A reference to a work with an editor:

Lewis's *Till We Have Faces* illustrates an important point: "that Christianity has resources of insight and wisdom not available to those who deny transcendence or the reality of Christian revelation" (Van Der Weele 192).

Notice that you cite the author of the article and not the editor of the work. Your purpose, remember, is to direct your reader first of all to the originator of the idea you cite and secondly to the place where you found the idea.

Bibliography

The same footnote entries are arranged alphabetically according to the following format under the heading *Bibliography* or *List of Sources* or *Works Cited and Consulted*. The bibliography may be broader than your footnote references, including, for example, all the works you researched rather than just those from which you quoted. This sample bibliography is based on the forms found in the second edition of the *MLA Handbook for Writers of Research Papers*.

Bibliography

Boccaccio, Giovanni. *The Decameron*. Trans. Richard Aldington. New York:Dell Publishing Company, 1962.

Broyles, William, Jr. "The Road to Hill 10." *The Atlantic* Apr. 1985: 90–118.

(**Note:** A bibliography gives the complete pagination of an article from a journal or newspaper. If the article is broken up by advertisements, it is normally numbered continuously. If it is broken up by other articles, with some of the essay appearing later in the magazine, the page numbers are divided according to the pagination of the article: 89–101, 114–18.)

Christopher, Robert C. "Let's Give Pearl Harbor a Rest." *Newsweek* 14 Oct. 1985: 24.

"50 Protesters March Against Abortion." *Grand Rapids Press* 7 May 1985: A2.

Frye, Northrop. *Anatomy of Criticism: Four Essays*. Princeton: Princeton University Press, 1957.

Harp, Richard L. "The Christian Reader and the Christian Life." *Christianity and Literature* 25.3 (1976): 9–17.

Lewis, C. S. *The Last Battle*. 1956. New York: Macmillan, 1970.

Lewis, C. S. *The Lion, the Witch and the Wardrobe*. 1950. New York: Macmillan, 1974.

Mulder, Rodney J. and John H. Timmerman, eds. *Markings on a Long Journey: Writings of John J. Timmerman*. Grand Rapids: Baker Book House, 1982.

Reichardt, Paul F. "Gawain and the Image of the Wound." *PMLA* 99 (1984): 154–61.

Van Der Weele, Steve J. "From Mt. Olympus to Glome: C. S. Lewis's Dislocation of Apuleius's 'Cupid and Psyche' in *Till We Have Faces*." *The Longing for a Form: Essays on the Fiction of C. S. Lewis*. Ed. Peter J. Schakel. Kent: Kent State University Press, 1977. 182–92.

Woodward, Bob and Carl Bernstein. *The Final Days*. New York: Simon and Schuster, 1976.

PART 2

Reading

8

Defining a Worldview

Religion

Q. What is your only comfort in life and in death?
A. That I am not my own, but belong body and soul in life and
   in death to my faithful Savior Jesus Christ.

—Heidelberg Catechism

We find insufficient evidence for belief in the existence of a
supernatural; it is either meaningless or irrelevant to the
question of the survival and fulfillment of the human race. As
non-theists we begin with humans, not God, nature, not deity.
But we can discover no divine purpose or providence for the
human species. While there is much we do not know, humans
are responsible for what we are or will become. No deity will
save us; we must save ourselves.

—Humanist Manifesto II

Those days recorded in Luke 9 had been wearying ones for Jesus. As
word of his miracles and message spread, crowds grew about him.
Always there was the urgency of their need pressing upon him.

One can imagine the rumors that buzzed through the crowds as he
responded to their need. Some were saying that this was John, raised
from the dead. Others said that this was Elijah or one of the other Old
Testament prophets, come back in power to establish the kingdom of

God. When Jesus finally found time to be alone with his disciples, he asked them, "Who do the people say that I am?" They repeated the rumors they had heard. It was insufficient then, and remains so today, to answer Jesus' question simply as a voice echoing the words of a vast crowd. We must answer for ourselves, alone with the Savior and his question. So it is that Jesus confronts the disciples individually: "But who do you say that I am?"

He asks the same of everyone, and the answer that each of us gives serves as the foundation of our worldview, our way of seeing the world so that it is meaningful. As in Jesus' time, so too today many different answers arise in response to his question. One person answers, "My Lord and my King." Another, troubled by the aristocratic connotations of the titles *lord* and *king*, says, "My Savior." Another person calls him a great moral teacher; yet another terms him a hoax. The Buddhist calls him a *Bodhisattva*, one who has attained enlightenment, but who postpones Nirvana in order to help others. The Jehovah's Witness names him as God's son, but not God. The variety of responses to this question is misleading, however. There really are but two answers; either we call him God, or we do not.

The answer each of us gives determines who we are, for it is an answer that determines our place in the world. Saint Augustine describes the choice as one between two cities, one earthly, the other heavenly. Each has been formed by a different love, "the earthly by the love of self, even to the contempt of God; the heavenly by the love of God, even to the contempt of self" (*The City of God*). Augustine's use of the word *cities* here is important, for our answer to the question entails more than words; it affects the way we live. As Augustine explains, "The former, in a word, glories in itself, the latter in the Lord. For the one seeks glory from men; but the greatest glory of the other is God, the witness of conscience. The one lifts up its head in its own glory; the other says to its God, 'Thou art my glory, and the lifter up of mine head.'" The choice is that of Romans 1:25—between worship of the Creator and the created.

Flannery O'Connor portrays this truth in her short story "A Good Man Is Hard to Find." One of the characters, an escaped criminal named The Misfit, clearly identifies the consequences of responding to Jesus. "Jesus was the only One that ever raised the dead," says The Misfit, "and he shouldn't have done it. He thrown everything off balance. If He did what he said, then it's nothing for you to do but throw away everything and follow Him, and if He didn't then it's nothing for you to do but enjoy the few minutes you got left the best way you can— by killing somebody or burning down his house or doing some other meanness to him." Like The Misfit, we must decide between belief and obedience or disbelief and self-indulgence.

While in one sense this choice is as old as the gospel, in another it is a peculiarly modern choice. The debate over the merits of Christianity in the essays of Bertrand Russell and C. S. Lewis that are included in this chapter would have been very different a little over a hundred years ago. Then, most of Western culture believed in the existence of God and in historical Christianity. Certainly, there were dissenters; yet European and American culture were largely Christian. During the nineteenth century, however, developments in the culture increasingly led people to question the existence of God and the authenticity of the Bible. Charles Darwin's *Origin of Species*, published in 1859, raised questions about creation. In the 1880s, a new version of the Bible, the first in more than 250 years, led many people to raise new questions about the authority and inspiration of Scripture. In the United States the divisive terror of the Civil War raised questions about God's providence through political structures, questions that sharpened during the wars of our own century. More recently, discoveries in science and technology have led many to question whether there is a need for a God at all.

Each of the authors in this section responds to some aspect of this elementary choice. In "Dover Beach," Matthew Arnold captures that moment in the nineteenth century when Western civilization began to ponder life without God. James W. Fowler sets forth a theory for the development of faith. Emily Dickinson, M. Howard Rienstra, and Dorothy M. Johnson give accounts of individual experiences of God or of trials of faith. Stephen V. Monsma ponders the application of his faith in the world of politics. Each of these, we will notice, makes conclusions out of his or her fundamental understanding of who Jesus is.

Dover Beach

Matthew Arnold

One of the major figures of the Victorian era, Matthew Arnold wrote literary and social criticism, as well as poetry. As this poem suggests, he was interested in discovering meaning in a world where religion no longer provided satisfaction. His response to such a world is one that has echoed through the twentieth century.

The sea is calm tonight.
The tide is full, the moon lies fair
Upon the straits—on the French coast the light
Gleams and is gone; the cliffs of England stand,
Glimmering and vast, out in the tranquil bay.
Come to the window, sweet is the night-air!
Only, from the long line of spray
Where the sea meets the moon-blanched land,
Listen! you hear the grating roar
Of pebbles which the waves draw back, and fling,
At their return, up the high strand,
Begin, and cease, and then again begin,
With tremulous cadence slow, and bring
The eternal note of sadness in.

Sophocles long ago
Heard it on the Aegean, and it brought
Into his mind the turbid ebb and flow
Of human misery; we
Find also in the sound a thought,
Hearing it by this distant northern sea.

The Sea of Faith
Was once, too, at the full, and round earth's shore
Lay like the folds of a bright girdle furled.

But now I only hear
Its melancholy, long, withdrawing roar,
Retreating, to the breath
Of the night-wind, down the vast edges drear
And naked shingles of the world.

Ah, love, let us be true
To one another! for the world, which seems
To lie before us like a land of dreams,
So various, so beautiful, so new,
Hath really neither joy, nor love, nor light,
Nor certitude, nor peace, nor help for pain;
And we are here as on a darkling plain
Swept with confused alarms of struggle and flight,
Where ignorant armies clash by night.

Discussion

1. Examine the poem for places where the language or the style of the poem seems to reinforce the sense of the lines.
2. In the margin list the key images of the poem, and note how they contribute to the progression and meaning of the poem. How is the title important to how the poem works?
3. Elsewhere Arnold writes this about his poetry and his times: "The future of poetry is immense, because in poetry, where it is worthy of its high destinies, our race, as time goes on, will find an ever surer and surer stay. There is not a creed which is not shaken, not an accredited dogma which is not shown to be questionable, not a received tradition which does not threaten to dissolve." Those are strong words. What had happened in Victorian England to shake religion and tradition? Do you see any similarities between the ideas of the poem and those of the quotation?

Why I Am Not a Christian

Bertrand Russell

Christianity is outdated, an empty myth that some persist in believing even though it is rationally exposed as a fraud. So argues Bertrand Russell, a twentieth-century British philosopher, noted for his empirical emphasis in philosophy. As you will see in his critique of Christianity, Russell generally sought to base his thought—whether philosophical, mathematical, or ethical—on actual experience. He objected to beliefs held on the basis of faith. "The important thing," he said, "is not what you believe, but how you believe it."

Nowadays . . . we have to be a little more vague in our meaning of Christianity [than were people in former times]. I think, however, that there are two different items which are quite essential to anybody calling himself a Christian. The first is one of a dogmatic nature—namely, that you must believe in God and immortality. If you do not believe in those two things, I do not think that you can properly call yourself a Christian. Then, further than that, as the name implies, you must have some kind of belief about Christ. The Mohammedans, for instance, also believe in God and in immortality, and yet they would not call themselves Christians. I think you must have at the very lowest the belief that Christ was, if not divine, at least the best and wisest of men. If you are not going to believe that much about Christ, I do not think you have any right to call yourself a Christian. Of course, there is another sense, which you find in *Whitaker's Almanack* and in geography books, where the population of the world is said to be divided into Christians, Mohammedans, Buddhists, fetish worshipers, and so on; and in that sense we are all Christians. The geography books count us all in, but that is a purely geographical sense, which I suppose we can ignore. Therefore I take it that when I tell you why I am not a Christian I have to tell you two different things: first, why I do not believe in God and in immortality; and, secondly, why I do not think that Christ was the best and wisest of men, although I grant him a very high degree of moral goodness.

But for the successful efforts of unbelievers in the past, I could not take so elastic a definition of Christianity as that. As I said before, in olden days it had a much more full-blooded sense. For instance, it included the belief in hell. Belief in eternal hell-fire was an essential item of Christian belief until pretty recent times. In this country, as you know, it ceased to be an essential item because of a decision of the Privy Council, and from that decision the Archbishop of Canterbury and the Archbishop of York dissented; but in this country our religion is settled by Act of Parliament, and therefore the Privy Council was able to override their Graces and hell was no longer necessary to a Christian. Consequently I shall not insist that a Christian must believe in hell.

The Existence of God

To come to this question of the existence of God: it is a large and serious question, and if I were to attempt to deal with it in any adequate manner I should have to keep you here until Kingdom Come, so that you will have to excuse me if I deal with it in a somewhat summary fashion. You know, of course, that the Catholic Church has laid it down as a dogma that the existence of God can be proved by the unaided reason. That is a somewhat curious dogma, but it is one of their dogmas. They had to introduce it because at one time the freethinkers adopted the habit of saying that there were such and such arguments which mere reason might urge against the existence of God, but of course they knew as a matter of faith that God did exist. The arguments and the reasons were set out at great length, and the Catholic Church felt that they must stop it. Therefore they laid it down that the existence of God can be proved by the unaided reason and they had to set up what they considered were arguments to prove it. There are, of course, a number of them, but I shall take only a few.

The First-Cause Argument

Perhaps the simplest and easiest to understand is the argument of the First Cause. (It is maintained that everything we see in this world has a cause, and as you go back in the chain of causes further and further you must come to a First Cause, and to that First Cause you give the name of God.) That argument, I suppose, does not carry very much weight nowadays, because, in the first place, cause is not quite what it used to be. The philosophers and the men of science have got going on cause, and it has not anything like the vitality it used to have; but, apart from that, you can see that the argument that there must be a First Cause is one that cannot have any validity. I may say that when I was a young man and was debating these questions very seriously in my mind, I for a long time accepted the argument of the First Cause, until one day, at the age of eighteen, I read John Stuart Mill's Auto-biography, and I there found this sentence: "My father taught me that the question 'Who made me?' cannot be answered, since it imme-diately suggests the further question 'Who made God?'" That very simple sentence showed me, as I still think, the fallacy in the argument of the First Cause. If everything must have a cause, then God must have a cause. If there can be anything without a cause, it may just as well be the world as God, so that there cannot be any validity in that argu-ment. It is exactly of the same nature as the Hindu's view, that the world rested upon an elephant and the elephant rested upon a tortoise; and when they said, "How about the tortoise?" the Indian said, "Suppose we change the subject." The argument is really no better than that. There is no reason why the world could not have come into being without a cause; nor, on the other hand, is there any reason why it should not have always existed. There is no reason to suppose that the world had a beginning at all. The idea that things must have a beginning is really due to the poverty of our imagination. Therefore, perhaps, I need not waste any more time upon the argument about the First Cause.

Defects in Christ's Teaching

Historically it is quite doubtful whether Christ ever existed at all, and if He did we do not know anything about Him, so that I am not concerned with the historical question, which is a very difficult one. I am concerned with Christ as He appears in the Gospels, taking the Gospel narrative as it stands, and there one does find some things that do not seem to be very wise. For one thing, He certainly thought that His second coming would occur in clouds of glory before the death of all the people who were living at that time. There are a great many texts that prove that. He says, for instance, "Ye shall not have gone over the cities of Israel till the Son of Man be come." Then He says, "There are some standing here which shall not taste death till the Son of Man comes into His kingdom"; and there are a lot of places where it is quite clear that He believed that His second coming would happen during the lifetime of many then living. That was the belief of His earlier followers, and it was the basis of a good deal of his moral teaching. When He said, "Take no thought for the morrow," and things of that sort, it was very largely because He thought that the second coming was going to be very soon, and that all ordinary mundane affairs did not count. I have, as a matter of fact, known some Christians who did believe that the second coming was imminent. I knew a parson who frightened his congregation terribly by telling them that the second coming was very imminent indeed, but they were much consoled when they found that he was planting trees in his garden. The early Christians did really believe it, and they did abstain from such things as planting trees in their gardens, because they did accept from Christ the belief that the second coming was imminent. In that respect, clearly He was not so wise as some other people have been, and He was certainly not superlatively wise.

The Moral Problem

Then you come to moral questions. There is one very serious defect to my mind in Christ's moral character, and that is that He believed in hell. I do not myself feel that any person who is really profoundly humane can believe in everlasting punishment. Christ certainly as depicted in the Gospels did believe in everlasting punishment, and one does find repeatedly a vindictive fury against those people who would not listen to His preaching—an attitude which is not uncommon with preachers, but which does somewhat detract from superlative excellence. You do not, for instance, find that attitude in Socrates. You find him quite bland and urbane toward the people who would not listen to him; and it is, to my mind, far more worthy of a sage to take that line than to take the line of indignation. You probably all remember the sort of things that Socrates was saying when he was dying, and the sort of things that he generally did say to people who did not agree with him.

You will find that in the Gospels Christ said, "Ye serpents, ye generation of vipers, how can ye escape the damnation of hell." That was said to people who did not like His preaching. It is not really to my mind quite the best tone, and there are a great many of these things about hell. There is, of course, the familiar text about the sin against the Holy Ghost: "Whosoever speaketh against the Holy Ghost it shall not be forgiven him neither in this World nor in the world to come." That text has caused an unspeakable amount of misery in the world, for all sorts of people have imagined that they have committed the sin against the

Holy Ghost, and thought that it would not be forgiven them either in this world or in the world to come. I really do not think that a person with a proper degree of kindliness in his nature would have put fears and terrors of that sort into the world.

Then Christ says, "The Son of Man shall send forth His angels, and they shall gather out of His kingdom all things that offend, and them which do iniquity, and shall cast them into a furnace of fire; there shall be wailing and gnashing of teeth"; and He goes on about the wailing and gnashing of teeth. It comes in one verse after another, and it is quite manifest to the reader that there is a certain pleasure in contemplating wailing and gnashing of teeth, or else it would not occur so often. Then you all, of course, remember about the sheep and the goats; how at the second coming He is going to divide the sheep from the goats, and He is going to say to the goats, "Depart from me, ye cursed, into everlasting fire." He continues, "And these shall go away into everlasting fire." Then He says again, "If thy hand offend thee, cut it off; it is better for thee to enter into life maimed, than having two hands to go into hell, into the fire that never shall be quenched; where the worm dieth not and the fire is not quenched." He repeats that again and again also. I must say that I think all this doctrine, that hell-fire is a punishment for sin, is a doctrine of cruelty. It is a doctrine that put cruelty into the world and gave the world generations of cruel torture; and the Christ of the Gospels, if you could take Him as His chroniclers represent Him, would certainly have to be considered partly responsible for that.

There are other things of less importance. There is the instance of the Gadarene swine, where it certainly was not very kind to the pigs to put the devils into them and make them rush down the hill to the sea. You must remember that He was omnipotent, and He could have made the devils simply go away; but He chose to send them into the pigs. Then there is the curious story of the fig tree, which always rather puzzled me. You remember what happened about the fig tree. "He was hungry; and seeing a fig tree afar off having leaves, He came if haply He might find anything thereon; and when He came to it He found nothing but leaves, for the time of figs was not yet. And Jesus answered and said unto it: 'No man eat fruit of thee hereafter for ever' . . . and Peter . . . saith unto Him: 'Master, behold the fig tree which thou cursedst is withered away.'" This is a very curious story, because it was not the right time of year for figs, and you really could not blame the tree. I cannot myself feel that either in the matter of wisdom or in the matter of virtue Christ stands quite as high as some other people known to history. I think I should put Buddha and Socrates above Him in those respects.

The Emotional Factor

As I said before, I do not think that the real reason why people accept religion has anything to do with argumentation. They accept religion on emotional grounds. One is often told that it is a very wrong thing to attack religion, because religion makes men virtuous. So I am told; I have not noticed it. You know, of course, the parody of that argument in Samuel Butler's book, *Erewhon Revisited.* You will remember that in *Erewhon* there is a certain Higgs who arrives in a remote country, and after spending some time there he escapes from that country in a balloon. Twenty years later he comes back to that country and finds a new religion in which he is worshiped under the name of the "Sun Child," and it is said that he ascended into heaven. He finds that the Feast of the Ascension is about to be celebrated, and he hears Professors Hanky and Panky say to each other that they never set eyes on the man Higgs, and they hope they never will; but they are the high priests of the religion of the Sun Child. He is very indignant, and he comes up to them, and he says, "I am going to expose all this humbug and tell the people of Erewhon that it was only I, the man Higgs, and I went up in a balloon." He was told, "You must not do that, because all the morals of this country are bound round this myth, and if they once know that you did not ascend into heaven they will all become wicked"; and so he is persuaded of that and he goes quietly away.

That is the idea—that we should all be wicked if we did not hold to the Christian religion. It seems to me that the people who have held to it have been for the most part extremely wicked. You find this curious fact, that the more intense has been the religion of any period and the more profound has been the dogmatic belief, the greater has been the cruelty and the worse has been the state of affairs. In the so-called ages of faith, when men really did believe the Christian religion in all its completeness, there was the Inquisition, with its tortures; there were millions of unfortunate women burned as witches; and there was every kind of cruelty practiced upon all sorts of people in the name of religion.

You find as you look around the world that every single bit of progress in humane feeling, every improvement in the criminal law, every step toward the diminution of war, every step toward better treatment of the colored races, or every mitigation of slavery, every moral progress that there has been in the world, has been consistently opposed by the organized churches of the world. I say quite deliberately that the Christian religion, as organized in its churches, has been and still is the principal enemy of moral progress in the world.

How the Churches Have Retarded Progress

You may think that I am going too far when I say that that is still so. I do not think that I am. Take one fact. You will bear with me if I mention it. It is not a pleasant fact, but the churches compel one to mention facts that are not pleasant. Supposing that in this world that we live in today an inexperienced girl is married to a syphilitic man; in that case the Catholic Church says, "This is an indissoluble sacrament. You must stay together for life." And no steps of any sort must be taken by that woman to prevent herself from giving birth to syphilitic children. That is what the Catholic Church says. I say that that is fiendish cruelty, and nobody whose natural sympathies have not been warped by dogma, or whose moral nature was not absolutely dead to all sense of suffering, could maintain that it is right and proper that that state of things should continue.

That is only an example. There are a great many ways in which, at the present moment, the church, by its insistence upon what it chooses to call morality, inflicts upon all sorts of people undeserved and unnecessary suffering. And of course, as we know, it is in its major part an opponent still of progress and of improvement in all the ways that diminish suffering in the world, because it has chosen to label as morality a certain narrow set of rules of conduct which have nothing to do with human happiness; and when you say that this or that ought to be done because it would make for human happiness, they think that has nothing to do with the matter at all. "What has human happiness to do with morals? The object of morals is not to make people happy."

Fear, the Foundation of Religion

Religion is based, I think, primarily and mainly upon fear. It is partly the terror of the unknown and partly, as I have said, the wish to feel that you have a kind of elder brother who will stand by you in all your troubles and disputes. Fear is the basis of the whole thing—fear of the mysterious, fear of defeat, fear of death. Fear is the parent of cruelty, and therefore it is no wonder if cruelty and religion have gone hand in hand. It is because fear is at the basis of those two things. In this world we can now begin a little to understand things, and a little to master them by help of science, which has forced its way step by step against the Christian religion, against the churches, and against the opposition of all the old precepts. Science can help us to get over this craven fear in which mankind has lived for so many generations. Science can teach us, and I think our own hearts can teach us, no longer to look around for imaginary supports, no longer to invent allies in the sky, but rather to look to our own efforts here below to make this world a fit place to live in, instead of the sort of place that the churches in all these centuries have made it.

What We Must Do

We want to stand upon our own feet and look fair and square at the world—its good facts, its bad facts, its beauties, and its ugliness; see the world as it is and be not afraid of it. Conquer the world by intelligence and not merely by being slavishly subdued by the terror that comes from it. The whole conception of God is a conception derived from the ancient Oriental despotisms. It is a conception quite unworthy of free men. When you hear people in church debasing themselves and saying that they are miserable sinners, and all the rest of it, it seems contemptible and not worthy of self-respecting human beings. We ought to stand up and look the world frankly in the face. We ought to make the best we can of the world, and if it is not so good as we wish, after all it will still be better than what these others have made of it in all these ages. A good world needs knowledge, kindliness, and courage; it does not need a regretful hankering after the past or a fettering of the free intelligence by the words uttered long ago by ignorant men. It needs a fearless outlook and a free intelligence. It needs hope for the future, not looking back all the time toward a past that is dead, which we trust will be far surpassed by the future that our intelligence can create.

Discussion

1. List the presuppositions of Russell's attack on Christianity. Does understanding them help you to imagine ways of responding to the article?
2. A number of Russell's points against Christianity depend on his experience of it (e.g., his tongue-in cheek point about belief in hell). Is he wrong to base his attack on his personal experience of his subject? How would you attempt to understand another religion, Buddhism, for example?
3. Can you rebut the argument Russell makes about the defects in Christ's teaching? Sometimes background information can help you shape a response; for example, the *NIV Study Bible* offers this note on the incident of Jesus and the fig tree: "Fig trees around Jerusalem normally begin to get leaves in March or April but do not produce figs until their leaves are all out in

June. This tree was an exception in that it was already, at Passover time, full of leaves."

4. For an argument to be convincing, it must be logical. Do you spot any flaws in logic in Russell's analysis? For example, he argues that it was not kind of Jesus to drive the demons into the pigs in the case of the Gadarene demoniac. But isn't that miraculous act, which Russell accepts, in itself a sign of Jesus' divine nature—which premise Russell denies?

5. Is Russell right in any of his criticisms?

6. What is your response to the statement that fear is the foundation of religion? Can you support your response with Scripture?

What Christians Believe

C. S. Lewis

Perhaps best known for his children's novels set in the imaginary land of Narnia, C. S. Lewis also wrote numerous other works of fiction and nonfiction, including his famous apology for the Christian religion, Mere Christianity. *This excerpt from that work can be read as a response to Russell's attack on Christian belief. Both seek to present a clear argument that the layperson could accept; however, their different assumptions lead them in different directions, and to different conclusions.*

The Rival Conceptions of God

I have been asked to tell you what Christians believe, and I am going to begin by telling you one thing that Christians do not need to believe. If you are a Christian you do not have to believe that all the other religions are simply wrong all through. If you are an atheist you do have to believe that the main point in all religions of the whole world is simply one huge mistake. If you are a Christian, you are free to think that all these religions, even the queerest ones, contain at least some hint of the truth. When I was an atheist I had to try to persuade myself that most of the human race have always been wrong about the question that mattered to them most; when I became a Christian I was able to take a more liberal view. But, of course, being a Christian does mean thinking that where Christianity differs from other religions, Christianity is right and they are wrong. As in arithmetic—there is only one right answer to a sum, and all other answers are wrong: but some of the wrong answers are much nearer being right than others.

The first big division of humanity is into the majority, who believe in some kind of God or gods, and the minority who do not. On this point,

Christianity lines up with the majority—lines up with ancient Greeks and Romans, modern savages, Stoics, Platonists, Hindus, Mohammedans, etc., against the modern Western European materialist.

Now I go on to the next big division. People who all believe in God can be divided according to the sort of God they believe in. There are two very different ideas on this subject. One of them is the idea that He is beyond good and evil. We humans call one thing good and another thing bad. But according to some people that is merely our human point of view. These people would say that the wiser you become the less you would want to call anything good or bad, and the more clearly you would see that everything is good in one way and bad in another, and that nothing could have been different. Consequently, these people think that long before you got anywhere near the divine point of view the distinction would have disappeared altogether. We call a cancer bad, they would say, because it kills a man; but you might just as well call a successful surgeon bad because he kills a cancer. It all depends on the point of view. The other and opposite idea is that God is quite definitely "good" or "righteous," a God who takes sides, who loves love and hates hatred, who wants us to behave in one way and not in another. The first of these views—the one that thinks God beyond good and evil—is called Pantheism. It was held by the great Prussian philosopher Hegel and, as far as I can understand them, by the Hindus. The other view is held by Jews, Mohammedans and Christians.

And with this big difference between Pantheism and the Christian idea of God, there usually goes another. Pantheists usually believe that God, so to speak, animates the universe as you animate your body: that the universe almost *is* God, so that if it did not exist He would not exist either, and anything you find in the universe is a part of God. The Christian idea is quite different. They think God invented and made the universe—like a man making a picture or composing a tune. A painter is not a picture, and he does not die if his picture is destroyed. You may say, "He's put a lot of himself into it," but you only mean that all its beauty and interest has come out of his head. His skill is not in the picture in the same way that it is in his head, or even in his hands. I expect you see how this difference between Pantheists and Christians hangs together with the other one. If you do not take the distinction between good and bad very seriously, then it is easy to say that anything you find in this world is a part of God. But, of course, if you think some things really bad, and God really good, then you cannot talk like that. You must believe that God is separate from the world and that some of the things we see in it are contrary to His will. Confronted with a cancer or a slum the Pantheist can say, "If you could only see it from the divine point of view, you would realise that this also is God." The

Christian replies, "Don't talk damned nonsense." For Christianity is a fighting religion. It thinks God made the world—that space and time, heat and cold, and all the colours and tastes, and all the animals and vegetables, are things that God "made up out of His head" as a man makes up a story. But it also thinks that a great many things have gone wrong with the world that God made and that God insists, and insists very loudly, on our putting them right again.

And, of course, that raises a very big question. If a good God made the world why has it gone wrong? And for many years I simply refused to listen to the Christian answers to this question, because I kept on feeling "whatever you say, and however clever your arguments are, isn't it much simpler and easier to say that the world was not made by any intelligent power? Aren't all your arguments simply a complicated attempt to avoid the obvious?" But then that threw me back into another difficulty.

My argument against God was that the universe seemed so cruel and unjust. But how had I got this idea of *just* and *unjust*? A man does not call a line crooked unless he has some idea of a straight line. What was I comparing this universe with when I called it unjust? If the whole show was bad and senseless from A to Z, so to speak, why did I, who was supposed to be part of the show, find myself in such violent reaction against it? A man feels wet when he falls into water, because man is not a water animal: a fish would not feel wet. Of course I could have given up my idea of justice by saying it was nothing but a private idea of my own. But if I did that, then my argument against God collapsed too—for the argument depended on saying that the world was really unjust, not simply that it did not happen to please my private fancies. Thus in the very act of trying to prove that God did not exist—in other words, that the whole of reality was senseless—I found I was forced to assume that one part of reality—namely my idea of justice—was full of sense. Consequently atheism turns out to be too simple. If the whole universe has no meaning, we should never have found out that it has no meaning: just as, if there were no light in the universe and therefore no creatures with eyes, we should never know it was dark. *Dark* would be without meaning.

The Invasion

Very well then, atheism is too simple. And I will tell you another view that is also too simple. It is the view I call Christianity-and-water, the view which simply says there is a good God in Heaven and everything is all right—leaving out all the difficult and terrible doctrines about sin and hell and the devil, and the redemption. Both these are boys' philosophies.

It is no good asking for a simple religion. After all, real things are not simple. They look simple, but they are not. The table I am sitting at looks simple: but ask a scientist to tell you what it is really made of— all about the atoms and how the light waves rebound from them and hit my eye and what they do to the optic nerve and what it does to my brain—and, of course, you find that what we call "seeing a table" lands you in mysteries and complications which you can hardly get to the end of. A child saying a child's prayer looks simple. And if you are content to stop there, well and good. But if you are not—and the modern world usually is not—if you want to go on and ask what is really happening—then you must be prepared for something difficult. If we ask for something more than simplicity, it is silly then to complain that the something more is not simple.

Very often, however, this silly procedure is adopted by people who are not silly, but who, consciously or unconsciously, want to destroy Christianity. Such people put up a version of Christianity suitable for a child of six and make that the object of their attack. When you try to explain the Christian doctrine as it is really held by an instructed adult, they then complain that you are making their heads turn round and that it is all too complicated and that if there really were a God they are sure He would have made "religion" simple, because simplicity is so beautiful, etc. You must be on your guard against these people for they will change their ground every minute and only waste your time. Notice, too, their idea of God "making religion simple": as if "religion" were something God invented, and not His statement to us of certain quite unalterable facts about His own nature.

Besides being complicated, reality, in my experience, is usually odd. It is not neat, not obvious, not what you expect. For instance, when you have grasped that the earth and the other planets all go round the sun, you would naturally expect that all the planets were made to match— all at equal distances from each other, say, or distances that regularly increased, or all the same size, or else getting bigger or smaller as you go farther from the sun. In fact, you find no rhyme or reason (that we can see) about either the sizes or the distances; and some of them have one moon, one has four, one has two, some have none, and one has a ring.

Reality, in fact, is usually something you could not have guessed. That is one of the reasons I believe Christianity. It is a religion you could not have guessed. If it offered us just the kind of universe we had always expected, I should feel we were making it up. But, in fact, it is not the sort of thing anyone would have made up. It has just that queer twist about it that real things have. So let us leave behind all these boys' philosophies—these oversimple answers. The problem is not simple and the answer is not going to be simple either.

What is the problem? A universe that contains much that is obviously bad and apparently meaningless, but containing creatures like ourselves who know that it is bad and meaningless. There are only two views that face all the facts. One is the Christian view that this is a good world that has gone wrong, but still retains the memory of what it ought to have been. The other is the view called Dualism. Dualism means the belief that there are two equal and independent powers at the back of everything, one of them good and the other bad, and that this universe is the battlefield in which they fight out an endless war. I personally think that next to Christianity Dualism is the manliest and most sensible creed on the market. But it has a catch in it.

The two powers, or spirits, or gods—the good one and the bad one— are supposed to be quite independent. They both existed from all eternity. Neither of them made the other, neither of them has any more right than the other to call itself God. Each presumably thinks it is good and thinks the other bad. One of them likes hatred and cruelty, and the other likes love and mercy, and each backs its own view. Now what do we mean we call one of them the Good Power and the other the Bad Power? Either we are merely saying that we happen to prefer the one to the other—like preferring beer to cider—or else we are saying that, whatever the two powers think about it, and whichever we humans, at the moment, happen to like, one of them is actually wrong, actually mistaken, in regarding itself as good. Now if we mean merely that we happen to prefer the first, then we must give up talking about good and evil at all. For good means what you ought to prefer quite regardless of what you happen to like at any given moment. If "being good" meant simply joining the side you happened to fancy, for no real reason, then good would not deserve to be called good. So we must mean that one of the two powers is actually wrong and the other actually right.

But the moment you say that, you are putting into the universe a third thing in addition to the two Powers: some law or standard or rule of good which one of the powers conforms to and the other fails to conform to. But since the two powers are judged by this standard, then this standard, or the Being who made this standard, is farther back and higher up than either of them, and He will be the real God. In fact, what we meant by calling them good and bad turns out to be that one of them is in a right relation to the real ultimate God and the other in a wrong relation to Him.

The same point can be made in a different way. If Dualism is true, then the bad Power must be a being who likes badness for its own sake. But in reality we have no experience of anyone liking badness just because it is bad. The nearest we can get to it is in cruelty. But in real life people are cruel for one of two reasons—either because they are sadists, that is, because they have a sexual perversion which makes cruelty a cause of sensual pleasure to them, or else for the sake of something they are going to get out of it—money, or power, or safety. But pleasure, money, power, and safety are all, as far as they go, good things. The badness consists in pursuing them by the wrong method, or in the wrong way, or too much. I do not mean, of course, that the people who do this are not desperately wicked. I do mean that wickedness, when you examine it, turns out to be the pursuit of some good in the wrong way. You can be good for the mere sake of goodness: you cannot be bad for the mere sake of badness. You can do a kind action when you are not feeling kind and when it gives you no pleasure, simply because kindness is right; but no one ever did a cruel action simply because cruelty is wrong—only because cruelty was pleasant or useful to him. In other words badness cannot succeed even in being bad in the same way in which goodness is good. Goodness is, so to speak, itself: badness is only spoiled goodness. And there must be something good first before it can be spoiled. We called sadism a sexual perversion; but you must first have the idea of a normal sexuality before you can talk of its being perverted; and you can see which is the perversion, because you can explain the perverted from the normal, and cannot explain the normal from the perverted. It follows that this Bad Power, who is supposed to be on an equal footing with the Good Power, and to love badness in the same way as the Good Power loves goodness, is a mere bogy. In order to be bad he must have good things to want and then to pursue in the wrong way: he must have impulses which were originally good in order to be able to pervert them. But if he is bad he cannot supply himself either with good things to desire or with good impulses to pervert. He must be getting both from the Good Power. And if so, then he is not independent. He is part of the Good Power's world: he was made either by the Good Power or by some power above them both.

Put it more simply still. To be bad, he must exist and have intelligence and will. But existence, intelligence and will are in themselves good. Therefore he must be getting them from the Good Power: even to be bad he must borrow or steal from his opponent. And do you now begin to see why Christianity has always said that the devil is a fallen angel? That is not a mere story for the children. It is a real recognition of the fact that evil is a parasite, not an original thing. The powers which enable evil to carry on are powers given it by goodness. All the things which enable a bad man to be effectively bad are in themselves good things—resolution, cleverness, good looks, existence itself. That is why Dualism, in a strict sense, will not work.

But I freely admit that real Christianity (as distinct from Christianity-and-water) goes much nearer to Dualism than people think. One of the things that surprised me when I first read the New Testament seriously was that it talked so much about a Dark Power in the universe—a mighty evil spirit who was held to be the Power behind death and disease, and sin. The difference is that Christianity thinks this Dark Power was created by God, and was good when he was created, and went wrong. Christianity agrees with Dualism that this universe is at war. But it does not think this is a war between independent powers. It thinks it is a civil war, a rebellion, and that we are living in a part of the universe occupied by the rebel.

Enemy-occupied territory—that is what this world is. Christianity is the story of how the rightful king has landed, you might say landed in disguise, and is calling us all to take part in a great campaign of sabotage. When you go to church you are really listening-in to the secret wireless from our friends: that is why the enemy is so anxious to prevent us from going. He does it by playing on our conceit and laziness and intellectual snobbery. I know someone will ask me, "Do you really mean, at this time of day, to re-introduce our old friend the devil—hoofs and horns and all?" Well, what the time of day has to do with it I do not know. And I am particular about the hoofs and horns. But in other respects my answer is "Yes, I do." I do not claim to know anything about his personal appearance. If anybody really wants to know him better I would say to that person, "Don't worry. If you really want to, you will. Whether you'll like it when you do is another question."

The Shocking Alternative

Christians, then, believe that an evil power has made himself for the present the Prince of this World. And, of course, that raises problems. Is this state of affairs in accordance with God's will or not? If it is, He is a strange God, you will say: and if it is not, how can anything happen contrary to the will of a being with absolute power?

But anyone who has been in authority knows how a thing can be in accordance with your will in one way and not in another. It may be quite sensible for a mother to say to the children, "I'm not going to go and make you tidy the schoolroom every night. You've got to learn to keep it tidy on your own." Then she goes up one night and finds the Teddy bear and the ink and the French Grammar all lying in the grate. That is against her will. She would prefer the children to be tidy. But on the other hand, it is her will which has left the children free to be untidy. The same thing arises in any regiment, or trade union, or school. You make a thing voluntary and then half the people do not do it. That is not what you willed, but your will has made it possible.

It is probably the same in the universe. God created things which had free will. That means creatures which can go either wrong or right. Some people think they can imagine a creature which was free but had no possibility of going wrong; I cannot. If a thing is free to be good it is also free to be bad. And free will is what has made evil possible. Why, then, did God give them free will? Because free will, though it makes evil possible, is also the only thing that makes possible any love or goodness or joy worth having. A world of automata—of creatures that worked like machines—would hardly be worth creating. The happiness which God designs for His higher creatures is the happiness of being freely, voluntarily united to Him and to each other in an ecstasy of love and delight compared with which the most rapturous love between a man and a woman on this earth is mere milk and water. And for that they must be free.

Of course God knew what would happen if they used their freedom the wrong way: apparently He thought it worth the risk. Perhaps we feel inclined to disagree with Him. But there is a difficulty about disagreeing with God. He is the source from which all your reasoning power comes: you could not be right and He wrong any more than a stream can rise higher than its own source. When you are arguing against Him you are arguing against the very power that makes you able to argue at all: it is like cutting off the branch you are sitting on. If God thinks this state of war in the universe a price worth paying for free will—that is, for making a live world in which creatures can do real good or harm and something of real importance can happen, instead of a toy world which only moves when He pulls the strings—then we may take it it is worth paying.

When we have understood about free will, we shall see how silly it is to ask, as somebody once asked me: "Why did God make a creature of such rotten stuff that it went wrong?" The better stuff a creature is made of—the cleverer and stronger and freer it is—then the better it will be if it goes right, but also the worse it will be if it goes wrong. A cow cannot be very good or very bad; a dog can be both better and worse; a child better and worse still; an ordinary man, still more so; a man of genius, still more so; a superhuman spirit best—or worst of all.

How did the Dark Power go wrong? Here, no doubt, we ask a question to which human beings cannot give an answer with any certainty. A reasonable (and traditional) guess, based on our own experiences of going wrong, can, however, be offered. The moment you have a self at all, there is a possibility of putting yourself first—wanting to be the centre—wanting to be God, in fact. That was the sin of Satan: and that was the sin he taught the human race. Some people think the fall of man had something to do with sex, but that is a mistake. (The story in the Book of Genesis rather suggests that some corruption in our sexual nature followed the fall and was its result, not its cause.) What Satan put into the heads of our remote ancestors was the idea that they could "be like gods"—could set up on their own as if they had created themselves—be their own masters—invent some sort of happiness for themselves outside God, apart from God. And out of that hopeless attempt has come nearly all that we call human history—money, poverty, ambition, war, prostitution, classes, empires, slavery—the long terrible story of man trying to find something other than God which will make him happy.

The reason why it can never succeed is this. God made us: invented us as a man invents an engine. A car is made to run on gasoline, and it would not run properly on anything else. Now God designed the human machine to run on Himself. He Himself is the fuel our spirits were designed to burn, or the food our spirits were designed to feed on. There is no other. That is why it is just no good asking God to make us happy in our own way without bothering about religion. God cannot give us a happiness and peace apart from Himself, because it is not there. There is no such thing.

That is the key to history. Terrific energy is expended—civilisations are built up—excellent institutions devised; but each time something goes wrong. Some fatal flaw always brings the selfish and cruel people to the top and it all slides back into misery and ruin. In fact, the machine conks. It seems to start up all right and runs a few yards, and then it breaks down. They are trying to run it on the wrong juice. That is what Satan has done to us humans.

And what did God do? First of all He left us conscience, the sense of right and wrong: and all through history there have been people trying (some of them very hard) to obey it. None of them ever quite succeeded. Secondly, He sent the human race what I call good dreams: I mean those queer stories scattered all through the heathen religions about a god who dies and comes to life again and, by his death, has somehow given new life to men. Thirdly, He selected one particular people and spent several centuries hammering into their heads the sort of God He was—that there was only one of Him and that He cared about right conduct. Those people were the Jews, and the Old Testament gives an account of the hammering process.

Then comes the real shock. Among these Jews there suddenly turns up a man who goes about talking as if He was God. He claims to forgive sins. He says He has always existed. He says He is coming to judge the world at the end of time. Now let us get this clear. Among Pantheists, like the Indians, anyone might say that he was a part of God, or one with God: there would be nothing very odd about it. But this man, since He was a Jew, could not mean that kind of God. God, in their language, meant the Being outside the world Who had made it and was infinitely different from anything else. And when you have grasped that, you will see that what this man said was, quite simply, the most shocking thing that has ever been uttered by human lips.

One part of the claim tends to slip past us unnoticed because we have heard it so often that we no longer see what it amounts to. I mean the claim to forgive sins: any sins. Now unless the speaker is God, this is really so preposterous as to be comic. We can all understand how a man forgives offences against himself. You tread on my toe and I forgive you, you steal my money and I forgive you. But what should we make of a man, himself unrobbed and untrodden on, who announced that he forgave you for treading on other men's toes and stealing other men's money? Asinine fatuity is the kindest description we should give of his conduct. Yet this is what Jesus did. He told people that their sins were forgiven, and never waited to consult all the other people whom their sins had undoubtedly injured. He unhesitatingly behaved as if He was the party chiefly concerned, the person chiefly offended in all offences. This makes sense only if He really was the God whose laws are broken and whose love is wounded in every sin. In the mouth of any speaker who is not God, these words would imply what I can only regard as a silliness and conceit unrivalled by any other character in history.

Yet (and this is the strange, significant thing) even His enemies, when they read the Gospels, do not usually get the impression of silliness and conceit. Still less do unprejudiced readers. Christ says that He is "humble and meek" and we believe Him; not noticing that, if He were merely a man, humility and meekness are the very last characteristics we could attribute to some of His sayings.

I am trying here to prevent anyone saying the really foolish thing that people often say about Him: "I'm ready to accept Jesus as a great moral teacher, but I don't accept His claim to be God." That is the one thing we must not say. A man who was merely a man and said the sort of things Jesus said would not be a great moral teacher. He would either be a lunatic—on a level with the man who says he is a poached egg—or else he would be the Devil of Hell. You must make your choice. Either this man was, and is, the Son of God: or else a madman or something worse. You can shut Him up for a fool, you can spit at Him and kill Him as a demon; or you can fall at His feet and call Him Lord and God. But let us not come with any patronising nonsense about His being a great human teacher. He has not left that open to us. He did not intend to.

Discussion

1. Do you agree with Lewis when he says that Christians don't have to believe that other religions are wrong all through? If not, why not? If so, suggest some good things about other religions.
2. Do you see any elements of pantheism in our culture? Apply Lewis's discussion of pantheism and the Christian view of creation to Psalm 19.
3. What do you think of Lewis's response to the hypothetical pantheist: "Don't talk damned nonsense"? Is his language appropriate for a Christian?
4. Contrast Russell's view of hell and Lewis's view of what he calls a "Christianity-and-water" religion devoid of hell.
5. What does Lewis mean when he says that Christianity is a fighting religion? Do you agree?
6. List the ten best and the ten worst things man has done since creation and discuss the implications of your list for determining whether man is bad or good.
7. What passages in the Bible might make unbelievers think Christ to be, in Lewis's terms, a lunatic?

Stages of Faith
and Human Becoming

James W. Fowler

> *Just as Jean Piaget, Erik Erikson, and Lawrence Kohlberg
> have presented pioneering theories on human
> development, so James W. Fowler has offered a theory
> on the development of faith. His* Stages of Faith *is built
> on ten years of research into the developmental
> patterns of faith. Although some may quarrel with his
> definition of faith as "a person's way of seeing himself
> or herself against a background of shared meaning and
> purpose," his theory has proved valuable in a number
> of contexts, including that of the development of
> Christian educational materials.*

In the analysis of . . . faith development interviews, which may last
up to three hours with adults, we have found suggestive grounds for
proposing a sequence of stagelike ways of being in faith in order to
describe a general pattern of development in faith. These stages, which
try to describe uniform and predictable *ways* of being in faith, are not
primarily matters of the *contents* of faith. We are not suggesting that a
person goes through a succession of world views and value systems, if
we mean by those terms substantive beliefs, themes, images, and stories of faith. Rather, we are trying to identify and communicate differences in the *styles*, the *operations of knowing and valuing*, that
constitute the action, the way of being that is faith. Our stages describe
in formal terms the structural features of faith as a way of construing,
interpreting, and responding to the factors of contingency, finitude,
and ultimacy in our lives.

Let's look at the seven stages of faith that we have identified.

Primal Faith. We start as infants, you and I. Someone picks us up,
wipes off our afterbirth, and provides a nipple with breast or bottle,
and we are launched as human beings. Prior to the event of birth itself,

we have enjoyed one of the most remarkable of symbiotic relationships. Somatically, we likely have already derived from our life in the womb some sense of whether the world that welcomes us has meaning and purpose, and whether it intended and rejoices in our presence, or whether we come as intruders. Birth itself is a trauma. Students of the birth process tell us that even in the twenty-minute passage through the birth canal in a normal birth, we nearly smother. There is a threat of negation in our emergence into life. We are bruised and squeezed into life; we gasp our way into community.

During the first year, the mutual tasks of the baby and those providing care involve bonding and attachment, as well as the generation of a trusting give-and-take. Such a wondrous process! The baby's early efforts at relating and making the self at home have the effect, when things go well, of recruiting tenderness and mobilizing energetic care. In the mutuality of need and the need to be needed, the baby forms a rudimentary but deep sense of the rhythms of intimacy and of the texture of his or her environment. . . . Primal faith arises in the roots of confidence that find soil in the ecology of relations, care, and shared meanings that welcome a child and offset our profound primal vulnerability.

The first symbols of faith are likely to take primitive form in the baby's hard-won memories of maternal and paternal presence. As dependable realities who go away but can be trusted to return, our primary care givers constitute our first experiences of superordinate power and wisdom, as well as our dependence. These primal others, in their mixtures of rigidity and grace, of arbitrary harshness and nurturing love, are doubtless present in the images of God that take more or less conscious form by our fourth or fifth years. (See Ana Marie Rizzuto, *The Birth of the Living God* [Chicago: University of Chicago Press, 1979].)

Intuitive-Projective Faith. About age two a revolution begins to happen for the child. Language emerges to mediate relations to the world and others in new ways. Important preparation for this emergence has gone on in the interchanges between the child and those providing primary care, where—as videotapes of mother-child interactions show—each is teaching the other to talk. The mothers' imitations of the facial expressions and vocal experiments of their babies seem to provide a crucial mirror—both visually and vocally. And as the children match sounds and objects, they gain new leverage in communication and in the interpretation of the world. Language makes possible a qualitatively new reflectiveness on the environment and a qualitatively new reflexiveness with regard to the self.

The child, now able to walk freely and question everything, daily encounters novelties and newness. Whether we remember the vividness of our daily (and nightly) delights and terrors at three, four, and five or whether we have access to it only by observing others now in childhood, we know that the active, inquiring mind of the child will never again be so fresh and free of preformed constructions. Perception, feelings, and imaginative fantasy make up children's principal ways of knowing—and transforming—their experiences. The ordering tendencies of logical operations will come later. For now, stimulated by experience and by stories, symbols, and examples, children form deep and long lasting images that hold together their worlds of meaning and wonder. . . .

Here we see the Intuitive-Projective child's awakening to the mystery of death. We see the awakening to a world of reality beyond, around, and penetrating the everyday. We see lively imagination grasping the world, endeavoring to give it unity and sense. The preschool child who has access to the symbols, stories, and shared liturgical life of a religious tradition awakens to an expanded horizon of meanings. Though such symbols, in their archetypal power, can be misused, . . . they also enrich the child's stores of meaning and can provide powerful identification and aspirations, as well as sources of guidance and reassurance.

Mythic-Literal Faith. At about the time a child starts to school (six or seven, give or take a year), we see the beginnings of a new stage. Part of the groundwork for this revolution in knowing and valuing relates to the development of what Piaget called "concrete operational thinking." Stable categories of space, time, and causality make the child's constructions of experience much less dependent on feeling and fantasy. Now able to reverse processes of thought and to coordinate more than one feature of a situation at a time, the world becomes more linear, orderly, and predictable. Children in this stage routinely take the perspectives of others on matters of mutual interest, and they recognize others' perspectives as different from their own. This means that they can tell stories with new accuracy and richness. It also means that in their thinking about right and wrong, good and evil, they can develop a strong sense of fairness based on reciprocity (this means elevating the associations of reward for doing good and punishment for doing bad to the level of cosmic principle).

Faith becomes a matter of reliance on the stories, rules, and implicit values of the family's community of meanings. Where the family (or its substitute) is related to a larger community of shared traditions and meanings, faith involves valuing the stories, practices, and beliefs of that tradition. *Narrative* or story is the important idea here. With the abilities to take the perspectives of others and with a much-improved grasp of causal relations and consequences, narrative seems to be the favored and most powerful way of gathering and expressing personal and shared meanings. Knowing the stories of "our people" becomes an important index of identification and of evaluation of self and others and their groups. . . .

A substantial number of adolescents share [this] way of constructing their images of self, others, and ultimate environment. From this stage on, we are dealing with ways of being in faith that *can* typify adults as well as the age groups where they most typically have their rise.

Synthetic-Conventional Faith. We come now to a stage that typically begins to emerge in early adolescence. Before we discuss its particular features, it may be helpful to inject a few observations about the phenomenon of stage transition. It would be a mistake to think of the movement from one faith stage to another as analogous to climbing stairs or ascending a ladder, for two reasons: (1) It unnecessarily locks us into a kind of "higher"-"lower" mentality in thinking about the stages, when the real issue has to do with a successive progression of more complex, differentiated, and comprehensive modes of knowing and valuing. (2) The stair or ladder analogy, further, might lead us to think of transition as a matter of the self clambering from one level or rung to another, essentially unchanged. Faith stage transitions represent significant alterations in the structures of one's knowing and valuing and, therefore, in the basic orientation and responses of the self. In the process of transition we have the feeling, as one character in the film *Green Pastures* put it, that "everything nailed down is coming loose." Because of new operations and comprehensiveness in our knowing and valuing, both our previous knowledge and values and our very ways of verifying and justifying our perspectives and our actions undergo change and must be reworked. Our very life meanings are at stake in faith stage transitions. In relation to the transition we are just considering—from the Mythic-Literal to the Synthetic-Conventional stage—let me share an example. We have interviewed a number of what we have come to call "eleven-year-old atheists." These young people, almost on the cusp between concrete operational thinking and formal operational thinking (a Piagetian term we will examine more fully in a moment), begin to experience the breakdown of the moral principle of reciprocity that they frequently have used to compose their images of God. By observation and experience, they have found that either God is powerless, with regard to punishing evil people and rewarding the good, or God is, as one morally sensitive girl put it, "asleep." The God, therefore, who is constructed on the basis of moral reciprocity effectively dies and must be replaced. Such an experience involves, to a greater or lesser degree, coming to terms with feelings of anguish, struggle, and possibly guilt and grief. This is the stuff of which faith stage transitions are made.

Now to Synthetic-Conventional faith. The key to our understanding the structure and dynamics of this stage is an appreciation for a revolution that adolescence typically brings in cognitive development. In formal operational thinking the mind takes wings. No longer is it limited to the mental manipulation of concrete objects or representations and of observable processes. Now thinking begins to construct all sorts of ideal possibilities and hypothetical considerations. Faced with the challenge of developing the perfect mousetrap, the formal operational mind doesn't limit itself to modifying and perfecting the type of mousetraps it has seen, but it starts with the fundamental problem of disposing of a household pest and imagines a great variety of ways the problem might be solved. Imagination, one writer has said, is intelligence at play. Formal operational thinking makes possible the generation and use of abstract concepts and ideals. It makes it possible to think in terms of systems. And it enables us to construct the perspectives of others on ourselves—to see ourselves as others see us. Part of the confusion and difficulty of adolescence can be traced to the new self-consciousness I have summed up with the following couplet:

> I see you seeing me . . .
> I see the me I think you see. . . .

And its reciprocal:

> You see you according to me . . .
> You see the you you think I see. . . .

Putting these two together as elements of consciousness (which takes a period of several months, at least) results in what students of perspective taking have called "mutual interpersonal perspective taking." This emergence accounts for the "self-consciousness" of adolescence. It accounts for the rather sudden new depth of awareness and interest in the interiority (emotions, personality patterns, ideas, thoughts, and experiences) of persons—others and oneself. It makes for a newly "personal" young woman or man.

Synthetic, as we use the term here, does not mean *artificial*. Rather it means pulling together and drawing disparate elements into a unity, a synthesis. The drawing together in question is twofold. Due to the rich new possibilities of interpersonal perspective taking, the young person now has available a variety of reflections or mirrorings of the self. In every significant face-to-face relation, he or she has access to someone's construction of the self he/she is becoming. Like distorting mirrors in an amusement park fun house, the images of self that one discerns that others have constructed do not necessarily fit nicely together. Nor are they necessarily congruent with one's own felt images of self. Saint Augustine, writing about his own adolescent experience in this stage, said, "And I became a problem to myself." Synthesis, in the first instance then, means a drawing together, an integration into one, of that viable sense in selfhood that we have come to call "identity."

The other aspect of synthesis crucial to the forming of the Synthetic-Conventional stage has to do with the drawing together of one's stories, values, and beliefs into a supportive and orienting unity. In this stage a person struggles with composing a "story of my stories"—a sense of the meaning of life generally and of the meaning and purpose of her/his life in particular. Our research suggests that this involves a process of drawing together into an original unity a selection of the values, beliefs, and orienting convictions that are made available to the adolescent through her/his significant face-to-face relations. Although each person's world-view synthesis in this stage is in some degree unique, we describe it as "conventional" for two important reasons: (1) It is a synthesis of belief and value elements that are derived from one's significant others. The elements themselves, then, are conventional, although they may be formed into a novel, individual configuration. (2) It is a synthesis of belief and value that has, in this stage, a largely "tacit" (as opposed to "explicit") character. By this we mean that the beliefs, values, and stories that compose a person's faith outlook and support her/his emerging identity are not yet objectified for critical reflection by that person. The synthesis is supportive and sustaining; it is deeply felt and strongly held; but it has not yet become an object of (self) critical reflection and inquiry. In this stage one is *embedded* in her/his faith outlook, and one's identity is derived from membership in a circle of face-to-face relations. . . .

Individuative-Reflective Faith. In the previous stage it is very difficult to engage in pulling together unified images of identity and faith and at the same time to critically reflect on those images. This is what accounts for the tacit character of the faith of persons best described as Synthetic-Conventional.

The rise of Individuative-Reflective faith is occasioned by a variety of experiences that make it necessary for persons to objectify, examine, and make critical choices about the defining elements of their identity and faith. Two fundamental movements are at the heart of a transition to this stage: (1) There must be a shift in the sense of the grounding and orientation of the self. From a definition of self derived from one's relations and roles and the network of expectations that go with them, the self must now begin to be and act from a new quality of self-authorization. There must be the emergence of an "executive ego"—a differentiation of the self *behind* the personae (masks) one wears and the roles one bears, from the composite of roles and relations through which the self is expressed. (2) There must be an objectification and critical choosing of one's beliefs, values, and commitments, which come to be taken as a systemic unity. What were previously tacit and unexamined convictions and beliefs must now become matters of more explicit commitment and accountability.

The following composite statement from a young adult woman should give this description more concreteness. She might well be our fifteen-year-old girl from the last stage, only ten years later.

It is important to me to be able to know and state my beliefs and my values. I have had to face and struggle toward and answer to the question "Who am I when I'm not defined by being my parents' daughter, the friend of my friends, by my job, or by any other of the roles I play?" There is an "I" that *has* these roles but is not identical with any of them. I guess it is this I that organizes the many roles I play and the relations I have. And I have had to struggle hard to get it established!

I went through a time when I realized that there are many different groups of people with many different life-styles and value systems. For a while I came to believe that these matters—life-styles and belief systems—were all matters of relativity. While I didn't like the idea, I was not sure that my reasons for being committed to my values and beliefs were any better than those of anyone else. Maybe, I thought, relativism *is* the only truth. But I found that I couldn't live that way.

So I have made choices—choices about my beliefs and values, about life-style, and about the groups I will be part of and those I won't. I feel like I have "gotten it together," as they say. And now I am working to bring my beliefs and my living together.

In the process of clarifying my beliefs, I have had to examine some of the doctrines and myths of my religious tradition. I have learned that literalism or disbelief are not the only alternatives for dealing with the biblical story of creation or with the miracles of Jesus. The important thing is the *meanings* that are being conveyed in these stories from another cultural time. These meanings are valuable and indispensable. But they are separable, in some sense, from the outmoded, mythical world views that contain them in the Bible.

So I'm trying to achieve integrity in my faith. It's not so easy. And a lot of people think that I'm crazy to hang in with religion. Others in my church think that I raise too many questions and rock the boat too much.

But I've found a few people who share my questions—and some of my answers—and we make our way.

While this young woman has struggled toward the Individuative stage in her early and midtwenties, for many others this transition comes, if at all, only later. When individuals in their thirties or forties face this transition, it can be quite disturbing to the whole network of roles and relations they have formed. Sometimes people will work through only one of the two shifts we examined above. They will carry out the critical examination of beliefs and values and make choices in that regard but will not evolve the self-authorization of the "executive ego." Or they will evolve this sense of self-authorization but will not carry out a critical examination and regrounding of his system of values and beliefs. In either case, they will exhibit a kind of stabilized transitional position that is not fully describable by either the Synthetic or the Individuative position but is truly somewhere in between.

Conjunctive Faith. For some persons whom we have interviewed, at mid-life or beyond there seems to be a transition to a stage I have come to call "Conjunctive faith." This name can be traced to Nicholas of Cusa (1401–1464), whose greatest work, *De Docta Ignorantia*, developed the idea of God as the *coincidentia oppositorum*—"the coincidence of opposites"—the being wherein all opposites and contradictions meet and are reconciled. . . . The stage of faith that emerges with mid-life or beyond involves the integration of elements in ourselves, in society, and in our experience of ultimate reality that have the character of being apparent contradictions, polarities, or at the least, paradoxical elements. Let me explain.

The hard-won integrity of the individuative stage is based upon a clear sense of reflective identity, a firm set of ego boundaries, and a confident regard for one's *conscious* sense of self as though it were virtually exhaustive of one's total selfhood. The experience of reaching mid-life (age thirty-five and beyond) for some people marks the onset of new dimensions of awareness that can precipitate the movement to a new stage, the stage of Conjunctive faith. In this transition the firm boundaries of the previous stage begin to become porous and permeable. The confident conscious ego must develop a humbling awareness of the power and influence of aspects of the unconscious on our reactions and behavior—the individual, the social, and the archetypal unconscious. Moreover, having lived with ourselves as adults for twenty years or more, we begin to have to come to terms with certain of our patterns of behavior that we may never be able fully to change.

By this time one has begun to have to deal with a new sense of the reality and the power of death. Peers and some who are younger have died. Perhaps parents, and certainly many of their generation, have died. One recognizes that he/she may have lived more than half of an expectable lifetime, and the unmistakable signs of irreversible aging are both felt and visible. One's children may now be teenagers or young adults. One probably feels the full weight of being a member of the "bridge" generation, the linking group between the elders, who are gradually passing off the scene, and the youth, who are just beginning to seek and find their entering points in being the generation of the future.

Hallmarks of the transition to Conjunctive faith include the following: (1) An awareness of the need to face and hold together several unmistakable *polar tensions* in one's life: the polarities of being both *old* and *young* and of being both *masculine* and *feminine*. Further, it means integrating the polarity of being both *constructive* and *destructive* and the polarity of having both a *conscious* and a *shadow self*. (2) Conjunctive faith brings a felt sense that truth is more multiform and complex than most of the clear, either-or categories of the Individuative stage can properly grasp. In its richness, ambiguity, and multidimensionality, truth must be approached from at least two or more angles of vision simultaneously. Like the discovery in physics that to explain the behavior of light requires two different and unreconcilable models—one based on the model of packets of energy and one based on the model of wave theory—Conjunctive faith comes to cherish paradox and the apparent contradictions of perspectives on truth as intrinsic to that truth. (3) Conjunctive faith moves beyond the reductive strategy by which the Individuative stage interprets symbol, myth, and liturgy into conceptual meanings. Beyond demythologization and the critical translation of the mythic and symbolic to propositional statements, Conjunctive faith gives rise to a "second naivete," a postcritical receptivity and readiness for participation in the reality brought to expression in symbol and myth. This means (4) a genuine openness to the truths of traditions and communities other than one's own. This openness, however, is not to be equated with a relativistic agnosticism (literally, a "not knowing"). Rather, it is a disciplined openness to truths of those who are "other," based precisely on the experience of a deep and particular commitment to one's own tradition and the recognition that truth requires a dialectical interlay of such perspectives. Put another way, Conjunctive faith exhibits a combination of committed belief in and through the particularities of a tradition, while insisting upon the humility that knows that the grasp on ultimate truth that any of our traditions can offer needs continual correction and challenge. This is to help overcome blind spots (blind *sides*) as well as the tendencies to idolatry (the overidentification of our symbolizations of transcending truth with the reality of truth), to which all of our traditions are prone. . . .

Conjunctive faith combines deep, particular commitments with principled openness to the truths of other traditions. It combines loyalty to one's own primary communities of value and belief with loyalty to the reality of a community of communities. Persons of Conjunctive faith are not likely to be "true believers," in the sense of an undialectical, single-minded, uncritical devotion to a cause or ideology. They will not be protagonists in holy wars. They know that the line between the righteous and the sinners goes through the heart of each of us and our communities, rather than between us and them.

Universalizing Faith. The person or community of Conjunctive faith lives in paradox and in the tension of ironic consciousness and commitment. In an analogy with revolutionary theory, they can see the corruption and vulnerability of the old regime, even as they can also see and rejoice in the possibility of a new order, one more replete with a balance of equality and justice, of inclusion and corporate devotion to the common good. They recognize the imperative that all things be made new, yet they are deeply invested in the present order of things. They have attachments and commitments that make revolutionary alignment too costly and frightening to entertain. So they live divided in tension, working for amelioration and evolution toward justice, but deeply aware of their own implication in the unjust structures that they oppose.

The temptation of Conjunctive faith, thus, is to become immobilized in its compassion. The polarities in its loves and loyalties can seem to cancel each other. Persons of Conjunctive faith long for transforming newness; yet their integrity involves keeping steadfast commitments to institutions and persons in the present. They see the possibility, even the imperative, of lives lived in solidarity with *all* being. Yet their wills, affections, and actions manifest tension, splitness, and disunity. Being in but not of the world, they feel a cosmic homelessness and loneliness. For some, this longing and discomfort becomes the means by which they are called and lured into a transformed and transforming relation to the ultimate conditions of life—and to themselves and everyday existence with the neighbor. This transforming and transformed relation we call Universalizing faith.

The movement toward Universalizing faith is marked by the radical completion of two tendencies we have seen developing in the course of earlier stages. The first involves *decentration from self*. The radical decentration from self in Universalizing faith has several dimensions. The first is epistemological. We have seen in the description of development from one stage to another that each new stage brings a qualitative expansion in *perspective taking*. With each later stage, the circle of "those who count" in one's way of finding or giving meaning to life expands. From primal relations in intimate family, we gradually widen our circle of awareness and regard to extended family and friends, to those who share our political and/or religious identifications, and finally beyond those to humankind or Being, in an inclusive sense. Decentration from self in the epistemological sense means the gradual qualitative extension of the ability and readiness to balance one's own perspective with those others included in an expanding radius. It means "knowing" the world through the eyes and experiences of persons, classes, nationalities, and faiths quite different from one's own.

A second dimension of decentration that comes to a radical completion in Universalizing faith has to do with valuing and valuation. The developmental history of our devotion to values and centers of value parallels the course of decentration in our perspective taking. We invest in or commit to values that give our lives meaning and value. We "rest our hearts" on centers of value that confirm our identities and confer significance on our sense of selfhood. Put another way, we become attached to causes, persons, institutions, possessions, and the like precisely because they seem to promise to ground us in worth. Likewise, we tend to attach ourselves to certain appearances and promises of power. These sources of power, which promise to preserve our interests and values, help us deal with our fears and our insecurities as finite persons in a dangerous world of power. Across the stages of faith development, as the boundaries and identity of the self undergo clarification, each successive stage requires an expansion of the groups and interests whose valuing—based on *their* fears and anxieties about worth, significance, and survival—gradually become matters of our concern as well. This process reaches a kind of completion in Universalizing faith, for there a person decenters in the valuing process to such an extent that he/she participates in the valuing of the Creator and values other beings—and being—from a standpoint more nearly identified with the love of Creator for creatures than from the standpoint of a vulnerable, defensive, anxious creature.

From the paradoxical attachments and polar tensions of Conjunctive faith, the person best described by Universalizing faith has assented to a radical decentration from the self as an epistemological and valuational reference point for construing the world and has begun to manifest the fruits of a powerful kind of *kenosis* or emptying of self. Often described as "detachment" or "disinterestedness," the kenosis—literally, the "pouring out" or emptying of self described here—is actually the fruit of having one's affections powerfully drawn beyond the finite centers of value and power in our lives that promise meaning and security. "Perfect love casts out fear," as it says in I John 4:18. The transvaluation of values and the relinquishing of perishable sources of power that are part of the movement to Universalizing faith are the fruit of a person's total and pervasive response in love and trust to the radical love of God.

Let us listen to a voice representative of this stage and to the sacred text that guided the formation of this person's way of seeing and being:

> There comes a time when an individual becomes irresistible and his action becomes all-pervasive in its effect. This comes when he reduces himself to zero.
>
> For a nonviolent person, the whole world is one family. He will thus fear none, nor will others fear him.
>
> It is not nonviolence if we merely love those that love us. It is non-violence only when we love those that hate us. I know how difficult it is to follow this grand law of love. But are not all great and good things difficult to do? Love of the hater is the most difficult of all. But by the grace of God even this most difficult thing becomes easy to accomplish if we want to do it.
>
> By detachment I mean that you must not worry whether the desired results follow from your action or not, so long as your motive is pure, your means correct. Really, it means that things will come right in the end if you take care of the means and leave the rest to him.
>
> The last eighteen verses of the Second Chapter of the *Gita* give in a nutshell the secret of the art of living:
>
> > . . . When you keep thinking about sense-objects
> > Attachment comes. Attachment breeds desire,
> > The lust of possession which, when thwarted,
> > Burns to anger. Anger clouds the judgment
> > And robs you of the power to learn from past
> > Mistakes. Lost is the discriminative
> > Faculty, and your life is utter waste.
> >
> > But when you move amidst the world of sense
> > From both attachment and aversion freed,
> > There comes the peace in which all sorrows end,
> > And you live in the wisdom of the Self . . .
> >
> > He is forever free who has broken
> > Out of the ego-cage of *I* and *mine*
> > To be united with the Lord of Love.
> > This is the supreme state. Attain thou this
> > And pass from death to immortality.
>
> Love never claims, it ever gives. Love ever suffers, never resents, never revenges itself.

Have I that nonviolence of the brave in me? My death alone will show that. If someone killed me and I died with prayer for the assassin on my lips and God's remembrance and consciousness of His living presence in the sanctuary of my heart, then alone would I be said to have had the nonviolence of the brave.

The foregoing quotes from the writings of Gandhi and from the *Bhagavad Gita* provide fitting expressions for Universalizing faith. I could have used examples from Buddhist, Christian, or Jewish sources and from a few honest humanist mystics and militants. Universalizing faith, in its authentic form, is recognizable in any culture or tradition. Despite differences in the metaphysical convictions and imagery used to express them and despite differences in their understandings of the relation of being and time, the quality of the lives of persons of Universalizing faith from whatever time or tradition are demonstrably similar in spirit and in power.

Discussion

1. What is Fowler's definition of a worldview? Use his terms to describe your own worldview.
2. For the last two stages here, Fowler provides a narrative that exemplifies that stage. Without worrying about mechanics, try writing such a narrative for one of the earlier stages.
3. Do you have any memories of religious symbols or concepts that you "misused" or misunderstood as a child?
4. Why does Fowler urge you not to think of faith stages as rungs on a ladder? Is it possible to escape the notion of hierarchy? Why or why not? Can you think of any images or models that might replace that of the ladder? What about concentric circles? A spiral?
5. When describing the conjunctive stage, Fowler suggests that here the person realizes that truth must be approached from two directions simultaneously. Can you think of any examples to illustrate this?
6. Are relationships built on power, as Fowler, and the passage from the *Gita* quoted here, suggest? If so, how should a Christian try to limit that power? If not, what are relationships built on?
7. Can a Christian attain the last two stages Fowler describes and remain a Christian?

Who Is in Control?

M. Howard Rienstra

We all long for a sense of being in control of our own lives. Yet the control we exert is merely superficial, a lease of power from God. M. Howard Rienstra, before his death a prominent historian at Calvin College, explores the tension at the heart of this paradox in this personal narrative of his encounter with approaching death. Professor Rienstra succumbed in his long battle with cancer on June 16, 1986.

The realization that one is dying comes slowly. Six years ago I was diagnosed as having cancer. I have non-Hodgkins lymphoma. I was assured that although I was third stage, yet it was treatable. It has been and on two occasions I was in remission. At one point I lost most of my hair and I have done an awful lot of vomiting over these years. Yet I seemed to be in control. I knew that the vomiting was only temporary and I could feel the lymph nodes return to normal as the chemotherapy took effect. I accepted the reality of my cancer, but I denied that I had lost control over my own life. This paradox will be explored more fully below, but basically it seemed as if I were not yet dying.

The beginnings of a change came near midnight on January 30 [1985]. My fever had risen to 104 and Mary was driving me to the hospital for the second time this year. I said to her, "You know, don't you, that one of these times when I go to the hospital I won't return?" She quietly said, "Yes." Without using the words "death" or "dying" we came to acknowledge the reality of it and that I was losing control—but still reluctantly.

Since my first two hospitalizations produced no clear reasons for my continuing fever and lung problems, it was decided to do an out-patient lung biopsy. A tube was placed in my lungs through which the doctor could both visually examine the lung and take small tissue samples for analysis. At the end I was supposed to return home, but my

109

fever flared to 103 and so I was back in the hospital. The first biopsy also failed to give any clear reason for my difficulties, so it was decided to do an open chest biopsy. At this point the doctors were expecting to find cancer in the lung, but they were pleasantly surprised not to. The only certain thing was a mildly severe fibrosis of the lungs.

Failing to find anything specific to treat the suspicion again was focused on the general condition of my cancer. I returned home, coughing and running intermittently high fevers. Mary and I recognized my worsening condition. We decided on the basis of the three hospitalizations that I would not return to the hospital again just to treat my fever and cough. We decided that I would die at home. We, in other words, were trying to regain control over my life, and even my death. How wrong we were!

Because I had not received any chemotherapy since January 3, it was decided to begin a new kind of chemo, VP16, and on Thursday, May 2 an attempt was made. But my veins couldn't handle it and only half a dose was administered. It was decided that I would have to have a Hickman catheter or a Port-a-Cath placed in my chest so that I could receive further chemo and quickly. Out-patient surgery was scheduled for the next Monday for putting in a Port-a-Cath.

Little did we know what would be the consequences of that decision. It seemed merely to be another decision made so I could stay in control. Dozens of such decisions had been made over the years. And this did not violate our no-hospitalization resolve since I would walk in around noon and walk out by 4 P.M. having the procedure done with local anesthesia. Very simple. I was in control.

I was in the operating room promptly at 1 P.M. and after the usual preliminaries and administering of local anesthesia the cutting in my neck began. The surgeon had externally seen and palpitated a vein which he thought would be appropriate. Upon exposing that vein, however, he discovered it was too small to receive the catheter tubing. He then turned to other deeper veins. Let me anticipate questions by saying that I am an oddity. The veins in my neck, as it turns out, are not positioned as in an anatomy textbook. This structural oddity would soon have profound consequences.

The surgeon found a large vein which he assumed to be the external jugular vein. For most people it would have been. But as he put the catheter in that vein it could not be positioned correctly. It ran off either to my left or right arm, but it wouldn't go straight down no matter what he tried. A properly structured external jugular vein would have gone down as far as it had to for the successful operation of the Port-a-Cath, but this one wouldn't.

At this point, about two hours into the surgery, some dramatic things began to happen. I'll relate them as I experienced them at that moment even though I now recognize the limits of my understanding of the experience.

I began to think that I was going to die. I heard my surgeon begin to call for another surgeon to come to assist him. And the surgeons he named were the big names of Grand Rapids surgeons. At that point I began gasping for breath. In my perception I was panicking in the face of death. I said to Mary the next day, "I couldn't breathe and they didn't know what to do about it." My whole body was shaking as I desperately fought for air. I asked for oxygen and was given it, but since I was breathing so shallowly it took a while for even breathing to return and for my panic in the face of what I then thought was my imminent death to subside. Before what finally was a four and a half hour operation was over I went through two more similar episodes of panic and gasping for breath. I was scared to death and scared to die. I tried to pray, but I couldn't. I tried to recite to myself my favorite childhood hymn, "What a Friend We Have in Jesus," but the words seemed empty in my fright of the moment. I was convinced I was dying, and I recognized more clearly than ever before in my life that I was no longer in even apparent control. The loss of control came to me in the most crude way as I voided my urine during each of the three episodes of panic and gasping for breath.

Meanwhile the second surgeon, an open-heart specialist, came in and observed, confirmed the oddity of my vein structure, then scrubbed and took over the operation. He decided to go after the internal jugular vein which lies more deeply in the neck. It was not easy, but after about an hour he had the catheter successfully placed and the operation was then finished by the first surgeon.

I now know the alternative explanation of what I experienced. I have been assured that I didn't really panic, but that my body was in fact seriously deprived of oxygen. Oxygen deprivation rather typically produces both the gasping for breath and the sense of panic. That is the medical explanation. I was also informed that if I had not been able to regain even breathing they would simply have given me a general anesthesia in addition to the local I was receiving. I accept these scientific explanations and it would be very tempting to substitute them for what I had experienced. I could again think I was in control. But more lessons were to come.

After four and a half hours of surgery I obviously was not going to walk out of the hospital that day. In fact, they kept me on 6 liters of oxygen; my fever continued to flare; and I was coughing up heavy sputum. They ran a culture on that sputum and remarkably for the first time since January a specific infection was identified. It was pseudomonis, a rather bad infection of the lungs. It is a treatable disease and the treatment is in progress as I write. It is being treated successfully at the moment, but it would not have been if I had not stayed in the hospital. Rather I would have gone home and the next afternoon, with the help of Tylenol, I would have attended the semi-annual meeting of the Governing Board of the Meeter Center for Calvin Studies. In fact, I would not have seen a doctor until Thursday when the second stage of my new chemo was to be administered through my new Port-a-Cath. Speculation is always dangerous about things that did not happen, but it could be that if the chemo had been administered the pseudomonis could have advanced to a fatal stage. By trying to stay in control I could in fact have been committing suicide. Thus the experience of dying which I had on the operating room table was really God's way of extending my life and His clear demonstration to me that He and not I was in control.

Paradoxes are always difficult to understand. The paradox of good coming out of bad reminds me of John Milton's paradox of the "Fortunate Fall." Briefly, the fortunate fall argument is that if man had not fallen into sin we would never have known the infinite love and mercy of God in Jesus Christ. In my case paradoxes abound. If when I was born I had a normal structure to my veins I would now possibly be dying of pseudomonis without treatment. If my veins hadn't collapsed on Thursday I would not have had the Monday surgery with the same consequences. And even during the surgery if I had not experienced the panic and gasping for breath I would not have been willing to lose control. I had to be beaten out of my arrogant, selfish, and unbelieving sense of self-control.

Thus the primary benefit—the real good that came out of the apparent evil—is neither physical nor psychological, but spiritual. My belief has been strengthened and my faith deepened as dying seemed so near and God so far away. Some background explanation is probably appropriate.

I have always believed, or so it seems. I have always had a sense of God leading and directing my life. From the time of my adoption at age ten there could be no doubt about that. Probability theory would be quite inadequate as an explanation of my life. I have had a strong faith and understanding of God's presence in my life—but that faith and understanding was not, as I learned on the operating table, the full assurance of my salvation. To put it in terms that were popular a few years ago, I was still on the throne of my life rather than Christ. Intellectually I affirmed the Reformed faith without doubt and I took great delight in defending it. I have never intellectually doubted in the slightest the doctrines of the incarnation and resurrection of Christ, and I would with only slight provocation explain and defend them. And I have always known and taught the distinction between believing *that* Jesus Christ is God and believing *in* Jesus Christ. Salvation comes only from the latter.

What then went wrong? Knowing all that, teaching all that, and even trying in the practice of life to live justly, I still was trying to keep control. I refused to give myself over to Christ completely. I had to be broken for the comforting assurance of the first question and answer of the Heidelberg catechism to become a reality. It had always been real intellectually, and even psychologically, but not spiritually because I wanted to belong to myself—to keep control. Perhaps the best example of that is my never having prayed during these past six years for my own healing. I could pray for others, but not for myself. To pray for healing for myself would be to lose control—and God who knows the secrets of our hearts would surely not receive the prayers of one who was yet resisting him.

My brokenness began on the operating table on Monday and continued on Tuesday as I confessed my resistance in tearful prayer with Mary, and then continued the same with both Rev. Botts and Vermaire. The assurance of salvation began to become a reality as I experienced God's pursuing grace so vividly. I am not, except in the most common biblical sense, a saint, nor do I anticipate changes in belief or in the practice of life that will be visible to others. But I have been spiritually transformed by the grace of God coming through these paradoxical experiences. I now know more than intellectually that I am not in control, that I do not belong to myself. I have the comfort of the Heidelberg catechism and of God's real presence. And all this because of an odd neck.

Discussion

1. Repeatedly, Rienstra uses the construction *it was decided* to indicate medical decisions. How does this strategy contribute to the main topic of the piece?
2. After describing his sensations during surgery, Rienstra describes a temptation he experienced. What was it? Have you ever experienced similar temptations after praying for something and receiving an answer?
3. This essay mentions several paradoxes. What are some other significant ones that are a part of the Christian life?

Two Ways of Looking at God

Emily Dickinson

> *Reared in a Calvinist family in Amherst, Massachusetts, in the mid-nineteenth century, Emily Dickinson offers invigorating views of humanity, God, and nature in her brief and strangely modern poems. Here she presents two ways of seeing God that make us reconsider conventional views.*

I.

He fumbles at your Soul
As Players at the Keys
Before they drop full Music on—
He stuns you by degrees—
Prepares your brittle Nature
For the Ethereal Blow
By fainter Hammers—further heard—
Then nearer—Then so slow
Your Breath has time to straighten—
Your Brain—to bubble Cool—
Deals—One—imperial—Thunderbolt—
That scalps your naked Soul—

When Winds take Forests in their Paws—
The Universe—is still—

Discussion

1. Like many of the psalms in the Bible, this poem presents a frank account of an experience of God. What does it suggest about the way we sometimes encounter God? Does this relate a positive or a negative experience? Are you comfortable talking about God in these terms?

2. After listing the metaphors that Dickinson uses to capture this event, list others that you think capture aspects of God's character.

II.

Some keep the Sabbath going to Church—
I keep it, staying at Home—
With a Bobolink for a Chorister—
And an Orchard, for a Dome—

Some keep the Sabbath in Surplice—
I just wear my Wings—
And instead of tolling the Bell, for Church,
Our little Sexton—sings.

God preaches, a noted Clergyman—
And the sermon is never long,
So instead of getting to Heaven, at last—
I'm going, all along.

Discussion

1. Dickinson's choice of worship reveals some of her attitudes toward the formal worship of her day. What does she dislike about religious conventions in Amherst?
2. Underline instances of parallelism in the poem and suggest ways in which each instance contributes to the meaning of the poem.
3. What does Dickinson mean by the allusion to her "getting to Heaven . . . all along"? Is that a feeling that all Christians should have?
4. Like many of her poems, this one is written in common meter. Scan the poem to discover this pattern and then try singing the poem to the tune of a common-meter hymn like "Amazing Grace."

Why I Ran for Congress

Stephen V. Monsma

> *Is our religious worldview something private, or is it in fact a view by which we serve in the world? Here is the essential question for the Christian. Do our beliefs make a difference in how we live? Stephen V. Monsma believes that his religious views affect both his decisions and behavior in the sometimes bitter and antagonistic arena of politics. That belief determines his actions. In the following essay, Monsma, a former professor of political science at Calvin College and an eight-year Michigan legislator, discusses how his beliefs affected his campaign for national office.*

It was almost 2 A.M. and I was physically and mentally exhausted. I was at the end of a year-long campaign for Congress in Michigan's Fifth Congressional District, and as the late evening had stretched into early morning, it had become increasingly clear that I was going to lose a close race.

I had made a brief statement to a couple hundred supporters who had kept watch until the bitter end. Then a television reporter asked me to respond to a few questions on live television. He first asked for my reaction to a statement made earlier that evening by the county chairman of the opposing political party, to the effect that "the trouble with Monsma is that he thought he was running for Pope instead of for Congress."

My foggy brain cleared for an instant and I shot back, "If that means running for Congress must involve putting aside one's ideals and moral beliefs, then I reject it totally."

That exchange encapsulated much of what my campaign for Congress had been about. I had entered the arena of electoral politics because I was convinced that those of us who accept the full gospel of Jesus Christ must bring that gospel and its justice-promoting light to bear on the injustices and evils of the world. At times it must have appeared as though I indeed were a candidate for church office.

Almost a year has passed now since my campaign. As I have gained perspective, a three-part conclusion has emerged in my mind: it is important, difficult, and possible for Christians to run *as Christians* for high public office.

My experience of running for Congress, as well as the eight years I served in the Michigan legislature, has driven home the importance of Christians running for electoral office. The issues elected officials deal with are critical and Christians have something to offer to our nation's debate on them.

The issues are many and complex: How to help assure employment opportunities for those who want work. How to deal with a welfare system seemingly more dedicated to keeping people on welfare than enabling them to become self-sufficient. How to use our energy and other natural resources wisely. How to prevent the ultimate horror of nuclear war. What about world hunger? Or racism at home? Abortion? Gay rights?

The government, for good or bad, touches our lives in constant, pervasive ways. Holding public office is one crucial way—perhaps *the* way—for Christians to affect issues such as these in a justice-promoting biblical manner.

First, the Christian office holder approaches issues on their merit. Many in the political arena view issues merely as a means of gaining personal power. For such, the constant goal is manipulating issues to one's own advantage. Whether people are helped or hurt, whether justice is served or set back, the only question is what will improve one's chances for election.

Second, Christian politicians have a firm vision of a more just society. If truly running as Christians, they will not accept uncritically the standard liberal or conservative program of their party or the biases of their personal social and economic background.

It is not often clear exactly how biblical justice should be applied in concrete situations, which is why equally dedicated Christians will sometimes disagree on the proper response to specific cases. But even so, they will be contributing to the political process by raising the debate above the politics of self-interest.

As I look back on my campaign it is hard even for me to comprehend the enormous output of time, energy, and money that went into it. We raised $250,000 from almost 2,000 persons and organizations; we printed and distributed one million pieces of literature; 1,000 volunteers worked on the campaign; I personally worked 14 to 18 hours a day, every day except Sunday, for most of 1983. Waging a campaign for high public office is an all-consuming, exhausting struggle.

But all this does not yet touch on the moral struggles through which one goes. The system by which major public offices are filled is such that the temptations to run a fundamentally dishonest campaign are nearly irresistible. To maintain one's integrity and the integrity of one's campaign is a daily struggle. One does not have to be an especially evil person to fail in this struggle—only an ordinary, imperfect person doing what everyone, the whole system, expects him or her to do.

The danger is that one's actions and one's campaign will bear little relationship to one's true beliefs and intentions. When this happens, a campaign is little more than one big con game. The appearances being created operate on one track; while what one really is in favor of and what one really intends to do once elected operate on an entirely separate track.

Negative campaigning fits into this "two track" type of campaigning. The guiding spirit is to portray your opponent in as bad a light as possible.

To take an example, for approximately two and one-half weeks my opponent ran a very extensive television campaign that consisted of nothing but attacks on me. By broad generalizations and facts taken out of context, I was shown as soft on crime, against education and business, for more government spending and taxes. The fact that these charges did not fit my record as a state Senator made no difference. What counted was the emotional impact on viewers.

The most disturbing point about our electoral system is that there are few, if any, forces which discourage this dishonest two-track campaigning. No credit is given to those who refuse to engage in such methods. The whole system—political parties, special interest groups, the general public, and the media—says this is the way the game is played. "What are you complaining about? You're in politics, aren't you?" is the prevailing attitude. Running for public office is indeed difficult.

No one should take the preceding comments to imply that Christians can be elected to high office only under the most unusual circumstances. If I could have run a little stronger campaign and avoided several errors I made, I could very well have won. Mark Hatfield, U.S. Senator from Oregon, stands as a shining example of a dedicated Christian who has run successfully for office without sacrificing his Christian commitment.

Time and again the encouragement and prayers my campaign received exceeded my hopes. Requests for financial help to those on mailing lists of several evangelical organizations resulted in an out-pouring of contributions that far exceeded our expectations. Many of our volunteers put in countless hours because of their commitment to greater political justice. The election results clearly showed that in those areas of the district where members of my own denomination are concentrated I ran significantly stronger (relative to the rest of my party's ticket) than I did in other areas.

I came away from my campaign with the very clear impression that many evangelical Christians have a genuine, deep concern about the injustices in our world and are ready and willing to translate their concern into political action. The loyalty and support of these Christians has the potential for giving a Christian candidate a huge advantage in the race.

But having said this, it is important to remember that the Christian's standard of success is not the same as the world's. Charles Colson, in a Wheaton College commencement address last year, said, "You are called not to be successful or to meet any of the other counterfeit standards of the world, but to be faithful, and to be expended in the cause of serving the risen and returning Christ."

Colson is right. One could win an election but lose it in the profound sense of having sacrificed one's beliefs and integrity. Or one could lose an election and yet win by having run an honest, vigorous campaign which spoke to the crucial issues in a justice-promoting manner.

God demands paradoxical qualities of his servants he calls in the political realm. We are called to struggle, to expend ourselves in the dogged pursuit of a lofty goal . . . and then we are asked to let go, to let God do what he pleases with the effort. This is difficult. But that is what we are called to do. We are not called to be successful according to this world's standards. We are called to be faithful. No more, and no less.

Discussion

1. Monsma believes that his religious beliefs affect his motivation for and vision of both political office and the way in which he campaigned. Consider those two areas as developed in the essay. Are there other areas in Christian life where Christian vision and pragmatic behavior seem to conflict?

2. A common view in political circles today is that of pluralism, the belief that the officeholder serves people of many religious beliefs and therefore should keep his or her personal religious beliefs private. The officeholder should not let personal religious beliefs affect decisions for the common good. How legitimate is this view? It is commonly raised, for example, in

abortion issues. Here the officeholder may express personal disapproval of abortion, but refuses to vote to pass legislation opposing abortion because of the pluralistic nature of the constituency.

3. Would you say that Monsma simply isn't realistic, that he failed to "work within the system to beat the system"?

4. List some biblical models for political activism. Do they suggest reasons for voting for certain candidates rather than others?

Scars of Honor

Dorothy M. Johnson

> *Dorothy M. Johnson grew up in the small town of Whitefish in the northwest corner of Montana, a place where the legends and history of the Cheyenne Indians, of miners and trappers, of mountain men and drifters, still held a powerful grip on life. For fifteen years after her graduation from the University of Montana, she worked as an editor in New York. After visiting Whitefish for a vacation, she determined to remain. Her authentic, historically-rooted fiction has earned numerous awards, including the 1957 Spur Award. In "Scars of Honor" Johnson tells a simple story of a people's effort to observe old traditions in a changing world.*

Charley Lockjaw died last summer on the reservation. He was very old—a hundred years, he had claimed. He still wore his hair in braids, as only the older men do in his tribe, and the braids were thin and white. His fierce old face was like a withered apple. He was bent and frail and trembling, and his voice was like a wailing of the wind across the prairie grass.

Old Charley died in his sleep in the canvas-covered tepee where he lived in warm weather. In the winter he was crowded with the younger ones among his descendants in a two-room log cabin, but in summer they pitched the tepee. Sometimes they left him alone there, and sometimes his great-grandchildren scrambled in with him like a bunch of puppies.

His death was no surprise to anyone. What startled the Indian agent and some of Charley's own people, and the white ranchers when they heard about it, was the fact that some of the young men of the tribe sacrificed a horse on his grave. Charley wasn't buried on holy ground;

he never went near the mission. He was buried in a grove of cotton-woods down by the creek that is named for a dead chief. His lame great-grandson, Joe Walking Wolf, and three other young Indians took this horse out there and shot it. It was a fine sorrel gelding, only seven years old, broke fairly gentle and nothing wrong with it. Young Joe had been offered eighty dollars for that horse.

The mission priest was disturbed about the killing of the horse, justifiably suspecting some dark pagan significance, and he tried to find out the reason the young men killed it. He urged Joe's mother, Mary, to find out, but she never did—or if she did, she never told. Joe only said, with a shrug, "It was my horse."

The white ranchers chuckled indulgently, a little shocked about the horse but never too much upset about anything Indians did. The rancher who told the story oftenest and with most interest was the one who had made the eighty-dollar offer to Joe Walking Wolf. Joe had said to him: "Ain't my horse." But Joe was the one who shot it on old Charley's grave, and it didn't belong to anyone else.

But the Indian agent guessed what had been going on. He knew more about Indians than the Federal Government required him to know. The horse was not government property nor the tribe's common property; everybody knew it belonged to Joe. The agent did not investi-gate, figuring it was none of his business.

That was last summer, when old Charley died and the young men took the horse out to where he was buried.

The story about the killing of the horse begins, though, in 1941, before that horse was even born. The young men were being drafted then, and the agent explained it all, over and over again, through an interpreter, so nobody would have an excuse for not understanding. In the agent's experience, even an Indian who had been clear through high school could fail completely to understand English if he didn't happen to want to.

Some of the white ranchers explained it, too. Some of them were expecting to go, or to have their sons or hired cowboys go, and the draft was a thing they mentioned casually to the Indians who worked for them at two or three dollars a day, digging irrigation ditches or hoeing in the kitchen garden or working in the hay fields. So the Indians understood the draft all right, with everybody talking about it.

The agent kept telling them, "In the World War you were not citi-zens, so you did not have to go in the Army." (He meant the First World War, of course. The United States hadn't got into the second one yet; there was only the draft.) "Many of your fathers enlisted in the Army anyway and they were good fighters. They did not have to go, but they wanted to. Now you are citizens, you can vote, and some of you will have to go in the Army. When the letters come for you, we will talk about it again."

Well, some of the young men didn't want to wait until the letters came. Fighting was part of their tradition. It was in the old men's stories, and the names of their long-dead warriors were in history books, as well as in the stories the old men told around the cabin stoves when snow was deep outside and the cabins were crowded with many people and the air foul with much breathing and not much bathing. (Long ago, before any of these young men were born, their forefathers had bathed every morning in rivers or creeks, even if they had to break the ice, but that custom had passed with their glory.)

The middle-aged men of the tribe remembered the white man's war they had fought in, and some of them still had parts of their old uniforms put away. But the stories they told were of places too distant for understanding, foreign places with no meaning except for the men who had been there. The stories the grandfathers told were better. They were about the stealthy approach through the grass after the men had prayed and painted, the quick, sharp action on riverbanks that were familiar still or in tepee camps where white men now live in brick houses.

The grandfathers' stories were of warriors who never marched or drilled but walked softly in moccasins or rode naked on fleet war ponies. They had no uniforms; they wore mystic painted symbols on face and body. In those battles there was the proud waving of eagle-feathered war bonnets and the strong courage of warriors who dared to carry a sacred buffalo shield, although a man who carried one pledged not to retreat. They were battles without artillery, but with muzzle-loading rifles and iron-tipped lances and the long feathered arrows hissing out from a horn bow. Killing was not paramount in those old battles; more important was proof of a man's courage in the face of death, and the bravest were those few who dared to carry no weapon at all, but only a whip, for counting coup on a living, unhurt enemy. Nobody was drafted for those battles, and death was often the price of glory.

Only two or three of the old men remembered so far back. One of them was Charley Lockjaw. He was suddenly important. If he had not lived two generations too late, he would have been important simply because he was old. His people would have taken it for granted that he was wise, because his medicine had protected him for so long against death. They would have listened respectfully when he spoke. There was a time when it was a good thing to be an Indian, and old. But Charley was cheated—almost—of his honors, because he lived at the wrong time.

Suddenly he was needed. He was sitting in front of his summer tepee, nodding in the sun, with the good warmth seeping into his joints, when four young men came to him. They were modern Indians, with white men's haircuts. They wore torn blue jeans and faded shirts and white men's boots, because they were all cowboys, even the lame one, his great-grandson, Joe.

Charley looked up, ready to be angry, expecting some disrespectful, hurried greeting, like "Hey, grampa, look here."

They did not say anything for a while. Embarrassed, they shuffled their boots in the dust. Joe Walking Wolf took off his broad-brimmed hat, and the other three took their hats off, too, and laid them on the ground.

Joe cleared his throat and said in Cheyenne, "Greetings, my grand-father." It was the way a young man talked to a wise old one in the buffalo years that were gone.

Old Charley blinked and saw that Joe was carrying, with awkward care, an ancient ceremonial pipe of red stone.

Joe asked gravely, "Will you smoke with us, my grandfather?"

Charley was at first indignant, thinking they meant to tease him, because they were atheists who did not believe in the old religion or any of the new ones. He railed at them and said, "Goddam!" in English. But they did not go away; they stood there respectfully with their heads bent, accepting what he said and, in the old, courteous way, not interrupting.

He looked at their sober faces and their steady eyes, and he was ashamed for his own lack of courtesy. When he understood that they were sincere, he would have done anything for them, anything they asked. There was not much he could do any more, and nobody had asked him to do anything for a long time.

If he took the pipe and smoked, that said, "I will do whatever you ask." He did not know what they were going to ask, but he would have let them cut him into pieces if that was what they wanted, because his heart was full at being approached in the remembered, ceremonial way, clumsy as these modern Indians were about it. He answered in his reedy voice, "I will smoke with you."

They were going to do it all wrong. One of the young men brought out a sack of tobacco, and that was all right if there was none that had been raised with the right prayers said over it. But Joe pulled out a pocket lighter a white man had given him and another young man brought out some kitchen matches and old Charley could not endure such innovations.

He made them build a fire in the center of his summer tepee, under the fire hole in the peak, and he sat down with a groan of stiffness at the back, in the honor seat, the place of the lodge owner. The young men were patient. They sat where he told them to, on the old ragged carpet his granddaughter had put on the earth floor.

He filled the pipe with pinches of tobacco without touching the bowl and lighted it with a coal from the fire. With slow, remembered ceremony he offered the pipestem to Heammawihic, the Wise One Above, to Ahktunowihic, the power of the earth below, and to the spirits of the four directions—where the sun comes up, where the cold wind goes to, where the sun comes over and where the cold wind comes from.

He spoke reverently to each of these. Then he himself took four puffs and passed the pipe, slowly, carefully, holding the stem upright, to young Yellowbird, who was on his left.

Yellowbird smoked, though awkwardly, in the sacred manner and passed the pipe to Joe Walking Wolf. When Joe had finished, he stood up to take the pipe to the two young men on the other side of Charley, but the old man corrected him patiently. The pipe must not cross the doorway of the lodge; it must be passed back from hand to hand, first to Robert Stands in Water and then on to Tom Little Hand.

The young men were humble when he corrected them. They thanked him when he told them how to do things right.

When he signified that the time had come for them to talk, young Joe, the lame one, said formally in Cheyenne, "My grandfather has told of the old times long ago, and we have listened. He has told how the warriors used to go on a hilltop with a wise old man and stay there and dream before they went on the warpath."

Old Charley said, "I told you those things and they were true. I dreamed on a hilltop when I was young."

Joe Walking Wolf said, "We want to dream that way, my grandfather, because we are going to war."

The old man did not have to promise to help them. He had promised when he took the pipe. He sat for a while with his eyes closed, his head bowed, trying to remember what his instructors had said to him the three times he had gone through the *wu-wun*, the starving. How would anyone know the right way if the old men had forgotten? But he was able to remember, because he remembered his youth better than yesterday.

He remembered the chanted prayers and the hunger and thirst and the long waiting for mystery to be revealed. He remembered the grave warnings, the sympathetic teaching of the wise old men seventy years before.

"It is a hard thing to do," he told the young men. "Some men cannot do it. Alone on a high place for four days and four nights, without food or water. Some men dream good medicine, and some dream bad medicine, and some have no dream. It is good to finish this hard thing, but it is no disgrace not to finish.

"A man lies on a bed of white sage," he told them, "and he is alone after his teacher, his grandfather, has taught him what to do. After four days, his grandfather goes up the hill and gets him—if he has not come back before that time."

Charley Lockjaw remembered something else that was important and added firmly, "The young men bring the grandfather a gift."

And so they went through the *wu-wun*, each of them alone on a high hill, hungering and thirsting for four days and nights. First they brought Charley gifts: four silver dollars from one, new moccasins from another, and two bottles of whiskey. (After the ordeals were over, he spent the four silver dollars for whiskey, too, getting it with difficulty through a man who was going off the reservation and who did not look like an Indian, so he could buy it, though it was against the law. An Indian could vote and be drafted, but he could not buy whiskey.)

The whole thing was secret, so that no one would complain to anybody who might want to interfere. Charley Lockjaw had been interfered with so much that he was suspicious. All his long life, white men had been interfering with him and, he thought, his own granddaughter might go to the priest if she knew what was going on, or the other young men's families might make trouble. No good would come of telling what went on.

Because of the secrecy, the old man had to ride horseback several times. Usually he had to be helped into a saddle because his joints were stiff and his legs hurt, so that if he did not stop himself and remember that now he could be proud again, he might groan.

He took each young man out separately to a hill chosen because of its height, its loneliness and its location. It had to be south or west of a river; that had always been the rule. He had never known the reason, and neither did anyone else. It was one of the things that was right, that was all, and he was very anxious to do everything right.

At the foot of the hill he and the young man left the horses hobbled. The young man helped Charley up the hill, respectfully and with great patience. He made a bed of white sage, and Charley sang his prayers to the Spirit above.

He added a humble plea that had not been in the ritual when he was young. "If I make a mistake," he cried to the blue sky, "it is because I am old. Do not blame the young man. He wants to do right. If he does wrong, it is my fault. Give him good medicine."

Then he stumbled down the hill and got on the borrowed horse by himself and rode home. If the young man should give up before his time had passed, he could catch up the horse that was left.

None of them gave up, and none of them cheated. Each of them lay alone on the sage bed on the hill, singing the songs Charley Lockjaw had taught him, sometimes watching the sky (and seeing airplanes more often than wheeling eagles) and three times a day smoking the sacred pipe.

The first was Joe Walking Wolf. Charley was proud of him when he toiled up the hill with the canteen of water and a chunk of dry bread. He was proud when the boy first splashed water on his face and then drank, unhurriedly, from the canteen.

When Joe's tongue was moistened enough so he could talk, he said briefly, "I dreamed a horse was kicking me."

"I do not know what that means," Charley told him. "Maybe you will know after you think about it."

He was afraid, though, that the dream was bad. The reason Joe limped was that a horse had kicked him when he was three years old.

The second man was Yellowbird. He was impatient. He was standing up, watching, when Charley Lockjaw came in sight on his bag-of-bones, borrowed horse, and he came down the hill to gulp the water the old man had brought. But he had endured the four days.

He said in English, "I dreamed I was dead and gone to hell." Then he said it in Cheyenne, except "hell," and Charley knew what that word was. There was no hell for Cheyennes after they were dead, according to the old religion.

Charley said, "That may be good medicine. I do not know."

The third man was Robert Stands in Water. He was sick and he vomited the first water he drank, but he got better in a little while and they went home. He didn't say what his dream was.

The fourth and last was Tom Little Hand, a laughing young man except when there were white people around. He was a proud rider and a dandy; he wore green sunglasses when he went outdoors, and tight shirts like the white cowboys. When Charley brought him the water, he was no dandy any more. Naked to the waist, he lay flat on the sage bed, and the old man had to help him sit up so he could drink and eat.

"There was a bright light," he said when he felt like talking. "It floated in the air and I tried to catch it."

Charley didn't know what kind of medicine that was, but he said Tom Little Hand would probably be able to understand it after a while.

Anyway, they had all done the best they could, the right thing, and they were ready to be warriors. They had endured in the old fashion.

When they got back to the cabin settlement beside the creek that is named for a dead chief, old Charley dug up his whiskey and went into his lodge and drank, and slept, and drank some more. A teacher is worthy of his hire, and Charley Lockjaw was tired out from all that riding and climbing of high hills. For all that time, four days for four men, sixteen days altogether, he had not slept very much. He had been singing in his lodge or in front of it, in his reedy voice like the wailing of the wind across the prairie. The little boys had not bothered him by crowding in to tumble around like puppies. They were afraid of him.

While Charley was having his drunk, the four young men went down to town to enlist in the Army. He did not know that. When he was sober again, two of them had come back—his grandson Joe and Tom Little Hand, the dandy.

Tom said, "They don't want me. I don't see so good."

Joe Walking Wolf didn't say anything. He went around with his bad limp and got a job for a few days on a white man's ranch, sawing branches off some trees in the yard. The cook gave him his meals separate from the white hired hands, but he heard them talking about the draft and joking with each other about being 4F. Some were 4F because cowboys get stove up by bad horses. Joe felt better, knowing he was not the only one.

In the winter the war clouds broke with lightning and thunder, and the Army decided Tom Little Hand could see plenty well enough to go to war. The Army began to take some married men, too, and almost all the single ones except lame Joe Walking Wolf, and a couple who had an eye disease, and six who had tuberculosis and one who was stone-deaf.

Then for a couple of years old Charley Lockjaw wasn't important any more. The people who were important were those who could read the letters that came to the cabin settlement, and those who could write the answers.

Some of the young men came back on furlough, hitch-hiking eighty miles from the railroad. In wartime people would pick up a soldier, even if he was an Indian. They strolled around the settlement and rode over to the agency in their uniforms and went to the white men's store, and some of the white ranchers went out of their way to shake hands with them and say, "Well boy, how goes it?" They were important, the fledgling warriors.

Old Charley, sitting in front of his peaked lodge in the summer, saw them strut, saw the shawl-wrapped, laughing girls hang around them. He saw them walk down the road after dark, and he felt bad about some of the girls. When he was a young man, the Cheyennes took pride in the virtue of their women. His first wife had worn the rope of chastity until he removed it himself, the fourth night after her father had accepted his gift of captured horses.

He was ashamed of the Cheyenne girls, but not of the young warriors. He pitied them a little, remembering the proud nodding eagle-feathered war bonnets and the tall, straight men who wore them. He remembered his own courting; for five years it had gone on. There were many other gallants who had stood in front of the girl's lodge, blanket-wrapped, waiting for her to come out.

One of the letters that came to the reservation had bad news in it. It was in a yellow envelope, and the agent brought it over himself and explained it to the mother of Tom Little Hand.

Tom had been wounded, it said, and was in a hospital.

The next morning Joe Walking Wolf, the lame one, made a ceremonial visit to old Charley, carrying the old stone pipe. He was not embarrassed this time, because he knew how to smoke in the sacred way.

Charley drew in a breath sharply and was ashamed because he trembled.

"The gift for that, to the grandfather," he cautioned, "must be a big gift, because it is a hard ceremony."

"The gift is outside with the pole," Joe said humbly.

And outside was picketed Joe's good sorrel colt.

There was a time when the Cheyennes, the Cut Arm people, could be lordly in their generosity with gifts of captured horses, sometimes bought with their blood. They could be splendid in their charity, giving buffalo meat to the needy and fine robes to the poor. But that time was when Charley Lockjaw was young. He had not owned a horse of his own for thirty years. And this was the only horse his great-grandson had, for the old mare this colt belonged to had died.

Charley blinked at the horse, a beautiful colt without a blemish. He walked over to stroke his neck, and the colt threw its head back and tried to get away. Charley spoke to it sharply, with approval. The colt was no stable pet, but used to running across the prairie with its mane flying in the wind and the snow. It would throw a rider before it was broke, Charley thought.

He nodded and said, "The gift is enough."

When he was a young man, he had paid many fine horses to the old one who taught him the ceremony for swinging at the pole and whose hard, gentle hands had supported him when he fainted. But he had had many horses to give, and plenty of them left. This was a finer present than he had given, because it was all Joe had.

"We will have to wait," Charley said. "We cannot do this thing today. We will wait four days."

He chose four because it was the sacred number and because he needed time to remember. He had been a pupil for this sacrifice, but never a teacher.

"Come back in four days," he said.

In the time while he was remembering and praying for a return, in some part, of his old strength and steadiness, he fasted for one whole day. His granddaughter fretted and murmured, coming out to the lodge to bring soup because he said he was sick and could not eat.

"I will send one of the children to tell the nurse at the agency," she decided, but he waved her away, promising, "I will be well tomorrow."

He was afraid, not only because he might forget something important or his hand might slip, but because someone might find out and try to stop him. Somebody was always interfering. For years the old religion had been outlawed by the government in Washington. For years no one dared even to make the Medicine Lodge when the grass was tall in summer, so those years passed without the old, careful ceremony of prayer and paint and reverence that brought new life to the tribe and honor to the Lodge Maker.

This was no longer true by the time of the Second World War, though. Every year now the Medicine Lodge was made by some man who could afford it and wanted to give thanks for something. Perhaps his child had been sick and was well again. A man who made the Lodge, who learned the ritual, could teach another man. So that was not lost, though some of it had changed and some was forgotten, and it was very hard to find a buffalo skull to use in the ceremony.

The white ranchers and their guests came to the reservation in July to watch the making of the Lodge and see the prayer cloths waving from the Thunderbird's nest, and Charley took part in those ceremonies. The white people vaguely approved of the Indians keeping their quaint old customs.

But the Medicine Lodge, the Sun Dance, was a public ceremony. Swinging at the pole, as Joe Walking Wolf wanted to do it, was private suffering.

It was a long time since a young man had wished to swing at the pole. There was no one left in the tribe, except Charley Lockjaw, who could instruct a pupil in the ceremony. No one could teach it except a man who had himself endured it. And only Charley had on his withered breast the knotted scars of that ordeal.

Now that Joe was going to do it, Charley could not keep this great thing to himself. A man who suffered at the pole gained honor—but how could he be credited if no one knew what he had done?

At sunrise on the fourth day, Joe and Charley rode far out to a safe place among the sandstone cliffs.

Then Charley was shaken by terror. He denied his gods. He said, "Do not be too sure about this thing. Maybe the spirits will not hear my voice or yours. Maybe they are all dead and will never hear anything any more. Maybe they starved to death."

Joe Walking Wolf said, "I will do it anyway. Tom Little Hand has a bad wound, and he is my friend. I will make this sacrifice because maybe it will help him get well. Anyway, I will know what it is to be wounded. I did not go to war."

Charley dug a hole to set the pole in. He told Joe how to set up the pole and fasten a lariat to it, and all the time he was thinking about long ago. He could not remember the pain any more. He remembered his strong voice crying out prayers as he jerked against the thong. He had not flinched when the knife cut or when the thong jerked the skewers in the bloody flesh.

He said, "I did this to pay a pledge. My wife, Laughing Woman—my first wife—she was very sick, and I pledged this sacrifice. The baby died, because it was winter and the white soldiers chased our people through the snow in the bitter cold. Lots of people died. But Laughing Woman lived, and in the spring I paid what I had promised."

He had Joe make a bed of white sage. When everything was ready, Joe said, "Fasten it to my back. I don't want to see it."

Charley said, "Kneel on the sage bed."

He made his gnarled hands as steady as he could and pinched up the skin on Joe's right shoulder. He tunneled through the pinched part with a sharp knife, and the bright blood sprang to the dark skin. Through the tunnel he thrust a wooden skewer three inches long. Joe did not move or murmur. Kneeling on the sage bed, with his head bowed, he was silent as a stone.

Charley put another skewer under the skin on the left shoulder, and over each skewer he put a loop of rawhide, which he tied to the lariat that hung from the pole. The skewers would never be pulled out as they had been put in.

He lifted Joe to his feet and made him lean forward to see that the rope was tight and the pull even. Joe walked a quarter of a circle to the right four times, and back, sagging forward hard on the lariat's pull, trying to tear the skewers through. Then he walked four times to the left, with his blood running down his back.

Charley left the red stone pipe where he could reach it and said, "Three times before the sun goes down, stop and smoke for a little while."

His heart was full of Joe's pain. He ached with tenderness and pride.

"Break away if you can," he urged, "but if you cannot, there is no wrong thing done. If you cannot break away, I will cut you free when the sun goes down. Nobody can take away the honor."

Joe said, "I am not doing it to get honor. I am doing it to make Tom Little Hand get well again."

He kept walking with his bad limp and pulling mightily, but he could not break through the tough flesh that stretched like rubber.

"I will come back when the sun goes down," Charley Lockjaw said.

Back in the settlement he went around and told a few safe, religious men what was happening in the sandstone cliffs. They said their hearts were with Joe, and Charley knew that Joe would have his honor among his people.

When he went back to the pole at sunset, Joe was still walking, still pulling.

Charley asked, "Did you have a dream?"

Joe said, "I saw Tom Little Hand riding a horse."

"What a man dreams when he swings at the pole," Charley told him, "is sure to come true. I saw myself with thin, white braids, and I have lived to be old instead of being killed in battle." He got out his knife and said, "Kneel down."

He cut out a small piece of skin from the right shoulder and the left, freeing the skewers, and laid the bits of bloody skin on the ground as an offering.

He touched Joe's arm and said gently, "It is ended."

Joe stood up, not even giving a deep breath to show he was glad the suffering was over.

Charley did something new then. He bandaged the wounds as well as he could, with clean gauze and tape from the white man's store. These were new things, not part of the ceremony, but he saw that some new things were good as long as there were young men strong enough to keep the old ones.

"Tonight," he said, "you sleep in my lodge and nobody will bother you." In the sagging bed in the cabin where Joe slept, there were also two or three children who might hurt those wounds.

"Now," Charley said, "I am going to give you something."

He brought from a hiding place, behind a rock, a pint whiskey bottle, still half full, and said, "I am sorry there is not more here."

He told Joe, "Now you can teach the ritual of swinging at the pole. Two men can teach it, you and I, if anyone wants to learn. It will not be forgotten when my shadow walks the Hanging Road across the stars."

The spirits may be dead, he thought, but the strong hearts of the Cheyenne people still beat with courage like the steady sound of drums.

Charley never rode his sorrel horse, but when it was three years old, Joe broke it. The horse threw him two or three times, and the old man cackled, admiring its spirit, while Joe picked himself up from the dust, swearing. Joe used the horse, but he never put a saddle on that sorrel without first asking Charley's permission.

Some of the short-haired young men never did come back from the Army, but Joe's three friends came back, wearing their uniforms and their medals. Tom Little Hand walked on crutches the first time he came home, with a cane the second time, but when he came home to stay he needed only a brace on that leg that had been wounded, and a special shoe on that foot.

The three soldiers went to the agency to show off a little, and to the white man's store off the reservation, to buy tobacco and stand around. The white ranchers, coming in for the mail, shook hands with them and called each one by name and said, "Glad to see you back, boy! Sure glad to see you back!"

The Indian soldiers smiled a little and said, "Yeah."

The ranchers never thought of shaking hands with Joe Walking Wolf. He had been around all the time, and the marks of his honor were not in any medals but in the angry scars under his faded shirt.

After all the girls had had a chance to admire the uniforms, the young men took off their medals, to be put away with the broken-feathered war bonnets and the ancient, unstrung bows. They wore parts of their uniforms to work in, as the white veterans did, and they went back to raising cattle or doing whatever work they could get.

Tom Little Hand, that proud rider, never wore his old cowboy boots again because of the brace on his leg. He could not even wear moccasins, but always the special shoe. But he walked and he rode, and pretty soon he married Joe's sister, Jennie, whose Cheyenne name was Laughing Woman, the same as her great-grandmother's.

That's all there is to the story, except that last summer Charley Lockjaw died. He had thought he was a hundred years old, but his granddaughter told the Indian agent that he had always said he was born the year a certain treaty was made with the white chiefs. The agent knew what year that treaty was, and he figured out that Charley must have been ninety when he died.

The agent was interested in history, and so he asked, "Was Charley in the fight with Yellow Hair at the Little Big Horn?" Charley's granddaughter said she didn't know.

Her son, Joe Walking Wolf, knew but did not say so. Charley Lockjaw had been there, a warrior seventeen years old, and had counted coup five times on blue-coated soldiers of the Seventh Cavalry that June day when General Custer and his men died in the great victory of the Cheyennes and the Sioux. But Joe did not tell everything Charley Lockjaw had told him.

When Charley died, he left his horse to Joe. So Joe wasn't lying when, after he shot the beautiful eighty-dollar sorrel on Charley's grave, he simply said, "It was my horse."

The three other young men were there when Joe killed it. That was the right thing to do, they agreed soberly, because in the old days when a warrior died, his best horse was sacrificed for him. Then he would have it to ride as he went along the Hanging Road to the place were the shadows of the Cheyenne people go. The place is neither heaven nor hell, but just like earth, with plenty of fighting and buffalo and horses, and tall peaked lodges to live in, and everybody there who has gone before. It is just like earth, as Charley Lockjaw remembered earth from his young days.

When Joe had shot the horse, the young men took the sharp knives they had brought along and peeled the hide off. They butchered the carcass and took the great hunks of horse meat home to their families.

Because the buffalo are gone from earth now, and in the dirt-roofed cabins of the Cheyennes, the conquered people, there is not often enough food to get ready a feast.

Discussion

1. What is the meaning of the title of the story?
2. Johnson parenthetically introduces comments, often historical, sometimes as an opinion, on the narrative details. What is the effect of this parenthetical insertion, particularly in the early stages of the story?
3. Many of the western Indian tribes, like the Cheyenne depicted in this story, had highly developed religions. Do you observe similarities between the Cheyenne religious customs and those of Christianity? How does this support Lewis's contention that all religions contain parts of the one true Christianity?
4. When Charley Lockjaw instructs the four men in the ways of the sacred ceremony, he has difficulty remembering reasons for the laws of the ritual, but he dutifully follows the laws. Explore this tension in the story. Somehow, the spirit of the ceremony breaks through even when the guiding laws are not entirely clear. How does the story reveal the relation between law and spirit, ritual and faith, and how might that relate to modern Christianity?
5. Is the sacrifice of the horse simply a meaningless ritual? How does Johnson suggest the religious significance of it? How do religious traditions conflict in the story?
6. All religions rely to a certain extent upon certain rituals which make religious belief familiar and commonplace. The danger of any ritual is that it becomes empty and meaningless. Consider the place and importance of ritual in your own religious tradition.

Writing Assignments for Chapter 8

1. Write a letter to Bertrand Russell in which you respond to the charges he makes in his essay. Pay special attention to matters of audience and persona; that is, remember Russell's like of personal experience and make sure your persona acknowledges and is sensitive to him as a person.
2. Perhaps, like M. Howard Rienstra, you have had a religious experience that would edify others if you would write about it. Perhaps it is the story of your conversion. Perhaps it is the story of God's healing in your life. Perhaps it is some other significant event. Whatever it is, write a narrative that presents the event while making clear its significance for others.
3. Write an article that provides a critique of James W. Fowler's theory of the stages of faith. Choose as your audience a popular religious magazine like *Moody Monthly, Eternity,* or *Christianity Today.*
4. Write a letter to a friend or to your parents in which you describe your own religious development in Fowler's terms.
5. Choose a religion other than Christianity and analyze it in the way that C. S. Lewis examines other worldviews in "Why I Am a Christian." Here you will need to begin with Lewis's assumption that there is a glimmer of good in all religions. Remember to consider carefully the values of your audience as you proceed.

9

Living Morally
Ethics

Thus says the LORD:
"Keep justice, and do righteousness,
for soon my salvation will come,
    and my deliverance be revealed."
                    —Isaiah 56:1

What does it profit, my brethren, if a man says he has faith but
has not works? Can his faith save him?

                                        —James 2:14

How one travels on the way of life, makes the difference and
the difference of the way.

                        —Søren Kierkegaard

Sometimes it may seem that ethics is simply a series of questions
leading to still more questions. For example, is it wrong to kill, to steal,
to lie? One would say that, yes, killing, stealing, and lying are acts that
are intrinsically wrong. Until more questions arise. If those bad acts
are prompted by good motives—that is, killing to save another's life,

stealing to ward off starvation, lying to protect a friend or even a country—can the bad acts become good acts? The cycle of questions can whirl on and on until one gets dizzy trying to connect answers in systematic, logical patterns.

However worthwhile it may be to ponder such questions, ethics more appropriately should be understood as a world-and-life view, a way of understanding life itself. Ethics is so frequently understood only as trying to answer sets of often conflicting and confusing questions that many people claim to have nothing to do with living ethically. But it isn't that easy, for that claim in and of itself constitutes an ethical stance. Ethics entails making choices, and even a choice to make no choice is a choice. It is important in ethics, then, to know where you stand, to establish a position from which intelligent choices may be made.

While the philosophical tradition of ethics is nearly as complex as the questions it raises, several fundamental alternatives emerge. In his book *Personal Ethics in an Impersonal World* (Philadelphia: Westminster, 1967), C. Eugene Conover has detailed several contemporary ethical stances, summarized as follows.

The Existential Ethic holds that the individual stands alone, and is free and responsible only to one's self in making choices. The task for such a person is to be "authentic" to one's own self. In fact, one acts in "bad faith" whenever one acts according to what others want, if it is contrary to personal freedom. No absolute standards of good exist, since good is determined individually. The only restriction upon individual choices is the understanding that others are also free to choose and one's choices should not infringe upon the free choice of others. Other than that, one's own values are of paramount importance.

The Situational Ethic seeks to make the existential ethic more precise and socially responsible by stressing concern for one's neighbor. It emphasizes more heavily the impact of our choices upon others, stressing that all actions are interpersonal in nature. Therefore one must take a social point of view in solving whatever problems a situation poses. Whereas the first ethical view emphasizes individual choices, this view emphasizes social welfare.

The Cultural Morality Ethic asserts that, since society is the dominant reality in any individual's life, and since any individual choice inevitably affects others, the individual should therefore accept the standards and discipline of the larger social organism as a guide to moral choices. Clearly this ethic asserts more rigorous control over individual behavior, but it also introduces other issues. How much freedom do cultures within larger societies have?

The Universal Principle Ethic, recognizing possible conflicts among social groups and cultures, holds that certain obligations and principles are valid for all humans everywhere. These are not relative to individuals, or situations, or cultures. One such guide would be this: it is a universal principle to avoid harm to others. Another would be a utilitarian point of view that seeks to find the right act, the good act, for the greatest number of people involved. A third variation on this ethical view would be the so-called deontological ethic which argues that there are moral obligations required of us which may in fact make many people unhappy. For example, people are taxed to fulfill an obligation to care for the suffering. Here the right is more important than the many.

The Theological Ethic differs from the Universal Principle Ethic largely in that it finds the universal principles not first of all in a human sense of obligation but in a divine being who has given directions for the way humans should live. In such an ethic, humans start with faith—the acceptance of a divine being as authority, and move to obedience—the adherence to the will of that divine being. Christians believe, for example, that God has commanded humans to love, and therefore all of the Christian's choices and actions will be grounded in love, both loving God and loving one's neighbor. Any act not based on love, and therefore transgressing the commandments of a loving God, is a wrong act.

Within this broad categorizing of fundamental ethical perspectives exists some degree of variation. That variation, in fact, becomes clear in the readings selected for this section. But repeatedly you will observe how one's ethical place to stand determines one's choices and actions.

On Good and Evil

Saint Augustine

> Saint Augustine, born in North Africa in 354, is one of the most influential thinkers in Christianity. For many years a non-Christian who lived a wanton and self-indulgent life, Augustine later became a bishop in the church. His genius as a writer and theologian is clear in many works, but his primary effort was The City of God, to which he devoted some fourteen years of labor. In the work he contrasts two cities—the City of the World which is characterized by desire of the flesh, pride, competition with others, and war; and the City of God which is characterized by desire of the spirit, humility, unity with others, and peace. In the following excerpt from book 14 of The City of God Augustine sets forth his view of the origin of sin.

Chapter 11

Since God foresaw all things and, hence, that man would sin, our conception of the supernatural City of God must be based on what God foreknew and forewilled, and not on human fancies that could never come true, because it was not in God's plan that they should. Not even by his sin could man change the counsels of God, in the sense of compelling Him to alter what He had once decided. The truth is that, by His omniscience, God could foresee two future realities: how bad man whom God had created good was to become, and how much good God was to make out of this very evil.

Though we sometimes hear the expression, "God changed His mind," or even read in the figurative language of Scripture that "God repented" (Gen. 6:6; Exod. 32:14; 1 Sam. 15:11), we interpret these sayings not in reference to the decisions determined on by Almighty

God but in reference to the expectations of man or to the order of natural causes. So, we believe, as Scripture tells us (Eccl. 7:30) that God created man right and, therefore, endowed with a good will, for without a good will he would not have been "right."

The good will, then, is a work of God, since man was created by God with a good will. On the contrary, the first bad will, which was present in man before any of his bad deeds, was rather a falling away from the work of God into man's own works than a positive work itself; in fact, a fall into bad works, since they were "according to man" and not "according to God." Thus, this bad will or, what is the same, man in so far as his will is bad is like a bad tree which brings forth these bad works like bad fruit.

A bad will, however, contrary as it is to nature and not according to nature, since it is a defect in nature, still belongs to the nature of which it is a defect, since it has no existence apart from this nature. This nature, of course, is one that God has created out of nothing, and not out of Himself, as was the case when He begot the Word through whom all things have been made (John 1:3). Though God has fashioned man from the dust of the earth, that same dust, like all earthly matter, has been made out of nothing. And it was a soul made out of nothing which God united to the body when man was created.

In the long run, however, the good triumphs over the evil. It is true, of course, that the Creator permits evil, to prove to what good purpose His providence and justice can use even evil. Nevertheless, while good can exist without any defect, as in the true and supreme God Himself, and even in the whole of that visible and invisible creation, high in the heavens above this gloomy atmosphere, evil cannot exist without good, since the natures to which the defects belong, in as much as they are natures, are good. Moreover, we cannot remove evil by the destruction of the nature or any part of it, to which the damage has been done. We can only cure a disease or repair the damage by restoring the nature to health or wholeness.

Take the case of the will. Its choice is truly free only when it is not a slave to sin and vice. God created man with such a free will, but, once that kind of freedom was lost by man's fall from freedom, it could be given back only by Him who had the power to give it. Thus, Truth tells us: "If therefore the Son makes you free, you will be free indeed" (John 8:36). He might equally have said: "If, therefore, the Son saves you, you will be saved indeed." For the same reason that God's Son is our Saviour He is also our Liberator.

Thus, man once lived according to God in a Paradise that was both material and spiritual. Eden was not merely a place for the physical needs of the body, but had a spiritual significance as food for the soul.

On the other hand, it was not so purely spiritual as to delight only the soul, and not also a place where man could get enjoyment for his bodily senses. It was both, and for both purposes.

However, the joy of Eden was short-lived because of the proud and, therefore, envious spirit who fell from the heavenly Paradise when his pride caused him to turn away from God to his own self and the pleasures and pomp of tyranny, preferring to rule over subjects than be subject himself.

This Lucifer, striving to insinuate his sly seductions into the minds of man whose fidelity he envied, since he himself had fallen, chose for his spokesman a serpent in the terrestrial Paradise, where all the animals of earth were living in harmless subjection to Adam and Eve. It was suited for the task because it was a slimy and slippery beast that could slither and twist on its tortuous way. So, subjecting it to his diabolical design by the powerful presence of his angelic nature and misusing it as his instrument, he, at first, parleyed cunningly with the woman as with the weaker part of that human society, hoping gradually to gain the whole. He assumed that a man is less gullible and can be more easily tricked into following a bad example than into making a mistake himself. This was the case with Aaron. He did not consent to the making of idols for his erring people, but he gave an unwilling assent when he was asked by the people to do so (Exod. 32:2, 21:24); and it is not to be thought that Solomon was deceived into believing in the worship of idols, but was merely won over to this sacrilege by feminine flattery (3 Kings 11:4). So, too, we must believe that Adam transgressed the law of God, not because he was deceived into believing that the lie was true, but because in obedience to a social compulsion he yielded to Eve, as husband to wife, as the only man in the world to the only woman. It was not without reason that the Apostle wrote: "Adam was not deceived but the woman was deceived" (1 Tim. 2:14). He means, no doubt, that Eve accepted the serpent's word as true, whereas Adam refused to be separated from his partner even in a union of sin—not, of course, that he was, on that account, any less guilty, since he sinned knowingly and deliberately. That is why the Apostle does not say: "He did not sin," but "he was not deceived." Elsewhere, he implies that Adam did sin: "Through one man sin entered into the world." And a little further on, even more plainly, he adds: "After the likeness of the transgression of Adam" (Rom. 5:12, 14). The distinction is here made between those who, like Adam, sin with full knowledge and those who are deceived because they do not know that what they are doing is a sin. It is this distinction which gives meaning to the statement: "Adam was not deceived."

Nevertheless, in so far as he had had no experience of the divine severity, Adam could be deceived in believing that his transgression was merely venial. And, therefore, he was at least not deceived in the same way that Eve was; he was merely mistaken concerning the judgment that would follow his attempt to excuse himself. "The woman you placed at my side gave me fruit from the tree and I ate" (Gen. 3:12).

To summarize briefly: though not equally deceived by believing the serpent, they equally sinned and were caught and ensnared by the Devil.

Chapter 12

Someone may be puzzled by the fact that other sins do not change human nature in the way that the transgression of our first parents not merely damaged theirs but had the consequence that human nature, ever since, has been subject to death, to the great corruption which we can see and experience, and to so many and such opposing passions which disturb and disorder it, which was not the case in Eden before there was sin, even though the human body was animal then as now. However, no one has a right to be puzzled, on the assumption that our first parents' sin must have been a small, venial sin, since it involved merely a matter of food—a thing good and harmless in itself apart from being forbidden as everything else was good which God had created and planted in that place of perfect happiness.

However, what is really involved in God's prohibition is obedience, the virtue which is, so to speak, the mother and guardian of all the virtues of a rational creature. The fact is that a rational creature is so constituted that submission is good for it while yielding to its own rather than its Creator's will is, on the contrary, disastrous. Now, this command to refrain from a single kind of food when they were surrounded by an abundance of every other kind of food was so easy to obey and so simple to remember for anyone still free from passion resisting the will (as would be the case later on, in punishment for sin) that the sinfulness involved in breaking this precept was so very great precisely because the difficulty of submission was so very slight.

Chapter 13

Moreover, our first parents only fell openly into the sin of disobedience because, secretly, they had begun to be guilty. Actually, their bad deed could not have been done had not bad will preceded it; what is more, the root of their bad will was nothing else than pride. For, "pride is the beginning of all sin" (Eccl. 10:15). And what is pride but an appetite for inordinate exaltation? Now, exaltation is inordinate when the soul cuts itself off from the very Source to which it should keep close and somehow makes itself and becomes an end to itself. This takes place when the soul becomes inordinately pleased with itself, and such self-pleasing occurs when the soul falls away from the unchangeable Good which ought to please the soul far more than the soul can please itself. Now, this falling away is the soul's own doing, for, if the will had merely remained firm in the love of that higher immutable Good which lighted its mind into knowledge and warmed its will into love, it would not have turned away in search of satisfaction in itself and, by so doing, have lost that light and warmth. And thus Eve would not have believed that the serpent's lie was true, nor would Adam have preferred the will of his wife to the will of God nor have supposed that his transgression of God's command was venial when he refused to abandon the partner of his life even in a partnership of sin.

Our first parents, then, must already have fallen before they could do the evil deed, before they could commit the sin of eating the forbidden fruit. For such "bad fruit" could come only from a "bad tree" (Cf. Matt. 7:18). That the tree became bad was contrary to its nature, because such a condition could come about only by a defection of the will, which is contrary to nature. Notice, however, that such worsening by reason of a defect is possible only in a nature that has been created out of nothing. In a word, a nature is a nature because it is something made by God, but a nature falls away from That which Is because the nature was made out of nothing.

Yet, man did not so fall away from Being as to be absolutely nothing, but, in so far as he turned himself toward himself, he became less than he was when he was adhering to Him who is supreme Being. Thus, no longer to be in God but to be in oneself in the sense of to please oneself is not to be wholly nothing but to be approaching nothingness. For this reason, Holy Scripture gives another name to the proud. They are called "rash" and "self willed" (Cf. 2 Pet. 2:10). Certainly, it is good for the heart to be lifted up, not to oneself, for this is the mark of pride, but to God, for this is a sign of obedience which is precisely the virtue of the humble.

There is, then, a kind of lowliness which in some wonderful way causes the heart to be lifted up, and there is a kind of loftiness which makes the heart sink lower. This seems to be a sort of paradox, that loftiness should make something lower and lowliness lift something up. The reason for this is that holy lowliness makes us bow to what is above us and, since there is nothing above God, the kind of lowliness that makes us close to God exalts us. On the other hand, the kind of loftiness which is a defection by this very defection refuses this subjection to God and so falls down from Him who is supreme, and by falling comes to be lower. Thus it comes to pass, as Scripture says, that "when they were lifting themselves up thou hast cast them down" (Cf. Ps. 72:18). Here, the Psalmist does not say: "When they had been lifted up," as though they first lifted themselves up and afterwards were cast down, but "when they are lifting themselves up, at that moment they were cast down," which means that their very lifting themselves up was itself a fall.

Hence it is that just because humility is the virtue especially esteemed in the City of God and so recommended to its citizens in their present pilgrimage on earth and because it is one that was particularly outstanding in Christ, its King, so it is that pride, the vice contrary to this virtue, is, as Holy Scripture tells us, especially dominant in Christ's adversary, the Devil. In fact, this is the main difference which distinguishes the two cities of which we are speaking. The humble City is the society of holy men and good angels; the proud city is the society of wicked men and evil angels. The one City began with the love of God; the other had its beginnings in the love of self.

The conclusion, then, is that the Devil would not have begun by an open and obvious sin to tempt man into doing something which God had forbidden, had not man already begun to seek satisfaction in himself and, consequently, to take pleasure in the words: "You shall be as Gods" (Gen. 3:5). The promise of these words, however, would much more truly have come to pass if, by obedience, Adam and Eve had kept close to the ultimate and true Source of their being and had not, by pride, imagined that they were themselves the source of their being. For, created gods are gods not in virtue of their own being but by a participation in the being of the true God (Cf. above, 9:23). For, whoever seeks to be more than he is becomes less, and while he aspires to be self-sufficing he retires from Him who is truly sufficient for him.

Thus, there is a wickedness by which a man who is self-satisfied as if he were the light turns himself away from that true Light which, had man loved it, would have made him a sharer in the light; it was this wickedness which secretly preceded and was the cause of the bad act which was committed openly. It has been truly written that "before destruction, the heart of a man is exalted: and before he be glorified, it is humbled" (Cf. Prov. 18:12). The "destruction which is not seen precedes the "destruction" which is seen, though the former is not looked upon as such. For, who would think of exaltation as a ruin; yet there is a fall the moment that the will turns away from the Highest. On the other hand, everyone can recognize the ruin when a command has been openly and unmistakably violated.

Therefore, God forbade that which, when committed, could be defended by no pretense of sanctity. And I am willing to say that it is advantageous for the proud to fall into some open and manifest sin, and so become displeasing to themselves, after they had already fallen by pleasing themselves. For, when Peter wept and reproached himself, he was in a far healthier condition than when he boasted and was satisfied with himself. A verse of the psalm expresses this truth: "Fill their faces with shame; and they shall seek thy name, O Lord" (Ps. 82:17), meaning, "May those who pleased themselves in seeking their own glory find pleasure in Thee by seeking Thy name."

Discussion

1. In Augustine's view, what accounts for sin? What is its counterpart in his view of the City of God?
2. What does Augustine mean by a "fall from freedom"? What are the implications of this for New Testament Christians?
3. Augustine argues in the final paragraph that it is good for some people to fall into sin for they will thereby learn to dislike themselves as sinners and be motivated to turn to God for renewal. Does this view seem to be accurate in your perception of modern life? Do people loathe their sin? Some people seem to rejoice in it. How genuine is such joy?
4. In chapter 11, Augustine seems to imply that sin can be cured and that sinners therefore should not be destroyed. Does this correspond to your view of sin? What are the implications of Augustine's view for capital punishment or warfare?
5. In a later chapter of *The City of God*, Augustine argues that "peace is the calm that comes of order," knowing ourselves in relation to God. Can you find a personal or biblical support for this argument?

Why Get Married?

Lewis B. Smedes

> *Lewis B. Smedes, professor of ethics at Fuller Theological Seminary, is well known for his careful articulation of contemporary ethical problems and insightful application of biblical responses to them. His book* Forgive and Forget *(San Francisco: Harper and Row, 1984) has been a national best seller. The excerpts reprinted here, which deal with a biblical view of marriage and sex, are from* Sex for Christians: The Limits and Liberties of Sexual Living.

We asked who was qualified for sexual intercourse. The New Testament answered: people who intend to live together. We asked why. And Paul answered: sexual intercourse signifies and seals a personal life-union. We asked how. But Paul did not answer; he simply told us that when two people copulate they do something that binds them in a life-partnership, which the Hebrews called being "one flesh." Still, while the relationship between sexual intercourse and life-partnership was not precise, it was definite enough to tell us that only people who intend the latter were qualified for the former. Therefore, liking each other a lot is not enough. Enriching a personal relationship is not enough. Only a commitment to a total and permanent partnership is enough to qualify people for sexual intercourse.

For most of us, a commitment to a life-partnership is the same as "getting married." But some of our sons and daughters do not make the same connection. "Living together" has become almost as common on larger campuses and in larger cities as "going steady" used to be. While it is still rare in smaller towns and on the smaller—especially Christian—campuses, cohabitation has become an accepted life-style wherever college-age people live away from home and where the college does not act as substitute parent. And even if it has not been digested into the style of the Christian campus, it is likely to become a minority practice there eventually.

The ground rules of cohabitation without a license vary. They run the gamut from going very steady to quasi-marriage. I will skip the more subtle nuances and point to two options. First, the young people who live together—full-time or most of the time—without pretending anything permanent like marriage have a partnership that is much more than "going steady"; but they do not mean it even as a prelude to marriage or a trial marriage. They are not trying marriage on "for size." The deal is completely open-ended: either partner can call it quits whenever he or she wishes. They make love but do not make commitments. They want more than casual sex but less than life-union. What they want lies somewhere between the uncertainties and anxieties of "going steady" and the certainty and commitment of marriage.

Before pronouncing moral judgment on this kind of life-style, we should at least try to understand. Compassion should be the cutting edge of moral judgment and understanding the cutting edge of compassion. In the first place, cohabitation is probably not a lustful lunge for sex on a regular basis. In our culture, young people can find enough sex without having to live together to get it. What, then, is the main motive? I think the main motive is a need for personal closeness, for a relaxed, open, dependable and deep relationship with another person. Sexual intercourse is an ingredient of such a relationship, and its importance varies from couple to couple. But what is valued highest is the satisfaction of being close to someone who cares but who does not make heavy demands.

If this is true, "living together" is the young person's answer to one of the deep needs of our time. We have all come to put a high value on personal relationships, mainly because they are so hard to come by. Our neighborhoods do not give them to us; institutions are large and impersonal; friendships are *ad hoc*, depending on the temporary associations of business and sports; deep and personal ties are not even easily formed in church. We live in what Vance Packard rightly called a "nation of strangers." So we value most consciously what we miss and need most deeply. We are all hungry for closeness.

Young people feel the need most urgently. They grew up in neighborhoods of indifference; they have often felt alienated from their parents' styles and values; and they are lonely within the huge information factories called universities. Besides, they have become skeptical about the institutional side of life in general—and of marriage in particular. So why not find closeness in the simplest way, a sexual partnership without the bondage of commitment or bother of legality? Furthermore, there is a certain logic that moves from a romantic definition of marriage to "living together" for the time being. If love is what marriage is all about, why can one not have all the experience of love without a marriage license? Besides, since love is what marriage is all about, partners choose each other without interference from their families. Marriage, once a merger of families, is now only a merger of two people. And if this is true, why should not the two people choose their own style of arranging their lives together? Whether or not the argument is sound, it has a convincing ring to young people.

Finally, sexual intercourse has lost its moral mystique. Young people, as far as I can tell, tend to think of it on a more practical basis. It may still be a special form of getting close, but it is not necessarily an expression of a total life-union. Paul's belief that sexual intercourse makes two people "one flesh" simply does not get through to the average secular young person. The traditional rules are ignored; but, more importantly, the biblical insight into the moral meaning of sexual intercourse is not even a conscious option.

From the Christian viewpoint, "living together" on an open-ended basis is morally inappropriate. There is no way to justify it on New Testament grounds. This is not simply a matter of breaking traditional rules: it is a matter of one's view of the deeper meaning of sexual intercourse. It may also have important practical hazards that raise many questions. Does it lock people into a deep relationship they are not ready for? Does it trigger emotional attachments on the part of one of the partners that the other does not share? What, in short, is the potential for emotional pain? Does open-ended cohabitation condition young people to shun all permanent commitments? And will it, for that reason, make their eventual marriage a shaky partnership from the beginning? Does it tend to reduce sexual intercourse to a mere expression of close friendship and so open doors to extramarital affairs after marriage? Does it delude young people with the fantasy that living together for a while is really like marriage? Does it keep them in the illusion that deep and total partnership can come without struggle, agony, disappointment, and constantly renewed will to create a true partnership? Does it, in short, give a cheap answer to the problem of loneliness and alienation? I suspect it does. I suspect that open-ended cohabitation is an infantile solution because it grabs the goodies of life without the long-term responsibilities of life. It achieves instant closeness but avoids the tensions and conflicts that are built into a life partnership that is achieved only by a love that is willing to struggle.

We can put all these questions to the young people involved, but in the long run they will not be powerful considerations. For every red flag we wave they can find a green light to counter it. Cohabitation, they will argue, can be a useful preparation for marriage. It may make young people less impulsive and more rational in choosing their mates for marriage. And, within the new sexual ethos, having sexual intercourse does not trigger either strong commitment or deep guilt. In the end, the practical factors leave parents and young people in a standoff. The only question that can finally decide the issue *morally* is: what is the real meaning of sexual intercourse?

We have been talking about people who live together without commitment to each other. But many people live together with a kind of commitment, and yet do not want to get married. These are the people this chapter is mainly about. They intend something like marriage, and they do not see why a piece of legal paper filed in a clerk's office could make their partnership more meaningful, moral, or real than it is. The fact that they do not get married seems to betray some reservation in their commitment; but they feel as though it is a real one nonetheless. We could say that their commitment is more intensive than extensive. Their sharing is total, even though they do not want it institutionally extended into permanent wedlock. It is as permanent as they can make it at this point, but they are unwilling to gamble on a long-term future. Their relationship is not stable enough to fit the label of a "common law" marriage, but it is as stable as they can manage for now.

Why couples do not want to get married varies with each partnership, so we can speak only in generalities. But often these people are simply not able, within themselves, to make a permanent commitment. Their entire lives have been spent in uncertainty about the future; how can they now sincerely place their persons-in-relationship on the line for as long as they live? They also hate to contemplate the hassle of divorce should they not be able to keep their partnership going. If it should come to that, they want to be able to split without the nasty complications of a legal divorce. Some of them are no doubt reacting to the hypocrisies of many modern marriages. Serial monogamy, they see, is not prevented by legal or even church weddings. Some of them grew up in homes where the hallowed ceremony was an initiation into a cold war. Furthermore, a cynicism about all social institutions filters through their rejection of a wedding. These and many other motives lie behind their reluctance to gather the clan for a festive and solemn wedding ceremony.

Against this background, we must ask about the morality of weddings as the right way to begin a sexual partnership. And in so doing we must admit that weddings are often moral farces. Moreover, the institution planted in a wedding is often an empty shell that binds two people together for a while in a hell of hostility or a purgatory of boredom. People do get married with little more than a hope that things will work out; and a hope is not a commitment to life together

as long as that "life shall last." We must also understand that there is
no moral law that tells us how we must begin a marriage. Marriages
are not created only by the words of a justice of the peace or a preacher.
Myriads of splendid marriages have begun without anything like what
we would recognize as a wedding in our culture. And who knows how
many weddings have legalized sham marriages? The Bible has a lot to
say about marriage, but it has little or nothing to say about how marriages must begin. There is a theology of marriage, but there is no
divine morality of weddings. Marriage is an invention of God; weddings are inventions of cultures. So when we ask why young people
ought to "get married," we are asking why they should submit to a
cultural custom that changes as culture changes. We will have to put
up with an answer that carries less weight than divine law.

It seems to me that the correct moral category to use in fluid situations like this is responsibility. We do not always have clear moral law
at our disposal but persons are always called to responsibility. The
responsible person is one who responds with human sensitivity and
intelligence to each situation as it calls for a decision. We respond
when we take stock of the claims our life-situation makes on us, interpret their meanings, and calculate the effects of our action. We respond
when we use our wills and determine to be accountable for our actions.
In the absence of rules, being responsible means giving the most fitting
and helpful response we can to the situation that calls for a decision. A
responsible Christian person will respond to his total situation as he
sees it in the light of what Christ wills for him and for all who are
affected by his actions. Thus, when he asks, "Why should we get married?" the responsible person will give his response in the light of such
factors within his situation as the claims the state has on him, the
claims of the church, the claims of his family, the claims of his partner,
and the claims his own future has on him.

Moreover, our response has to be given in our own situation. A young
man and woman living in the simpler days of Abraham would only
have had to look tenderly into each other's eyes, go off by themselves to
a tent, and make love; they then would be married. In that culture a
network of clearly understood—though unwritten—laws, plus the
supporting closeness of the clan or tribe, would have held them together in a marriage more stable than are most marriages in a society
crisscrossed by detailed legal codes. But today's young people cannot
be responsible within Abraham's culture; they can be responsible only
within their own. If the same couple were alone on a desert island, they
could be truly married without intervention of church or state. But
most couples are not alone on an island. They can be responsible only
in their situation: they have to do the humanly and Christianly responsi-

ble thing in the advanced and legally complex culture of the twentieth century. How it is done in Samoa settles nothing for a couple in Chicago.

There are two essential issues that involve every couple in "getting married": (a) whether they will play the game according to the rules set by the state; and (b) whether the couple is willing to begin a new relationship with a public declaration.

First, a responsible person will at least give a serious answer to the claims that legalities have on him. Civil laws concerning marriage require records to be kept because married life in modern societies becomes complicated. There will be children, property and income taxes, deaths, burials, inheritances, possibly divorces, and many other contingencies. Future decisions may need to rely on records of the people involved. Legal marriages are for the benefit of married people: they protect people against disease, involvement in bigamy, and other technical disasters. Legal marriage also safeguards the privacy and intimacy of the couple; it guards the rights of the married couple against unwanted intrusions by third parties into their partnership. And it guards the rights of children if one partner should die or leave.

Furthermore, the laws of the state are there as an expression of an ordered community. If everyone made marriage only a matter of the heart, only a private thing in the hearts and minds of two people, a large dimension of society would be in a chaotic mess, and many people would suffer unfairly. The so-called institution of marriage supports, not diminishes, the possibilities of personally creative marriages. So the claims of the state are really protective claims. The occasional "unmarried" partnership is feasible only in a society where most people do honor the claims of society. Therefore, the question of whether to get married must be decided in response to the claims of the community on married couples.

Second, there is the matter of a public declaration. A responsible person will want his "style" to fit the real ingredients of his action. If it is true that when two people marry they are creating a new social entity within the community, their style ought to fit this fact. In the Christian view, a marriage is not only a private affair between two people who happen to live under the same roof. These two people form a new unit, and as a unit their relationship to the community is not the same as it was when they acted simply as individuals. They can pretend to be two individuals who happen to live together; but in fact they have formed a new social entity and have accepted a new status in the community as a married partnership. If this is true, what is the responsible way of initiating the partnership? Getting married is a couple's way of affirming publicly that they intend to accept the responsibilities of what their marriage makes them: a new social unit within a society of such social units.

For Christian couples there is another community involved: the fellowship of Christian people in the church. The church is a supporting and disciplining community. When Christian people get married and thus form a social unit within that community, it is their way of openly accepting the community's support and discipline. When a couple gets married "in the sight of God and these witnesses," they are saying that they seek and accept the prayers, the counsel, and the discipline of the church. And the responsible couple will by their wedding declare in community that they are prepared to live as a partnership within the supportive fellowship.

Finally, there is one more thing about marriage that asks for a wedding: it is the human need for festivity. Human life seems to need moments set apart for celebration and partying. We mark birthdays, anniversaries, graduations, births and any other special event in our lives by breaking the routine of our life-style with a party. A person needs something to make toasts to; so does the community. And weddings are festivals celebrating the beginning of a new adventure. God's blessing on a marriage, given at a wedding, is really an act of celebration; the wedding affirms that a good and important thing is taking place. But again, there is no specific morality involved. Responsible moral decisions are made when persons size up the total picture and respond to it in a fitting way. Weddings are the public beginning of a new enterprise, which is at its heart the original private enterprise. Like all private enterprises, it needs the support and the restraint of a community. Weddings are not society's trick to keep young people in line with custom; they are this society's method of receiving a new enterprise of love into its midst.

There is no moral law that demands a wedding, and it is perverse to identify real marriage with weddings. A marriage without a wedding is not *per se* an immoral arrangement, and a marriage begun with a wedding is not *per se* a moral one. But being Christian and human implies a calling for persons to give an accountable response to all the dimensions of their actions. In view of that calling, a cogent case can be made that getting married is more responsible than living together without bothering with the institution.

Discussion

1. In another section of *Sex for Christians,* Smedes states that we are "forever *becoming* married," always moving toward a perfect unity initiated in the marriage ceremony. In what way is his statement true? How do traditional marriage vows suggest this?

2. In what ways does the New Testament conviction that "in Christ you are free indeed" apply to marriage and sexuality?
3. Smedes writes that "we are all hungry for closeness." Think about ways of showing affection in your own family. Some of us show affection physically; some by a word or gesture. In 1 Thessalonians 5:26 Paul orders us to "greet all the brethren with a holy kiss." What prevents us from doing this? In what ways can we satisfy the "hunger for closeness" in others?
4. Smedes uses a formal *persona,* the so-called editorial *we.* What is the effect of this in his discussion?

A Quiet Conversion

Cathy Stentzel

> Sojourners *magazine has for some years been a leading voice for pacifism in evangelical Christianity. In a startling special issue published in November 1980, many of the editors and writers of* Sojourners *explained how their views on pacifism led them to positions, and sometimes radically changed positions, on the issue of abortion. The writers challenged themselves to develop a consistent ethical view, and quite often were surprised at what the challenge demanded of them. The following essay by Cathy Stentzel, assistant to the editor of* Sojourners, *details her radical transformation.*

I have not always been pro-life. In the years of the late '60s and the decade of the '70s I was for abortion. It was the popular opinion of everyone I knew. I accepted the doctrinal orthodoxy of the women's movement which states that the right to abortion is an absolute necessity for liberation and equality with men. In this view we women must have full control of our bodies and reproductive lives; by not being saddled with pregnancies and children, we could have the freedom men do to reap the rewards of the system so long denied us.

My religious outlook led me to think that legalized abortion was far better than the horror and ugliness of "back-alley" or self-induced abortions. I reasoned that legalizing abortion would actually *save* lives. Abortion seemed a positive and humane solution for poor women who could not afford another mouth to feed—humane for the child as well as the mother.

After abortion was legalized in this country in 1973, I found myself looking down on women who kept having baby after baby: "Even if their birth control failed, they could have had an abortion," I thought. I couldn't imagine someone willingly raising more children than she wanted. The question of the possible elitism of that attitude didn't bother me. In the same way I unquestioningly accepted aborting potentially retarded or handicapped babies, unknowingly presuming the superiority of the hearing, the sighted, and the intellectually able.

Admittedly, I was a little shocked to hear a friend tell of having an abortion because she and her husband didn't want any more children. Though I thought myself a feminist, I saw abortion as a solution for the poor and unmarried. I thought that the life produced by two committed married people (i.e., people I knew) should be allowed to live. They could afford to make arrangements and changes in their lives.

But eventually even these misgivings were quelled by a steadily growing secularism in my attitude toward sex, marriage, and family, in line with the popular culture. Abortion was the reasoned, pragmatic, safe, convenient answer to untimely or unwanted pregnancies, even when the need for it sprang from an inherent materialism that put a career, mortgage, or reputation ahead of life itself.

Spouting the slogan, "People before profits," I took part in demonstrations against real-estate speculators or multinational corporations and never saw the inconsistency in the fact that I wasn't bothered that many women got abortions for quite profit-oriented reasons. I agreed with the Supreme Court that a fetus is not a person and therefore didn't qualify for my protection or advocacy.

I remember feeling intense emotion when faced with the anti-abortion point of view. I thought that people who opposed abortion had no right to do violence to my mind (and other people's minds) with their brochures carrying color photos of aborted fetuses. When I was librarian at Tokyo Union Church in 1974, I took a stack of anti-abortion tracts and threw them in the waste basket in disgust.

The question of the value of life itself never came to mind, even though I had had one child and adopted another. I did not even see the connection between our being able to adopt our daughter in Japan, a country which had had legalized abortion since the end of World War II, and the fact that her 15-year-old mother had not had an abortion.

Even after coming to Sojourners in the summer of 1977, I held on to my belief, adamantly and at times vocally. At one point, the magazine staff had to decide whether to print an anti-abortion article. We had a highly charged debate but could not reach consensus about abortion itself. We agreed not to print anything then, and we let the subject drop. It came up briefly twice a year when we met to plan future issues, but until last spring the response was always, "We're not ready to say anything yet."

It's not easy to trace the strands of reason and faith that led me to a change of mind and heart on this question. Being pro-life now seems all one piece with my life itself and the deeper experience of God's life I have found in community. But the conversion has been slow and quiet.

The first and earliest strand was a long-held belief in nonviolence—that killing and the use of force are wrong. Born a female in this culture, the abhorrence of violence was an ingrained part of my being. But there were deeper reasons for embracing nonviolence. One was Christian conviction: an innate knowledge that the killing of Christ should have been the last killing; that to live a Christ-like life is to live peaceably, without defense.

Another was the influence of historical events, allowing my feelings to be engaged by the atrocities of my world. I read about the holocaust in Europe, feeling the weight of the evil that had happened in my lifetime. I was at Columbia University in the spring of 1968 when police charged into lines of students holding the campus in protest against research being conducted for the Department of Defense. I was in Hiroshima on August 6, 1972, and experienced the shock of the reality of nuclear war depicted in the museum there. And of course there was the war in Vietnam, the assassinations of the Kennedys and Martin Luther King, the war in Biafra, Kent State, the hanging of the PRP in South Korea, the killing of Steve Biko.

Since I've come to Sojourners, the reality of being a pacifist has taken on new and deeper meaning. This is a function of our peace witness and study, and a deepening of my understanding of Christ's life and the gospel message of peace. It is also a matter of seeing nonviolent lives actually being lived out.

It was in reading such people as Gordon Zahn, Daniel Berrigan, Juli Loesch, and others presented in this issue of *Sojourners* that I came to see the connections between nonviolence and a "pro-life" position on abortion. It was hard to admit that I had been inconsistent. I was a nonviolent person who winced even killing roaches, and at the same time I was adamantly in favor of abortion. I had not allowed my feelings to be involved where abortion was concerned.

It was an intellectual matter for me, one which did not consider the life being taken but only the rights of the already-born. I think now that a believer in nonviolence must view life from both sides and plead on behalf of the already-conceived, as well as for justice and freedom from want and fear for the mother.

The most important strand in my conversion from pro-abortion to pro-life was the acknowledgment that the being growing in the womb was life, that life in all its fullness was apparent from conception. I think most women who have borne children will acknowledge this in our souls. It doesn't matter what name we give to this life to distance ourselves from it and make it sound like not-life, part of us still knows what it is.

I know it is life and has a right to live because I have come to know its Creator. In the last three years at Sojourners I have been on a journey of continuous conversion, a turning and returning to God. Through prayer and contemplation, in the reading of Scriptures and in the life of the Eucharist, at the most personal and intimate level, I have come to know the value of my own life. At the center of my life I meet God and am named. What I know in prayer has been made real in the life of the community through the love and acceptance I receive from my sisters and brothers here.

My experience of healing from depression, anxiety, and a sense of failure and not being "good enough" has helped me see more clearly that a pro-life stance must start with a belief in the ultimate worth of our own lives. If I do not love myself, if at the core of my life I have no meaning or hope, no belief in life's goodness and joy, I could project that despair on a massive scale: Any new life in me is not worth living; the lives of the poor are even worse than mine—surely *they* are not worth living. In such a view, death becomes more desirable than the pain of life.

In community I have experienced Christ's healing love and have been allowed to be me, without the masks that cover pain and inadequacy. This healing is gradual; no one comes to it overnight. It is an experience that allows me to say, "My suffering has become my joy." I think that too often abortion is seen as the only solution to problem pregnancies, the quick fix, the lesser pain which is preferable to facing the myriad of unknown larger pains that a new life might bring.

It is by now a cliche to say that as a society we are intent on seeking pleasure and avoiding pain at almost any price. But as Christians we bear witness to the One who bore the supreme pain of rejection and death, and rose to life again. We know that life is joy as well as pain, and that in being able to accept and live through our places of suffering, we grow and come to know the fullness of life. I do not want to say glibly that "suffering is good for you" and use that as a rationale for opposing abortion. But I do think it is important that we not forget Christ's teaching that it is only in losing our lives, giving them in service to others, that we truly find them. It is apparent that in many cases an inherent selfishness is what brings a woman to the abortion clinic—her own selfishness, that of her man, or the selfish preoccupations of our society as a whole. Healing also comes when we are able to accept the results of our choices, to take responsibility for our life and other lives.

The third strand in my pro-life cloth is having come to depend very deeply on God for my security. I can trust the maker of heaven and earth with my life and the life of the world. In Jesus' words, I do not have to be anxious about what I will eat, or drink, or wear, for God in heaven knows I need these things.

When we come to know that security in our deepest selves, we are able to offer it to others, even to the smallest of our sisters and brothers just being formed in the womb. We can stop acting like jealous siblings who view each new life as a threat to getting our share of love and the necessities of life.

The last strand of my conversion is my new understanding of feminism. In the paradox of community, I have begun to live a more truly feminist lifestyle than the one I gave lip service to in pre-Sojourners days. Being really liberated means being free to know myself as a daughter of God and to stand whole in that knowledge. In our women's group we studied feminist theologians and biblical scholars, and I learned that Jesus affirmed the wholeness of women, that in Christ we are already equal with men.

Of course we must be aware of our socialization that causes us to feel unworthy, to seek second place, or to give in to male dominance. We must not only begin to believe we are equal, we must act on that belief. But true liberation comes from God and is given in abundance to us all. I do not need to take and grasp it. Under the illusion of "being in control" of their lives, women have bought into the abortion mystique in a way that in the end will beget only emptiness for themselves and perhaps for our whole culture.

I am wholeheartedly in support of the Equal Rights Amendment. Feminists who use a pro-choice position on abortion as a litmus test for membership in the women's movement must re-examine that position. There have been almost seven million abortions in this country since 1973. As a woman and a Christian I do not want to be identified with that measure of liberation.

Just like the arms race, abortion is a product of our society's collective anxiety and insecurity about the future. Women need to step out of that anxiety. We must at least begin to see that abortion, convenient as it is for a woman's "problem," is often more convenient for the lover, or boss, or husband, or father of that woman. Our own liberation must not be based on destroying our children, but on reaching out to our brothers, offering them the word of life, and insisting that they begin to assume their responsibility for the care and nurture of those children. In that way both parents can have equal opportunity to discover their individual gifts and talents.

Perhaps I have made the conversion from pro-abortion to pro-life sound too smooth, as if there were no struggle or conflict. On the contrary, I experienced intense struggle and resistance to change. Abortion even became part of my sleeping life late last summer in dreams that showed my insecurity in having to defend my new belief to others who would see it as right wing. Other conflicts were brought up at our women's group meeting here in the community the night we talked about abortion. For some, saying that abortion was wrong or a sin seemed absolutist; such a view didn't seem to take into considera-tion the complexities of our world and its social realities. Didn't we have to ask prior questions about sexual morality and birth control, the plight of the genuinely poor, or even "when does life begin?" Did saying abortion was wrong mean we were judging women who had had abortions or not showing compassion for the agonizing decisions they had to make? What would be our commitment to women in difficult situations who choose not to abort?

We talked about the difficult choices in our own lives and the lives of women we knew personally, and what it means to give up control of our lives to the Spirit of God working in us. We shared our convictions and listened to our doubts. The spirit of sisterhood was strong among us as we realized that there was space for the struggle and for listening to and loving those who disagreed with us.

To attempt to live a life according to the gospel of Christ, one has to be an idealist. Taking a stand against abortion is very similar to pro-testing the arms race or trying to live a life of voluntary poverty. We will be seen by many as naive, simplistic, or hopelessly idealistic. But that is a small risk if we can begin a dialogue that will help others struggle more deeply with the issue. Whether we have been "pro-choice" or "pro-life" or "somewhere in the middle" in the past, I believe God is calling us now to choose life.

Discussion

1. In the first-person narration, the thesis often evolves in the essay with the story of the narrator. The thesis is not always neatly announced at the outset, but the reader discovers the thesis through the experience of the narrator. What would you say is the thesis of this essay?
2. What is the significance of the essay's title?
3. How did the writer's change in ethical perspective affect her decisions? What specific items caused the change?

4. How does the writer attempt an inclusive world-and-life view from her particular ethical stance? How, specifically, does she apply her views to other issues? Are these applications consistent with her ethical stance?

The Death of Infant Doe: Jesus and the Neonates

Mark 10:13–16

Allen Verhey

> *Allen Verhey, professor of religion at Hope College, has written and lectured extensively on the relationship between medicine and Christian ethics. His study of New Testament ethics,* The Great Reversal, *was published by Eerdmans Publishing Company in 1984. In "The Death of Infant Doe: Jesus and the Neonates," Professor Verhey examines different ethical responses to the landmark Bloomington, Indiana, case and carefully distinguishes the value of the Christian ethical response.*

I imagine it was a hot and sunny day, the kind of day when kids seem to have such boundless energy and grownups seem to wilt. The disciples, I suppose, were quite glad for the rest; at least they were a little peevish when women and children threatened to interrupt it. They rebuked them, the story says. "Can't you see Jesus is an important person? What business do you have bothering him? Get back to your ovens, women! Return to your toys, children! Stay out of our way."

The disciples' response was conventional enough; surely understandable. Women and children just were not that important. They were numbered among the heathen and illiterate, with sinners and those who know not the law, with slaves and property. They were not numbered at all when the members of the synagogue were counted. You needed ten *adult males* for a synagogue. Women and children just didn't count for much. The disciples knew that and told them to go away.

Jesus gets angry, too, but not with the women, not with the children. He gets angry with the disciples. He turns the conventional rules of pomp and protocol upside down. Those who don't count count with him! He makes the last first! When will his disciples ever learn that? He says to them, "Let the children come to me. Do not hinder them. To them belongs the kingdom of God."

The disciples must have been more than a little dumbfounded. Other strange behavior of this Galilean teacher had *hardly* prepared them for this.

There must have been babies there, and more than one dirty diaper. And Jesus takes them in his arms. There must have been toddlers and youngsters, curious and energetic, crying occasionally and interrupting often. "Women are meant to deal with them," the disciples thought, but Jesus blesses them. And there must have been boys and girls, taking an infrequent break from playing tag and catch, and some who stood on the sidelines because of a limp or a disease or something else that made them unwelcome in the game. And Jesus lays his hands on them.

And as though all this is not enough, Jesus says, "If you want to enter the kingdom become *like one* of these children." People have speculated endlessly about how we are supposed to be like children. It is their *trust*, some say; their *dependence*, others say; their *joy*, still others say; or their *simplicity*. There is perhaps some truth in each of those comparisons, but I really think they are beside the point. Jesus says in other places, "If any would be first of all, let him be last of all and the servant of all." And that's what he says here too. Become *like* one of these children means simply "become last—for *such* are first with me." That's the shocking thing. Jesus exalts the humble and humbles the exalted. He makes the last first. Those who don't count count with him. He *blesses* kids: dirty-diapered, sweaty, silly, obnoxious kids. He rebukes the disciples, impressed with their own importance and conventional prestige. And Jesus makes it clear that to *be* his disciple, to welcome the kingdom, will mean to welcome, to serve and to help, these little children. Who is greatest in the kingdom? These little children and those who bless and serve them.

After the death and resurrection of Jesus, soon that story was being told again and again in the young church. Pentecost had convinced them that Jesus continued to abide with his church, and that he continued to address his church in their memory of what he had said once or had done once. Even as the church awaited the new creation, the redemption of their bodies and their adoption as sons, as Paul says, the church was constantly informed and reformed by the stories about Jesus. Imagine, for example, Peter telling the story to settle the question of whether the children of believing parents should be baptized. Or Andrew telling the story in a slightly different way to exhort his hearers to a childlike faith. Or again, imagine some unknown preacher telling the story to protest the neglect and abandonment of children that were practiced in the Roman empire. The story found its way finally into Mark's gospel alongside sayings about marriage and riches to provide guidance for a Christian household.

The story continues to be told in the churches, of course. It is told in countless stained glass windows. You've all seen them. The only thing wrong with these windows is that the kids are too *angelic*. There are no snotty noses or bruised knees or any imperfection to be found in the stained glass representations of the story.

The story has indeed become so familiar that we have to make an effort to stop and think about it, to contemplate what it would mean to make this story our story, to be informed and reformed by this story. I invite you to make that effort, specifically to think about what this story might mean for our care of neonates.

To do that there is another story that I want you to think about. It is a familiar story, too. It's the story of Infant Doe. It happened in Bloomington, Indiana. Now, Bloomington is a pleasant little city set in the lovely hills of southern Indiana. Bloomington Hospital is typical of hospitals in pleasant little cities; the daily human events of giving birth, suffering, and dying are attended to with the ordinary measure of professional competence and compassion. It seems unlikely that the story of birth, suffering, and death of a baby in Bloomington would capture national attention.

On April 9, 1982, a boy was born in Bloomington Hospital with Down's syndrome and esophageal atresia. Down's syndrome is a fairly common genetic defect which causes varying degrees of mental retardation and physical deformity. Esophageal atresia is a malformation of the esophagus, so that food taken orally cannot enter the stomach and instead causes choking.

The parents of this baby refused to consent to the surgical procedure necessary to correct the esophageal atresia. The obstetrician who had initially presented such "benign neglect" as one of the medical options supported the parents in that decision. A pediatrician who had been consulted to confirm the diagnosis dissented from such a course of "treatment." The Circuit Court in Bloomington and subsequently the Indiana Supreme Court in Indianapolis refused to override the parents' decision and to order the surgery to correct the esophagus of "Infant Doe." The baby lay in Bloomington Hospital for six days until his starving yielded to his death on April 15.

The obstetrician and the pediatrician disagreed not only about the recommended treatment but also about the chances for successful esophageal surgery, about the likelihood of other serious physical problems, and about the prognosis of retardation. The obstetrician, in presenting the options to the parents, said that the chances for successful surgery were about fifty-fifty, that other physical defects, including congenital heart disease, would subsequently have to be surgically corrected, and that the child would certainly be severely retarded. The pediatrician insisted that the likelihood of successful surgery was more like ninety per cent, that there was no evidence of congenital heart disease, and that it was impossible to determine the severity of the retardation Infant Doe would have. The conflicting medical opinions and recommendations weighed heavily in the courts' decisions not to intervene, not to play either doctor or parent to the child.

The courts' hesitancy to pretend to either medical competence or parental compassion can be appreciated (especially by those schooled in something called "sphere sovereignty"). Moreover, the competence of the doctors and the compassion of the parents were widely attested. Still, the medical recommendation of the obstetrician and the decisions by the parents and by the justices were morally wrong—not just tragic, but wrong.

Decisions are tragic when goods come into conflict, when any decision brings in its train some wrong. This was not such a decision. The right decision would have been to do the surgery.

I will undertake to defend that judgment in ways that are standard in medical ethics, in ways that rely on impartial rationality to formulate judgments and to solve dilemmas. One need not be a Christian to see that the decision not to treat Infant Doe was wrong. But I will also undertake to show that impartial rationality is inadequate, that it can provide only a minimal account of morality, and that when its minimalism is not acknowledged it can distort the moral life. Finally, because the conventional approach is inadequate, I will undertake another approach, a candidly Christian approach, an approach which owns the Christian story, including the story of Jesus and the children, as *our* story also in cases like Infant Doe's.

First, then, one need not be a Christian to see that the right decision would have been to perform the surgery to correct the esophagus so that Infant Doe could be fed. The impartial rational justification for saying this might be provided in a number of different ways. The most telling in my view is that, if a "normal" child had been born with esophageal atresia, the surgery would have been performed—even if the obstetrician were right about the risks and the additional physical problems. The reason for "treating" Infant Doe differently was an irrelevant one, Infant Doe's Down's syndrome. (The obstetrician was simply wrong about the ability to predict the extent of retardation caused by Down's syndrome so early.)

Suppose that on April 9 two other babies were born in Bloomington. Suppose "Infant Smith" was born without Down's syndrome but with esophageal atresia. The consent to operate would surely have been given or ordered, and Infant Smith would probably be alive today. Suppose "Infant Jones" was born with Down's syndrome but without any life-threatening malformations of the esophagus. No consent to operate would have been necessary, and Infant Jones would probably be alive today. The difference between Infant Doe and Infant Smith, the difference between life and death, is that Infant Doe had Down's syndrome, nothing else. The difference between Infant Doe and Infant Jones, also the difference between life and death, is that Infant Doe had esophageal atresia in addition to Down's syndrome. If we ought to preserve and cherish the life of Infants Smith and Jones, then we ought also to have preserved and cherished the life of Infant Doe. The differences among these infants are irrelevant to the obligation to sustain their lives and to nurture their bodies and spirits.

This is not to deny that different conditions among infants may indicate different treatments or even in some cases the cessation of treatment. If a condition is terminal and if treatment would only prolong the child's dying and exacerbate his or her suffering, then treatment is not indicated. Anencephalic newborns are a clear case of legitimate neglect. There are tragic cases where a child's suffering from a disease and from the treatment of the disease is so profound as to put it outside the reach of human caring, let alone human curing. Such, however, was not the case with Infant Doe or other Down's syndrome youngsters. Down's syndrome is not a terminal condition; and if people who have it suffer more, it is not because surgery pains them more but because "normal" people can be cruel and spiteful. A Down's child can experience and delight in the reach and touch of human caring.

The neglect of Infant Doe was morally wrong. His death was caused by "natural causes," to be sure, but it was both possible and obligatory to interfere with those "natural causes." If a lifeguard neglected a drowning swimmer whom he recognized as his competition for his lover's affection, we would say he did wrong. That the drowned man died of "natural causes" would not prevent us from seeing the wrong done to him—or from invoking the category "murder." If the same lifeguard neglected a drowning wader whom he recognized as an infant with Down's syndrome, we should also say he did wrong. That the infant died of "natural causes" should not prevent us from seeing the wrong done to him—or from invoking the category "murder."

Someone may argue that "lifeguard" is a well-defined role with specific responsibilities and a tradition involving certain technical skills and moral virtues, and that the obligation to rescue the swimmer and the wader is really a role-obligation. Two replies might be made to this objection to our analogy. First, we might say that any person—lifeguard or not—who sees an infant stumble and fall face down in the water is obliged to attempt to rescue the child, Down's syndrome or not. The decision to neglect Infant Doe, by analogy, is simply morally wrong. The second reply is to acknowledge that "lifeguard" is a special role with special responsibilities and a tradition, and to insist that "physician" and "parent" are also such roles. But here impartial rationality begins to fail us, for it tends to reduce role relations—for example, the relation of the doctors to Infant Doe or his parents or the relation of the parents to Infant Doe—to *contractual* arrangements between independent individuals. That is a minimal account of such roles at best, and when its minimalism is not acknowledged, it is an account which distorts the moral life and the covenants of which it is woven. The stance of impartial rationality cannot nurture any moral wisdom about these roles or sustain any moral traditions concerning them. And it is our confusion about these roles, our diminishing sense of a tradition concerning them that accounts for the failure of a competent physician, compassionate parents, and duly humble justices to make the morally right decision with respect to the care of Infant Doe.

There are other inadequacies in the stance of impartial rationality which bore on the story of Infant Doe. The stance of impartial rationality tends to emphasize the procedural question, the question of who decides, rather than the substantive question of what should be decided. The first and final question in the care of Infant Doe was who should decide, and the answer was consistently that the parents should decide. I am not saying that that question or that answer is wrong, but I am saying that it provides only a minimal account of the moral issues, and that if its minimalism is forgotten or ignored, the moral life and particular moral issues can be distorted. I am saying that a fuller account of morality would focus as well on substantive questions, on the question of *what* should be decided, and on questions of character and virtue, on the question of *what* the person who decides should *be*.

Let me call attention to one other weakness (or inadequacy) of the approach of impartial rationality. This approach requires alienation from ourselves, from our own moral interests and loyalties, from our own histories and communities in order to adopt the impartial point of view. We are asked, nay, obliged, by this approach to view our own projects and passions as though we were outside objective observers.

The stories which we own as our own, which provide our lives a narrative and which develop our own character, we are asked by this approach to disown—and for the sake of morality. Now, to be made to pause occasionally, and for the sake of analysis and judgment to be asked to view things as impartially as we can is not only legitimate but salutary, but neither physicians nor parents nor any Christian can finally live their moral lives like that with any integrity.

These remarks about the inadequacies of impartial rationality allow us to turn an important corner in this paper. My concern is not merely to make a moral judgment about the care of Infant Doe. The decision not to treat him was wrong, but the more interesting questions—and finally the more important questions, from my point of view are: How could a competent physician, compassionate parents, and duly humble justices make such a decision? What stories and tradition make sense of such a decision? And how can the Christian story and explicitly the story of Jesus and the children be brought to bear on such decisions? Can we begin to write a story of Jesus and the neonates? Let's examine briefly the stories and traditions of medicine, of parenting, and society's attitude toward the handicapped.

The obstetrician, however competent and skillful he may have been, had apparently not been initiated into the tradition of medical care which insists that the practice of medicine involves more than techniques and skills, that it serves and embodies certain intrinsic goods. According to one witness to that tradition, the Hippocratic Oath, the end of medicine is "the benefit of the sick," not some extrinsic good like money or fame or the wishes of the medical "consumer."

The benefit of the sick does not stand as a motive for taking up certain ethically neutral skills. It does not identify an extrinsic good to be accomplished by means of ethically neutral technical means. Rather, the benefit of the sick is the "intrinsic" good of medicine. It governs the practice of medicine and entails certain standards which define medicine as a moral art. Medicine in this tradition intends to heal the sick, to protect and nurture health, to maintain and restore a measure of physical well-being. All the powers of medicine are guided and limited by those ends, and they may not be used to serve alien ends—and death is an alien end. In this sad world death will win its victories finally, but medicine which has identified with the tradition to which the Hippocratic Oath witnesses will not serve death or practice hospitality toward it.

Such medicine has its own stories, of course, stories about the great Hippocrates initiating his students into the art with an oath that they will indeed practice medicine for "the benefit of the sick," stories about dedicated physicians braving the elements or the opposition to help some sick scoundrel without worrying about the social utility of his patient or of his profession.

Medicine, formed and informed by such *stories*, would and should have stood in the service of Infant Doe, the sick one, the patient, after all, and braved the claims of any and all who wanted him dead. A physician initiated into such a *tradition* would not present the choice between possible life with Down's syndrome or certain death without esophageal surgery as an option to be contemplated for his patient, nor would she support the choice of death. The obstetrician's failure to embody these stories is symptomatic of our society's diminishing appreciation of this tradition of medicine and a growing confusion about the physician's role. These stories of medicine—let's call them the Hippocratic stories—are today considered sometimes naive, sometimes foolish, both by physicians and by society. Properly impressed by modern medicine's technological accomplishments, we are tempted to view medicine as a collection of skills to get what we want, as a value-free enterprise which may be bought and sold to satisfy consumer desires, hired to do the autonomous bidding of the one who pays. A new story is used to understand medicine—that omnipresent American story of the *marketplace*, where you get rich by supplying what the buyer wants. The decision about Infant Doe is understandable, I think, within the marketplace story of medicine. But we are uncomfortable with the marketplace story for understanding medicine—and properly so—for the medical skills alone can make one either a good healer or a crafty murderer. Medicine formed by such a story—the story of the marketplace—cannot and will not sustain the disposition of care and trust which have defined the characters of doctor and patient in the Hippocratic stories; the marketplace story will *end* with medicine in the service of the rich and powerful, while the poor and weak watch and pray.

Infant Doe was too young to pray but not too young to groan with the rest of us "as we wait for the redemption of our bodies" as Paul says. The points are these: the technical skills and competence of a physician provide no wisdom about a morally right decision. The story of medicine that a physician and a society make their own story will govern such decisions. And the Christian story, including the story of Jesus and the children, provides a resource to support the fragile Hippocratic tradition of medicine—for it enlists us on the side of life and health in a world where death and evil still apparently reign. It makes us suspicious of and repentant for human capacities for pride and sloth with respect to medical technology. And it calls us to identify with and to serve especially the sick and poor and powerless and despised, those who do not measure up to conventional standards.

A note must be added with respect to another community that evidently has the resources to support the fragile tradition of medicine—nurses. Nurses at Bloomington Hospital who were first charged with the "care" of Infant Doe refused to participate in his non-treatment masquerading as care. It violated the ends of nursing as they understood it; it compromised their integrity as members of a nursing community and as heirs of a medical tradition. The immediate consequence of their protest was not great: Infant Doe was simply moved from the nursery to a private room on a surgical floor. But a worthy tradition of medicine was represented and protected by their action. These nurses and others like them are a precious resource if the medical professions and society are to remember and relearn the medical moral tradition.

Our society is also confused about the role of parent. The parents of Infant Doe, however compassionate they may have been, had apparently not been initiated into a tradition of parental care which insists that parents have a duty not only to care "about" their children but to care "for" them, to tend to their physical, emotional, moral, and spiritual needs, not because they "measure up," but because they are their children.

The parents' failure to represent this tradition is symptomatic of our society's growing confusion about parenting. The tradition has always been challenged by the contrary opinion (now usually unstated) that children are the property of parents to be disposed of as they wish, that children exist for the happiness of parents. Today, however, especially among the compassionate, the tradition is being challenged by a contrary opinion: the view that parents have the awesome responsibility to produce "perfect" children and to assure them a happy and successful life or at least the capacity to attain to and conform to the American ideal of "the good life."

All of us who are parents know we want our children to be perfect. And all of us who are children know the pain that can sometimes be caused by that desire. The story of making perfect children and making children perfect will allow—or finally require—the abortion of the unborn who do not meet our standards and the neglect of newborns with diminished capacities to achieve *our* ideal of "the good life."

Such a view of parenting will finally reduce our options to a perfect child or a dead child. The Infant Doe decision is understandable, I think, within a story of making perfect children and making children perfect, but that story will not and cannot sustain the disposition of uncalculating nurturance and basic trust which have defined the relation of parent and child within the Christian story.

It is a commonplace to assert that the institution of the family is in crisis, but it can receive little support from conventional modern moral theory, whether utilitarian or formalist. Both have some power in dealing with our relation with strangers, but neither can deal adequately with the family or sustain it in a time of crisis. Family loyalties are an embarrassment to our calculations of "the greatest happiness for the greatest number" and to our assertions of autonomy. The tradition of the family—and experience in a family—reminds us both that "happiness" is not what it's all about and that we are not as independent, self-sufficient, and autonomous as we sometimes claim.

The fragile tradition of the family, too, may be and should be supported by the Christian story, for the Father's uncalculating nurturance is still the place to learn parenting. Infant Doe's groans awaited not only "the redemption of our bodies" but "our adoption as sons." In the Christian vision the family is seen as a gift and a vocation, providing opportunities to learn to love the *im*perfect, the snotty-nosed, and the just plain snotty. The story of a Lord who welcomed little children (and the sick and women and sinners and all others who did not measure up) is a resource for that sort of uncalculating nurturance that can love the child who is there, that would and should insist on the support of others to enable that child to live and—within the limits of his condition and the world's fallenness—to flourish. Parental nurturance formed and informed by the story of Jesus and the children would think it *curious*—at best—to be told it was *optional* to do the surgery necessary for the child's life and flourishing—as though one has a choice whether to attend to those things necessary for one's child's life and flourishing or to neglect and starve one's child.

The fundamental point is this: although the parents were, by all accounts, compassionate individuals, love is *not* all you need—no matter what popular songs and popular preaching may tell us. Compassion exercised outside the moral tradition of parenting is quite capable of pitying and killing ("mercy-killing," some would call it) those who do not measure up to the perfection we want for and from our children. Joseph Fletcher—whom no one may accuse of not emphasizing love enough—has (in spite of himself) at least one moral rule: "No unwanted child should ever be born." Compassion by itself may be quite capable of formulating another, "No unwanted child need be fed."

The duly humble Indiana judges were properly hesitant to intervene in the private arena of medical and parental decisions about the appropriate care of "defective neonates" (itself a neologism to help us forget that it is our children we are talking about). As we have observed, the decision not to treat is sometimes perfectly legitimate and sometimes legitimately controverted. In such cases that decision is best left to the parents and to the advice of physicians. The decision not to treat Infant Doe, however, was immoral; yet the court did not have the resources to call it illegal.

In part the court could not judge the decision illegal because of the simple lack of law governing such cases. But it is also true that the predominant legal theory today, quite self-consciously impartial and rational, emphasizes autonomy and privacy and contract in ways which make it difficult to give legal support to the interdependencies of a family or the moral roles in which there is no formal contract. I do not deny the moral importance of this legal theory or the pluralism it sponsors and sustains, but I do claim that it can give only a minimal account of the moral life and that society (and the courts) dangerously distort the moral life and endanger our life together when they reduce morality to such legality.

The courts might still have intervened if not for our confusion about the rights of the handicapped and the rights of others to be free from contact with them. Society is confused about the handicapped, and that confusion helps to explain judicial restraint in the Infant Doe case. On the one hand, there is physical evidence everywhere—ramps, special bathrooms, barrier-free doorways—of legislation to *integrate* the handicapped into our social life. On the other hand, many such people remain *segregated* in institutions acknowledged to be inhumane; and a 1981 Supreme Court decision, *Pennhurst v. Haldemann*, overturned a state court's order to close one such institution and to establish smaller facilities integrated into the state's residential communities.

Integration versus segregation, the rights of a minority versus the rights of a majority not to be confronted with them—it all has a dismally familiar ring. In the case of Infant Doe and others like him, integration would entail welcoming their life without celebrating or romanticizing their condition. It would mean acknowledging that even if we call them "defective neonates" they remain our children, and that attempts to cut off emotional and role relations with them are self-deceptive. And it would mean a willingness to pay the additional *taxes* necessary to support the care and nurturance of such children.

Segregation, on the other hand, would mean a refusal to practice hospitality toward them or toward their lives, seceding from the obligations of community with them, and asserting our independence from them.

The duly humble decision of the justices not to decide the case is understandable in terms of the segregationist story and—however unwittingly—it strengthened the segregationist tradition.

The Christian story—including the story of Jesus and the children—would support and sustain a tradition of including and welcoming society's outcasts, of serving and helping those who are last. If we keep telling the story of Jesus we may yet learn and live a story of joyful acceptance of people, including little people, who—in other stories and other views—don't count for much.

A competent physician, compassionate parents, and duly humble justices failed to make the right decision. The problem was not that the decision was extraordinarily difficult, a real moral dilemma. The problem was not that these people were mean-spirited or evil. The problem was rather that they had—however unwittingly or unconsciously—made the wrong stories of medicine and parenting and relations with the handicapped *their* stories. This is not altogether their fault: those traditions are fragile in contemporary culture. But those traditions have not completely broken down. Witness the statement of the pediatrician, "As a father and physician I can't make the decision to let the baby die." Witness the response of the nurses. Witness the offers to adopt Infant Doe.

Yet the traditions are weak. Babies are not as fragile as the moral traditions that protect them. And the courts are apparently powerless to preserve these traditions. Infant Doe and all of us are dependent on moral traditions and communities, on covenants, which can neither be reduced to contracts nor rendered legally enforceable means to legally enforceable ends.

Infant Doe now rests in peace. The sleep of many others is still disturbed by thoughts of his brief but real suffering and his calculated death. To judge these parents or these physicians will not ease our restlessness. But to resist the erosion of some ancient traditions about medicine and parenting and to establish a tradition of including the handicapped in our community is today part of our Christian vocation and our cultural mandate. Christians can, sometimes do, and should preserve and cherish a tradition about medicine that gives to doctors the worthy calling of healer, not the demeaning role of hired hand to do a consumer's bidding. Christians can, sometimes do, and should preserve and cherish a tradition about the family that gives parents the vocation of uncalculating nurturance and rescues them from the impossible obligation of making their children either perfect or "happy." Christians can, sometimes do, and should welcome and include those whom it is too much our impulse to shun and neglect.

Such medicine and such families and such a community may not always be "happy," but they will always be capable of being surprised by joy in caring for one they cannot cure. They will learn to tell and live a story of Jesus and the neonate. And when the groanings of all creation cease, they may hear, "As you did it to one of the least of these my brethren, you did it unto me."

Discussion

1. "The Death of Infant Doe" presents a fine example of the use of a first-person narrator in a formal essay. What is the effect of the narrator on the argument? Does it give the writer greater or lesser freedom in the essay? For example, in the opening paragraph the first-person narrator "imagines" what it was like to be at Jesus' side while he was on earth. What is the effect on the reader? What qualities characterize the first-person narrator in this essay? How would you describe him?

2. Professor Verhey writes about "stories" that shape our ethical decisions. What exactly does he mean by story? Is it just a fabrication or an excuse to act in a certain way? Or, can story mean our understanding of what is true and right? In your journal, detail your own story and its effect on your ethical decisions.

3. What distinction does Professor Verhey see between love and compassion? Can you make other applications of the distinction to ethical choices?

No Man Is an Island

John Donne

> *John Donne (1572–1631) is one of the best-known poets and essayists of the seventeenth century, but he was also a formidable preacher and religious thinker with the rare ability to make facts and reason pertinent to everyday life. His own life was not free from severe trial. Before his wife, Anne, died in 1617, they had twelve children, five of whom died. He was troubled by a sense of loss and loneliness, and wrote many of his devotional meditations during his own serious illness. In this powerful meditation, Donne reflects on loss, and on his unity with all of mankind.*

Devotion No. 17

Now, this Bell tolling softly for another, saies to me, Thou must die.

Meditation

Perchance hee for whom this *Bell* tolls, may be so ill, as that he knows not it tolls for him; And perchance I may thinke my selfe so much better than I am, as that they who are about mee, and see my state, may have caused it to toll for mee, and I know not that. The *Church* is *Catholike, universall,* so are all her *Actions; All* that she does, belongs to *all.* When she *baptizes a child,* that action concernes mee; for that child is thereby connected to that *Head* which is my *Head* too, and engraffed into that *body,* whereof I am a *member.* And when she *buries a Man,* that action concerns me: All *mankinde* is of one *Author,* and is one *volume;* when one Man dies, one *Chapter* is not *torne* out of the *booke,* but *translated* into a better *language;* and every *Chapter* must be so *translated;* God emploies several *translators;* some peeces are translated by *age,* some by *sickness,* some by *warre,* some by *justice;* but *Gods* hand is in every *translation;* and his hand shall binde up all our scattered leaves againe, for that *Librarie* where every *booke* shall lie open to one another: As therefore the *Bell* that rings to a *Sermon,* calls not upon the *Preacher* onely, but upon the *Congregation* to come; so this *Bell* calls us all: but how much more mee, who am brought so neere the *doore* by this *sicknesse.* There was a *contention* as farre as a *suite,* (in which both *pietie* and *dignitie, religion,* and *estimation,* were mingled) which of the religious *Orders* should ring to *praiers* first in the *Morning;* and it was *determined,* that *they should ring first that rose earliest.* If we understand aright the *dignitie* of this *Bell* that tolls for our *evening prayer,* wee would bee glad to make it ours, by rising early, in that *application,* that it might bee ours, as wel as his, whose indeed it is. The *Bell* doth toll for him that *thinkes* it doth; and though it *intermit* againe, yet from that *minute,* that that occasion wrought upon him, hee is united to *God.* Who casts not up his *Eie* to the *Sunne* when it rises? but who takes off his *eie* from a *Comet* when that breakes out? Who bends not his *eare* to any *bell,* which upon any occasion rings? but who can remove it from that *bell,* which is passing a *peece of himselfe* out of this *world?* No man is an *Iland,* intire of it selfe; every man is a peece of the *Continent,* a part of the *maine,* if a *Clod* bee washed away by the *Sea, Europe* is the lesse, as well as if a *Promontorie* were, as well as if a *Mannor* of thy *friends* or of *thine owne were;* any mans *death* diminishes *me,* because I am involved in *Mankinde;* And therefore never send to know for whom the *bell* tolls; It tolls for *thee.* Neither can we call this a *begging* of *Miserie* or a *borrowing* of *Miserie,* as though we were not miserable enough of our selves, but must fetch in more from the next house, in taking upon us the *Miserie* of our *Neighbours.* Truly it were an excusable *covetousnesse* if wee did; for *affliction* is a *treasure,* and scarce any man hath *enough* of it. No man hath *affliction* enough that is not matured, and ripened by it, and made fit for *God* by that *affliction.* If a man carry *treasure* in *bullion,* or in a *wedge* of gold, and have none coined into *currant Monies,* his *treasure* will not defray him as he travells. *Tribulation* is *Treasure* in the *nature* of it, but it is not *currant money* in the *use* of it, except wee get nearer and nearer our *home, Heaven,* by it. Another man may be *sicke* too, and sick to *death,* and this *affliction* may lie in his *bowels,* as *gold* in a *Mine,* and be of no use to him; but this *bell,* that tells me of his *affliction,* digs out, and applies that *gold* to *mee:* if by this consideration of anothers danger, I take mine owne into contemplation, and so secure my selfe, by making my recourse to my *God,* who is our onely *securitie.*

Discussion

1. In his essay Donne makes use of figurative language. Can you identify and explain his use of imagery in the essay?

2. How does Donne's view that we are all part of one body both reflect scriptural teaching and also affect our ethical choices?
3. In your journal, rewrite Donne's essay in modern prose. Is the effect of the essay different?

A Place to Stand

Henri J. M. Nouwen

The idea of living as a Trappist monk had been in Henri Nouwen's mind for some years. The well-known teacher and author had pondered questions that found no immediate answers, and he sought a quiet place from which to search for those answers. As he states it, the decision to join the Abbey of Genesee on June 1, 1974, for a period of seven months was preceded by "many years of restless searching." His remarkable Genesee Diary, begun on June 2, records the questions and the answers he found during those months.

Thursday, 13

This afternoon I worked a few hours alone in the river carrying heavy granite rocks to the bank and making piles. While doing this, I realized how difficult "nepsis"—the control of thoughts—about which I read this morning, really is. My thoughts not only wandered in all directions, but started to brood on many negative feelings, feelings of hostility toward people who had not given me the attention I wanted, feelings of jealousy toward people who received more than I, feelings of self-pity in regard to people who had not written, and many feelings of regret and guilt toward people with whom I had strained relationships. While pulling and pushing with the crowbar, all these feelings kept pulling and pushing in me, and I often looked at the curve of the river, wondering if Brian would come to keep me company and help me to quiet them.

My reading about the spirituality of the desert has made me aware of the importance of "nepsis." Nepsis means mental sobriety, spiritual attention directed to God, watchfulness in keeping the bad thoughts away, and creating free space for prayer. While working with the rocks I repeated a few times the famous words of the old desert fathers: *"fuge, tace, et quiesce"* (live in solitude, silence, and inner peace), but only God knows how far I am, not only from this reality but even from this desire.

Once in a while I cursed when the rock was too heavy to carry or fell out of my arms into the water, making a big splash. I tried to convert my curse into a prayer: "Lord, send your angels to carry these stones," but nothing spectacular happened. I heard some red-winged black-birds making some ugly noises in the air. My muscles felt strained, my legs tired. When I walked home I realized that it was exactly the lack of spiritual attention that caused the heaviness in my heart. How true it is that sadness is often the result of our attachments to the world.

Friday, 12

When you keep going anxiously to the mailbox in the hope that someone "out there" has thought about you; when you keep wondering if and what your friends are thinking of you; when you keep having hidden desires to be a somewhat exceptional person in this commu-nity; when you keep having fantasies about guests mentioning your name; when you keep looking for special attention from the abbot or any one of the monks; when you keep hoping for more interesting work and more stimulating events—then you know that you haven't even started to create a little place for God in your heart.

Saturday, 13

I have always had a strange desire to be different than other people. I probably do not differ in this desire from other people. Thinking about this desire and how it has functioned in my life, I am more and more aware of the way my life-style became part of our contemporary desire for "stardom." I wanted to say, write or do something "different" or "special" that would be noticed and talked about. For a person with a rich fantasy life, this is not too difficult and easily leads to the desired "success." You can teach in such a way that it differs enough from the traditional way to be noticed; you can write sentences, pages, and even books that are considered original and new, you can even preach the Gospel in such a way that people are made to believe that nobody had thought of that before. In all these situations you end up with applause because you did something sensational, because you were "different."

In recent years I have become increasingly aware of the dangerous possibility of making the Word of God sensational. Just as people can watch spellbound a circus artist tumbling through the air in a phosphorized costume, so they can listen to a preacher who uses the Word of God to draw attention to himself. But a sensational preacher stimulates the senses and leaves the spirit untouched. Instead of being the way to God, his "being different" gets in the way.

The monastic experience attacks this type of attention drawing. It asks you to say, write, and do things not differently but the same. It asks you to be obedient to age-long traditions and to form your mind and heart according to often proved and approved principles. In the spiritual literature I have read since I came here, there is a remarkable attempt to be faithful to the Gospel, to the words of the early fathers, to the insights of the spiritual director of the time, and an equally remarkable avoidance of trying to be different, sensational, and original. It seems that all the great spiritual writers are saying, "You cannot be original. If anything you say is worth saying, you will find its origin in the Word of God and his saints." What this place is calling me to be is— the same, and *more* of the same. The same as the monks, the same as the saints, the same as Jesus, the same as the heavenly Father. The rule of St. Benedict—the returning rhythm of the day, the continuous recitation of the 150 psalms and the uniformity of dress, food, and place—slowly makes you aware of a powerful sameness that transcends time and place and unifies you with the one God who is the Father of all people, all places, and all times, and who is the same through ages unending.

The monastic life is indeed very unsensational. I keep catching myself with the desire to do something special, to make a contribution, to add something new, and have to remind myself constantly that the less I am noticed, the less special attention I require, the less I am different, the more I am living the monastic life. Maybe—when you have become fully aware that you have nothing to say that has not already been said—maybe then a monk might be interested in listening to you. The mystery of God's love is that in this sameness we discover our uniqueness. That uniqueness has nothing to do with the "specialties" we have to offer that glitter like the artificial silver balls on a Christmas tree, but has everything to do with our most personal and most intimate relationship with God. When we have given up the desire to be different and experienced ourselves as sinners without any right to special attention, only then is there space to encounter our God who calls us by our own name and invites us into his intimacy.

Jesus, the only son of the Father, emptied himself "and being as we are, he was humbler yet, even to accepting death, death on a cross. But

God raised him high and gave him the name which is above all other names" (Ph. 2:7–9). Only through ultimate sameness was Jesus given his unique name. When St. Paul calls us to have the mind of Jesus Christ, he invites us to that same humility through which we can become brothers of the Lord and sons of the heavenly Father.

Today was the feast of St. Henry. All the attention went to Brother Henry. I guess I had hoped for a little extra attention. Not getting it helped me to give a little more "flesh" to my meditation on sameness.

Painting was my afternoon job. The weather was beautiful—sunny and cool. I enjoyed scraping away the peeling paint, sandpapering and repainting the damaged spot, and looking out over the field from the vantage point where I was working. A big wasp kept me company the whole afternoon and did not sting. Brother Pascal said, "Don't make panicky moves. Just be gentle and it won't bother you." He proved to be right.

Monday, 15

When I went to see John Eudes today my head seemed so filled with questions that I wondered how we could focus a little bit and bring some order into the chaos of concerns.

When I left I had the feeling that many things had indeed come together by focusing on the glory of God. The question, "How to live for the glory of God and not for your own glory?" has become very important to me. During the last weeks I have realized more and more that even my seemingly most spiritual activities can be pervaded with vainglory. There is something special and in some people's eyes "heroic" about going to the Trappists, and I wondered if it is really God I am seeking. Even my most intense attention to the ascetic and mystical writings of the early fathers easily turns into ideas and insights to be used for others' conversion instead of my own. Yes, there is a great temptation to make even God the object of my passion and to search for him not for his glory but for the glory that can be derived from smart manipulation of godly ideas.

John Eudes wasn't very surprised by my worries. He welcomed them as important enough to worry about, to think about, to live through.

How to dispel the passions that make us manipulate instead of worship? Well, the first thing to realize is that you *are* the glory of God. In Genesis you can read: "Yahweh God fashioned man of dust from the soil. Then he breathed into his nostrils a breath of life, and thus man became a living being" (Gen. 2:7). We live because we share God's breath, God's life, God's glory. The question is not so much, "How to live for the glory of God?" but, "How to live who we are, how to make true our deepest self?"

With a smile John Eudes said, "Take this as your koan: 'I am the glory of God.' Make that thought the center of your meditation so that it slowly becomes not only a thought but a living reality. You are the place where God chose to dwell, you are the *topos tou theou* (God's place) and the spiritual life is nothing more or less than to allow that space to exist where God can dwell, to create the space where his glory can manifest itself. In your meditation you can ask yourself, 'Where is the glory of God? If the glory of God is not there where I am, where else can it be?'"

Obviously, all this is more than an insight, an idea, a way of seeing things. That is why it is a subject for meditation and not so much for study. But once you start "realizing" in this very intimate and personal way that you indeed are the glory of God, then everything is different, then your life takes a decisive turn. Then, for instance, your passions which seemed so real, more real than God, show their illusory nature to you and sort of dwindle away.

These thoughts led us to a short conversation about the experience of God. I told John Eudes that for many years, I had the fantasy that one day God just might break through the hard shell of my resistance and reveal himself to me in such an intensive and convincing way that I finally would be able to let my "idols" go and commit myself unconditionally to him. John Eudes, not too surprised by the fantasy, said, "You want God to appear to you in the way your passions desire, but these passions make you blind to his presence now. Focus on the nonpassionate part of yourself and realize God's presence there. Let that part grow in you and make your decisions from there. You will be surprised to see how powers that seem invincible shrivel away."

We talked about many more things, but what I remember best of the final part of our conversation was the idea that I should be happy to be part of the battle, independent of the question of victory. The battle is real, dangerous, and very crucial. You risk all you have; it is like fighting a bull in a bull ring. You will only know what victory is when you have been part of the battle. People who have tasted real victory are always very modest about it because they have seen the other side and know that there is little to brag about. The powers of darkness and the powers of light are too close to each other to offer the occasion for vainglory. That's what a monastery is all about. In the many little things of everyday life we can recognize the battle. It can be as small as a desire for a letter or a craving for a glass of milk. By staying at one place you get to know the battlefield quite well.

Wednesday, 24

I would like to think a little more about love. This monastery definitely exudes a real atmosphere of love. You can indeed say, the monks love each other. I even dare to say they show a real love to me. I think that this is a very important experience because they not only make me feel love but also help me to understand love better.

My first inclination has been, and in many ways still is, to connect love with something special in me that makes me lovable. When people are kind and friendly toward me, I feel happy because I think that they are attracted to me and like me in a special way. This more or less unconscious attitude got me into trouble here since the monk who is nice and good to me proves to be just as nice and good to everyone else. So it becomes hard to believe that he loves me because of something special that I have and others do not have. I am obviously not more or less attractive than others. This experience was in the beginning a painful one. I tended to react by thinking, "Well, if he is just as friendly to everyone else as he is to me, his friendliness cannot be real. It is just one of those poses, one of those 'frozen smiles.' He is friendly because he is supposed to be friendly. He is just following the rule. His love is only the result of obedience. It is not natural, not spontaneous, not real. Underneath his friendly surface he probably couldn't care less about me as an individual."

But these ruminations were exactly that: ruminations. I knew that I was fooling myself, that there was something very important I was missing. I knew it simply because the story I told myself was not true. The monks who show me love, show love to me not as an abstraction but as a real individual with his own strengths and weaknesses, habits and customs, pleasant and unpleasant sides. The love they show me is very alert, awake, and based on the real me. When I ask something, they listen with attention and try to help me, and when I show a need for support, information, or interest, they offer me as well as they can what I need. So although their love for me is not exclusive, particular, or unique, it is certainly not general, abstract, impersonal, or just an act of obedience to the rule.

It is important for me to realize how limited, imperfect, and weak my understanding of love has been. Not my theoretical understanding but my understanding as it reveals itself in my emotional responses to concrete situations. My idea of love proves to be exclusive: "You only love me truly if you love others less"; possessive: "If you really love me, I want you to pay special attention to me"; and manipulative: "When you love me, you will do extra things for me." Well, this idea of love easily leads to vanity: "You must see something very special in me"; to jealousy: "Why are you now suddenly so interested in someone else and not in me?" and to anger: "I am going to let you know that you have let me down and rejected me."

But love is "always patient and kind; it is never jealous; love is never boastful or conceited; it is never rude or selfish; it does not take offense, and is not resentful" (I Cor. 13:4–5).

It is this understanding of love that I must slowly learn. But how? It seems that the monks know the answer, "You must love the Lord your God with all your heart, with all your soul, with all your mind." This is the greatest and the first commandment. It seems that the life the monks are living is a witness to the importance of keeping the first commandment first so that the second, "which resembles it" can be realized as well: "You must love your neighbor as yourself" (Mt. 22:37–39). I am beginning to experience that an unconditional, total love of God makes a very articulate, alert, and attentive love for the neighbor possible. What I often call "love for neighbor" too often proves to be a tentative, partial, or momentary attraction, which usually is very unstable and does not last long. But when the love of God is indeed my first concern, a deep love for my neighbor can grow.

Two more considerations may clarify this. First of all, I discover *myself* in a new way in the love of God. St. Bernard of Clairvaux describes as the highest degree of love the love of ourselves for God's sake. Thomas Merton commenting on this says: "This is the high point of Bernard's Christian humanism. It shows that the fulfillment of our destiny is not merely to be lost in God, as the traditional figures of speech would have it, like a 'drop of water in a barrel of wine or like iron in the fire' but found in God in all our individual and personal reality, tasting our eternal happiness not only in the fact that we have attained to the possession of his infinite goodness, but above all in the fact that we see his will done in us."

Secondly, it is not only ourselves we discover in our individuality but our fellow human beings as well, because it is God's glory itself that manifests itself in his people in an abundant variety of forms and styles. The uniqueness of our neighbors is not related to those idiosyncratic qualities that only they and nobody else have, but it is related to the fact that God's eternal beauty and love become visible in these unique, irreplaceable, finite human beings. It is exactly in the preciousness of the individual person that the eternal love of God is refracted and becomes the basis of a community of love.

When we have found our own uniqueness in the love of God and have been able to affirm that indeed we are lovable since it is God's love that dwells in us, then we can reach out to others in whom we discover a new and unique manifestation of the same love and enter into an intimate communion with them.

Sunday, 28

What do you do when you are always comparing yourself with other people? What do you do when you always feel that the people you talk to, hear of, or read about are more intelligent, more skillful, more attractive, more gentle, more generous, more practical, or more contemplative than you are? What do you do when you can't get away from measuring yourself against others, always feeling that they are the real people while you are a nobody or even less than that?

It is obvious that these feelings are distorted, out of proportion, the result of projections, and very damaging for a healthy spiritual life, but still they are no less real and can creep up on you before you are aware of it. Before you know it you are comparing other people's age and accomplishments with your own, and before you know it you have entered into a very harmful psychological competition and rivalry.

I talked about this with John Eudes today. He helped me analyze it a little more. We talked about the vicious circle one enters when one has a low self-esteem or self-doubt and then perceives other people in such a way as to strengthen and confirm these feelings. It is the famous self-fulfilling prophecy all over again. I enter into relationships with some apprehension and fear and behave in such a way that whatever the others say or do, I experience them as stronger, better, more valuable persons, and myself as weaker, worse, and not worth talking to. After a while the relationship becomes intolerable, and I find an excuse to walk away feeling worse than when I started it. My general abstract feeling of worthlessness becomes concrete in a specific encounter, and there my false fears increase rather than decrease. So real peer relationships become difficult, if not impossible, and many of my emotions in relation to others reveal themselves as the passive-dependent sort.

What do you do? Analyze more? It is not hard to see the neurotic dynamism. But it is not easy to break through it to a mature life. There is much to say about this and much has been said by psychologists and psychotherapists. But what to say about it from a spiritual perspective?

John Eudes talked about that moment, that point, that spot that lies before the comparison, before the beginning of the vicious circle or the self-fulfilling prophecy. That is the moment, point, or place where meditation can enter in. It is the moment to stop reading, speaking, socializing, and to "waste" your time in meditation. When you find your mind competing again, you might plan an "empty time" of meditation, in this way interrupting the vicious circle of your ruminations and entering into the depth of your own soul. There you can be with him who was before you came, who loved you before you could love, and who has given you your own self before any comparison was possible. In meditation we can come to the affirmation that we are not created by other people but by God, that we are not judged by how we compare with others but how we fulfill the will of God.

This is not as easy as it sounds because it is in meditation itself that we become painfully aware how much we have already been victimized by our own competitive strivings and how much we have already sold our soul to the opinions of others. By not avoiding this realization, however, but by confronting it and by unmasking its illusory quality, we might be able to experience our own basic dependency and so dispel the false dependencies of our daily life.

The more I think about this, the more I realize how central the words of St. John are, words so central also in St. Bernard's thought: "Let us love God because God has loved us first."

Monday, 26

Talked with John Eudes about obedience. I said, "I don't think I ever could become a monk because of my problem with obedience. If you or anyone else told me to go collect stones every day while I was deeply convinced that I should write, read, study, or whatever, I would not be able to take it and would become so restless and hostile that I would leave sooner or later."

He said, "The reasons you give not only would make you a poor monk but also a poor diocesan priest. Your problem is not that specific for monks. If you cannot be detached from all you do and like to do, you cannot live a full spiritual life."

So we talked about obedience. It was helpful because John Eudes made me see that the problem of obedience is a problem of intimacy. "Obedience becomes hard when you have to be vulnerable to the other who has authority. You can play the obedience game in such a way that you never disobey any rule while keeping from your guide and director, your abbot or superior those things about which you do not want to hear a 'no.' You need a lot of trust to give yourself fully to someone else, certainly to someone to whom you owe obedience. Many people adapt very quickly but are not really obedient. They simply don't want to make waves and instead go along with the trend. That is not obedience. That is just adaptation."

If I were able to trust more, to open myself more easily, to be more vulnerable, then obedience would not be so hard. I would be able to disagree without fear of rejection, to protest without resentment, to express different viewpoints without self-righteousness, and to say after all arguments: "If I am still asked to do something I do not like to do, perhaps I must be open to the idea of God's preparing me for something greater and more important than I can imagine."

With that attitude, life in obedience indeed can be quite exciting since you never really know what is next. But I have a long way to go to develop that attitude in my innermost self.

Monday, 23

Often I have said to people, "I will pray for you" but how often did I really enter into the full reality of what that means? I now see how indeed I can enter deeply into the other and pray to God from his center. When I really bring my friends and the many I pray for into my innermost being and feel their pains, their struggles, their cries in my own soul, then I leave myself, so to speak, and become them, then I have compassion. Compassion lies at the heart of our prayer for our fellow human beings. When I pray for the world, I become the world; when I pray for the endless needs of the millions, my soul expands and wants to embrace them all and bring them into the presence of God. But in the midst of that experience I realize that compassion is not mine but God's gift to me. I cannot embrace the world, but God can. I cannot pray, but God can pray in me. When God became as we are, that is, when God allowed all of us to enter into his intimate life, it became possible for us to share in his infinite compassion.

In praying for others, I lose myself and become the other, only to be found by the divine love which holds the whole of humanity in a compassionate embrace.

Tuesday, 24

Yesterday I shared with John Eudes some of my thoughts about prayer for others. He not only confirmed my thoughts but also led me further by saying that compassion belongs to the center of the contemplative life. When we become the other and so enter into the presence of God, then we are true contemplatives. True contemplatives, then, are *not* the ones who withdrew from the world to save their own soul, but the ones who enter into the center of the world and pray to God from there.

Discussion

1. What answers did Nouwen find for his life? What roles did physical labor, quiet reflection, and discussion play in finding them?
2. What is the significance of obedience in learning peace?
3. Can peace be learned or acquired?
4. Does the last sentence in the selection support or contradict Nouwen's experience in the monastery?
5. Write your own spiritual journal for a limited period of time, say a week or a month. How can the act of writing focus questions and help locate answers?

Writing Assignments for Chapter 9

1. Since ethical issues frequently surface as themes in literary works, this section serves as an excellent area for the essay of literary analysis. For example, William Golding's *Lord of the Flies* explores what happens to a group of boys stranded on an island and stripped of all authority. Faced with the loss of rules, of stated guidelines for proper behavior, what will become of human choices and actions? The tension between rules and human will can be carefully examined in the novel. Similarly, Aldous Huxley's *Brave New World* raises the question of what constitutes happiness. Is it complete freedom of choice with the attendant danger of wrong choices? Or is it the security of having one's life carefully programmed? How much freedom are you willing to give up for security?
2. Write an essay on how a particular contemporary issue is viewed from a particular ethical position. For example, how has the issue of censorship become subject to the Cultural Morality Ethic? Examine federal and local laws for support. How would each of the other ethical views described in the introduction to this chapter regard censorship? (In doing research for this essay, you will want to limit the issue of censorship to a particular kind, that is, pornography, speech, or behavior.) The same kind

of examination may be applied to other contemporary ethical issues, and often the debate surrounding such issues may be clarified by understanding the ethical arguments involved.

3. Write an essay of argumentation, in which you select the ethical view which most nearly represents your own, and argue the value of that ethic over the others. What specific items emerge as weaknesses in the other ethical theories? You should give concrete, specific examples to demonstrate those weaknesses.

10

Exercising Stewardship

Environmental Issues

And God blessed them, and God said to them, "Be fruitful and multiply, and fill the earth and subdue it; and have dominion over the fish of the sea and over the birds of the air and over every living thing that moves upon the earth."
> —Genesis 1:28

> He speaks. The lake in front becomes a lawn;
> Woods vanish, hills subside, and vallies rise:
> And streams, as if created for his use,
> Pursue the track of his directing wand.
> > —William Cowper, *The Task*

The American Axe! It has made more real and lasting conquests than the sword of any warlike people that ever lived; but they have been conquests that have left civilization in their train instead of havoc and destruction.
> —James Fenimore Cooper,
> *The Chainbearer*

In wildness is the preservation of the world.
> —Henry David Thoreau

Ability to see the cultural value of wilderness boils down, in the last analysis, to a question of intellectual humility. The shallow-minded modern who has lost his rootage in the land assumes that he has already discovered what is important; it is such who prate of empires, political or economic, that will last a thousand years. . . . It is only the scholar who understands

why the raw wilderness gives definition and meaning to the
human enterprise.

—Aldo Leopold, *A Sand County*
Almanac

In Psalm 19, David exclaims that "the heavens are telling the glory of
God," that "the firmament proclaims his handiwork." Theologians
point to the fact that the creation reveals attributes of God, a revelation
that complements the revelation of Scripture. In his *Institutes of the
Christian Religion,* John Calvin calls the universe "a sort of mirror in
which we can contemplate God, who is otherwise invisible." God has
done this, writes Calvin, so that people will not miss his goodness. God
has shaped creation so that man is without excuse, for "upon his individual works he has engraved unmistakable marks of his glory, so clear
and prominent that even unlettered and stupid folk cannot plead the
excuse of ignorance" (1.5.1).

Yet, despite Calvin's confidence in the clarity of this revelation, people often respond incorrectly to it. Paul identifies this problem in his
letter to the Romans as the confusion of Creator with created. This
confusion usually manifests itself in one of two ways when people
respond to the natural world: they either covet and misuse the items
God created, or they worship them as though the items *per se* were
God.

God gives us dominion over the earth (Gen. 1:28), yet too often we
have read this mandate as one which gives us absolute right to use the
earth's resources any way we choose. And too often we have used this
right to hoard and abuse those resources, instead of to regulate and
nurture them. Instead of imitating the loving-kindness of God in the
exercise of our dominion, we imitate the selfishness of Satan. Instead
of cultivating these resources so that future generations will know
God's goodness in creation, we use our oil, our metals, our land, and
our water as though we were the only generation that mattered.

Environmentalists are correct to point out, as Lynn White, Jr., does
in his essay, the abuses that have developed out of a misdirected Christian stewardship. But in their response to the creation, environmentalists often err in a different way. In their enthusiastic appreciation
for the beauty of creation they mistake the qualities of God revealed in
nature with God himself. Such an error is exemplified by Ralph Waldo
Emerson in his essay "Nature." He writes that upon going to the woods,
he becomes "a transparent eye-ball," through which "the currents of
the Universal Being circulate." By standing in creation, he becomes
"part or particle of God."

A popular hymn of the church declares that "in the rustling grass I hear Him pass." The hymn does not mean that God literally passes by, like the wind in the grass, but that God's grace and something of his nature are revealed through the natural world he has fashioned. Just as we know a certain book, *Huckleberry Finn*, for example, is written by Mark Twain by finding his familiar craft and theme revealed in its pages, so too we know something of God by studying the revelation of nature. How do we study it? How do we perceive and preserve it? His gift of natural beauty, splendid but intricate, is given into our keeping as a cherished instrument of revelation.

How then can we act as good stewards? Somewhere between the extremes of exploitation and pantheism lies the answer: the issues considered in this chapter will help you find it.

The Historical Roots of Our Ecological Crisis

Lynn White, Jr.

According to many historians, the mandate in Genesis 1:28 for man to subdue the earth spawned the Western practice of exploitation of natural resources. In this essay, Lynn White, Jr., acknowledges that legacy as he analyzes the historical view of man toward nature, but he also proposes what he terms an alternative Christian view.

Medieval View of Man and Nature

Until recently, agriculture has been the chief occupation even in "advanced" societies; hence, any change in methods of tillage has much importance. Early plows, drawn by two oxen, did not normally turn the sod but merely scratched it. Thus, cross-plowing was needed and fields tended to be squarish. In the fairly light soils and semi-arid climates of the Near East and Mediterranean, this worked well. But such a plow was inappropriate to the wet climate and often sticky soils of northern Europe. By the latter part of the seventh century after Christ, however, following obscure beginnings, certain northern peasants were using an entirely new kind of plow, equipped with a vertical knife to cut the line of the furrow, a horizontal share to slice under the sod, and a moldboard to turn it over. The friction of this plow with the soil was so great that it normally required not two but eight oxen. It attacked the land with such violence that cross-plowing was not needed, and fields tended to be shaped in long strips.

In the days of the scratch-plow, fields were distributed generally in units capable of supporting a single family. Subsistence farming was the presupposition. But no peasant owned eight oxen: to use the new and more efficient plow, peasants pooled their oxen to form large plow-teams, originally receiving (it would appear) plowed strips in proportion to their contribution. Thus, distribution of land was based no

192

longer on the needs of the family but, rather, on the capacity of a power machine to till the earth. Man's relation to the soil was profoundly changed. Formerly man had been part of nature; now he was the exploiter of nature. Nowhere else in the world did farmers develop any analogous agricultural implement. Is it coincidence that modern technology, with its ruthlessness toward nature, has so largely been produced by descendants of these peasants of northern Europe?

This same exploitive attitude appears slightly before A.D. 830 in Western illustrated calendars. In older calendars the months were shown as passive personifications. The new Frankish calendars, which set the style for the Middle Ages, are very different: they show men coercing the world around them—plowing, harvesting, chopping trees, butchering pigs. Man and nature are two things, and man is master.

These novelties seem to be in harmony with larger intellectual patterns. What people do about their ecology depends on what they think about themselves in relation to things around them. Human ecology is deeply conditioned by beliefs about our nature and destiny—that is, by religion. To Western eyes this is very evident in, say, India or Ceylon. It is equally true of ourselves and of our medieval ancestors.

The victory of Christianity over paganism was the great psychic revolution in the history of our culture. It has become fashionable today to say that, for better or worse, we live in "the post-Christian age." Certainly the forms of our thinking and language have largely ceased to be Christian, but to my eye the substance often remains amazingly akin to that of the past. Our daily habits of action, for example, are dominated by an implicit faith in perpetual progress which was unknown either to Greco-Roman antiquity or to the Orient. It is rooted in, and is indefensible apart from, Judeo-Christian teleology. The fact that Communists share it merely helps to show what can be demonstrated on many other grounds: that Marxism, like Islam, is a Judeo-Christian heresy. We continue today to live as we have lived for about 1700 years, very largely in a context of Christian axioms.

What did Christianity tell people about their relations with the environment?

While many of the world's mythologies provide stories of creation, Greco-Roman mythology was singularly incoherent in this respect. Like Aristotle, the intellectuals of the ancient West denied that the visible world had had a beginning. Indeed, the idea of a beginning was impossible in the framework of their cyclical notion of time. In sharp contrast, Christianity inherited from Judaism not only a concept of time as nonrepetitive and linear but also a striking story of creation.

By gradual stages a loving and all-powerful God had created light and darkness, the heavenly bodies, the earth and all its plants, animals, birds, and fishes. Finally, God had created Adam and, as an afterthought, Eve, to keep man from being lonely. Man named all the animals, thus establishing his dominance over them. God planned all of this explicitly for man's benefit and rule: no item in the physical creation had any purpose save to serve man's purposes. And, although man's body is made of clay, he is not simply part of nature: he is made in God's image.

Especially in its Western form, Christianity is the most anthropocentric religion the world has seen. As early as the second century both Tertullian and Saint Irenaeus of Lyons were insisting that when God shaped Adam he was foreshadowing the image of the Incarnate Christ, the Second Adam. Man shares, in great measure, God's transcendence of nature. Christianity, in absolute contrast to ancient paganism and Asia's religions (except, perhaps, Zoroastrianism), not only established a dualism of man and nature but also insisted that it is God's will that man exploit nature for his proper ends.

At the level of the common people this worked out in an interesting way. In antiquity every tree, every spring, every stream, every hill had its own *genius loci*, its guardian spirit. These spirits were accessible to men, but were very unlike men; centaurs, fauns, and mermaids show their ambivalence. Before one cut a tree, mined a mountain, or dammed a brook, it was important to placate the spirit in charge of that particular situation, and to keep it placated. By destroying pagan animism, Christianity made it possible to exploit nature in a mood of indifference to the feelings of natural objects.

It is often said that for animism the Church substituted the cult of saints. True; but the cult of saints is functionally quite different from animism. The saint is not *in* natural objects; he may have special shrines, but his citizenship is in heaven. Moreover, a saint is entirely a man; he can be approached in human terms. In addition to saints, Christianity of course also had angels and demons inherited from Judaism and perhaps, at one remove, from Zoroastrianism. But these were all as mobile as the saints themselves. The spirits *in* natural objects, which formerly had protected nature from man, evaporated. Man's effective monopoly on spirit in this world was confirmed, and the old inhibitions to the exploitation of nature crumbled.

When one speaks in such sweeping terms, a note of caution is in order. Christianity is a complex faith, and its consequences differ in differing contexts. What I have said may well apply to the medieval West, where in fact technology made spectacular advances. But the Greek East, a highly civilized realm of equal Christian devotion, seems to have produced no marked technological innovation after the late seventh century, when Greek fire was invented. The key to the contrast may perhaps be found in a difference in the tonality of piety and thought which students of comparative theology find between the Greek and the Latin churches. The Greeks believed that sin was intellectual blindness, and that salvation was found in illumination, orthodoxy—that is, clear thinking. The Latins, on the other hand, felt that sin was moral evil, and that salvation was to be found in right conduct. Eastern theology has been intellectualist, Western theology has been voluntarist. The Greek saint contemplates; the Western saint acts. The implications of Christianity for the conquest of nature would emerge more easily in the Western atmosphere.

The Christian dogma of creation, which is found in the first clause of all the Creeds, has another meaning for our comprehension of today's ecologic crisis. By revelation, God had given man the Bible, the Book of Scripture. But since God had made nature, nature also must reveal the divine mentality. The religious study of nature for the better understanding of God was known as natural theology. In the early Church, and always in the Greek East, nature was conceived primarily as a symbolic system through which God speaks to men: the ant is a sermon to sluggards; rising flames are the symbol of the soul's aspiration. This view of nature was essentially artistic rather than scientific. While Byzantium preserved and copied great numbers of ancient Greek scientific texts, science as we conceive it could scarcely flourish in such an ambience.

However, in the Latin West by the early thirteenth century natural theology was following a very different bent. It was ceasing to be the decoding of the physical symbols of God's communication with man and was becoming the effort to understand God's mind by discovering how his creation operates. The rainbow was no longer simply a symbol of hope first sent to Noah after the Deluge: Robert Grosseteste, Friar Roger Bacon, and Theodoric of Freiberg produced startlingly sophisticated work on the optics of the rainbow, but they did it as a venture in religious understanding. From the thirteenth century onward, up to and including Leibnitz and Newton, every major scientist, in effect, explained his motivations in religious terms. Indeed, if Galileo had not been so expert an amateur theologian he would have got into far less trouble: the professionals resented his intrusion. And Newton seems to have regarded himself more as a theologian than as a scientist. It was not until the late eighteenth century that the hypothesis of God became unnecessary to many scientists.

It is often hard for the historian to judge, when men explain why they are doing what they want to do, whether they are offering real reasons or merely culturally acceptable reasons. The consistency with which scientists during the long formative centuries of Western science said that the task and the reward of the scientists was "to think God's thoughts after him" leads one to believe that this was their real motivation. If so, then modern Western science was cast in a matrix of Christian theology. The dynamism of religious devotion, shaped by the Judeo-Christian dogma of creation, gave it impetus.

An Alternative Christian View

We would seem to be headed toward conclusions unpalatable to many Christians. Since both *science* and *technology* are blessed words in our contemporary vocabulary, some may be happy at the notions, first, that, viewed historically, modern science is an extrapolation of natural theology and, second, that modern technology is at least partly to be explained as an occidental, voluntarist realization of the Christian dogma of man's transcendence of, and rightful mastery over, nature. But, as we now recognize, somewhat over a century ago science and technology—hitherto quite separate activities—joined to give mankind powers which, to judge by many of the ecologic effects, are out of control. If so, Christianity bears a huge burden of guilt.

I personally doubt that disastrous ecologic backlash can be avoided simply by applying to our problems more science and more technology. Our science and technology have grown out of Christian attitudes toward man's relation to nature which are almost universally held not only by Christians and neo-Christians but also by those who fondly regard themselves as post-Christians. Despite Copernicus, all the cosmos rotates around our little globe. Despite Darwin, we are *not*, in our hearts, part of the natural process. We are superior to nature, contemptuous of it, willing to use it for our slightest whim. The newly elected governor of California, like myself a churchman, but less troubled than I, spoke for the Christian tradition when he said (as is alleged), "when you've seen one redwood tree, you've seen them all." To a Christian a tree can be no more than a physical fact. The whole concept of the sacred grove is alien to Christianity and to the ethos of the West. For nearly two millennia Christian missionaries have been chopping down sacred groves, which are idolatrous because they assume spirit in nature.

What we do about ecology depends on our ideas of the man-nature relationship. More science and more technology are not going to get us out of the present ecologic crisis until we find a new religion, or rethink our old one. The beatniks, who are the basic revolutionaries of our time, show a sound instinct in their affinity for Zen Buddhism, which conceives of the man-nature relationship as very nearly the mirror image of the Christian view. Zen, however, is as deeply conditioned by Asian history as Christianity is by the experience of the West, and I am dubious of its viability among us.

Possibly we should ponder the greatest radical in Christian history since Christ: Saint Francis of Assisi. The prime miracle of Saint Francis is the fact that he did not end at the stake, as many of his left-wing followers did. He was so clearly heretical that a general of the Franciscan Order, Saint Bonaventura, a great and perceptive Christian, tried to suppress the early accounts of Franciscanism. The key to an understanding of Francis is his belief in the virtue of humility—not merely for the individual but for man as a species. Francis tried to depose man from his monarchy over creation and set up a democracy of all God's creatures. With him the ant is no longer simply a homily for the lazy, flames a sign of the thrust of the soul toward union with God; now they are Brother Ant and Sister Fire, praising the Creator in their own ways as Brother Man does in his.

Later commentators have said that Francis preached to the birds as a rebuke to men who would not listen. The records do not read so: he urged the little birds to praise God, and in spiritual ecstasy they flapped their wings and chirped rejoicing. Legends of saints, especially the Irish saints, had long told of their dealings with animals but always, I believe, to show their human dominance over creatures. With Francis it is different. The land around Gubbio in the Apennines was being ravaged by a fierce wolf. Saint Francis, says the legend, talked to the wolf and persuaded him of the error of his ways. The wolf repented, died in the odor of sanctity, and was buried in consecrated ground.

What Sir Steven Ruciman calls "the Franciscan doctrine of the animal soul" was quickly stamped out. Quite possibly it was in part inspired, consciously or unconsciously, by the belief in reincarnation held by the Cathar heretics who at that time teemed in Italy and southern France, and who presumably had got it originally from India. It is significant that at just the same moment, about 1200, traces of metempsychosis are found also in western Judaism, in the Provencal *Cabbala*. But Francis held neither to transmigration of souls nor to pantheism. His view of nature and of man rested on a unique sort of pan-psychism of all things animate and inanimate, designed for the glorification of their transcendent Creator, who, in the ultimate gesture of cosmic humility, assumed flesh, lay helpless in a manger, and hung dying on a scaffold.

I am not suggesting that many contemporary Americans who are concerned about our ecologic crisis will be either able or willing to counsel with wolves or exhort birds. However, the present increasing disruption of the global environment is the product of a dynamic technology and science which were originating in the Western medieval world against which Saint Francis was rebelling in so original a way. Their growth cannot be understood historically apart from distinctive attitudes toward nature which are deeply grounded in Christian dogma. The fact that most people do not think of these attitudes as Christian is irrelevant. No new set of basic values has been accepted in our society to displace those of Christianity. Hence we shall continue to have a worsening ecologic crisis until we reject the Christian axiom that nature has no reason for existence save to serve man.

The greatest spiritual revolutionary in Western history, Saint Francis, proposed what he thought was an alternative Christian view of nature and man's relation to it: he tried to substitute the idea of the equality of all creatures, including man, for the idea of man's limitless rule of creation. He failed. But our present science and our present technology are so tinctured with orthodox Christian arrogance toward nature that no solution for our ecologic crisis can be expected from them alone. Since the roots of our trouble are so largely religious, the remedy must also be essentially religious, whether we call it that or not. We must rethink and refeel our nature and destiny. The profoundly religious, but heretical, sense of the primitive Franciscans for the spiritual autonomy of all parts of nature may point a direction. I propose Francis as a patron saint for ecologists.

Discussion

1. In the early portion of this selection, White suggests that changes in technology (the plow) shaped behavior. Can you think of ways that recent technological innovations have shaped the way that we behave or think?
2. Do we, as White and many others claim, "live in 'the post-Christian age'"?
3. White notes that the correlation between our attitudes and actions toward nature would be as obvious to an Eastern observer as that of an Indian would be to us. Imagine yourself as an Indian observer of American culture and describe the relationship between Judeo-Christian attitudes and environmental practices. Use as many specific examples as possible to support your observations.

4. Speculate on what White means in his claim that "Marxism, like Islam, is a Judeo-Christian heresy."
5. Are all creatures equal? Do you agree with White that such a view is necessary to Christian stewardship of the earth?

No Silent Spring

Jay Van Andel

In 1962, Rachel Carson, an American writer and marine biologist, published Silent Spring, a book that outlined the dangers involved in the use of insecticides. Carson warned that chemicals like DDT which infiltrate the ecosystem can work long-term harm and may, through the destruction of birds and other animal life, lead to a silent spring. Here Jay Van Andel, co-founder and chairman of the Amway Corporation, uses Carson's title in his effort to formulate a Christian response to environmental issues.

The struggle for adequate food, clothing, and shelter has been the principal concern of most of mankind since the beginning of time. Up until very recent years, most people have been too busy using whatever share they could get of the earth's resources to worry very much about conserving those resources. No matter how badly some sections of the earth's geography were misused, it was always possible to move on and make a fresh start. But the advent of the industrial society, with its great demands for energy and natural resources, plus the mushrooming growth of the earth's population, have rather suddenly made "conservation," "ecology," "pollution" and "environment" household words. In less than a decade we have seen concern for preservation of the environment move from a cause that involved only a few specialists with prophetic thoughts to a cause that now seems to involve almost every segment of society.

Students, farmers, businessmen, hunters, suburbanites, city dwellers, fishermen, politicians all have their views on pollution. And their views don't necessarily coincide. Since the definition of the problem varies with who is doing the defining, the proposed solutions often vary widely too.

Is there a Christian viewpoint that bridges these many variations of opinion? I think so. It seems to me that the Christian viewpoint of ecology is not one that subdivides into the views of the Christian businessman, Christian student, Christian farmer, and so on, but rather an overall view or slant that brings together all the separate views.

Here are some of the characteristics of the Christian's viewpoint toward preservation of the earth's material environment, as I see them.

1. *Reverence for God's creation:* It is God's earth, created by Him as a temporary home for man. He *intended* that we should use it. We *must* use it for our physical existence. From it must come all of our material welfare—most of it extracted with human energy and brainpower. But to waste it, to destroy it without need, is to fling God's gift back in His face. The Christian will use the earth as he would use the house or property of a friend. The friend would expect him to enjoy it—give it normal wear and tear—but return it in good order.

2. *Conservation for future generations:* No one knows how many more generations of mankind God will see fit to put on this earth. The Christian believes that God will not allow mankind to destroy the earth and make it uninhabitable for future generations. He knows he is only briefly here on earth, that the earth has been a temporary home for billions before him, and will possibly be so for billions yet to come. As in any temporary use of facilities, he has a responsibility to leave them in good repair for the next user. He therefore supports systems of using the earth's resources in ways that will make them available for reuse by future generations.

3. *Responsibility for waste disposal:* Birds pollute the air, fish the sea, and animals the land with the waste products of their existence. Yet they go about unconcerned, and the earth for them is automatically replenished with a self-balancing ecological system.

By God's decree, man must work to secure food, clothing, shelter, and to move about. The Christian expects to work. God has mandated it. The Christian expects no free ride. But work means not only gathering food and preparing a meal, it also means washing the dirty dishes and disposing of the garbage. So also in the use of the world's resources, the Christian expects to do the extra work involved in returning waste products to the earth in such a way that they do not pollute the environment, now or in the future. It takes extra work—costs extra effort reflected in higher prices and higher taxes—to completely treat sewage before returning it to waterways, to convert garbage to reusable compost, to convert sewage to usable fertilizer, to treat the causes of air pollution. The Christian accepts this as a cost of existence.

4. *God will provide:* There are those who predict calamity in the future when we exhaust the earth's resources of stored hydrocarbons for fuel. But God created the sun as the source of energy for the earth. Some of this energy He stored up in the form of coal and oil. Other comes daily in the form of water evaporated to rain to form rivers for hydroelectric power, or in plant photosynthesis. If God intends our industrial society to come to a halt sometime in the future for lack of energy availability, then it will do so in spite of man's efforts to the contrary. On the other hand, if He wants it to continue, He will see to it that man invents new ways of tapping the sun's energy to sustain his needs.

Some people want to slow down the world and return to a simpler agricultural existence to conserve resources. Yet the only resource we really consume that is unrecoverable is energy, and we get a whole new supply of that daily from the sun. All of the minerals or organic material we use are returned to the earth. The elements remain. They may not be in the exact form or distribution we found them, but they *are* there, and they *are* recoverable for reuse again and again.

God knew eons ago what our civilization today would be like. He knew what our modern-day airplanes, automobiles, and skyscrapers would be like, what we would need to build them and who would be here to do it. He knew what General Motors' latest offering would be like, how much fuel it would consume, and the materials needed to build it. He didn't place the materials we would need in neat little piles ready for use. The iron, the aluminum, the copper, the cement, the component chemicals of everything we manufacture, were dispersed widely in places often difficult, but not impossible, to work. But they were all there—everything we needed.

5. *Man's God-given intelligence expands usability of resources:* Man is not an animal. Animals merely consume what is provided on the earth for them. If the particular kind of food on which they depend, or the particular environment which they need in order to live, disappears, they die. Animals cannot invent anything. They cannot convert raw materials into something different to satisfy their needs. They cannot cultivate crops, make clothing, or build tools to multiply their efforts. They can only use what is provided for them ready-made in nature.

Only man, with the intelligence God gave him, can produce something that does not exist ready-made. With his energy, both muscular and mental, and with the tools he has invented, he can convert the earth's resources to new usable products. So his activities do not merely involve division of existing usable resources, as with the animals. He expands the usability and reusability of the earth's resources. He makes usable that which was not usable before. Cotton is in short supply? No matter—he invents nylon. Natural rubber supply limited? He invents synthetic. Metals limited? He invents plastic. Arable land needed? He irrigates the desert.

Our advanced technology does not deplete natural resources and result in less for all. Instead, by using man's God-given creative intelligence to convert substances unusable by themselves into useful and usable products, our society, aided by the competitive urge of the free enterprise system, provides more material wealth per hour of work so there is more available to all.

6. *Man is not a trespasser on earth:* Man is not an intruder upsetting the ecological balance of the earth. The earth was created with all man's uses of it in mind. Man was given dominion over the animals, and commanded by God to fill and subdue the earth. This is not an outdated "Judeo-Christian ethic." God has never rescinded that decree. Man was not an afterthought. The world without man would be like a house without occupants—a derelict without purpose.

On earth, man does not disrupt the natural order of things; he *is* the natural order of things.

Conclusion: Much of the ecological doomsday talk is purveyed by those who don't really believe that God rules the universe. Man has the responsibility, of course, to husband the earth's resources with care. He is going to have to continue to use all the aggregate mental capacity of the human race to meet the challenges of the future in using and reusing the earth's resources to satisfy his needs. He may even have to work harder to get the same results. Just as he thinks he has found new ways to give him more leisure and less work he'll probably find he has to work harder to extract the resources to support the new and more efficient systems.

His utopian dream of a world of ever more leisure and wealth will always remain a few jumps ahead, because he dreams of Eden and Eden is gone forever from the earth.

But the earth will remain, and there will never be a "Silent Spring." For God in Genesis 8 promised Noah, after the flood, "I will never again curse the ground because of man . . . neither will I ever again destroy every living creature as I have done. While the earth remains, seedtime and harvest, cold and heat, summer and winter, day and night, shall not cease."

Discussion

1. What are the five most serious environmental problems we are now facing? To what extent should Christians get involved in trying to solve them? What can we do?

2. Respond to Van Andel's assertion that the Christian should "use the earth as he would use the house or property of a friend." In concrete terms what might this mean?

3. In sections 4 and 5, Van Andel suggests that resources can be used over and over and that man can expand the "usability" of the earth's resources. Do you agree? What limits or constraints, if any, might apply to such activities? Where do God's provision and humanity's responsibility meet or diverge?

4. What does the free-enterprise system contribute to Van Andel's vision of stewardship? Is the notion of competition compatible with the rest of his argument?

5. Do you agree that "there will never be a 'Silent Spring'"? Why or why not?

But a Watch in the Night
A Scientific Fable

James C. Rettie

> Genesis 1:28 gives man dominion over the earth, but
> that phrase means different things to different people.
> To some it indicates a right, to others a responsibility.
> Yet, whatever it means, humankind has generally
> accepted it as a mandate to alter nature. This fable by
> James C. Rettie raises questions about the implications
> of those alterations.

Out beyond our solar system there is a planet called Copernicus. It came into existence some four or five billion years before the birth of our Earth. In due course of time it became inhabited by a race of intelligent men.

About 750 million years ago the Copernicans had developed the motion picture machine to a point well in advance of the stage that we have reached. Most of the cameras that we now use in motion picture work are geared to take twenty-four pictures per second on a continuous strip of film. When such film is run through a projector, it throws a series of images on the screen and these change with a rapidity that gives the visual impression of normal movement. If a motion is too swift for the human eye to see it in detail, it can be captured and artificially slowed down by means of the slow-motion camera. This one is geared to take many more shots per second—ninety-six or even more than that. When the slow-motion film is projected at the normal speed of twenty-four pictures per second, we can see just how the jumping horse goes over a hurdle.

What about motion that is too slow to be seen by the human eye? That problem has been solved by the use of the time-lapse camera. In this one, the shutter is geared to take only one shot per second, or one per minute, or even one per hour—depending upon the kind of movement that is being photographed. When the time-lapse film is projected at the normal speed of twenty-four pictures per second, it is possible to see a bean sprout growing up out of the ground. Time-lapse films are useful in the study of many types of motion too slow to be observed by the unaided human eye.

The Copernicans, it seems, had time-lapse cameras some 757 million years ago and they also had superpowered telescopes that gave them a clear view of what was happening upon this Earth. They decided to make a film record of the life history of Earth and to make it on the scale of one picture per year. The photography has been in progress during the last 757 million years.

In the near future, a Copernican interstellar expedition will arrive upon our Earth and bring with it a copy of the time-lapse film. Arrangements will be made for showing the entire film in one continuous run. This will begin at midnight of New Year's eve and continue day and night without a single stop until midnight December 31. The rate of projection will be twenty-four pictures per second. Time on the screen will thus seem to move at the rate of twenty-four years per second; 1,440 years per minute; 86,400 years per hour; approximately two million years per day; and 62 million years per month. The normal life-span of individual man will occupy about three seconds. The full period of Earth history that will be unfolded on the screen (some 757 million years) will extend from what the geologists call Pre-Cambrian times up to the present. This will, by no means, cover the full time-span of the Earth's geological history but it will embrace the period since the advent of living organisms.

During the months of January, February, and March the picture will be desolate and dreary. The shape of the land masses and the oceans will bear little or no resemblance to those that we know. The violence of geological erosion will be much in evidence. Rains will pour down on the land and promptly go booming down to the seas. There will be no clear streams anywhere except where the rains fall upon hard rock. Everywhere on the steeper ground the stream channels will be filled with boulders hurled down by rushing waters. Raging torrents and dry stream beds will keep alternating in quick succession. High mountains will seem to melt like so much butter in the sun. The shifting of land into the seas, later to be thrust up as new mountains, will be going on at a grand scale.

Early in April there will be some indication of the presence of single-celled living organisms in some of the warmer and sheltered coastal waters. By the end of the month it will be noticed that some of these organisms have become multicellular. A few of them, including the Trilobites, will be encased in hard shells.

Toward the end of May, the first vertebrates will appear, but they will still be aquatic creatures. In June about 60 percent of the land area that we know as North America will be under water. One broad channel will occupy the space where the Rocky Mountains now stand. Great deposits of limestone will be forming under some of the shallower seas. Oil and gas deposits will be in the process of formation— also under shallow seas. On land there will still be no sign of vegetation. Erosion will be rampant, tearing loose particles and chunks of rock and grinding them into sand and silt to be spewed out by the streams into bays and estuaries.

About the middle of July the first land plants will appear and take up the tremendous job of soil building. Slowly, very slowly, the mat of vegetation will spread, always battling for its life against the power of erosion. Almost foot by foot, the plant life will advance, lacing down with its root structures whatever pulverized rock material it can find. Leaves and stems will be giving added protection against the loss of the soil foothold. The increasing vegetation will pave the way for the land animals that will live upon it.

Early in August the seas will be teeming with fish. This will be what geologists call the Devonian period. Some of the races of these fish will be breathing by means of lung tissue instead of through gill tissues. Before the month is over, some of the lung fish will go ashore and take on a crude lizard-like appearance. Here are the first amphibians.

In early September the insects will put in their appearance. Some will look like huge dragon flies and will have a wingspread of 24 inches. Large portions of the land masses will now be covered with heavy vegetation that will include the primitive spore-propagating trees. Layer upon layer of this plant growth will build up, later to appear as the coal deposits. About the middle of this month, there will be evidence of the first seed-bearing plants and the first reptiles. Heretofore, the land animals will have been amphibians that could reproduce their kind only by depositing a soft egg mass in quiet waters. The reptiles will be shown to be freed from the aquatic bond because they can reproduce by means of a shelled egg in which the embryo and its nurturing liquids are sealed in and thus protected from destructive evaporation. Before September is over, the first dinosaurs will be seen—creatures destined to dominate the animal realm for about 140 million years and then to disappear.

In October there will be a series of mountain uplifts along what is now the eastern coast of the United States. A creature with feathered limbs—half bird and half reptile in appearance—will take itself into the air. Some small and rather unpretentious animals will be seen to bring forth their young in a form that is a miniature replica of the parents and to feed these young on milk secreted by mammary glands in the female parent. The emergence of this mammalian form of animal life will be recognized as one of the great events in geologic time. October will also witness the high water mark of the dinosaurs— creatures ranging in size from that of the modern goat to monsters like Brontosaurus that weighed some 40 tons. Most of them will be placid vegetarians, but a few will be hideous-looking carnivores, like Allosaurus and Tyrannosaurus. Some of the herbivorous dinosaurs will be clad in body armor for protection against their flesh-eating comrades.

November will bring pictures of a sea extending from the Gulf of Mexico to the Arctic in space now occupied by the Rocky Mountains. A few of the reptiles will take to the air on bat-like wings. One of these, called Pteranodon, will have a wingspread of 15 feet. There will be a rapid development of the modern flowering plants, modern trees, and modern insects. The dinosaurs will disappear. Toward the end of the month there will be a tremendous land disturbance in which the Rocky Mountains will rise out of the sea to assume a dominating place in the North American landscape.

As the picture runs on into December it will show the mammals in command of the animal life. Seed-bearing trees and grasses will have covered most of the land with a heavy mantle of vegetation. Only the areas newly thrust up from the sea will be barren. Most of the streams will be crystal clear. The turmoil of geologic erosion will be confined to localized areas. About December 25 will begin the cutting of the Grand Canyon of the Colorado River. Grinding down through layer after layer of sedimentary strata, this stream will finally expose deposits laid down in Pre-Cambrian times. Thus in the walls of that canyon will appear geological formations dating from recent times to the period when the earth had no living organisms upon it.

The picture will run on through the latter days of December and even up to its final day with still no sign of mankind. The spectators will become alarmed in the fear that man has somehow been left out. But not so; sometime about noon on December 31 (one million years ago) will appear a stooped, massive creature of man-like proportions. This will be Pithecanthropus, the Java ape man. For tools and weapons he will have nothing but crude stone and wooden clubs. His children will live a precarious existence threatened on the one side by hostile animals and on the other by tremendous climatic changes. Ice sheets—in places 4000 feet deep—will form in the northern parts of North America and Eurasia. Four times this glacial ice will push southward to cover half the continents. With each advance the plant and animal life will be swept under or pushed southward. With each recession of the ice, life will struggle to reestablish itself in the wake of the retreating glaciers. The wooly mammoth, the musk ox, and the caribou all will fight to maintain themselves near the ice line. Sometimes they will be caught and put into cold storage—skin, flesh, blood, bones and all.

The picture will run on through supper time with still very little evidence of man's presence on the Earth. It will be about 11 o'clock when Neanderthal man appears. Another half hour will go by before the appearance of Cro-Magnon man living in caves and painting crude animal pictures on the walls of his dwelling. Fifteen minutes more will bring Neolithic man, knowing how to chip stone and thus produce sharp cutting edges for spears and tools. In a few minutes more it will appear that man has domesticated the dog, the sheep and, possibly, other animals. He will then begin the use of milk. He will also learn the arts of basket weaving and the making of pottery and dugout canoes.

The dawn of civilization will not come until about five or six minutes before the end of the picture. The story of the Egyptians, the Babylonians, the Greeks, and the Romans will unroll during the fourth, the third and the second minute before the end. At 58 minutes and 43 seconds past 11:00 P.M. (just 1 minute and 17 seconds before the end) will come the beginning of the Christian era. Columbus will discover the new world 20 seconds before the end. The Declaration of Independence will be signed just 17 seconds before the final curtain comes down.

In those few moments of geologic time will be the story of all that has happened since we became a nation. And what a story it will be! A human swarm will sweep across the face of the continent and take it away from the . . . red men. They will change it far more radically than it has ever been changed before in a comparable time. The great virgin forests will be seen going down before ax and fire. The soil, covered for aeons by its protective mantle of trees and grasses, will be laid bare to the ravages of water and wind erosion. Streams that had been flowing clear will, once again, take up a load of silt and push it toward the seas. Humus and mineral salts, both vital elements of productive soil, will be seen to vanish at a terrifying rate. The railroads and highways and cities that will spring up may divert attention, but they cannot cover up the blight of man's recent activities. In great sections of Asia, it will be seen that man must utilize cow dung and every scrap of available straw or grass for fuel to cook his food. The forests that once provided wood for this purpose will be gone without a trace. The use of these agricultural wastes for fuel, in place of returning them to the land, will be leading to increasing soil impoverishment. Here and there will be seen a dust storm darkening the landscape over an area a thousand miles across. Man-creatures will be shown counting their wealth in terms of bits of printed paper representing other bits of a scarce but comparatively useless yellow metal that is kept buried in strong vaults. Meanwhile, the soil, the only real wealth that can keep mankind alive on the face of this Earth is savagely being cut loose from its ancient moorings and washed into the seven seas.

We have just arrived upon this Earth. How long will we stay?

Discussion

1. What does the title of the essay mean? Read Psalm 90 to inform your answer.
2. The essay depends heavily on an extended analogy. How successful is this strategy? What does it assume about the audience? Can you think of other ways of developing the essay to lead into the last two paragraphs?
3. How would you answer the question in the last sentence of the essay?

The Land Ethic

Aldo Leopold

> As a member of the National Forest Service in the first
> quarter of this century, Aldo Leopold campaigned
> successfully for policies that would preserve wilderness
> areas as part of that system. As a writer, he is best
> known for A Sand County Almanac *(1948), a collection
> made famous by its sensitive presentation of nature
> and by its early statements of environmental theory. In
> the following excerpt from one of the theoretical
> essays, he argues for a revision of our attitudes toward
> the land.*

When god-like Odysseus returned from the wars in Troy, he hanged all on one rope a dozen slave-girls of his household whom he suspected of misbehavior during his absence.

This hanging involved no question of propriety. The girls were property. The disposal of property was then, as now, a matter of expediency, not of right and wrong.

Concepts of right and wrong were not lacking from Odysseus' Greece: witness the fidelity of his wife through the long years before at last his black-prowed galleys clove the wine-dark seas for home. The ethical structure of that day covered wives, but had not yet been extended to human chattels. During the three thousand years which have since elapsed, ethical criteria have been extended to many fields of conduct, with corresponding shrinkages in those judged by expediency only.

The Ethical Sequence

This extension of ethics, so far studied only by philosophers, is actually a process in ecological evolution. Its sequences may be described

211

in ecological as well as in philosophical terms. An ethic, ecologically, is a limitation on freedom of action in the struggle for existence. An ethic, philosophically, is a differentiation of social from anti-social conduct. These are two definitions of one thing. The thing has its origin in the tendency of interdependent individuals or groups to evolve modes of co-operation. The ecologist calls these symbioses. Politics and economics are advanced symbioses in which the original free-for-all competition has been replaced, in part, by co-operative mechanisms with an ethical content.

The complexity of co-operative mechanisms has increased with population density, and with the efficiency of tools. It was simpler, for example, to define the anti-social uses of sticks and stones in the days of the mastodons than of bullets and billboards in the age of motors.

The first ethics dealt with the relation between individuals; the Mosaic Decalogue is an example. Later accretions dealt with the relation between the individual and society. The Golden Rule tries to integrate the individual to society; democracy to integrate social organization to the individual.

There is as yet no ethic dealing with man's relation to land and to the animals and plants which grow upon it. Land, like Odysseus' slave-girls, is still property. The land-relation is still strictly economic, entailing privileges but not obligations.

The extension of ethics to this third element in human environment is, if I read the evidence correctly, an evolutionary possibility and an ecological necessity. It is the third step in a sequence. The first two have already been taken. Individual thinkers since the days of Ezekiel and Isaiah have asserted that the despoliation of land is not only inexpedient but wrong. Society, however, has not yet affirmed their belief. I regard the present conservation movement as the embryo of such an affirmation.

An ethic may be regarded as a mode of guidance for meeting ecological situations so new or intricate, or involving such deferred reactions, that the path of social expediency is not discernible to the average individual. Animal instincts are modes of guidance for the individual in meeting such situations. Ethics are possibly a kind of community instinct in-the-making.

The Community Concept

All ethics so far evolved rest upon a single premise: that the individual is a member of a community of interdependent parts. His instincts prompt him to compete for his place in that community, but his ethics prompt him also to co-operate (perhaps in order that there may be a place to compete for).

The land ethic simply enlarges the boundaries of the community to include soils, waters, plants, and animals, or collectively: the land.

This sounds simple: do we not already sing our love for and obligation to the land of the free and the home of the brave? Yes, but just what and whom do we love? Certainly not the soil, which we are sending helter-skelter downriver. Certainly not the waters, which we assume have no function except to turn turbines, float barges, and carry off sewage. Certainly not the plants, of which we exterminate whole communities without batting an eye. Certainly not the animals, of which we have already extirpated many of the largest and most beautiful species. A land ethic of course cannot prevent the alteration, management, and use of these "resources," but it does affirm their right to continued existence, and, at least in spots, their continued existence in a natural state.

In short, a land ethic changes the role of *Homo sapiens* from conqueror of the land-community to plain member and citizen of it. It implies respect for his fellow-members, and also respect for the community as such.

In human history, we have learned (I hope) that the conqueror role is eventually self-defeating. Why? Because it is implicit in such a role that the conqueror knows, *ex cathedra*, just what makes the community clock tick, and just what and who is valuable, and what and who is worthless, in community life. It always turns out that he knows neither, and this is why his conquests eventually defeat themselves.

In the biotic community, a parallel situation exists. Abraham knew exactly what the land was for: it was to drip milk and honey into Abraham's mouth. At the present moment, the assurance with which we regard this assumption is inverse to the degree of our education.

The ordinary citizen today assumes that science knows what makes the community clock tick; the scientist is equally sure that he does not. He knows that the biotic mechanism is so complex that its workings may never be fully understood.

That man is, in fact, only a member of a biotic team is shown by an ecological interpretation of history. Many historical events, hitherto explained solely in terms of human enterprise, were actually biotic interactions between people and land. The characteristics of the land determined the facts quite as potently as the characteristics of the men who lived on it.

Consider, for example, the settlement of the Mississippi valley. In the years following the Revolution, three groups were contending for its control: the native Indian, the French and English traders, and the

American settlers. Historians wonder what would have happened if the English at Detroit had thrown a little more weight into the Indian side of those tipsy scales which decided the outcome of the colonial migration into the cane-lands of Kentucky. It is time now to ponder the fact that the cane-lands, when subjected to the particular mixture of forces represented by the cow, plow, fire, and axe of the pioneer, became bluegrass. What if the plant succession inherent in this dark and bloody ground had, under the impact of these forces, given us some worthless sedge, shrub, or weed? Would Boone and Kenton have held out? Would there have been any overflow into Ohio, Indiana, Illinois, and Missouri? Any Louisiana Purchase? Any transcontinental union of new states? Any Civil War?

Kentucky was one sentence in the drama of history. We are commonly told what the human actors in this drama tried to do, but we are seldom told that their success, or the lack of it, hung in large degree on the reaction of particular soils to the impact of the particular forces exerted by their occupancy. In the case of Kentucky, we do not even know where the bluegrass came from—whether it is a native species, or a stowaway from Europe.

Contrast the cane-lands with what hindsight tells us about the Southwest, where the pioneers were equally brave, resourceful, and persevering. The impact of occupancy here brought no bluegrass, or other plant fitted to withstand the bumps and buffetings of hard use. This region, when grazed by livestock, reverted through a series of more and more worthless grasses, shrubs, and weeds to a condition of unstable equilibrium. Each recession of plant types bred erosion; each increment to erosion bred a further recession of plants. The result today is a progressive and mutual deterioration, not only of plants and soils, but of the animal community subsisting thereon. The early settlers did not expect this: on the cienegas of New Mexico some even cut ditches to hasten it. So subtle has been its progress that few residents of the region are aware of it. It is quite invisible to the tourist who finds this wrecked landscape colorful and charming (as indeed it is, but it bears scant resemblance to what it was in 1848).

This same landscape was "developed" once before, but with quite different results. The Pueblo Indians settled the Southwest in pre-Columbian times, but they happened *not* to be equipped with range livestock. Their civilization expired, but not because their land expired.

In India, regions devoid of any sod-forming grass have been settled, apparently without wrecking the land, by the simple expedient of carrying the grass to the cow, rather than vice versa. (Was this the result of some deep wisdom, or was it just good luck? I do not know.)

In short, the plant succession steered the course of history; the pioneer simply demonstrated, for good or ill, what successions inhered in the land. Is history taught in this spirit? It will be, once the concept of land as a community really penetrates our intellectual life.

The Ecological Conscience

Conservation is a state of harmony between men and land. Despite nearly a century of propaganda, conservation still proceeds at a snail's pace; progress still consists largely of letterhead pieties and convention oratory. On the back forty we still slip two steps backward for each forward stride.

The usual answer to this dilemma is "more conservation education." No one will debate this, but is it certain that only the *volume* of education needs stepping up? Is something lacking in the *content* as well?

It is difficult to give a fair summary of its content in brief form, but, as I understand it, the content is substantially this: obey the law, vote right, join some organizations, and practice what conservation is profitable on your own land; the government will do the rest.

Is not this formula too easy to accomplish anything worth-while? It defines no right or wrong, assigns no obligation, calls for no sacrifice, implies no change in the current philosophy of values. In respect of land-use, it urges only enlightened self-interest. Just how far will such education take us? An example will perhaps yield a partial answer.

By 1930 it had become clear to all except the ecologically blind that southwestern Wisconsin's topsoil was slipping seaward. In 1933 the farmers were told that if they would adopt certain remedial practices for five years, the public would donate CCC labor to install them, plus the necessary machinery and materials. The offer was widely accepted, but the practices were widely forgotten when the five-year contract period was up. The farmers continued only those practices that yielded an immediate and visible economic gain for themselves.

This led to the idea that maybe farmers would learn more quickly if they themselves wrote the rules. Accordingly the Wisconsin Legislature in 1937 passed the Soil Conservation District Law. This said to farmers, in effect: *We, the public, will furnish you free technical service and loan you specialized machinery, if you will write your own rules for land-use. Each county may write its own rules, and these will have the force of law.* Nearly all the counties promptly organized to accept the proffered help, but after a decade of operation, *no county has yet written a single rule.* There has been visible progress in such practices as strip-cropping pasture renovation, and soil liming, but none in fencing woodlots against grazing, and none in excluding plow and cow from steep slopes. The farmers, in short, have selected those remedial practices which were profitable anyhow, and ignored those which were profitable to the community, but not clearly profitable to themselves.

When one asks why no rules have been written, one is told that the community is not yet ready to support them; education must precede rules. But the education actually in progress makes no mention of obligations to land over and above those dictated by self-interest. The net result is that we have more education but less soil, fewer healthy woods, and as many floods as in 1937.

The puzzling aspect of such situations is that the existence of obligations over and above self-interest is taken for granted in such rural community enterprises as the betterment of roads, schools, churches, and baseball teams. Their existence is not taken for granted, nor as yet seriously discussed, in bettering the behavior of the water that falls on the land, or in the preserving of the beauty or diversity of the farm landscape. Land-use ethics are still governed wholly by economic self-interest, just as social ethics were a century ago.

To sum up: we asked the farmer to do what he conveniently could to save his soil, and he has done just that, and only that. The farmer who clears the woods of a 75 percent slope, turns his cows into the clearing, and dumps its rainfall, rocks, and soil into the community creek, is still (if otherwise decent) a respected member of society. If he puts lime on his fields and plants his crops on contour, he is still entitled to all the privileges and emoluments of his Soil Conservation District. The District is a beautiful piece of social machinery, but it is coughing along on two cylinders because we have been too timid, and too anxious for quick success, to tell the farmer the true magnitude of his obligations. Obligations have no meaning without conscience, and the problem we face is the extension of the social conscience from people to land.

No important change in ethics was ever accomplished without an internal change in our intellectual emphasis, loyalties, affections, and convictions. The proof that conservation has not yet touched these foundations of conduct lies in the fact that philosophy and religion have not yet heard of it. In our attempt to make conservation easy, we have made it trivial.

Discussion

1. What does Leopold mean by the assertion that "disposal of property was then, as now, a matter of expediency, not of right and wrong"? Is such still the case?

2. If ethics evolve, do you see any evidence of the development of a land ethic in the almost fifty years since the composition of this essay?

3. How would you respond to the allusion to Abraham and the land of Canaan? Bear in mind Leopold's claim that "the assurance with which we regard this assumption is inverse to the degree of our education."

4. Using the land in your community as an example, list the advantages and disadvantages inherent in thinking of land as community, with man simply as one more organism in that community.

5. Would it be possible to apply such an ethic to life in other communities? Consider the implications for the business community, the church community, or the education community.

Pisces

Hugh Cook

> *Our understanding of nature often determines what we see in nature. In "Pisces" the understandings of several people clash during a one-week vacation on the shores of Lake Erie, a lake at one time considered to be ecologically doomed. Canadian writer Hugh Cook has published his stories in a variety of literary magazines and in a book-length collection—*Cracked Wheat and Other Stories.

> The power of the visible
> is in the invisible
> —Marianne Moore

Baars was so deep in his daydream that his wife had to ask her question three times before he heard her voice. They were driving towards Lake Erie with their twin boys, and what Baars was thinking about was their upcoming week at the lake, and then he certainly felt in good spirits. Lots of sun and water, plus some casual research with fish and algae around Erie. Through his mind ran the refrain of a song he'd heard on the radio earlier. He found it rather pleasant and sang it to himself over and over:

> Joy to the world,
> All the boys and girls,
> Joy to the fishes in the deep blue sea,
> Joy to you and me.

Baars liked that. The song's tone struck him as being entirely appropriate. After all, if the benefit of man's being crown of creation did not extend to the animals, then what *did* it mean? Yes, joy to the fishes of the deep blue sea, all right, even those of Lake Erie, if people would only listen to the voice of science.

It was then Baars finally heard his wife's question, and even so it did not register at first. He was only half aware of her, sitting uncomfortable and heavy with pregnancy on the opposite end of the front seat, when her voice broke his daydream. What motel had he reserved, she wanted to know. What motel indeed? Suddenly Baars felt as if he had just made a serious miscalculation in an experiment, with his whole graduate class looking on. What motel indeed?

He confessed that he had forgotten to make the reservation.

One hour later they stood at the town's last motel, the red neon sign glowing *No Vacancy* as a bright reminder of Baars' stupidity.

"Try anyway," his wife said, "you never know. Maybe the sign's wrong."

"Fat chance," Baars snorted, taking on a sour look, as if she had just asked him to make a public fool of himself. "This is ridiculous," he said.

"What's ridiculous," her voice snapped from the open car window, "is that you didn't write for reservations, like I suggested."

He stepped into the motel office, was told the sign was indeed correct, and emerged with a scowl on his face. He felt very angry at himself for not having made the reservation, not only for the inconvenience his error now caused, but especially because he had always considered efficient, rational planning his most outstanding trait. He felt both irritated and mystified that it had momentarily deserted him. What had possessed him to forget?

"We've tried all the motels, now what?" Hume wailed from the back seat.

"Maybe we can rent one of the cottages around here," Baars said, hoping to salvage his respect.

"That means we won't have a swimming pool!"

"And what's wrong with having a beach? All you've got here is the whole of Lake Erie!"

"It's polluted," David complained. "My teacher says there's nothin' in it but dead fish."

"Well, your teacher just happens to be wrong. Scientists have been working on it, and I ought to know."

He drove slowly away from the town, away from the resort area. At the first intersection, he saw that the road to the left followed the lake and that it was lined with cottages. He turned onto it.

"Dike Road," David groaned, reading the road sign. "Dike Road. What a hick place."

"Yeah," Hume chimed in, "who wants to spend their vacation on a stupid onion farm." The road was narrow, without a centre white line.

On the right the pavement was fringed by a tangle of tall grass and blooming dandelions, the ground dropping off sharply to a broad, water-filled ditch. Beyond the ditch lay fields of black dirt bisected by row after straight row of onions.

Baars dropped the visor above him to shield his eyes from the late afternoon sun. "What do you suggest?" his wife asked, arching her eyebrows.

"Let's just take a look down here," he said, stalling.

On the left, green lawns separated the road from the cottages, a few of which stood farther back shaded by maples and willows and elms. Far beyond Baars saw the keen edge of the lake's horizon slice sharply against the sky. What surprised him, however, was the narrowness of the neck of land between the cottages and the lake, as if half the beach had been cut away. I'd have given myself a bit more room, he thought. Then he saw two cottagers lifting rocks into wire-mesh cages piled on top of each other along the lake shore. Others built walls with sand-bags, like the besieged villagers in Holland Baars remembered from the War. So that was it: the lake must have been high. Half a mile farther a row of cottages stood perilously close to the lake, then a number of them had been jarred from their moorings and tossed aside, torn to splintered boards. Waves dashed through the caved-in walls, flinging spray as high as the roofs. Then the road itself veered close to the lake, and water flew over the pavement.

"Gol!" one of the boys shouted as a wave crashed, tossing spume against the windshield.

This is getting close, Baars thought. He drove slowly.

A hundred yards farther on the air smelled suddenly putrid, the car filling with the stench of decay, and after a moment Baars saw why. In a marsh, littered among the spiked reeds and muddied spears of grass, lay the decomposing bodies of hundreds of dead carp.

"Peeyew!" the boys groaned, rolling up their windows.

"Let's turn back," Baars' wife said, closing her eyes and turning away.

"How come they're dead, Dad?" Hume asked.

"High winds must have raised the water level, and when the lake receded the fish were trapped." He turned the car around. When he had almost reached the road leading back to town his wife said, "Maybe you should ask that lady over there if any of these cottages are for rent."

He did not want to do any such thing, but realizing he had little choice he slowed the car. Ahead the motels were full; behind him the sun began to sink lower, reflecting an angry glare in his rear view mirror. The woman was down on her hands and knees weeding a bed of purple zinnias. Her cottage was much larger than the others and was

built of white stucco rather than wood siding. On the front lawn gera-
niums bloomed inside two car tires that had been turned inside out
and painted white. Baars stopped the car and stepped out, feeling
uncomfortably like a door-to-door salesman.

The woman had seen the car and was waiting on all fours. Her body
was huge and she wore a white kerchief tied in two knots that stuck out
like horns from her forehead, so that she resembled a bull irritated at
being interrupted while feeding.

"Excuse me, ma'am," Baars said, "but could you tell me if any of
these cottages are for rent?"

The woman eyed him a moment, then craned her neck to look past
him at the car. "How long are you thinking of?" she said.

"Oh, a week, maybe."

She stood up, brushed the hair out of her face with a gloved hand,
then slowly removed the gloves, all the while eyeing Baars and the car.
She spoke with a European accent, asking him why he wanted a cottage over here rather than a motel in town, and whether the boys were
good boys and not destructive. Baars answered, not telling the whole
story of the motel but saying they wanted to stay away from the commercialized area. He felt interrogated and wanted to retreat to the car,
convinced he had made a mistake. He turned to go.

"Mr. Cragg next door sometimes rents his cottage," the woman said,
pointing.

Baars looked at her, then over at the cottage. It was painted white
with green shutters and trim. It looked neat enough. He thanked the
woman and walked across the lawn, wondering whether he should
have walked around it on the road. Ahead of him the sun hung red as a
bruised berry in the trees in the west.

Baars pressed the doorbell but no one answered. From inside he
heard the broadcast of a baseball game. He tried knocking. Immediately the sound inside was turned down and the door opened. Again
Baars wondered whether he had made a mistake. Before him stood an
old man whose nose and cheeks were bulbous and red, criss-crossed
with dark purple veins. His hair lay greased on his head, the thin front
of it pushed forward in a rakish wave. He wore a white T-shirt and
beneath it his pants hung low, the belt buckle hidden under a sagging
belly.

He agreed to let Baars and his wife look through the cottage. They
were satisfied with it and decided to rent it for a week.

"Just give me a sec to move my stuff into the garage," Cragg said.
"I've got it all decked out for when I rent out the place."

They spent the evening unpacking the station wagon, Baars carrying suitcases inside where his wife emptied them. Later, after they had

put the boys to bed, they sat at the kitchen table. Baars' wife sat straight in her chair, one hand cupped over the top of her protruding stomach.

"Beat?" Baars asked.

"Sort of," she said, then placed her hand over his on the table as if to atone for her snappishness that afternoon. "First the long drive, then the looking for a place." Her sentence trailed off, and they sat silently.

He was in his fourth year at the University of Guelph when they'd married, while she was just a year out of high school. She had worked five years in a bank supporting them while he did graduate studies. They had tried to have children then, when he was finished, but were unsuccessful, and finally the doctor had advised them to adopt. Soon after, they had received the twin boys from the agency. Now, eight years later, she had suddenly become pregnant. She was a good mother but Baars, assuming that the complexity of his research lay beyond her comprehension, shared little of his work with her, and he was aware of her dissatisfaction over how little he seemed to need her.

They had debated whether to have a vacation this summer, what with her pregnancy—her first, after all—and had decided that perhaps a quiet week in a motel by the lake would not prove too strenuous for her. Which made his failure to make the reservation all the more serious, and as it crossed his mind again he was filled anew with embarrassment.

"I think we'll enjoy it here," he said. "The boys will have plenty to do."

She smiled wanly. "You're not going to spend all your time doing research, though, are you?"

"I promise. But there are a few things I want to look at."

Fatigue showed on her face, and she suggested they go to bed.

"I don't think I can sleep yet," he said, "you go ahead. I'll just grab some fresh air a moment and then be right in," and he kissed her.

When he stepped outside he saw Cragg sitting against the garage smoking. Baars sat down on a stump beside him. "Nice evening," he said. He looked up and saw a half a moon in the sky, the dark half faintly visible like a shrivelled and black-green globe of fruit.

"What do you do, Baars?" Cragg asked.

"I'm a biologist. Ph.D. from Guelph."

"How about that. And you decided to come here for your vacation."

"Mostly. I haven't been to this part of the lake for a while, and I thought I'd do some poking around. You know, kill two stones with one bird," and he chuckled, but Cragg did not laugh. "Looks like you've been hit though," he began again.

"I'll tell ya," Cragg said, "she's been nasty. Had us a few good storms this spring. I think the beach is ten foot higher 'n what it was. Had a willow down there by the dock at one time. Not no more. Snapped right off, like it was a toothpick. You're sittin' on it now. But we been lucky compared with down the road. Care for a beer?"

He disappeared into the garage without waiting for Baars to reply and after a moment came out with two bottles.

"I noticed the people sandbagging," Baars said.

"Won't do no good," Cragg scoffed. "I seen her throw trees like they was nothin', and she don't pay no more attention to us. Best thing for us is to stay out of her way. As far as the water itself is concerned, I suppose it's been gettin' better. Can see bottom now at two feet. And they're back fishin' on it, commercial, I mean."

"It shows you what responsible science can do," Baars said. "Course, it helps that Erie is small. Takes just seven years for it to change its water completely. The other four are bigger so they take much longer."

Cragg seemed duly impressed with this information.

"How about you, Mr. Cragg, what do you do?"

"Call me Don. Me? I'm retired now. Ph.D. from Michigan. Economics."

"You don't say," Baars said. Maybe he had misjudged this Cragg.

"Naw, I'm kiddin' ya. I went to the school a hard knocks. Worked thirty years in the Ford plant in Detroit."

"Are you an American then?" Strange fellow, Cragg.

"Nope. Canadian as hell. From Moose Jaw."

"How did you end up in Detroit?"

"I played hockey. Got a tryout long time ago with the Red Wings."

"I see," Baars said, skeptical now. He did not intend to get hooked twice.

Cragg, however, seemed serious. "That was in the days of Delvecchio and Abel and them boys, though. No way I was going to crack that lineup, not before expansion. Somehow I never left Detroit. Played some industrial hockey, bought the cottage in the meantime, then when the wife died four years ago I decided to sell the place in Detroit and live here. How about you, sounds like you got an accent—German?"

Baars laughed. "No, Dutch."

"Well, I had you figured wrong then. Ever since the War I can't stand them Germans. But I got to introduce you to Thelma next door. She's Belgian. Same thing, right?"

"Almost. Actually, I met her already. She's the one who told me about your place."

"Mmm, wonder what made her do that. Usually she's pretty leery of me gettin' someone in here. Bit of a kook, if you ask me. Inta horoscopes and ouija boards and all that. You believe in that?"

Baars laughed again. "Wouldn't look too good for a scientist, would it." He felt the evening chill and rose to go. "Thanks for the beer."

"That's O.K. Maybe tomorra your boys can get some fishin' in. You fish?"

"A little."

"Tell ya what. One a these days I'll take ya out in my boat and we'll catch us a mess of perch. You cut yours open and look inside. I'd rather eat mine!"

"O.K., Don," he laughed. "See you tomorrow."

Despite the boys' earlier fears, Baars saw that they had a good time at the lake. They found that the ditch across the road contained small gold carp and spent hours trying to catch them. David fashioned a net from some wire and netting, stationed himself at a narrow point in the ditch, and had Hume try to herd the carp toward him, but the fish were elusive, darting back in a flash of gold. Cragg took the boys to the onion farm to find worms under logs, then pointed out some good fishing spots, teaching them how to cast into the lake. Baars watched, envious of Cragg's easy manner with the boys, glad, however, that it freed him to do some research. He stopped in at the commercial fishery in town to see what fish were now being caught and left with some skin tissues of perch and whitefish. He collected some water samples along the lake shore, which he would check for concentration of blue-green algae.

He felt in his element then. The last few years he had become somewhat disenchanted with teaching, wondering whether he should quit and do research for industry. Students weren't the same anymore. Drugs, science fiction, Zen this and that—just a bunch of mystics. The trouble with them was that they had no appreciation for two thousand years of Western culture.

Cragg, however, seemed an interested pupil. "So that's what causes that, eh?" he said when Baars explained the reason for the foam on the beach. "You know I've seen the layer of scum in the middle of the lake to be a mile wide? And so thick I swear you could of walked right there on the water. How'd that be for a trick! But you fellas think you can fix all that, huh?"

"We can go a long way," Baars said. "But unless we stop dumping toxic wastes and using mercury for fungicide, we're going to have a hard time." He had said the words often. Classes at the university, speeches to service clubs and church groups, at all of them he had spread his view of a scientific approach to the environment. He felt proud knowing that man possessed the knowledge to improve his world, and that science stood in the forefront of this progress.

His words didn't have the effect on Cragg that he had hoped, however. "You're way beyond me already," Cragg chuckled. "Toxic wastes and fungawhatnots—I'll leave that up to you boys. The only mercury I know is the kind with four wheels on it. Hell, I've paid my dues. All I want's my pension from Ford and I'm happy." He rose from the willow stump. "I'll let you fellas clean up the world. Wanna beer?"

Baars was reading *The Journal of Marine Biology* under the parasol of the picnic table, oblivious to his wife sunning in a lawn chair to his left. A white summer top hung taut over her stomach, and the skin of her arms and shoulders glistened under a coating of baby oil.

"What time is it, dear?" she asked.

Baars glanced at his watch. "Pretty well three o'clock," he said.

"Oh, we've got to get ready then. I forgot to mention it to you, but Thelma asked us over for a cold drink this afternoon."

Baars looked at her. "I wish you would have checked with me first," he said. He had hoped to avoid Thelma. He felt she was a suspicious old woman. He had noticed her watching him from her window as he worked with his samples. His mind had been nagged, moreover, by the notion that she was not only unpleasant but even, perhaps—well, sinister. It was something Cragg had said about her.

"Oh come on, don't be so anti-social," his wife said, struggling to rise from her chair. "She's a very nice lady. Besides, I'm about ready for a cold drink."

So was Baars, but it did not make him feel any better as they walked over.

Thelma met them at the door, wearing a flowing silky dress with a pattern of turquoise flowers, a dress which Baars thought was rather low-cut for her age. A kerchief of the same material tied her hair and flowed down her back. Thin golden hoops dangled from her ears to her shoulders.

"It's so nice to have you two stop by," she sang, ushering them in.

The living room they stepped into was cool, with a slight breeze from the lake rustling the print curtains, but Baars felt uneasy. The walls were painted a deep blue and in the room hung a strange odour which he could not identify. It wasn't the zinnias or chrysanthemums or asters which stood in vases everywhere; the smell was more like incense, and Baars felt as if he had just stepped into an alien Eastern shrine. He wished he were back in his white lab with its familiar formaldehyde smell.

"Please sit down," Thelma said. "Would you like a lime and vodka?"

"Oh, that would be nice," Baars' wife said.

Baars could tell by its interior finish that the house was more than a summer cottage. The smooth blue walls and gold carpeted floor gave an air of permanence and solidity, unlike Cragg's cottage with its white-washed, bare stud walls and linoleum-covered, sloping floors.

"Well here we are," Thelma crowed as she glided in carrying a tray with three tall glasses and a dish of chocolate candies.

"Your place is nicely built," Baars said. "Looks like it's been here a while."

"Why thank you. My father built it a long time ago. Actually, it was the first house on Dike Road. Isn't it a beautiful setting?"

Baars' wife said it looked lovely.

"I'm afraid the area has deteriorated terribly the last little while, though," Thelma said. "People are building just any kind of cottages now, it's such a shame. And everything in town has become so commercialized, and the black folks coming from Detroit, fishing everywhere—I know we Tauruses are terribly possessive, but . . . Anyway, I hope you're all enjoying your stay?"

"Yes, it's turned out very well," Baars' wife said, "although I was worried for a while, not being able to get a motel," and she glanced at her husband. Baars looked straight ahead.

"You're a biologist I take it, Mr. Baars, the things I see you doing around the lake. Have you found what you came for?"

"Oh, I've just been doing some very informal things," he said.

"Well I just think it's dreadful what they've done to the lake," Thelma said. "And they tell me now that if someone throws a match into the Detroit river it'll actually burn. Can you imagine that?"

Baars' wife said she could not, and what were things coming to.

But Baars thought it time to set things straight, and started into his speech about toxic wastes and mercury in fungicide when Thelma interrupted him.

"But isn't it just a band-aid solution in the long run, Mr. Baars? I agree with you about not using our rivers and lakes as convenient garbage dumps, but **why** do we do it?"

Baars shrugged. "Mass carelessness."

Thelma shook her head. "I think it goes much deeper. I think it's because we've reduced reality to being nothing more than physical, giving us license to plunder."

"Granted," said Baars, "our materialism gets pretty crass—"

"That's not what I mean, Mr. Baars," Thelma broke in. "I'm talking about environmental rape."

"Oh, I don't know if it's as drastic as all that. If it's true what you're saying, that means we'd have to change the whole North American pattern of science and industry, and I—"

"That's **precisely** what I'm saying," Thelma urged. "Listen, we conscript boy scouts to comb the medians of our highways to pick up beer cans, but the fact is we produce them faster than all the boy scouts in the world combined can pick them up!"

Baars shifted uncomfortably in his seat. "I don't know," he said, "it just seems to me you're overstating it. There's been some irresponsible things done to our lakes by industry and agriculture, granted, but surely the way to remedy that is to apply some equally responsible and enlightened science."

"The kind that denies that nature is spiritual, I suppose."

"But what else can we do? Those are separate realms. What we see is what there is."

"But what do we choose to see?"

"Hard cold reality."

"That's all?"

"With our five senses, yes."

"Mr. Baars," Thelma said slowly, "that there's more to reality than what **you** see means only that you've shrivelled your vision, and that makes you no different from our friend Cragg. Are you an Aquarius by the way?"

Baars had expected the topic, but the question irritated him with its suddenness. "I'm sorry," he said curtly, "but I have no idea."

"Well, when's your birthday?"

There she goes interrogating again, Baars thought, not wanting to answer. "Early March," he said hoping his reply would be sufficiently vague.

"Pisces, then."

"For what it's worth."

"Oh, this drink is so refreshing!" Baars' wife exulted, putting down her glass.

"In that case, let me get us all another," Thelma said, gathering the empty glasses. She flowed to the kitchen in a rustle of silk.

Baars' wife turned to him when Thelma was gone. "Don't you get us into an argument now!" she hissed into his ear, but he only glared at her accusingly, as if to say, "**You're** the one who got us here!"

Thelma returned with their drinks and the visit turned exactly into what Baars was afraid it would. Thelma continued her assault. Baars knew there was no hope of returning the conversation to mere pleasantries, and after a trying hour he left with his wife. It bothered him that Thelma had seemed to enjoy the visit.

Cragg threaded his hook through a dew worm the next day, his fingers slimy with the mucus the worm secreted as the steel barb punctured its body. "Hell," he said, "just think of the number of people who'd lose jobs in the auto industry alone, not to mention rubber and petroleum and steel."

Baars watched his bobber roll and toss twenty feet away with the swell of the waves. "That's exactly what I told her," he said.

"Shows you what happens when you let women run the world," Cragg said.

Baars looked at Cragg holding his rod with his elbows out, arms ready, as if something were playing with the bait. He glanced at the bobber and saw it sink, and Cragg gave his rod a strong upward sweep. It bent toward the water in a slight bow, jerking slightly as Cragg reeled in fast. "Whatever it is, it isn't very big," he said.

"Do you want the net?"

"Naw, I won't need it."

Then Baars saw the yellow shape of the fish as it glimmered near the surface.

"Lousy small perch," Cragg muttered as he lifted the fish out of the water. He let it crash into the boat and the perch landed on its back, white belly writhing, until it righted itself. Cragg took a knife out of his tacklebox, placed his foot on the fish's back, and drove the knifepoint through the top of its head. Baars winced as he heard the crunch of steel slicing through the cartilage. The perch flopped twice and lay still.

"Let's see what he did with my hook," Cragg said. He squeezed at the gills to open the mouth and looked inside. "Wouldn't you know it," he said, "happens all the time with these little buggers. Took it right down inside his bloody craw." He took the knife again, cut the corners of the fish's mouth, and sliced away the slimy flesh of the throat until the knifepoint reached the hook deep in the fish and cut it free. Blood dripped through Cragg's fingers. He threw the perch overboard and it landed with a slight splash, sending water circles widening, then it floated away upside down, creamy belly showing. "Can't stand those dinky ones," Cragg said. He reached over the side of the boat and washed his hands of the blood. Baars saw the perch's scales leave his hands and, catching the sun, float like pearls through the green water.

Baars did not feel like fishing anymore. Tomorrow would be their last day at the lake. Strange: for a man who had just had a vacation, he felt in desperate need of one. At least his boys had seemed to enjoy themselves. But on their own, without him. Cragg had seemed to engage their interest all right. When they got home he'd have to spend more time with the boys, playing—what? He realized with dismay that he hardly knew what games they played. Baseball and football, probably, and then he felt how little his own childhood in Holland, with its emphasis on soccer and gymnastics, had prepared him to play with the boys at their games.

And his wife, what kind of a week had she had? It struck him how little he really knew of her world, too, and then he felt suddenly alone. Or empty, as if an old friend had died and no new intimate had yet filled the void. He'd experienced the same feeling once after a conference in Montreal at which he had met a woman biologist with whom he'd had a number of animated conversations, and as he flew home he'd had the feeling that someone very close to him had died.

Monday he would be back in the lab. Perhaps the water samples and fish tissues he'd collected might produce some interesting results, but as he thought about it he felt no hurry to check them in the lab. Perhaps the familiar surroundings would help and he'd again be in the mood.

Perhaps, perhaps. No, he knew it was more than that, more than a passing funk caused by a week that failed to measure up to his expectations. It was more as if a long-held hypothesis had suddenly been found to be false, and years of work had come to nothing. He would have to think things through again. Or had the friend not died after all? Hang that Thelma!

He felt cold then and noticed that the lake lay in shadow, but when he looked toward the shoreline half a mile away he saw that just before the beach the sunlight began again, the water turning lighter green in a sharp line. The white cottages, too, stood in bright sunlight against the trees, warm and inviting.

He did not feel like waiting for the cloud to pass. "How many did we catch, Don?" he asked.

"About a dozen. Just enough for a fish fry."

"What do you say we call it a day."

"O.K. by me. It's too late in the afternoon now anyway."

They started reeling in their lines, Baars quickly so, his bobber skipping across the water in quick little spurts.

All at once it sank, and had it not been for the total deadness on the end of the line Baars might have thought he had a strike. "I'm snagged, Don," he said.

"Couldn't be. You weren't anywhere near the bottom."

"Must be some debris just below the surface. I'll see if I can work it loose," and he pulled the line taut.

"Don't break it, though," Cragg cautioned. "I'll row us there and have a look."

Baars continued yanking at the line, the rod bending in a sharp arc. Afraid to break the rod, he placed it in the boat, then he stood up and took the line in his hand, pulling hard, stretching the nylon like elastic.

"Better sit down," Cragg said.

Suddenly the hook broke free. The line flew through the air with a snap, and the hook struck Baars on the bare chest. Hands flying to the stinging pain, he lost his balance, struck his tacklebox with his right foot, and lurched backward out of the boat.

He was not a good swimmer. He lost sense of where he was, sinking backward, and as the water closed over him with a cold shock, he felt a sense of utter darkness and he was sure he was lost. Then, as he struggled to right himself in the water, he heard a moan as of a woman giving birth, and at that moment was revealed to him the groan of the creation in its bondage to decay.

He did not drown. He wrestled with the water until he broke loose, and as his head hit the surface, Cragg was there to haul him out.

"I did hear it!" Baars shouted, as if Cragg might not believe him. "It wasn't in my head. I actually heard the voice!"

"What voice?" Cragg said, "I didn't hear no voice. Listen, everything's all right, you're safe now."

Discussion

1. Baars' musing on the snippet of song at the start of the story implies that man's dominion over creation should bring joy to the world. In what way does that, or does that not, seem true?
2. Why is it that Baars feels like he needs a vacation even as he nears the end of his vacation?
3. Does Baars change over the course of the story? Speculate on whether his attitude toward his work might be any different when he comes home from vacation.
4. Try to think of examples from the real world that might serve as examples of the creation groaning. Relate the closing paragraphs of the story to Romans 8:22.

The Fixed

Annie Dillard

The essays in this section have, for the most part, presented ways of seeing the world. Annie Dillard demonstrates what it is like to experience the world itself, to let one's senses flow with the vigor of creation and to let one's ideas be stimulated by the divine Creator. In "The Fixed" from Pilgrim at Tinker Creek, *for which she won the Pulitzer Prize, Dillard introduces the reader to the praying mantis. In so doing, she also introduces us in a fresh way to the majesty of the created world in which we find ourselves.*

I have just learned to see praying mantis egg cases. Suddenly I see them everywhere; a tan oval of light catches my eye, or I notice a blob of thickness in a patch of slender weeds. As I write I can see the one I tied to the mock orange hedge outside my study window. It is over an inch long and shaped like a bell, or like the northern hemisphere of an egg cut through its equator. The full length of one of its long sides is affixed to a twig; the side that catches the light is perfectly flat. It has a deadstraw, deadweed color, and a curious brittle texture, hard as varnish, but pitted minutely, like frozen foam. I carried it home this afternoon, holding it carefully by the twig, along with several others— they were light as air. I dropped one without missing it until I got home and made a count.

Within the week I've seen thirty or so of these egg cases in a rose-grown field on Tinker Mountain, and another thirty in weeds along Carvin's Creek. One was on a twig of tiny dogwood on the mud lawn of a newly built house. I think the mail-order houses sell them to gardeners at a dollar apiece. It beats spraying, because each case contains between one hundred twenty-five to three hundred fifty eggs. If the eggs survive ants, woodpeckers, and mice—and most do—then you get the fun of seeing the new mantises hatch, and the smug feeling of knowing, all summer long, that they're out there in the garden devouring gruesome numbers of fellow insects all nice and organically. When a mantis has crunched up the last shred of its victim, it cleans its smooth green face like a cat.

In late summer I often see a winged adult stalking the insects that swarm about my porch light. Its body is a clear, warm green; its naked, triangular head can revolve uncannily, so that I often see one twist its head to gaze at me as it were over its shoulder. When it strikes, it jerks so suddenly and with such a fearful clatter of raised wings, that even a hardened entomologist like J. Henri Fabre confessed to being startled witless every time.

Adult mantises eat more or less everything that breathes and is small enough to capture. They eat honeybees and butterflies, including monarch butterflies. People have actually seen them seize and devour garter snakes, mice, and even *hummingbirds*. Newly hatched mantises, on the other hand, eat small creatures like aphids and each other. When I was in elementary school, one of the teachers brought in a mantis egg case in a Mason jar. I watched the newly hatched mantises emerge and shed their skins; they were spidery and translucent, all over joints. They trailed from the egg case to the base of the Mason jar in a living bridge that looked like Arabic calligraphy, some baffling text from the Koran inscribed down the air by a fine hand. Over a period of several hours, during which time the teacher never summoned the nerve or the sense to release them, they ate each other until only two were left. Tiny legs were still kicking from the mouths of both. The two survivors grappled and sawed in the Mason jar; finally both died of injuries. I felt as though I myself should swallow the corpses, shutting my eyes and washing them down like jagged pills, so all that life wouldn't be lost.

When mantises hatch in the wild, however, they straggle about prettily, dodging ants, till all are lost in the grass. So it was in hopes of seeing an eventual hatch that I pocketed my jackknife this afternoon before I set out to walk. Now that I can see the egg cases, I'm embarrassed to realize how many I must have missed all along. I walked east through the Adams' woods to the cornfield, cutting three undamaged egg cases I found at the edge of the field. It was a clear, picturesque day, a February day without clouds, without emotion or spirit, like a beautiful woman with an empty face. In my fingers I carried the thorny stems from which the egg cases hung like roses; I switched the bouquet from hand to hand, warming the free hand in a pocket. Passing the house again, deciding not to fetch gloves, I walked north to the hill by the place where the steers come to drink from Tinker Creek. There in the weeds on the hill I found another eight egg cases. I was stunned—I cross this hill several times a week, and I always look for egg cases here, because it was here that I had once seen a mantis laying her eggs.

It was several years ago that I witnessed this extraordinary procedure, but I remember, and confess, an inescapable feeling that I was watching something not real and present, but a horrible nature movie, a "secrets-of-nature" short, beautifully photographed in full color, that I had to sit through unable to look anywhere else but at the dimly lighted EXIT signs along the walls, and that behind the scenes some amateur moviemaker was congratulating himself on having stumbled across this little wonder, or even on having contrived so natural a setting, as though the whole scene had been shot very carefully in a terrarium in someone's greenhouse.

I was ambling across this hill that day when I noticed a speak of pure white. The hill is eroded; the slope is a rutted wreck of red clay broken by grassy hillocks and low wild roses whose roots clasp a pittance of topsoil. I leaned to examine the white thing and saw a mass of bubbles like spittle. Then I saw something dark like an engorged leech rummaging over the spittle, and then I saw the praying mantis.

She was upside-down, clinging to a horizontal stem of wild rose by her feet which pointed to heaven. Her head was deep in dried grass. Her abdomen was swollen like a smashed finger; it tapered to a fleshy tip out of which bubbled a wet, whipped froth. I couldn't believe my eyes. I lay on the hill this way and that, my knees in thorns and my cheeks in clay, trying to see as well as I could. I poked near the female's head with a grass; she was clearly undisturbed, so I settled my nose an inch from that pulsing abdomen. It puffed like a concertina, it throbbed like a bellows; it roved, pumping, over the glistening, clabbered surface of the egg case testing and patting, thrusting and smoothing. It seemed to act so independently that I forgot the panting brown stick at the other end. The bubble creature seemed to have two eyes, a frantic little brain, and two busy, soft hands. It looked like a hideous, harried mother slicking up a fat daughter for a beauty pageant, touching her up, slobbering over her, patting and hemming and brushing and stroking.

The male was nowhere in sight. The female had probably eaten him. Fabre says that, at least in captivity, the female will mate with and devour up to seven males, whether she has laid her egg cases or not. The mating rites of mantises are well known: a chemical produced in the head of the male insect says, in effect, "No, don't go near her, you fool, she'll eat you alive." At the same time a chemical in his abdomen says, "Yes, by all means, now and forever yes."

While the male is making up what passes for his mind, the female tips the balance in her favor by eating his head. He mounts her. Fabre describes the mating, which sometimes lasts six hours, as follows: "The male, absorbed in the performance of his vital functions, holds the female in a tight embrace. But the wretch has no head; he has no neck; he has hardly a body. The other, with her muzzle turned over her shoulder continues very placidly to gnaw what remains of the gentle swain. And, all the time, that masculine stump, holding on firmly, goes on with the business! . . . I have seen it done with my own eyes and have not yet recovered from my astonishment."

I watched the egg-laying for over an hour. When I returned the next day, the mantis was gone. The white foam had hardened and browned to a dirty suds; then, and on subsequent days, I had trouble pinpointing the case, which was only an inch or so off the ground. I checked on it every week all winter long. In the spring the ants discovered it; every week I saw dozens of ants scrambling over the sides, unable to chew a way in. Later in the spring I climbed the hill every day, hoping to catch the hatch. The leaves of the trees had long since unfolded, the butterflies were out, and the robins' first broods were fledged; still the egg case hung silent and full on the stem. I read that I should wait for June, but still I visited the case every day. One morning at the beginning of June everything was gone. I couldn't find the lower thorn in the clump of three to which the egg case was fixed. I couldn't find the clump of three. Tracks ridged the clay, and I saw the lopped stems: somehow my neighbor had contrived to run a tractor-mower over that steep clay hill on which there grew nothing to mow but a few stubby thorns.

So. Today from this same hill I cut another three undamaged cases and carried them home with the others by their twigs. I also collected a suspiciously light cynthia moth cocoon. My fingers were stiff and red with cold, and my nose ran. I had forgotten the Law of the Wild, which is, "Carry Kleenex." At home I tied the twigs with their egg cases to various sunny bushes and trees in the yard. They're easy to find because I used white string; at any rate, I'm unlikely to mow my own trees. I hope the woodpeckers that come to the feeder don't find them, but I don't see how they'd get a purchase on them if they did.

Night is rising in the valley; the creek has been extinguished for an hour, and now only the naked tips of trees fire tapers into the sky like trails of sparks. The scene that was in the back of my brain all afternoon, obscurely, is beginning to rise from night's lagoon. It really has nothing to do with praying mantises. But this afternoon I threw tiny string lashings and hitches with frozen hands, gingerly, fearing to touch the egg cases even for a minute because I remembered the Polyphemus moth.

I have no intention of inflicting all my childhood memories on any-one. Far less do I want to excoriate my old teachers who, in their bungling, unforgettable way, exposed me to the natural world, a world covered in chitin, where implacable realities hold sway. The Poly-phemus moth never made it to the past; it crawls in that crowded, pellucid pool at the lip of the great waterfall. It is as present as this blue desk and brazen lamp, as this blackened window before me in which I can no longer see even the white string that binds the egg case to the hedge, but only my own pale, astonished face.

Once, when I was ten or eleven years old, my friend Judy brought in a Polyphemus moth cocoon. It was January; there were doily snow-flakes taped to the schoolroom panes. The teacher kept the cocoon in her desk all morning and brought it out when we were getting restless before recess. In a book, we found what the adult moth would look like; it would be beautiful. With a wingspread of up to six inches, the Poly-phemus is one of the few huge American silk moths, much larger than, say, a giant or tiger swallowtail butterfly. The moth's enormous wings are velveted in a rich, warm brown, and edged in bands of blue and pink delicate as a water-color wash. A startling "eyespot," immense, and deep blue melding to an almost translucent yellow, luxuriates in the center of each hind wing. The effect is one of a masculine splendor foreign to the butterflies, a fragility unfurled to strength. The Poly-phemus moth in the picture looked like a mighty wraith, a beating essence of the hardwood forest, alien-skinned and brown, with spread, blind eyes. This was the giant moth packed in the faded cocoon. We closed the book and turned to the cocoon. It was an oak leaf sewn into a plump oval bundle; Judy had found it loose in a pile of frozen leaves.

We passed the cocoon around; it was heavy. As we held it in our hands, the creature within warmed and squirmed. We were delighted, and wrapped it tighter in our fists. The pupa began to jerk violently, in heart-stopping knocks. Who's there? I can still feel those thumps, urgent through a muffling of spun silk and leaf, urgent through the swaddling of many years, against the curve of my palm. We kept pass-ing it around, When it came to me again it was hot as a bun; it jumped half out of my hand. The teacher intervened. She put it, still heaving and banging, in the ubiquitous Mason jar.

It was coming. There was no stopping it now, January or not. One end of the cocoon dampened and gradually frayed in a furious battle. The whole cocoon twisted and slapped around in the bottom of the jar. The teacher fades, the classmates fade, I fade: I don't remember any-thing but that thing's struggle to be a moth or die trying. It emerged at last, a sodden crumple. It was a male; his long antennae were thickly plumed, as wide as his fat abdomen. His body was very thick, over an inch long, and deeply furred. A gray, furlike plush covered his head; a long, tan furlike hair hung from his wide thorax over his brown-furred, segmented abdomen. His multijointed legs, pale and powerful, were shaggy as a bear's. He stood still, but he breathed.

He couldn't spread his wings. There was no room. The chemical that coated his wings like varnish, stiffening them permanently, dried, and hardened his wings as they were. He was a monster in a Mason jar. Those huge wings stuck on his back in a torture of random pleats and folds, wrinkled as a dirty tissue, rigid as leather. They made a single nightmare clump still wracked with useless, frantic convulsions.

The next thing I remember, it was recess. The school was in Shadyside, a busy residential part of Pittsburgh. Everyone was playing dodgeball in the fenced playground or racing around the concrete schoolyard by the swings. Next to the playground a long delivery drive sloped downhill to the sidewalk and street. Someone—it must have been the teacher—had let the moth out. I was standing in the driveway, alone, stock-still, but shivering. Someone had given the Polyphemus moth his freedom, and he was walking away.

He heaved himself down the asphalt driveway by infinite degrees, unwavering. His hideous crumpled wings lay glued and rucked on his back, perfectly still now, like a collapsed tent. The bell rang twice; I had to go. The moth was receding down the driveway, dragging on. I went; I ran inside. The Polyphemus moth is still crawling down the driveway, crawling down the driveway hunched, crawling down the driveway on six furred feet, forever.

Shading the glass with a hand, I can see how shadow has pooled in the valley. It washes up the sandstone cliffs on Tinker Mountain and obliterates them in a deluge; freshets of shadow leak into the sky. I am exhausted. In Pliny I read about the invention of clay modeling. A Sicyonian potter came to Corinth. There his daughter fell in love with a young man who had to make frequent long journeys away from the city. When he sat with her at home, she used to trace the outline of his shadow that a candle's light cast on the wall. Then, in his absence she worked over the profile, deepening it, so that she might enjoy his face, and remember. One day the father slapped some potter's clay over the gouged plaster; when the clay hardened he removed it, baked it, and "showed it abroad." The story ends here. Did the boy come back? What did the girl think of her father's dragging her lover all over town by the hair? What I really want to know is this: Is the shadow still there? If I went back and found the shadow of that face there on the wall by the fireplace, I'd rip down the house with my hands for that hunk.

The shadow's the thing. Outside shadows are blue, I read, because they are lighted by the blue sky and not the yellow sun. Their blueness bespeaks infinitesimal particles scattered down inestimable distance. Muslims, whose religion bans representational art as idolatrous, don't observe the rule strictly; but they do forbid sculpture, because it casts a shadow. So shadows define the real. If I no longer see shadows as "dark marks," as do the newly sighted, then I see them as making some sort of sense of the light. They give the light distance; they put it in its place. They inform my eyes of my location here, here O Israel, here in the world's flawed sculpture, here in the flickering shade of the nothingness between me and the light.

Now that shadow has dissolved the heavens' blue dome, I can see Andromeda again; I stand pressed to the window, rapt and shrunk in the galaxy's chill glare. "Nostalgia of the Infinite," di Chirico: cast shadows stream across the sunlit courtyard, gouging canyons. There is a sense in which shadows are actually cast, hurled with a power, cast as Ishmael was cast, *out*, with a flinging force. This is the blue strip running through creation, the icy roadside stream on whose banks the mantis mates, in whose unweighed waters the giant water bug sips frogs. Shadow Creek is the blue subterranean stream that chills Carvin's Creek and Tinker Creek; it cuts like ice under the ribs of the mountains, Tinker and Dead Man. Shadow Creek storms through limestone vaults under forests, or surfaces anywhere, damp, on the underside of a leaf. I wring it from rocks; it seeps into my cup. Chasms open at the glance of an eye; the ground parts like a wind-rent cloud over stars. Shadow Creek: on my least walk to the mailbox I may find myself knee-deep in its sucking, frigid pools. I must either wear rubber boots, or dance to keep warm.

Discussion

1. One reviewer wrote of *Pilgrim at Tinker Creek* that "there is no way to avoid *seeing* again after you have read Annie Dillard" (Doris Grumbach, *The New Republic*). Part of the reason for this lies in Dillard's rhetorical achievement. How does she bring the reader onto the scene so that the reader *sees*, that is, grasps with the creative imagination and understanding as well as with the senses? Note examples of analogy and anecdote. Note also examples of figurative language, particularly use of simile.

2. Dillard's view of nature is not romantic. She sees the violence and battle in nature also. You might contrast her prose, for example, to some of the English Romantic poets of the early nineteenth century. How does this realism affect her persona? What does she assume about her audience?

3. Dillard's essay may be described as expository prose, but does she also achieve a story in it? How does she create suspense, for example?

4. Natural imagery greatly enhances some types of writing. For a writing exercise you might do a descriptive paragraph on a natural object, employing images in the description.

Writing Assignments for Chapter 10

1. Write the ecological history of a piece of land that you know well. One strategy to consider is that of writing from the perspective of an earlier inhabitant of that area. An approach similar to James C. Rettie's might also work well. Whatever you do, however, make sure that you have your facts straight; adopting a novel strategy does not give you permission to write fiction.

2. Several of the authors in this section blame our culture's environmental abuses on the Judeo-Christian worldview. Respond to that charge in an editorial written for a specific publication.

3. Consider this hypothetical situation. An avenue in your city is lined with massive oak trees, each of them over a hundred years old. The city, however, feels that the trees pose a danger to motorists and wishes to cut them down and widen the road, much to the chagrin of the local neighborhood association. Enter into the debate on this issue by writing a letter to the local newspaper arguing for or against the removal of the trees.

4. Several of the authors in this section call for an expansion of our environmental conscience. But given the nature of man, is such an expansion possible? In one sense, this is simply a more narrowly focused version of the question of whether it is possible to legislate morality. Write an essay in which you answer one or both of these questions.

11

Responding to Science

The capacity to blunder slightly is the real marvel of DNA. Without this special attribute, we would still be anaerobic bacteria and there would be no music.

—Lewis Thomas

Faith—an illogical belief in the occurrence of the improbable.

—H. L. Mencken

If the work of God could be comprehended by reason, it would be no longer wonderful.

—Pope Gregory I

For now we see in a mirror dimly, but then face to face. Now I know in part; then I shall understand fully, even as I have been fully understood.

—1 Corinthians 13:12

Science carries us into zones of speculation, where there is no habitable city for the mind of man.

—Robert Louis Stevenson

It is perhaps inevitable that the disciplines of science and religion should be in conflict at times. To some degree they do attempt to answer some of the same basic questions. Both treat the origins of the

239

universe; both address the nature of man; both speculate on the future of mankind. Yet both operate very differently. Where religion demands spiritual faith, science demands empirical knowledge. And so, despite their common interests, the two often stand at odds, looking in different directions for the answers to these similarly basic questions. Yet we question whether such a split is necessary.

One modern scientist who has contributed significantly to widening the split between science and religion is Francis Crick, a winner of the Nobel Prize in Medicine in 1962 for his work in DNA molecular structure. Shortly after receiving the award, Crick set forth his views on scientific inquiry in *Of Molecules and Men* (Seattle: University of Washington Press, 1966). Here Crick announces his "great news" that life evolved according to Darwinian principles and "that we need not involve a special 'life force' or 'intelligence' to direct this process." Thus Crick dispenses with *vitalism*, any concept of divinely ordained and directed life, in favor of explaining "all biology in terms of physics and chemistry." Vitalism, he argues, has been an excuse, a way of explaining what we don't know, but excuses are no longer necessary as the mysteries of life are rolled back in the laboratory: "When facts come in the door, vitalism flies out the window."

Crick is pleased to open the window wide. The first thing he wants to throw out of the classroom, for example, is religion. God didn't ordain life, according to Crick. Life occurred "by chance." Furthermore, he writes, "I . . . believe that the soul is imaginary." Therefore Crick concludes that "it is also regrettable that there is so much religious teaching . . . since much of this instruction, from the point of view of most educated men, is utter nonsense. . . ." It is interesting that he also wants to toss literature out of the modern educational system.

But, other scientists question, doesn't this make of science a kind of end in itself, a "sacred cow" as the chemist Anthony Standen says in his book *Science as a Sacred Cow*? Or, as C. S. Lewis argues, have we simply created a new religion called Scientism? Listen to one of this century's greatest scientists on this subject.

"You will hardly find one among the profounder sort of scientific minds," writes Albert Einstein, "without a religious feeling of his own." But what does this eminent thinker mean by "religious feeling"? Should we take this to mean that the popularly conceived schism between science and religion has been closed, that science is a means to faith? Such seems to be Einstein's intention, but the Christian needs to take exception to the claim, for the "religious feeling" of the scientist may be religious only in the loosest sense of that term, indicating, at best, a deistic sense of awe. Einstein explains that the feeling that keeps the scientist from selfishness "takes the form of a rapturous amazement at the harmony of natural law, which reveals an intelligence of such superiority that, compared with it, all the systematic thinking and acting of human beings is an utterly insignificant reflection." Here indeed seems to be worship of the "sacred cow," the advent of the new religion of Scientism.

If Christians take exception to Einstein's synthesis of science and religion, they should, nevertheless, appreciate his attempt at reconciliation. Despite the commonly held view, perhaps bolstered by widely publicized debates on creation and evolution, the two disciplines are neither incompatible nor independent. No doubt both non-Christian scientists and Christians have prolonged this misconception—the former by postulating unwarranted metaphysical views not based on scientific evidence and the latter by refusing to consider evidence.

As we approach scientific issues, we discover that our Lord has not left us without guidance. The Bible doesn't speak only of sacred matters, leaving us to decipher the secular on our own. Nor does it teach us to ignore our world to concentrate only on spiritual mysteries. On the contrary, although it does not offer a systematic treatment of scientific reality, it does present a framework in which to understand the origin and purpose of the material world. We know not only that Christ "is the image of the invisible God," but also that "in him all things were created," that "he is before all things, and in him all things hold together" (Col. 1:15–17).

Religion and Science

Albert Einstein

> *Best known for the discovery of the theory of relativity, Albert Einstein is known popularly as a scientist rather than a philosopher. Yet his theoretical work led him again and again to consider issues that involved disciplines other than physics. He wrote and spoke on such topics as epistemology, religion, economics, politics, and education. In this essay written for the* New York Times Magazine *in 1930, he categorizes religion and differentiates it from science according to its function.*

Everything that the human race has done and thought is concerned with the satisfaction of deeply felt needs and the assuagement of pain. One has to keep this constantly in mind if one wishes to understand spiritual movements and their development. Feeling and longing are the motive force behind all human endeavor and human creation, in however exalted a guise the latter may present themselves to us. Now what are the feelings and needs that have led men to religious thought and belief in the widest sense of the words? A little consideration will suffice to show us that the most varying emotions preside over the birth of religious thought and experience. With primitive man it is above all fear that evokes religious notions—fear of hunger, wild beasts, sickness, death. Since at this stage of existence understanding of causal connections is usually poorly developed, the human mind creates illusory beings more or less analogous to itself on whose wills and actions these fearful happenings depend. Thus one tries to secure the favor of these beings by carrying out actions and offering sacrifices which, according to the tradition handed down from generation to generation, propitiate them or make them well disposed toward a mortal. In this sense I am speaking of a religion of fear. This, though not created, is in an important degree stabilized by the formation of a special priestly caste which sets itself up as a mediator between the people and the beings they fear, and erects a hegemony on this basis. In many cases a leader or ruler or a privileged class whose position rests on other factors combines priestly functions with its secular authority in order to make the latter more secure; or the political rulers and the priestly caste make common cause in their own interests.

The social impulses are another source of the crystallization of religion. Fathers and mothers and the leaders of larger human communities are mortal and fallible. The desire for guidance, love, and support prompts men to form the social or moral conception of God. This is the God of Providence, who protects, disposes, rewards, and punishes; the God who, according to the limits of the believer's outlook, loves and cherishes the life of the tribe or of the human race, or even life itself; the comforter in sorrow and unsatisfied longing; he who preserves the souls of the dead. This is the social or moral conception of God.

The Jewish scriptures admirably illustrate the development from the religion of fear to moral religion, a development continued in the New Testament. The religions of all civilized peoples, especially the peoples of the Orient, are primarily moral religions. The development from a religion of fear to moral religion is a great step in peoples' lives. And yet, that primitive religions are based entirely on fear and the religions of civilized peoples purely on morality is a prejudice against which we must be on our guard. The truth is that all religions are a varying blend of both types, with this differentiation; that on the higher levels of social life the religion of morality predominates.

Common to all these types is the anthropomorphic character of their conception of God. In general, only individuals of exceptional endowments, and exceptionally high-minded communities, rise to any considerable extent above this level. But there is a third stage of religious experience which belongs to all of them, even though it is rarely found in a pure form: I shall call it cosmic religious feeling. It is very difficult to elucidate this feeling to anyone who is entirely without it, especially as there is no anthropomorphic conception of God corresponding to it.

The individual feels the futility of human desires and aims and the sublimity and marvelous order which reveal themselves both in nature and in the world of thought. Individual existence impresses him as a sort of prison and he wants to experience the universe as a single significant whole. The beginnings of cosmic religious feeling already appear at an early stage of development, e.g., in many of the Psalms of David and in some of the Prophets. Buddhism, as we have learned especially from the wonderful writings of Schopenhauer, contains a much stronger element of this.

The religious geniuses of all ages have been distinguished by this kind of religious feeling, which knows no dogma and no God conceived in man's image; so that there can be no church whose central teachings are based on it. Hence it is precisely among the heretics of every age that we find men who were filled with this highest kind of religious feeling and were in many cases regarded by their contemporaries as atheists, sometimes also as saints. Looked at in this light, men like Democritus, Francis of Assisi, and Spinoza are closely akin to one another.

How can cosmic religious feeling be communicated from one person to another, if it can give rise to no definite notion of a God and no theology? In my view, it is the most important function of art and science to awaken this feeling and keep it alive in those who are receptive to it.

We thus arrive at a conception of the relation of science to religion very different from the usual one. When one views the matter historically, one is inclined to look upon science and religion as irreconcilable antagonists, and for a very obvious reason. The man who is thoroughly convinced of the universal operation of the law of causation cannot for a moment entertain the idea of a being who interferes in the course of events—provided, of course, that he takes the hypothesis of causality really seriously. He has no use for the religion of fear and equally little for social or moral religion. A God who rewards and punishes is inconceivable to him for the simple reason that a man's actions are determined by necessity, external and internal, so that in God's eyes he cannot be responsible, any more than an inanimate object is responsible for the motions it undergoes. Science has therefore been charged with undermining morality, but the charge is unjust. A man's ethical behavior should be based effectually on sympathy, education, and social ties and needs; no religious basis is necessary. Man would indeed be in a poor way if he had to be restrained by fear of punishment and hope of reward after death.

It is, therefore easy to see why the churches have always fought science and persecuted its devotees. On the other hand, I maintain that the cosmic religious feeling is the strongest and noblest motive for scientific research. Only those who realize the immense efforts and, above all, the devotion without which pioneer work in theoretical science cannot be achieved are able to grasp the strength of the emotion out of which alone such work, remote as it is from the immediate realities of life, can issue. What a deep conviction of the rationality of the universe and what a yearning to understand, were it but a feeble reflection of the mind revealed in this world, Kepler and Newton must have had to enable them to spend years of solitary labor in disentangling the principles of celestial mechanics? Those whose acquaintance with scientific research is derived chiefly from its practical results easily develop a completely false notion of the mentality of the men who, surrounded by a skeptical world, have shown the way to kindred spirits scattered wide through the world and the centuries. Only one who has devoted his life to similar ends can have a vivid realization of what has inspired these men and given them the strength to remain true to their purpose in spite of countless failures. It is cosmic religious feeling that gives a man such strength. A contemporary has said, not unjustly, that in this materialistic age of ours the serious scientific workers are the only profoundly religious people.

Discussion

1. Explain what Einstein understands as the three varieties of religions. How would you respond to his assertion that "the Jewish scriptures admirably illustrate the development from the religion of fear to moral religion, a development continued in the New Testament"? How does his use of the word *admirably* affect the tone of the statement?
2. Is your conception of God anthropomorphic? Is that good or bad?
3. Like many proponents of Eastern religions, Einstein claims that the purest form of religious experience transcends an "anthropomorphic conception of God." How would you counter such a claim of superior religious experience?
4. What, according to Einstein, is the relationship between religion and science? Do you agree? How would you define the relationship? List ways that the two disciplines might complement each other and ways that they might antagonize each other.

Natural Selection

Charles Darwin

> *Few scientific writers have stirred as much discussion as Charles Darwin. His book* On the Origin of Species *revolutionized the way scientists perceive the natural world and influenced the way some social philosophers perceive relationships among people. Darwin's theory, as the subtitle of his book suggests, explored the origins of species "By Means of Natural Selection or the Preservation of Favoured Races in the Struggle for Life." In the passage that follows, he attempts to illustrate how natural selection works.*

In order to make it clear how, as I believe, natural selection acts, I must beg permission to give one or two imaginary illustrations. Let us take the case of a wolf, which preys on various animals, securing some by craft, some by strength, and some by fleetness; and let us suppose that the fleetest prey, a deer for instance, had from any change in the country increased in numbers, or that other prey had decreased in numbers, during that season of the year when the wolf was hardest pressed for food. Under such circumstances the swiftest and slimmest wolves would have the best chance of surviving and so be preserved or selected,—provided always that they retained strength to master their prey at this or some other period of the year, when they were compelled to prey on other animals. I can see no more reason to doubt that this would be the result, than that man should be able to improve the fleetness of his greyhounds by careful and methodical selection, or by that kind of unconscious selection which follows from each man trying to keep the best dogs without any thought of modifying the breed. I may add, that, according to Mr. Pierce, there are two varieties of the wolf inhabiting the Catskill Mountains, in the United States, one with a light greyhound-like form, which pursues deer, and the other more bulky, with shorter legs, which more frequently attacks the shepherd's flocks.

It should be observed that, in the above illustration, I speak of the slimmest individual wolves, and not of any single strongly-marked variation having been preserved. In former editions of this work I sometimes spoke as if this latter alternative had frequently occurred. I saw the great importance of individual differences, and this led me fully to discuss the results of unconscious selection by man, which depends on the preservation of all the more or less valuable individuals, and on the destruction of the worst. I saw, also, that the preservation in a state of nature of any occasional deviation of structure, such as a monstrosity, would be a rare event; and that if at first preserved, it would generally be lost by subsequent intercrossing with ordinary individuals. Nevertheless, until reading an able and valuable article in the "North British Review" (1867), I did not appreciate how rarely single variations, whether slight or strongly marked, could be perpetuated. The author takes the case of a pair of animals, producing during their lifetime two hundred offspring, of which, from various causes of destruction, only two on an average survive to procreate their kind. This is rather an extreme estimate for most of the higher animals, but by no means so for many of the lower organisms. He then shows that if a single individual were born, which varied in some manner, giving it twice as good a chance of life as that of the other individuals, yet the chances would be strongly against its survival. Supposing it to survive and to breed, and that half its young inherited the favourable variation; still, as the Reviewer goes on to show, the young would have only a slightly better chance of surviving and breeding; and this chance would go on decreasing in the succeeding generations. The justice of these remarks cannot, I think, be disputed. If, for instance, a bird of some kind could procure its food more easily by having its beak curved, and if one were born with its beak strongly curved, and which consequently flourished, nevertheless there would be a very poor chance of this one individual perpetuating its kind to the exclusion of the common form; but there can hardly be a doubt, judging by what we see taking place under domestication, that this result would follow from the preservation during many generations of a large number of individuals with more or less strongly curved beaks, and from the destruction of a still larger number with the straightest beaks.

It should not, however, be overlooked that certain rather strongly marked variations, which no one would rank as mere individual differences, frequently recur owing to a similar organisation being similarly acted on—of which fact numerous instances could be given with our domestic productions. In such cases, if the varying individual did not actually transmit to its offspring its newly-acquired character, it would undoubtedly transmit to them, as long as the existing conditions remained the same, a still stronger tendency to vary in the same manner. There can also be a little doubt that the tendency to vary in the same manner has often been so strong that all the individuals of the same species have been similarly modified without the aid of any form of selection. Or only a third, fifth, or tenth part of the individuals may have been thus affected, of which fact several instances could be given. Thus Graba estimates that about one-fifth of the guillemots in the Faroe Islands consist of a variety so well marked, that it was formerly ranked as a distinct species under the name of Uria lacrymans. In cases of this kind, if the variation were of a beneficial nature, the original form would soon be supplanted by the modified form, through the survival of the fittest.

To the effects of intercrossing in eliminating variations of all kinds, I shall have to recur; but it may be here remarked that most animals and plants keep to their proper homes, and do not needlessly wander about; we see this even with migratory birds, which almost always return to the same spot. Consequently each newly-formed variety would generally be at first local, as seems to be the common rule with varieties in a state of nature; so that similarly modified individuals would soon exist in a small body together, and would often breed together. If the new variety were successful in its battle for life, it would slowly spread from a central district, competing with and conquering the unchanged individuals on the margins of an ever-increasing circle.

It may be worth while to give another and more complex illustration of the action of natural selection. Certain plants excrete sweet juice, apparently for the sake of eliminating something injurious from the sap: this is effected, for instance, by glands at the base of the stipules in some Leguminosae, and at the backs of the leaves of the common laurel. This juice, though small in quantity, is greedily sought by insects; but their visits do not in any way benefit the plant. Now, let us suppose that the juice or nectar was excreted from the inside of the flowers of a certain number of plants of any species. Insects in seeking the nectar would get dusted with pollen, and would often transport it from one flower to another. The flowers of two distinct individuals of the same species would thus get crossed; and the act of crossing, as can be fully proved, gives rise to vigorous seedlings which consequently would have the best chance of flourishing and surviving. The plants which produced flowers with the largest glands or nectaries, excreting most nectar, would oftenest be visited by insects, and would oftenest be crossed; and so in the long-run would gain the upper hand and form a local variety. The flowers, also, which had their stamens and pistils placed, in relation to the size and habits of the particular insects which visited them, so as to favour in any degree the transportal of the pollen, would likewise be favoured. We might have taken the case of insects visiting flowers for the sake of collecting pollen instead of nectar; and as pollen is formed for the sole purpose of fertilisation, its destruction appears to be a simple loss to the plant; yet if a little pollen were carried, at first occasionally and then habitually, by the pollen-devouring insects from flower to flower, and a cross thus effected, although nine-tenths of the pollen were destroyed it might still be a great gain to the plant to be thus robbed; and the individuals which produced more and more pollen, and had larger anthers, would be selected.

When our plant, by the above process long continued, had been rendered highly attractive to insects, they would, unintentionally on their part, regularly carry pollen from flower to flower; and that they do this effectually, I could easily show by many striking facts. I will give only one, as likewise illustrating one step in the separation of the sexes of plants. Some holly-trees bear only male flowers, which have four stamens producing a rather small quantity of pollen, and a rudimentary pistil: other holly-trees bear only female flowers; these have a full-sized pistil, and four stamens with shrivelled anthers, in which not a grain of pollen can be detected. Having found a female tree exactly sixty yards from a male tree, I put the stigmas of twenty flowers, taken from different branches, under the microscope, and on all, without exception, there were a few pollen-grains, and on some a profusion. As the wind had set for several days from the female to the male tree, the pollen could not thus have been carried. The weather had been cold and boisterous, and therefore not favourable to bees, nevertheless every female flower which I examined had been effectually fertilised by the bees, which had flown from tree to tree in search of nectar. But to return to our imaginary case: as soon as the plant had been rendered so highly attractive to insects that pollen was regularly carried from flower to flower, another process might commence. No naturalist doubts the advantage of what has been called the "physiological division of labour"; hence we may believe that it would be advantageous to a plant to produce stamens alone in one flower or on one whole plant, and pistils alone in another flower or on another plant. In plants under culture and placed under new conditions of life, sometimes the male organs and sometimes the female organs become more or less impotent; now if we suppose this to occur in ever so slight a degree under nature, then, as pollen is already carried regularly from flower to flower, and as a more complete separation of the sexes of our plant would be advantageous on the principle of the division of labour, individuals with this tendency more and more increased, would be continually favoured or selected, until at last a complete separation of the sexes might be effected. It would take up too much space to show the various steps, through dimorphism and other means, by which the separation of the sexes in plants of various kinds is apparently now in progress; but I may add that some of the species of holly in North America, are, according to Asa Gray, in an exactly intermediate condition, or, as he expresses it, are more or less dioeciously polygamous.

Let us now turn to the nectar-feeding insects; we may suppose the plant, of which we have been slowly increasing the nectar by continued selection, to be a common plant; and that certain insects depended in main part on its nectar for food. I could give many facts showing how anxious bees are to save time: for instance, their habit of cutting holes and sucking the nectar at the bases of certain flowers, which, with a very little more trouble, they can enter by the mouth. Bearing such facts in mind, it may be believed that under certain circumstances individual differences in the curvature or length of the proboscis, etc., too slight to be appreciated by us, might profit a bee or other insect, so that certain individuals would be able to obtain their food more quickly than others; and thus the communities to which they belonged would flourish and throw off many swarms inheriting the same peculiarities. The tubes of the corolla of the common red and incarnate clovers (Trifolium pratense and incarnatum) do not on a hasty glance appear to differ in length; yet the hive-bee can easily suck the nectar out of the incarnate clover, but not out of the common red clover, which is visited by humble-bees alone; so that whole fields of red clover offer in vain an abundant supply of precious nectar to the hive-bee. That this nectar is much liked by the hive-bee is certain; for I have repeatedly seen, but only in the autumn, many hive-bees sucking the flowers through holes bitten in the base of the tube by humble-bees. The difference in the length of the corolla in the two kinds of clover, which determines the visits of the hive-bee, must be very trifling; for I have been assured that when red clover has been mown, the flowers of the second crop are somewhat smaller, and that these are visited by many hive-bees. I do not know whether this statement is accurate; nor whether another published statement can be trusted, namely, that the Ligurian bee which is generally considered a mere variety of the common hive-bee, and which freely crosses with it, is able to reach and suck the nectar of the red clover. Thus, in a country where this kind of clover abounded, it might be a great advantage to the hive-bee to have a slightly longer or differently constructed proboscis. On the other hand, as the fertility of this clover absolutely depends on bees visiting the flowers, if humble-bees were to become rare in any country, it might be a great advantage to the plant to have a shorter or more deeply divided corolla, so that the hive-bees should be enabled to suck its flowers. Thus I can understand how a flower and a bee might slowly become, either simultaneously or one after the other, modified and adapted to each other in the most perfect manner, by the continued preservation of all the individuals which presented slight deviations of structure mutually favourable to each other.

I am well aware that this doctrine of natural selection, exemplified in the above imaginary instances, is open to the same objections which were first urged against Sir Charles Lyell's noble views on "the modern changes of the earth, as illustrative of geology"; but we now seldom hear the agencies which we see at work, spoken of as trifling or insignificant, when used in explaining the excavation of the deepest valleys or the formation of long lines of inland cliffs. Natural selection acts only by the preservation and accumulation of small inherited modifications, each profitable to the preserved being; and as modern geology has almost banished such views as the excavation of a great valley by a single diluvial wave, so will natural selection banish the belief of the continued creation of new organic beings, or of any great and sudden modification in their structure.

Discussion

1. At one point Darwin refers to "the battle for life," revealing his assumption that life is essentially a struggle. Individual competes with individual; species competes with species. Do you agree with this assumption? Is it true for humans as well as for all organisms?

2. Darwin bases his theory of the origin of life on his observations of mutations. Can you reconcile his observations of the adaptation of organisms with the model of a created world?

3. In several places here, Darwin refers to animals or to natural phenomena in human terms. For example, he notes that the bees are "greedy" and that they are "anxious . . . to save time." The technical term for this practice is *anthropomorphism*. Can you find other instances of this type of reference? What effect does anthropomorphism have on Darwin's argument? Does it help or hinder it?

And the Trees Clap Their Hands

Virginia Stem Owens

While many Christians seek to distinguish the domains of science and religion, Virginia Stem Owens explores their common ground. Her effort is unique in that most such interdisciplinary efforts move in the direction of Eastern mysticism. Owens, on the other hand, draws on the mysteries inherent in a Christian model of creation and on biblical revelation to explore the metaphysics of the new physics.

From the moment of birth, each human creature embarks upon a lifelong task of figuring out the world. Even as he sucks in his first gulp of the world's air, he encounters a creation that constantly threatens to overwhelm his small craft of intelligence with the waves of stimuli that batter his brain in an unremitting storm. How is he ever to make sense of it all? Is there any sense to be made of it, or is there only the chaos of constant random motion? Is the meaning we make of it only a thin membrane we stretch to hold the world, precariously and provisionally, together?

The infant lives in the midst of a riot, a welter of physical stimuli. Yet if he intends to set up housekeeping on this shore where he's been so unaccountably cast up, he must, Crusoe-like, begin to construct some kind of shelter for his consciousness, a structure that will order the raw sensory stimuli.

Physics is one way of figuring out the world. It tries to wrestle down samples of the world long enough to discover what it's made of and how it works. All in all, it's a satisfying method. It gives one a sense of really getting to the root of things. But there are questions that come up in the course of pursuing matter that demand decisions. Where does one begin, for example—or end, for that matter? If one is eventually able to identify the ingredients in the cosmic cake, does that mean the recipe is equal to the reality? These annoyances that accompany figuring out the world are called metaphysics. The decisions these kinds of questions demand may be made offhandedly, desperately, or in a fit of pique. The important point is that they *are* made, and as soon as that happens, the investigator has committed himself, whether he acknowledges it or not, to certain assumptions. There is no physics without a corresponding metaphysics. One cannot even begin without deciding to begin. It is metaphysics that determines the very question about the physical world that an individual or an age allows itself to ask.

The evidence of this indissoluble connection between physics and metaphysics has in fact been documented by contemporary historians of science, who have traced it back at least as far as the pre-Socratic Greeks. Whether a culture has committed itself to a world view that emphasizes isolation, variety, and disjunction or to one that stresses unity, consonance, and correlation shows up not only in its science but also in its politics, economics, art, and spiritual enterprises.

For a good many generations, however, these annoying metaphysical decisions have been made mostly by default, and afterwards deliberately ignored. Their existence as a necessary part of the scientific undertaking has even been denied. Science, full of its intellectual oats and expanding its territory exponentially with new discoveries, grew fretful under the steady demands of its slower-paced partner. It tried to shake itself loose from its inconvenient alliance with metaphysics, like a successful businessman shedding his dowdy wife. The question of what the world "meant" was dismissed as not only irrelevant but impertinent. The only business of physics was to describe whatever was there, not to make judgments about it.

Then, unaccountably and almost with the perfect timing of poetic justice, the world began to dissolve in the hands of the scientists, to run through their fingers like water. The more fiercely they wrestled with the world, the closer they looked at the stuff it was made of, the further it receded from their grasp. No sooner had they concocted one way of describing it than it turned another and unexpected face toward them. The world, it appeared, was made of no-thing at all. Just an ultimately elusive sort of energy. Loren Eiseley has even reported that one poor fellow was driven to wearing snowshoes day and night so that he wouldn't fall through the insubstantial world. Today physicists continue to invent new names for the myriad "particles" they discover—clever and intriguing names such as "quark" and "strange"—but they hesitate to call them "things." They are more accurately described as necessary parts of a thought process.

For the first time in any of our lifetimes, physics has become flagrantly and self-consciously metaphysical. Ever since matter turned coy with its pursuers, physicists have had to coax it with questions of meaning. Indeed, interpretation is now such an integral part of the new physicists' understanding of the universe that it can no longer be ignored or made a mere philosophical afterthought to the description of the basic structure of being.

For centuries science has tried to operate as though the world and our understanding of it could be kept in two separate compartments. In one compartment were the bare facts; in another were the fairy tales those so inclined made up to explain why the facts were as they were. This included not only religion and poems and legends, but also the remnants of a good many civilizations that had wrecked themselves against the superior solidity of the scientific method.

The new physics, however, can no longer properly recognize such distinctions between kinds of truth. It tells us that, if we can know anything at all about the world, it is that everything is related to everything else. Truth cannot be compartmentalized. The implications of this are yet to be felt by a society that insists science and spirituality are separate disciplines to be pursued in separate facilities so that one may not contaminate the other.

Most of the metaphysics of this movement in science has so far taken a decidedly Eastern tone, as one can tell from the titles of the books published on the subject—*The Tao of Physics*, for example, and *The Dancing Wu Li Masters*. Even Fred Wolf in his award-winning book, *Taking the Quantum Leap*, claims that an understanding of the new physics should change one's life forever, in much the way we expect a religious conversion to alter one's perceptions.

Needless to say, Christians in this country have not exactly found the implications of the new physics a burning issue. Among Protestants, in fact, knowledge of the natural world has never been a high priority, and "natural theology" has been an empty category. They have taken as their touchstone the biblical pronouncement that the flesh availeth nothing, and thus have sought to approach the spirit directly, unmediated by matter. Even the sole mediation of Christ between God and humankind is understood as an entirely spiritual transaction, having nothing to do with matter.

All the natural imagery of Scripture that calls for creation to participate in the praise of its maker has been demoted to the level of mere metaphor and decorative figures of speech, or else seen as unfortunate vestiges of a primitive people's animism. For ever since the age of Newton and the classical laws of physics, civilized folk have agreed that matter is essentially a manipulable machine. No "spirit" or knowledge was observed to inhabit matter, regardless of the psalmist's assertion that the heavens proclaim the glory of God, that the day pours forth speech and the night declares knowledge. And Christians, as creatures of their culture, have been content to bump along with Newtonian laws of motion, adding an occasional vague reference to Einstein and the relativity of time and space.

To be sure, we have continued to beat the dead horse of the Enlightenment, blaming its intellectual errors for the immorality and arrogance of the secularism under which we all stoop today. But at the same time we have been only too eager to profit from the products such a pragmatically based science turns out. We have failed to see that by consuming the fruits of a science that denies the permeation of matter with meaning, we too have acquiesced in a science that leaves the world for dead.

Even the moralistic stewardship-of-the-earth understanding of our relation to the world reinforces this science to some extent. It reduces creation to capital, assets for us to expend as prudent market analysts. Protecting something we call the environment, like the moralistic monitors of society, simply leaves us with the unenviable job of keeping unruly exploiters in line. Thus we are tolerated because we provide a useful balance for society.

At present, however, the scientific community is preparing to line up on entirely different issues. On the one hand are those who see matter as fundamentally dead and dumb, inhabiting an equally dead void of space. Often they are the very ones who are intent on the possibilities of finding extraterrestrial life somewhere, out there, in space. The matter they see right here on earth, of which they themselves are made, they assume follows basic mechanical laws, completely passive under scientific investigation, with no "mind of its own." Any mysterious goings-on observed in it they dismiss as mysticism and folderol.

On the other hand are those scientists who have reason to suspect that matter itself is at some level sentient, informed with knowledge. In other words, that we are living in an at least potentially conscious cosmos.

Those in this second group find themselves unprovided with ways of thinking about such possibilities, except as they discover them in Eastern religions. The Christian tradition, even among Catholics, has almost abandoned the pursuit of God in the world's flesh. Whereas it used to be imperative for theologians to know as much as possible about the nature of matter, physical theories of the universe have become less and less cogent to theology.

Nevertheless, the Christian tradition does have means (buried pretty deep by now, to be sure) to appropriate new ways of figuring out the world. It was the Church, after all, that insisted no model of the universe, neither Galileo's nor Ptolemy's, could ever be equated with its total reality. But an age intent on the pragmatic side of science, on learning how to manipulate the controls of what it perceived as a vast machine, discarded that kind of intellectual rigor. Consequently, over the centuries, the Church, too, has almost forgotten its own concern for precision of thought and purity of science. Presented with a new model of the universe, it finds itself without a means of taking in this fresh, demechanized possibility. It cannot seem to lay its hands on the old treasures of thought it long ago put away as outdated and impractical.

The perceptual merits of the discipline of Zen, however, are readily apparent. The initial encounter with an imported spirituality foreign to one's culture can indeed shock the sensibilities into attending to reality in a new way. But the past, as the new physics itself testifies, is not so easily disposed of. The intellectual traditions and the imagery of the Christian Church are too closely intertwined with science to be torn asunder in such a cavalier fashion.

Yet unless we want to continue with the same religion/science schizophrenia our society has been supporting through the past few centuries, we need to incorporate somehow the fresh data the new physics is offering. . . .

Only a full embrace of the Incarnation can open our eyes to its interpenetration of all being, its redemption of the whole cosmos, which is the biblical claim. To see ourselves as separate and distinct from the physical world is our terrible inheritance from the Manichees. Such a heresy leads to the enormous excesses of our current technology.

The task begins with answering one of those annoying questions science thought it had left behind: how important is matter? The Manichean contempt for matter that early infected the Church still plagues it today, and indeed undermines all areas of human endeavor. We continue to imagine that we can exist as disembodied intelligences. The resurrection of the body has only the dimmest possible meaning for us. Such contempt for creation lays the groundwork for an unwitting alliance between religious spiritualizers, whether of the demythologizing or the supposedly literalist school, and a science that would have us believe that matter itself is dead and thus would strip everything "merely" material of significance. Even, ultimately, ourselves.

In a secular society such as ours, devoted to de-sacramentalizing and de-carnating the world, the very concept of "holy" becomes an empty category. Yet this vacuum cannot now be replenished by going back to a dualistic understanding of a "spiritual" world over against a "physical" world. It is not a case of mind over matter because mind *is* matter, and no less hallowed for that. As Owen Barfield has insisted, we can no longer be satisfied with a "religious" truth that fails to implicate matter—and vice versa.

An explication of the new physics that is only discursive, however, fails to give any indication of the urgency, elegance, and richness of the subject. It cannot show how all of life must incandesce and pulsate with this understanding of the universe that is growing in travail. We live a cosmic drama just by opening our eyes and metabolizing carbohydrates, and it is imperative to engage matter on those terms. . . .

I declare that the prophet's figure of trees clapping their hands is a living reality and that Paul's image of living Christ's life is simultaneously symbol and fact. This is the reality of matter we have not dared to dream. To declare this reality one must allow one's own life to flow into this tributary of testimony.

Discussion

1. Diction is an important component of style. Find examples of places where Owens's word choice helps her accomplish her purpose of identifying the errors of the past. Notice also her use of figurative language and its contribution to the tone of the essay.
2. Owens accuses the environmental movement of reducing "creation to capital." Do you agree with her assessment? Speculate on what her stance on environmental issues might be.
3. Respond to her statement that "only a full embrace of the Incarnation can open our eyes to its interpenetration of all being, its redemption of the whole cosmos, which is the biblical claim."
4. Try to define your own metaphysics by listing what is real and what is unreal in our world. Where does God fit in your scheme?

"Faith" Is a Fine Invention

Emily Dickinson

> *Emily Dickinson's poetry intrigues because it does so well what all poetry is supposed to do—to compress ideas into a specialized form and to charge the language with new meanings so that the reader is forced to think about experience in a new way. Here, in just sixteen words, she raises basic questions of faith and reason.*

"Faith" is a fine invention
When Gentlemen can *see*—
But *Microscopes* are prudent
In an Emergency.

Discussion

1. Before you can respond completely to this poem, you must decide what the tone of the piece is. Based on the diction (the words used) what do you think Dickinson's attitudes are toward religion and science?
2. Reared in a Calvinist family, Dickinson knew the Bible well. Do any biblical passages on seeing or sight add to the meaning of the poem? What kind of sight do you think she refers to here?
3. How does this notion of faith compare with the definition in Hebrews 11?
4. Another way to focus consideration of the issues of this poem is to compare our attitudes toward medical treatment. Does your reading of this poem change if you read it in that context? What would you say to someone who believed only in divine healing? What would you say to someone who trusted only human medical care?

In Defense of Pain

Philip Yancey

During the last few years Philip Yancey has written extensively about medical treatment of pain. His research into recent scientific discoveries about human physiology leads inevitably to spiritual issues. In this essay Yancey ponders the unsettling premise: pain has immense value, both physiologically and spiritually. A regular contributor to Christianity Today, *Philip Yancey has published several hundred articles and three books.*

The well-known German pastor and theologian Helmut Thielicke was once asked what was the greatest problem he had observed in the United States. He replied, "They have an inadequate view of suffering."

Ask any group of college students what they have against Christianity, and they'll likely echo variations on the theme of suffering: "I can't believe in a God who would allow Auschwitz and Vietnam"; "My teen-age sister died of leukemia despite all the Christians' prayers"; "One-third of the world went to bed hungry last night—how does that fit in with your Christianity?"

The problem of pain keeps popping up. Like Hercules' battle against the hydra, all our attempts to chop down arguments are met with writhing new examples of suffering. And the Christian's defense usually sounds like an apology (not in the classic theological sense of a well-reasoned defense, but in the red-faced, foot-shuffling, lowered-head sense of embarrassment).

I have never read a poem extolling the virtues of pain, nor seen a statue erected in its honor, nor heard a hymn dedicated to it. Pain is usually defined as "unpleasantness." In a dark, secret moment, many Christians would probably concede that pain was God's mistake. He really should have worked harder and invented a better way of alerting us to the world's dangers. I am convinced that pain gets a bad press.

Perhaps we *should* see statues, hymns, and poems to pain. Up close, under a microscope, the pain network is seen in an entirely different dimension.

In our embarrassment over the problem of pain, we seem to have forgotten a central fact which has been repeatedly brought to my attention by Dr. Paul Brand, a missionary surgeon who heads the rehabilitation branch of America's only leprosarium. "If I had one gift which I could give to people with leprosy, it would be the gift of pain," Dr. Brand says.

The gift of pain. An alien, paradoxical concept. One that might never have occurred to us but, as we shall see, one that flows naturally from the experience of a surgeon who treats leprosy victims.

Seen from this viewpoint, pain, like man and nature, is an essentially good creation which has been bent in the Fall. It fits neatly into the cosmic Christian scheme.

Consider earth, which brightly mirrors the handiwork of God: brilliant hues and delicate shadings of a sunset or a rainbow; the roiling foam and spray of a dependable ocean tide; the magnificent abstract designs on butterflies—ten thousand wild variations, all compressed into tiny swatches of flying fabric. Yet the sun which lavishes the sky with color can bake African soil into a dry, cracked glaze which may doom millions of people. The pounding, steady rhythm of a surf can, when fomented by a storm, roll in as a twenty-foot wall of death, obliterating towns, villages, even countries. And the harmless swatches of color which spend their lifetimes fluttering among flowers are snatched and destroyed in the daily, bloody ferocity of nature's life cycles. The world, though God's showplace, is also a rebel fortress. It is a good thing, bent.

Consider man: the country which produced Bach, Beethoven, Luther, Goethe, and Brahms also gave us Hitler, Eichmann, Goering. The country which fathered the Constitution of the United States brought us Watergate. In all of us, streaks of brilliance, creativity, talent, and compassion jostle with deceit, selfishness, and cruelty.

And so it is with pain. The nervous system which carries it makes possible man's noblest works. Have you ever watched a concert violinist? Each time his finger lowers on a string he has controlled the synchronized movement of a dozen muscles, supported by the balanced tension of scores of others. His fingers fly through the twelve positions, now falling with power and surety, now searching delicately for a harmonic on the E string, now plucking a loud pizzicato. The nervous system, with its intricate variations of pressure sensations, makes possible his performance.

Of course, you might say, the nervous system has good built within it. But what about when the circuits are shorted out, when a piercing shot of pain races to the brain, drowning the meek sounds of all other sensations? Can that be a gift?

Pain itself, the hurt of pain, is a gift. After years of working with leprosy patients Dr. Paul Brand learned to exult in the sensation of cutting a finger, turning an ankle, stepping into a too-hot bath. "Thank God for pain!" he says.

Doctors once believed the disease of leprosy caused the ulcers on hands and feet and face which eventually led to rotting flesh and the gradual loss of limbs. Mainly through Dr. Brand's research, it has been established that in 99 percent of the cases, leprosy only *numbs* the extremities. The decay of flesh occurs solely because the warning system of pain is absent.

How does the decay happen? Visitors to rural villages in Africa and Asia have sometimes observed a horrible sight: the person with leprosy standing by the heavy iron cooking pot watching the potatoes. As they are done, without flinching he thrusts his arm deep into the scalding water and recovers the cooked potatoes. Dr. Brand found that abusive acts such as this were the chief cause of body deterioration. The potato-watching leprosy victim had felt no pain, but his skin blistered, his cells were destroyed and laid open to infection. Leprosy had not destroyed the tissue; it had merely removed the warning sensors which alerted him to danger.

On one occasion, as Dr. Brand was still formulating this radical theory, he tried to open the door of a little storeroom, but a rusty padlock would not yield to his pressure on the key. A leprosy patient, an undersized, malnourished ten-year-old, approached him, smiling.

"Let me try, sahib doctor," he offered and reached for the key. He closed his thumb and forefinger on the key and with a quick jerk of the hand turned it in the lock.

Brand was dumbfounded. How could this weak youngster out-exert him? His eyes caught a telltale clue. Was that a drop of blood on the floor?

Upon examining the boy's fingers, Brand discovered the act of turning the key had slashed the finger open to the bone; skin and fat and joint were all exposed. Yet the boy was completely unaware of it! To him, the sensation of cutting a finger to the bone was no different from picking up a stone or turning a coin in his pocket.

The daily routines of life ground away at these patients' hands and feet; but without a warning system to alert them, they succumbed. If an ankle turned, tearing tendon and muscle, they would adjust and walk crookedly. If a rat chewed off a finger in the night, they would not discover it until the next morning. (In fact, Brand required his departing patients to take a cat home with them to prevent this common occurrence.)

His discovery revolutionized medicine's approach to leprosy. And it starkly illustrates why Paul Brand can say with utter sincerity, "Thank God for pain!" By definition, pain is unpleasant, so unpleasant as to *force* us to withdraw our finger from boiling water, lightning-fast. Yet it is that very quality which saves us from destruction. Unless the warning signal demands response, we might not heed it.

Brand's discovery in the physical realm closely parallels the moral argument for pain offered by C. S. Lewis in the *The Problem of Pain*. Just as physical pain is an early warning signal to the brain, it is a warning signal to the soul. Pain is a megaphone of God which, sometimes murmuring, sometimes shouting, reminds us that something is wrong. It is a "rumor of transcendence" that convinces us the entire human condition is out of whack. We on earth are a rebel fortress, and every sting and every ache reminds us.

We could (some people do) believe that the purpose of life here is to be comfortable. Enjoy yourself, build a nice home, engorge good food, have sex, live the good life. That's all there is. But the presence of suffering complicates that philosophy. It's much harder to believe that the world is here for my hedonistic fulfillment when a third of its people go to bed starving each night. It's much harder to believe that the purpose of life is to feel good when I see people smashed on the freeway. If I try to escape the idea and merely enjoy life, suffering is there, haunting me, reminding me of how hollow life would be if this world were all I'd ever know.

Something is wrong with a life of wars and violence and insults. We need help. He who wants to be satisfied with this world, who wants to think the only reason for living is to enjoy a good life, must do so with cotton in his ears; the megaphone of pain is a loud one.

Pain, God's megaphone, can drive me away from him. I can hate God for allowing such misery. Or, on the other hand, it can drive me to him. I can believe him when he says that this world is not all there is and take the chance that he is making a perfect place for those who follow him on pain-wracked Earth.

If you once doubt the megaphone value of suffering, visit the intensive-care ward of a hospital. It's unlike any other place in the world. All sorts of people will pace the lobby floors: rich and poor, beautiful and plain, black and white, smart and dull, spiritual and atheistic, white-collar and blue-collar. But the intensive-care ward is the one place in the world where none of those divisions makes a speck of difference, for all those people are united by a single awful thread—their love for a dying relative or friend. You don't see sparks of racial tension there. Economic differences, even religious differences, fade away. Often they'll be consoling one another or crying quietly. All of them are facing the rock-bottom emotions of life, and many of them call for a pastor or priest or rabbi for the first time ever. Only the megaphone of pain is strong enough to bring these people to their knees and make them reconsider life.

The concept of pain as a gift directly contradicts the common evangelical attitude of avoiding pain at all costs. We seem to reserve our shiniest merit badges for those who have been healed, with the frequent side-effect of causing unhealed ones to feel as though God has passed them by. The church needs to confront pain realistically and to affirm that a sick person is not unspiritual. A tornado bearing down on my house will not magically swerve and hop to the houses of pagans.

Nothing in Scripture hints that we Christians should expect life to be easier, more antiseptic, or safer. We need a mature awareness of the contributions of pain, and we need the courage to cling to God, Joblike, despite the world of pain and sometimes because of it. Christianity calls us to complete identification with the world—the *suffering* world—not an insulated scarfree pilgrimage through the world.

There are those for whom pain seems to be in revolt. Bodies wracked with cancer so that nerve cells scream in unison a message to the brain which cannot be heeded. Muscular athletes who suffer a freak accident which bruises the spinal cord and condemns them to a life of paralysis and excruciating misery. To these people, all philosophical explanations and all phrases like "the gift of pain" must sound hollow and sadistic. It is as if they are connected to the pain machine in *1984;* pain has left its natural cycle and becomes a Frankenstein.

There are two contributions to the problem of pain that hold true in any circumstance, whether healing or death ensues. The first is the simple fact of Jesus' coming. When God entered humanity, he saw and felt for himself what this world is like. Jesus took on the same kind of body you and I have. His nerve fibers were not bionic—they screamed with pain when they were misused. And, above all, Jesus was surely misused. This fact of history can have a large effect on the fear and helpless despair of sufferers.

The scene of Christ's death, with the sharp spikes and the wrenching thud as the cross was dropped in the ground, has been told so often that we, who shrink from a news story on the death of a race horse or of baby seals, do not flinch at its retelling. It was a bloody death, an execution quite unlike the quick, sterile ones we know today: gas chambers, electric chairs, hangings, injections. This one stretched on for hours in front of a jeering crowd.

Jesus' death is the cornerstone of the Christian faith, the most important fact of his coming. You can't follow Jesus without confronting his death; the gospels bulge with its details. He laid out a trail of hints and bald predictions about it throughout his ministry, predictions that were only understood after the thing had been done, when to the disciples the dream looked shattered. His life seemed prematurely wasted. His triumphant words from the night before surely must have cruelly haunted his followers as they watched him groan and twitch on the cross.

What possible contribution to the problem of pain could come from a religion based on an event like the Crucifixion? Simply this: we are not abandoned. The Alaskan boy with an amputated foot, grieving Salvadoran Christians, survivors of catastrophes—none has to suffer alone. Because God came and took a place beside us, he fully understands. Dorothy Sayers says:

> For whatever reason God chose to make man as he is—limited and suffering and subject to sorrows and death—He had the honesty and courage to take His own medicine. Whatever game He is playing with His creation, He has kept His own rules and played fair. He can exact nothing from man that He has not exacted from Himself. He has Himself gone through the whole of human experience, from the trivial irritations of family life and the cramping restrictions of hard work and lack of money to the worst horrors of pain and humiliation, defeat, despair, and death. When He was a man, He played the man. He was born in poverty and died in disgrace and thought it well worthwhile.

By taking it on himself, Jesus in a sense dignified pain. Of all the kinds of lives he could have lived, he chose a suffering one. Because of Jesus, I can never say about a person, "He must be suffering because of some sin he committed."

Jesus, who did not sin, also felt pain. And I cannot say, "Suffering and death must mean God has forsaken us; he's left us alone to self-destruct." Because even though Jesus died, his death became the great victory of history, pulling man and God together. God made a supreme good out of that day. T. S. Eliot wrote in *Four Quartets* (*Collected Poems 1909–1962*, p. 187):

> The wounded surgeon plies the steel
> That questions the distempered part;
> Beneath the bleeding hands we feel

The sharp compassion of the healer's art
Resolving the enigma of the fever chart.

That uniquely Christian contribution is a memory. But there is another one—a hope. To the person with unrequited suffering, it is the most important contribution of all. Christ did not stay on the cross. After three days in a dark tomb, he was seen alive again. Alive! Could it be? His disciples couldn't believe it at first. But he came to them, letting them feel his new body. Christ brought us the possibility of an afterlife without pain and suffering. All our hurts are temporary.

How can we imagine eternity? It's so much larger than our short life here that it's difficult even to visualize. You can go to a ten-foot blackboard and draw a line from one side to another. Then, make a one-inch dot in that line. To a microscopic germ cell, sitting in the midst of that one-inch dot, it would look enormous. The cell could spend its lifetime exploring its length and breadth. But you're a human, and by stepping back to view the whole blackboard you're suddenly struck with the largesse of the ten-foot line compared to the tiny dot the germ calls home.

Eternity compared to this life is that way. In seventy years we can develop a host of ideas about God and how indifferent he appears to be about suffering. But is it reasonable to judge God and his plan for the universe by the swatch of time we spend on earth? No more reasonable than for that germ cell to judge a whole blackboard by the tiny smudge of chalk where he spends his life. Have we missed the perspective of the timelessness of the universe?

Who would complain if God allowed one hour of suffering in an entire lifetime of comfort? Yet we bitterly complain about a lifetime that includes suffering when that lifetime is a mere hour of eternity.

In the Christian scheme of things, this world and the time spent here are not all there is. Earth is a proving ground, a dot in eternity—but a very important dot, for Jesus said our destiny depends on our obedience here. Next time you want to cry out to God in anguished despair, blaming him for a miserable world, remember: less than one-millionth of the evidence has been presented.

Let me use another analogy to illustrate the effect of this truth. Ironically, the one event that probably causes more emotional suffering than any other—death—is in reality a translation, a time for great joy when Christ's victory will be appropriated to each of us. Describing the effect of his own death, Jesus used the simile of a woman in travail, full of pain and agony until all is replaced by ecstasy.

Allow yourself to go back in time to an unremembered state—the sterile security of your mother's womb:

Your world is dark, safe, secure. You are bathed in warm liquid, cushioned from shock. You do nothing for yourself; you are fed automatically, and a murmuring heartbeat assures you that someone larger than you fills all your needs. Your life consists of simple waiting. You're not sure what to wait for, but any change seems far away and scary. You meet no sharp objects, no pain, no threatening adventures. A fine existence.

One day you feel a tug. The walls are falling in on you. Those soft cushions are now pulsing and beating against you, crushing you downwards. Your body is bent double, your limbs twisted and wrenched. You're falling, upside down. For the first time in your life you feel pain. You're in a sea of rolling matter. There is more pressure, almost too intense to bear. Your head is squeezed flat, and you are pushed harder, harder into a dark tunnel. Oh, the pain. Noise. More pressure.

You're hurting all over. You hear a groaning sound and an awful sudden fear rushes in on you. It is happening—your world is collapsing. You're sure it's the end. You see a piercing, blinding light. Cold, rough hands pull at you. A painful slap. A loud cry.

You have just experienced birth.

Death is like that. On this end of the birth canal, it seems fiercesome, portentous, and full of pain. Death is a scary tunnel and we are being sucked toward it by a powerful force. We're afraid. It's full of pressure, pain, darkness—the unknown. But beyond the darkness and the pain there's a whole new world outside. When we wake up after death in that bright new world, our tears and hurts will be mere memories. And the new world is so much better than this one that we have no categories to understand what it will be like. The best the Bible writers can tell us is that then, instead of the silence of God, we will have the presence of God and see him face to face. At that time we will be given a stone, and upon it will be written a new name, which no one else knows. Our birth into new creatures will be complete (Rev. 2:17).

Do you sometimes think God does not hear? God is not deaf. He is as grieved by the world's trauma as you are. His only son died here. But he has promised to set things right.

Let history finish. Let the orchestra scratch out its last mournful warm-up note of discord before it bursts into the symphony. As Paul said, "In my opinion whatever we may have to go through now is less than nothing compared with the magnificent future God has planned for us. The whole creation is on tiptoe to see the wonderful sight of the sons of God coming into their own. . . .

"It is plain to anyone with eyes to see that at the present time all created life groans in sort of a universal travail. And it is plain, too, that we who have a foretaste of the Spirit are in a state of painful tension, while we wait for that redemption of our bodies which will mean that at last we have realized our full sonship in Him" (Rom. 8:18, 19, 22, 23).

As we look back on the speck of eternity that was the history of this planet, we will be impressed not by its importance, but by its smallness. From the viewpoint of the Andromeda galaxy, the holocaustic destruction of our entire solar system would be barely visible, a match flaring faintly in the distance, then imploding in permanent darkness. Yet for this burnt-out match, God sacrificed himself. Pain can be seen, as Berkouwer puts it, as the great "not yet" of eternity. It reminds us of where we are, and creates in us a thirst for where we will someday be.

Discussion

1. What does Yancey mean by describing pain as a "paradox," and how does he develop this in the essay? Yancey provides examples of paradox from nature. Perhaps you can add your own examples to his.
2. We might expect an essay on pain to be a dull, plodding, scientific analysis. Yancey's essay bursts with energy. This reveals something about the author's attitude toward the subject. Notice how this energy is achieved by use of action verbs, unusual adjectives, and imagery.
3. Discuss Yancey's use of example and analogy as rhetorical devices.
4. C. S. Lewis calls pain "a megaphone of God." But what would you say is the purpose of God's calling to us in this way? What effects and purposes does Yancey see of this calling?
5. Erma Bombeck wrote a book titled *If Life Is a Bowl of Cherries, What Am I Doing in the Pits?* Could her question apply to Christian living? How does Yaney explain pain in the Christian life?

Writing Assignments for Chapter 11

1. Using Emily Dickinson's poem, "'Faith' Is a Fine Invention," as an epigraph, write an essay that argues for or against scientific medical treatments. Consider the rhetorical situation as you write. If you are writing as a Christian or if you are writing for a Christian audience, be sure to refer to relevant biblical passages on faith and healing.
2. Pretending that Albert Einstein's essay had just been written, write a letter to the *New York Times* responding to his views.

3. List the ten most important scientific discoveries of the last one hundred years. Then write an essay that examines their impact on our culture. Does such an examination lead to the conclusion that the culture is progressing? Have they promoted happiness? Do they, in C. S. Lewis's terms, provide a measure of "man's power over nature"?

12

Reading Literature

What has Horace to do with the Psalter, Virgil with the Gospel, Cicero with the Apostle?

—Abelard

You use a glass mirror to see your face; you use works of art to see your soul.

—George Bernard Shaw, *Back to Methuselah*

It is just the literature that we read for 'amusement,' or 'purely for pleasure' that may have the greatest and least suspected influence on us. It is the literature which we read with the least effort that can have the easiest and most insidious influence upon us. Hence it is that the influence of popular novelists, and of popular plays of contemporary life, requires to be scrutinized most closely.

—T. S. Eliot, "Religion and Literature"

Literature helps us see our lives. By showing us other worlds, it helps us understand our own. Every poem, every story, every play presents the writer's vision of life. When we read, then, we read for the pleasure that derives from seeing another world, but we also read to learn, to try to understand that writer's vision of reality.

As Christians we are particularly interested in what happens to us when we read. We are aware of being called to be in the world but not of it, and so desire to understand what happens to us as we participate in

269

these fictional worlds, these constructs of reality. Do we remain separate from these other worlds, or are we pulled in? And in either case, what are the consequences? If we stand as onlookers, can we watch and learn? And if we participate, if we identify with a character or characters—what then? If they sin will we be likely to imitate them?

The serious tone of these questions suggests our interest in books that offer more than escape. Entertaining diversion is necessary and worthwhile, but we are primarily interested in a meaningful encounter with life, rather than simple escape from it. The best books offer us an engagement with life so that we may understand it better or clarify our relation with the world around us.

This doesn't mean that stories must be fables, that everything we read must explicitly teach a lesson. Beauty and form contribute to a story's meaning and we would do ourselves a great disservice to neglect them when we read. In fact we should be looking for beauty as part of the truth that we seek. But what constitutes true beauty? Some may reply that true beauty lies in the ideas of the work. A work of art that stimulates noble thoughts or challenges the intellect presents true beauty. Others may argue that true beauty inheres in a faithful representation of life; the work is beautiful insofar as it corresponds to reality. Yet others may respond that this beauty appears in the provision of spiritual answers to human need. And still others may respond that the beauty of art lies in its structure, in the expert crafting of the work itself.

All of us face this question when we begin to read literature. But as we do so we should bear in mind T. S. Eliot's admonition in "Religion and Literature" that "in ages like our own, in which there is no . . . common agreement, it is the more necessary for Christian readers to scrutinize their reading, especially of works of imagination, with explicit ethical and theological standards." In other words, we should have a particular notion of what beauty is, and we should seek it in the literature we read. This is not to say that the stories, poems, and plays will necessarily be pretty, or nice, or happy, or any of the modern adjectives we use as synonyms for beauty; but this is to say that they will present an order or a harmony that is beautiful because it mirrors, however dimly, the divine reality. As we read, we should look for beauty, yet as we look, we should keep our knowledge of Scripture in mind, for the beauty that is truth will appear only in the light of the Bible.

Even so there are questions. For as Eliot also notes, "So far as we are taken up with the happenings in any novel in the same way that we are taken up with what happens under our eyes [in real life], we are acquiring at least as much falsehood as truth." How should we understand stories that present other worldviews? How should we deal with texts that focus on sinful or evil aspects of life? These questions may lead Christians to condemn soap opera-like fictions and pornographic literature, but such condemnations don't make the questions go away. Moreover, most books aren't soap operas or pornography. As the writers of this section demonstrate, the questions not only linger, but become more difficult. Each writer here attempts to establish criteria for judging whether a story is moral. Each comes with slightly different assumptions and presents a slightly different conclusion. You must decide who is right.

Censorship and the Nature of Art

Plato

> *Plato's* Republic *presents a series of dialogues between Socrates and his fellow Athenians on what the ideal society should be like. In these two excerpts from those conversations, the discussants consider issues of literature and censorship that are as relevant to our situation as they were to that of the Greeks of 450 B.C. In the section of* The Republic *which follows, Socrates initiates the conversation with Glaucon and Adeimantus.*

Come then, and let us pass a leisure hour in story-telling, and our story shall be the education of our heroes.

By all means.

And what shall be their education? Can we find a better than the traditional sort—and this has two divisions, gymnastic for the body, and music for the soul.

True.

Shall we begin education with music, and go on to gymnastic afterwards?

By all means.

And when you speak of music, do you include literature or not?

I do.

And literature may be either true or false?

Yes.

And the young should be trained in both kinds, and we begin with the false?

I do not understand your meaning, he said.

You know, I said, that we begin by telling children stories which, though not wholly destitute of truth, are in the main fictitious; and these stories are told them when they are not of an age for gymnastics.

Very true.

That was my meaning when I said that we must teach music before gymnastics.

Quite right, he said.

You know also that the beginning is the most important part of any work, especially in the case of a young and tender thing; for that is the time at which the character is being formed and the desired impression is more readily taken.

Quite true.

And shall we just carelessly allow children to hear any casual tales which may be devised by casual persons, and to receive into their minds ideas for the most part the very opposite of those which we should wish them to have when they are grown up?

We cannot.

Then the first thing will be to establish a censorship of the writers of fiction, and let the censors receive any tale of fiction which is good, and reject the bad; and we will desire mothers and nurses to tell their children the authorised ones only. Let them fashion the mind with such tales, even more fondly than they mould the body with their hands; but most of those which are now in use must be discarded.

Of what tales are you speaking? he said.

You may find a model of the lesser in the greater, I said; for they are necessarily of the same type, and there is the same spirit in both of them.

Very likely, he replied; but I do not as yet know what you would term the greater.

Those, I said, which are narrated by Homer and Hesiod, and the rest of the poets, who have ever been the great story-tellers of mankind.

But which stories do you mean, he said; and what fault do you find with them?

A fault which is most serious, I said; the fault of telling a lie, and what is more, a bad lie.

But when is this fault committed?

Whenever an erroneous representation is made of the nature of gods and heroes,—as when a painter paints a picture not having the shadow of a likeness to the original.

Yes, he said, that sort of thing is certainly very blameable; but what are the stories which you mean?

First of all, I said, there was that greatest of all lies in high places, which the poet told about Uranus, and which was a bad lie too,—I mean what Hesiod says that Uranus did, and how Cronus retaliated on him (Hesiod, *Theogony*, 154, 459). The doings of Cronus, and the sufferings which in turn his son inflicted upon him, even if they were true, ought certainly not to be lightly told to young and thoughtless persons; if possible, they had better be buried in silence. But if there is an absolute necessity for their mention, a chosen few might hear them in a mystery, and they should sacrifice not a common [Eleasinian] pig, but some huge and unprocurable victim; and then the number of the hearers may be very few indeed.

Why, yes, said he, those stories are extremely objectionable.

Yes, Adeimantus, they are stories not to be repeated in our State; the young man should not be told that in committing the worst of crimes he is far from doing anything outrageous; and that even if he chastises his father when he does wrong, in whatever manner, he will only be following the example of the first and greatest among the gods.

I entirely agree with you, he said; in my opinion those stories are quite unfit to be repeated.

Neither, if we mean our future guardians to regard the habit of quarrelling among themselves as of all things the basest, should any word be said to them of the wars in heaven, and of the plots and fightings of the gods against one another, for they are not true. No, we shall never mention the battles of the giants, or let them be embroidered on garments; and we shall be silent about the innumerable other quarrels of gods and heroes with their friends and relatives. If they would only believe us we would tell them that quarrelling is unholy, and that never up to this time has there been any quarrel between citizens; this is what old men and old women should begin by telling children; and when they grow up, the poets also should be told to compose for them in a similar spirit. But the narrative of Hephaestus binding Here his mother, or how on another occasion Zeus sent him flying for taking her part when she was being beaten, and all the battles of the gods in Homer—these tales must not be admitted into our State, whether they are supposed to have an allegorical meaning or not. For a young person cannot judge what is allegorical and what is literal; anything that he receives into his mind at that age is likely to become indelible and unalterable; and therefore it is most important that the tales which the young first hear should be models of virtuous thoughts.

There you are right, he replied; but if anyone asks where are such models to be found and of what tales are you speaking—how shall we answer him?

I said to him, You and I, Adeimantus, at this moment are not poets, but founders of a State: now the founders of a State ought to know the general forms in which poets should cast their tales, and the limits which must be observed by them, but to make the tales is not their business.

Very true, he said; but what are these forms of theology which you mean?

Something of this kind, I replied:—God is always to be represented as he truly is, whatever be the sort of poetry, epic, lyric or tragic, in which the representation is given.

Right.

And is he not truly good? and must he not be represented as such?

Certainly.

And no good thing is hurtful?

No, indeed.

And that which is not hurtful hurts not?

Certainly not.

And that which hurts not does no evil?

No.

And can that which does no evil be a cause of evil?

Impossible.

And the good is advantageous?

Yes.

And therefore the cause of well-being?

Yes.

It follows therefore that the good is not the cause of all things, but of the good only?

Assuredly.

Then God, if he be good, is not the author of all things, as the many assert, but he is the cause of a few things only, and not of most things that occur to men. For few are the goods of human life, and many are the evils, and the good is to be attributed to God alone; of the evils the causes are to be sought elsewhere, and not in him.

That appears to me to be most true, he said. . . .

Let this then be one of our rules and principles concerning the gods, to which our poets and reciters will be expected to conform,—that God is not the author of all things, but of good only.

That will do, he said.

And what do you think of a second principle? Shall I ask you whether God is a magician, and of a nature to appear insidiously now in one shape, and now in another—sometimes really changing and passing into many forms, sometimes deceiving us with the semblance of such transformations; or is he one and the same immutably fixed in his own proper image?

I cannot answer you, he said, without more thought.

Well, I said; but if we suppose a change in anything, that change must be effected either by the thing itself, or by some other thing?

Most certainly.

And things which are at their best are also least liable to be altered or discomposed; for example, when healthiest and strongest, the human frame is least liable to be affected by meats and drinks, and the plant which is in the fullest vigour also suffers least from winds or the heat of the sun or any similar causes.

Of course.

And will not the bravest and wisest soul be least confused or deranged by any external influence?

True.

And the same principle, as I should suppose, applies to all composite things—furniture, houses, garments: when good and well made, they are least altered by time and circumstances.

Very true.

Then everything which is good, whether made by art or nature, or both, is least liable to suffer change from without?

True.

But surely God and the things of God are in every way perfect?

Of course they are.

Then he can hardly be compelled by external influence to take many shapes?

He cannot.

But may he not change and transform himself?

Clearly, he said, that must be the case if he is changed at all.

And will he then change himself for the better and fairer, or for the worse and more unsightly?

If he change at all he can only change for the worse, for we cannot suppose him to be deficient either in virtue or beauty.

Very true, Adeimantus; but then, would any one, whether God or man, desire to make himself worse in any respect?

Impossible.

Then it is impossible that God should ever be willing to change; being, as is supposed, the fairest and best that is conceivable, every God remains absolutely and for ever in his own form.

That necessarily follows, he said, in my judgment.

Then, I said, my dear friend, let none of the poets tell us that

"The gods, taking the disguise of strangers from other lands, walk up and down cities in all sorts of forms" (Homer, *Odyssey*, xvii. 485); and let no one slander Proteus and Thetis, neither let anyone, either in tragedy or in any other kind of poetry, introduce Here disguised in the likeness of a priestess asking an alms

"For the life-giving daughters of Inachus the river of Argos";

—let us have no more lies of that sort. Neither must we have mothers under the influence of the poets scaring their children with a bad version of these myths—telling how certain gods, as they say, "Go about by night in the likeness of so many strangers in divers forms;" but let them take heed lest they make cowards of their children, and at the same time speak blasphemy against the gods.

Heaven forbid, he said.

But although the gods are themselves unchangeable, still by witchcraft and deception they may make us think that they appear in various forms?

Perhaps, he replied.

Well, but can you imagine that God will be willing to lie, whether in word or deed, to put forth a phantom of himself?

I cannot say, he replied.

Do you not know, I said, that the true lie, if such an expression may be allowed, is hated of all gods and men?

What do you mean? he said.

I mean that no one willingly deceived in that which is the truest and highest part of himself, or about the truest and highest matters; there, above all, he is most afraid of a lie having possession of him.

Still, he said, I do not comprehend you.

The reason is, I replied, that you attribute some profound meaning to my words; but I am only saying that deception, or being deceived or uninformed about the highest realities in the highest part of themselves, which is the soul, and in that part of them to have and to hold the lie, is what mankind least like;—that, I say, is what they utterly detest.

There is nothing more hateful to them.

And, as I was just now remarking, this ignorance in the soul of him who is deceived may be called the true lie; for the lie in words is only a kind of imitation and shadowy image of a previous affection of the soul, not pure unadulterated falsehood. Am I not right?

Perfectly right.

The true lie is hated not only by the gods, but also by men?

Yes.

Whereas the lie in words is in certain cases useful and not hateful; in dealing with enemies—that would be an instance; or again, when those whom we call our friends in a fit of madness or illusion are going to do some harm, then it is useful and is a sort of medicine or preventive; also in the tales of mythology, of which we were just now speaking—because we do not know the truth about ancient times, we make falsehood as much like truth as we can, and so turn it to account.

Very true, he said.

But can any of these reasons apply to God? Can we suppose that he is ignorant of antiquity, and therefore has recourse to invention?

That would be ridiculous, he said.

Then the lying poet has no place in our idea of God?

I should say not.

Or perhaps he may tell a lie because he is afraid of enemies?

That is inconceivable.

But he may have friends who are senseless or mad?

But no mad or senseless person can be a friend of God.

Then no motive can be imagined why God should lie?

None whatever.

Then the superhuman and divine is absolutely incapable of falsehood?

Yes.

Then is God perfectly simple and true both in word and deed; he changes not; he deceives not, either by sign or word, by dream or waking vision.

Your thoughts, he said, are the reflection of my own.

You agree with me then, I said, that this is the second type or form in which men should write and speak about divine things. The gods are not magicians who transform themselves, neither do they deceive mankind in any way.

I grant that.

Then, although we are admirers of Homer, we shall not admire the lying dream which Zeus sends to Agamemnon; neither will we praise the verses of Aeschylus in which Thetis says that Apollo at her nuptials

"Was celebrating in song her fair progeny, whose days were to be long, and to know no sickness. And when he had spoken of my lot as in all things blessed of heaven he raised a note of triumph and cheered my soul. And I thought that the word of Phoebus, being divine and full of prophecy, would not fail. And now he himself who uttered the strain, he who was present at the banquet, and who said this—he it is who has slain my son" (From a lost play).

These are the kind of sentiments about the gods which will arouse our anger; and he who utters them shall be refused a chorus; neither shall we allow teachers to make use of them in the instruction of the young, meaning, as we do, that our guardians, as far as men can be, should be true worshippers of the gods and like them.

I entirely agree, he said, in these principles, and promise to make them my laws. . . .

Of the many excellences which I perceive in the order of our State, there is none which upon reflection pleases me better than the rule about poetry.

To what do you refer?

To the rejection of imitative poetry, which certainly ought not to be received; as I see far more clearly now that the parts of the soul have been distinguished.

What do you mean?

Speaking in confidence, for I would not like to have my words repeated to the tragedians and the rest of the imitative tribe—but I do not mind saying to you, that all poetical imitations are ruinous to the understanding of the hearers, and that the knowledge of their true nature is the only antidote to them.

Explain the purport of your remark.

Well, I will tell you, although I have always from my earliest youth had an awe and love of Homer, which even now makes the words falter on my lips, for he is the great captain and teacher of the whole of that charming tragic company; but a man is not to be reverenced more than the truth, and therefore I will speak out.

Very good, he said.

Listen to me then, or rather, answer me.

Put your question.

Can you tell me what imitation is? for I really do not know.

A likely thing, then, that I should know.

Why not? for the duller eye may often see a thing sooner than the keener.

Very true, he said; but in your presence, even if I had any faint notion, I could not muster courage to utter it. Will you enquire yourself?

Well then, shall we begin the enquiry in our usual manner: Whenever a number of individuals have a common name, we assume them to have also a corresponding idea or form:—do you understand me?

I do.

Let us take any common instance; there are beds and tables in the world—plenty of them, are there not?

Yes.

But there are only two ideas or forms of them—one the idea of a bed, the other of a table.

True.

And the maker of either of them makes a bed or he makes a table for our use, in accordance with the idea—that is our way of speaking in this and similar instances—but no artificer makes the ideas themselves: how could he?

Impossible.

And there is another artist,—I should like to know what you would say of him.

Who is he?

One who is the maker of all the works of all other workmen.

What an extraordinary man!

Wait a little, and there will be more reason for your saying so. For this is he who is able to make not only vessels of every kind, but plants and animals, himself and all other things—the earth and heaven, and the things which are in heaven or under the earth; he makes the gods also.

He must be a wizard and no mistake.

Oh! you are incredulous, are you? Do you mean that there is no such maker or creator, or that in one sense there might be a maker of all these things but in another not? Do you see that there is a way in which you could make them all yourself?

What way?

An easy way enough; or rather, there are many ways in which the feat might be quickly and easily accomplished, none quicker than that of turning a mirror round and round—you would soon enough make the sun and the heavens, and the earth and yourself, and other animals and plants, and all the other things of which we were just now speaking, in the mirror.

Yes, he said; but they would be appearances only.

Very good, I said, you are coming to the point now. And the painter too is, as I conceive, just such another—a creator of appearances, is he not?

Of course.

But then I suppose you will say that what he creates is untrue. And yet there is a sense in which the painter also creates a bed? Is there not?

Yes, he said, but not a real bed.

And what of the maker of the bed? were you not saying that he too makes, not the idea which, according to our view, is the essence of the bed, but only a particular bed?

Yes, I did.

Then if he does not make that which exists he cannot make true existence, but only some semblance of existence; and if any one were to say that the work of the maker of the bed, or of any other workman, has real existence, he could hardly be supposed to be speaking the truth.

At any rate, he replied, philosophers would say that he was not speaking the truth.

No wonder, then, that his work too is an indistinct expression of truth.

No wonder.

Suppose now that by the light of the examples just offered we enquire who this imitator is?

If you please.

Well then, here are three beds: one existing in nature, which is made by God, as I think that we may say—for no one else can be the maker?

No.

There is another which is the work of the carpenter?

Yes.

And the work of the painter is a third?

Yes.

Beds, then, are of three kinds, and there are three artists who superintend them: God, the maker of the bed, and the painter?

Yes, there are three of them.

God, whether from choice or from necessity, made one bed in nature and one only; two or more such ideal beds neither ever have been nor ever will be made by God.

Why is that?

Because even if He had made but two, a third would still appear behind them of which they again both possess the form, and that would be the real bed and not the two others.

Very true, he said.

God knew this, and He desired to be the real maker of a real bed, not a particular maker of a particular bed, and therefore He created a bed which is essentially and by nature one only.

So we believe.

Shall we, then, speak of Him as the natural author or maker of the bed?

Yes, he replied; inasmuch as by the natural process of creation He is the author of this and of all other things.

And what shall we say of the carpenter—is not he also the maker of a bed?

Yes.

But would you call the painter a creator and maker?

Certainly not.

Yet if he is not the maker, what is he in relation to the bed?

I think, he said, that we may fairly designate him as the imitator of that which the others make.

Good, I said; then you call him whose product is third in the descent from nature an imitator?

Certainly, he said.

And the tragic poet is an imitator, and therefore, like all other imitators he is thrice removed from the king and from the truth?

That appears to be so.

Then about the imitator we are agreed. And what about the painter?—I would like to know whether he may be thought to imitate in each case that which originally exists in nature, or only the creations of artists?

The latter.

As they are or as they appear? you have still to determine this.

What do you mean?

I mean, that you may look at a bed from different points of view, obliquely or directly or from any other point of view, and the bed will appear different, but there is no difference in reality. And the same of all things.

Yes, he said, the difference is only apparent.

Now let me ask you another question: Which is the art of painting designed to be—an imitation of things as they are, or as they appear—of appearance or of reality?

Of appearance.

Then the imitator, I said, is a long way off the truth, and can do all things because he lightly touches on a small part of them, and that part an image. For example: A painter will paint a cobbler, carpenter, or any other artist, though he knows nothing of their arts; and, if he is a good artist, he may deceive children or simple persons when he shows them his picture of a carpenter from a distance, and they will fancy that they are looking at a real carpenter.

Certainly.

And whenever any one informs us that he has found a man who knows all the arts, and all things else that anybody knows, and every single thing with a higher degree of accuracy than any other man—whoever tells us this, I think that we can only imagine him to be a simple creature who is likely to have been deceived by some wizard or actor whom he met, and whom he thought all-knowing, because he himself was unable to analyse the nature of knowledge and ignorance and imitation.

Most true.

And so, when we hear persons saying that the tragedians, and Homer, who is at their head, know all the arts and all things human, virtue as well as vice, and divine things too, for that the good poet cannot compose well unless he knows his subject, and he who has not this knowledge can never be a poet, we ought to consider whether here also there may not be a similar illusion. Perhaps they may have come across imitators and been deceived by them; they may not have remembered when they saw their works that these were but imitations thrice removed from the truth, and could easily be made without any knowledge of the truth, because they are appearances only and not realities? Or, after all, they may be in the right, and good poets do really know the things about which they seem to the many to speak so well?

The question, he said, should by all means be considered.

Now do you suppose that if a person were able to make the original as well as the image, he would seriously devote himself to the image-making branch? Would he allow imitation to be the ruling principle of his life, as if he had nothing higher in him?

I should say not.

The real artist, who knew what he was imitating, would be interested in realities and not in imitations; and would desire to leave as memorials of himself works many and fair; and, instead of being the author of encomiums, he would prefer to be the theme of them.

Yes, he said, that would be to him a source of much greater honour and profit.

Then, I said, we must put a question to Homer; not about medicine, or any of the arts to which his poems incidentally refer: we are not going to ask him, or any other poet, whether he has cured patients like Asclepius, or left behind him a school of medicine such as the Asclepiads were, or whether he only talks about medicine and other arts at second-hand; but we have a right to know respecting military tactics, politics, education, which are the chiefest and noblest subjects of his poems, and we may fairly ask him about them. "Friend Homer," then we say to him, "if you are only in the second remove from truth in what you say of virtue, and not in the third—not an image maker or an imitator—and if you are able to discern what pursuits make men better or worse in private or public life, tell us what State was ever better governed by your help? The good order of Lacedaemon is due to Lycurgus, and many other cities great and small have been similarly benefited by others; but who says that you have been a good legislator to them and have done them any good? Italy and Sicily boast of Charondas, and there is Solon who is renowned among us; but what city has anything to say about you?" Is there any city which he might name?

I think not, said Glaucon; not even the Homerids themselves pretend that he was a legislator.

Well, but is there any war on record which was carried on successfully by him or aided by his counsel, when he was alive?

There is not.

Or is there any invention of his, applicable to the arts or to human life, such as Thales the Milesian or Anarcharsis the Scythian, and other ingenious men have conceived, which is attributed to him?

There is absolutely nothing of the kind.

But, if Homer never did any public service, was he privately a guide or teacher of any? Had he in his lifetime friends who loved to associate with him, and who handed down to posterity an Homeric way of life, such as was established by Pythagoras who was so greatly beloved for his wisdom and whose followers are to this day quite celebrated for the order which was named after him?

Nothing of the kind is recorded of him. For surely, Socrates, Creophylus, the companion of Homer, that child of flesh, whose name always makes us laugh, might be more justly ridiculed for his stupidity, if as is said is true, that Homer was greatly neglected by him and others in his own day when he was alive?

Yes, I replied, that is the tradition. But can you imagine, Glaucon, that if Homer had really been able to educate and improve mankind— if he had possessed knowledge and not been a mere imitator—can you imagine, I say, that he would not have had many followers, and been honoured and loved by them? Protagoras of Abdera, and Prodicus of Ceos, and a host of others, have only to whisper to their contemporaries: "You will never be able to manage either your own house or your own State until you appoint us to be your ministers of education"—and this ingenious device of theirs has such an effect in making men love them that their companions all but carry them about on their shoulders. And is it conceivable that the contemporaries of Homer, or again of Hesiod, would have allowed either of them to go about as rhapsodists, if they had really been able to make mankind virtuous? Would they not have been as unwilling to part with them as with gold, and have compelled them to stay at home with them? Or, if the master would not stay, then the disciples would have followed him about everywhere, until they had got education enough?

Yes, Socrates, that, I think, is quite true.

Then must we not infer that all these poetical individuals, beginning with Homer, are only imitators; they copy images of virtue and the like, but the truth they never reach? The poet is like a painter who, as we have already observed, will make a likeness of a cobbler though he understands nothing of cobbling; and his picture is good enough for those who know no more than he does, and judge only by colours and figures.

Quite so.

In like manner the poet with his words and phrases may be said to lay on the colours of the several arts, himself understanding their nature only enough to imitate them; and other people, who are as ignorant as he is, and judge only from his words, imagine that if he speaks of cobbling, or of military tactics, or of anything else, in metre and harmony and rhythm, he speaks very well—such is the sweet influence which melody and rhythm by nature have. And I think that you must have observed again and again what a poor appearance the tales of poets make when stripped of the colours which art puts upon them, and recited in simple prose.

Yes, he said.

They are like faces which were never really beautiful, but only blooming; and now the bloom of youth has passed away from them?

Exactly.

Here is another point: The imitator or maker of the image knows nothing of true existence; he knows appearances only. Am I not right?

Yes.

Then let us have a clear understanding, and not be satisfied with half an explanation.

Proceed.

Of the painter we say that he will paint reins, and he will paint a bit?

Yes.

And the worker in leather and brass will make them?

Certainly.

But does the painter know the right form of the bit and reins? Nay, hardly even the workers in brass and leather who make them; only the horseman who knows how to use them—he knows their right form.

Most true.

And may we not say the same of all things?

What?

That there are three arts which are concerned with all things: one which uses, another which makes, a third which imitates them?

Yes.

And the excellence and beauty and rightness of every structure, animate or inanimate, and of every action of man, is relative solely to the use for which nature or the artist has intended them.

True.

Then the user of them must have the greatest experience of them, and he must indicate to the maker the good or bad qualities which develop themselves in use; for example, the flute-player will tell the flute-maker which of his flutes is satisfactory to the performer; he will tell him how he ought to make them, and the other will attend to his instructions?

Of course.

The one knows and therefore speaks with authority about the goodness and badness of flutes, while the other, confiding in him, will do what is told by him?

True.

The instrument is the same, but about the excellence or badness of it the maker will only attain to a correct belief; and this he will gain from him who knows, by talking to him and being compelled to hear what he has to say, whereas the user will have knowledge?

True.

But will the imitator have either? Will he know from use whether or no his drawing is correct or beautiful? or will he have right opinion from being compelled to associate with another who knows and gives him instructions about what he should draw?

Neither.

Then he will no more have true opinion than he will have knowledge about the goodness or badness of his imitations?

I suppose not.

The imitative artist will be in a brilliant state of intelligence about his own creations?

Nay, very much the reverse.

And still he will go on imitating without knowing what makes a thing good or bad, and may be expected therefore to imitate only that which appears to be good to the ignorant multitude?

Just so.

Thus far then we are pretty well agreed that the imitator has no knowledge worth mentioning of what he imitates. Imitation is only a kind of play or sport, and the tragic poets, whether they write in Iambic or in Heroic verse, are imitators in the highest degree?

Very true.

And now tell me, I conjure you, has not imitation been shown by us to be concerned with that which is thrice removed from the truth?

Certainly.

And what is the faculty in man to which imitation is addressed?

What do you mean?

I will explain: The body which is large when seen near, appears small when seen at a distance?

True.

And the same objects appear straight when looked at out of the water, and crooked when in the water; and the concave becomes convex, owing to the illusion about colours to which the sight is liable. Thus every sort of confusion is revealed within us; and this is that weakness of the human mind on which the art of conjuring and of deceiving by light and shadow and other ingenious devices imposes, having an effect upon us like magic.

True.

And the arts of measuring and numbering and weighing come to the rescue of the human understanding—there is the beauty of them—and the apparent greater or less, or more or heavier, no longer have the mastery over us, but give way before calculation and measure and weight?

Most true.

And this, surely, must be the work of the calculating and rational principle in the soul?

To be sure.

And when this principle measures and certifies that some things are equal, or that some are greater or less than other, there occurs an apparent contradiction?

True.

But were we not saying that such a contradiction is impossible—the same faculty cannot have contrary opinions at the same time about the same thing?

Very true.

Then that part of the soul which has an opinion contrary to measure is not the same with that which has an opinion in accordance with measure?

True.

And the better part of the soul is likely to be that which trusts to measure and calculation?

Certainly.

And that which is opposed to them is one of the inferior principles of the soul?

No doubt.

This was the conclusion at which I was seeking to arrive when I said that painting or drawing, and imitation in general, when doing their own proper work, are far removed from truth, and the companions and friends and associates of a principle within us which is equally removed from reason, and that they have no true or healthy aim.

Exactly.

The imitative art is an inferior who marries an inferior, and has inferior offspring.

Discussion

1. Do you agree with Plato that children's books should be censored? If so, for what age group would you halt the censorship?
2. Plato's concern with erroneous representation is based on the assumption that people will imitate the behavior they encounter in art. Is this a reasonable assumption? List examples to support your response.

3. One "fiction" to which Plato objects is the suggestion that God made evil. The question he raises is a significant one; how would you answer if asked how evil was created if God made all things?
4. What, according to Plato, determines the beauty of an object? Do you agree?
5. Although Plato warns against literature because it stirs emotions that are not true, Aristotle and others argue that such a stimulus of emotion is one of the greatest values of literature because it allows the reader to gain emotional experience without exposure to the risks of real life. Who do you think is right?
6. Is Plato correct in suggesting that there is no value to art? Use examples to illustrate your point.

Moral Fiction

John Gardner

One of the strongest advocates of moral fiction in recent years has been John Gardner. Moral fiction, Gardner claims, possesses an enduring cultural effect by preserving models of decent behavior. But moral content does not necessarily constitute moral fiction; the method of composition must also, according to Gardner, reflect a mode of thought that is moral.

To maintain that true art is moral one need not call up theory; one need only think of the fictions that have lasted: *The Iliad* and *The Odyssey;* the tragedies of Aeschylus, Sophocles, and Euripides; Virgil's *Aeneid;* Dante's *Commedia;* the plays of Shakespeare and Racine; the novels of Tolstoy, Melville, Thomas Mann, James Joyce. Such works—all true works of art—can exert their civilizing influence century after century, long after the cultures that produced them have decayed. Yet it is clearly not true that the morality of art takes care of itself, the good, like gravity, inevitably prevailing. Good art is always in competition with bad, and though the long-run odds for good art are high, since cultures that survive almost by definition take pleasure in the good, even the good in a foreign tongue, the short-term odds are discouraging. The glories of Greece and Rome are now bones on old hills. Civilized virtue, in states or individuals, can easily become too complex for self-defense, can be forced simply to abdicate like those few late Roman emperors not murdered on the street. And like a civilized Roman, the creator of good art—the civilized artist—can easily fall into a position of disadvantage, since he can recognize virtues in the kind of art he prefers not to make, can think up excuses and justifications for even the cheapest pornography—to say nothing of more formidable, more "serious" false art—while the maker of trash, the barbarian, is less careful to be just. It is a fact of life that noble ideas, noble examples of human behavior, can drop out of fashion though they remain as real and applicable as ever—can simply come to be forgotten, plowed under by "progress."

I would not claim that even the worst bad art should be outlawed, since morality by compulsion is a fool's morality and since, moreover, I agree with Tolstoy that the highest purpose of art is to make people good by choice. But I do think bad art should be revealed for what it is whenever it dares to stick its head up, and I think the arguments for the best kind of art should be mentioned from time to time, because our appreciation of the arts is not wholly instinctive. If it were, our stock of bad books, paintings, and compositions would be somewhat less abundant.

I have said that wherever possible moral art holds up models of decent behavior; for example, characters in fiction, drama, and film whose basic goodness and struggle against confusion, error, and evil—in themselves and in others—give firm intellectual and emotional support to our own struggle. Sometimes, admittedly, the essentially moral artist may ignore this end, limiting his art to a search for information; that is, imaginative capture of what could not be known otherwise. A brilliantly imagined novel about a rapist or murderer can be more enlightening than a thousand psycho-sociological studies; and implied praise or condemnation in such a novel may be irrelevant or pettyminded. Work of this kind has obvious value and may even be beautiful in its execution, but it is only in a marginal sense art. At other times the moral model may be indirect, as when the confusion of Chaucer's Pardoner or Shakespeare's Macbeth leaves true morality at least partly to implication or at best in the hands of some minor character. Indirect models are hardly to be despised; nonetheless, it should be noticed that life's imitation of art is direct and not necessarily intelligent. After Marlon Brando appeared in *On the Waterfront*, an entire generation took to slumping, mumbling, turning up its collar, and hanging its cigarette casually off the lip. After the appearance of Roy Rogers, hordes of twelve-year-olds took to squinting. Today, though perhaps not in Shakespeare's day, the resolution never to behave like Macbeth does not inevitably carry any clear implication of what to do instead.

For the person who looks at fiction mainly from the point of view of the reader or critic, it is easy to get the idea that fiction is serious, thoughtful, or "philosophical" merely because—and merely in the sense that—some writers of fiction are intelligent thinkers who express their profound ideas through stories. Thus Henry James tells us about American innocence, Melville shows us how the quality of life is affected by the proposition of an indifferent universe, and so on. What literary critics claim is true: writers do communicate ideas. What the writer understands, though the student or critic of literature need not, is that the writer discovers, works out, and tests his ideas in the process of writing. Thus at its best fiction is, as I've said, a way of thinking, a philosophical method.

It must be granted at once that some good and "serious" fiction is merely first-class propaganda—fiction in which the writer knows before he starts what it is that he means to say and does not allow his mind to be changed by the process of telling the story. A good deal of medieval literature works in this way. The doctrine is stock, and the actions of ladies, gentlemen, and beasts are merely devices for communicating doctrine in a pleasing way. This is the method Boccaccio describes in his *Genealogy of the Gods* as the essential technique of allegory; it produces the kind of poetry Sidney defends in his *Defense: instruction clothed in delight. Pilgrim's Progress* and *Gulliver's Travels* (to some extent) are fictions of this kind, as are (to a large extent) such modern works as *Gravity's Rainbow*. Fiction of this sort, dogmatic or ironic-dogmatic fiction, may be highly entertaining, may be fully persuasive, may have the clear ring of art; but such fiction is closer to the sermon than to the true short story or novel, closer to the verse essay as practiced by Pope than to the Elizabethan play. Such fiction may be—and usually is—*moralistic*, and the writer, in creating it, may be morally careful—that is, may work hard at telling nothing but the truth; but in what I am describing as true moral fiction, the "art" is not merely ornamental: it controls the argument and gives it its rigor, forces the writer to intense yet dispassionate and unprejudiced watchfulness, drives him—in ways abstract logic cannot match—to unexpected discoveries and, frequently, a change of mind.

Moral fiction communicates meanings discovered by the process of the fiction's creation. We can see the process working when we look through the drafts of a certain kind of writer's work. Thus we see Tolstoy beginning with one set of ideas and attitudes in *Two Marriages*, an early draft of *Anna Karenina*—in which Anna, incredible as it seems, marries Vronsky—and gradually discovering, draft by draft, deeper and deeper implications in his story, revising his judgments, stumbling upon connections, reaching new insights, until finally he nails down the attitudes and ideas we find dramatized, with such finality and conviction that it seems to us unthinkable that they should not have burst full-grown from Tolstoy's head, in the published novel. So Dostoevski agonized over the better and worse implications of Myshkin's innocence and impotence. We see the same when we look at successive drafts of work by Kafka, or even the two drafts of Chaucer's *Troilus and Criseyde*.

The writing of a fiction is *not* a mode of thought when a good character and a bad one are pitted against each other. There is nothing inherently wrong with such fiction. It may be funny, or biting, or thrillingly melodramatic; it may be unspeakably witty, or grave, or mysterious, or something else; but it can contain only cleverness and preachments, not the struggle of thought. When fiction becomes thought—a kind of thought less restricted than logic or mere common sense (but also impossible to verify)—the writer makes discoveries which, in the act of discovering them in his fiction, he communicates to the reader.

He makes these discoveries in several ways. Much of what a writer learns he learns simply by imitation. Making up a scene, he asks himself at every step, "Would she really say that?" or "Would he really throw the shoe?" He plays the scene through in his imagination, taking all the parts, being absolutely fair to everyone involved (mimicking each in turn, as Aristotle pointed out, and never sinking to stereotype for even the most minor characters), and when he finishes the scene he understands by sympathetic imitation what each character has done throughout and why the fight, or accident, or whatever, developed as it did. The writer does the same with the total action. Throughout the entire chain of causally related events, the writer asks himself, would *a* really cause *b* and not *c*, etc., and he creates what seems, at least by the test of his own imagination and experience of the world, an inevitable development of story. Inevitability does not depend, of course, on realism. Some or all or the characters may be fabulous—dragons, griffins, Achilles' talking horses—but once a character is established for a creature, the creature must act in accord with it.

To learn about reality by mimicking it, needless to say, the writer must never cheat. He may establish any sort of *givens* he pleases, but once they are established he must follow where, in his experience, nature would lead if there really were, say, griffins. He cannot, for instance, make the reader accept some event on the basis of the writer's stylistic eloquence. By rhetoric any writer worth his salt can convince the reader than an eighty-pound griffin falls twice as fast as a forty-pound griffin, but if natural law in a world containing griffins is one of the premises the writer has accepted, the rhetoric is a betrayal of honest thought. Neither can the honest writer make the reader accept what he says took place if the writer moves from *a* to *b* by verbal sleight of hand; that is, by distracting the reader. It is easy for any clever writer to evoke and fully authenticate a situation (a), then digress to something else, then evoke and fully authenticate a situation which pretends to be the direct effect of *a*, a situation *b* which is in fact implausible as a result of *a* but does not seem implausible because the digression has blurred the real and inevitable effect of *a* in the reader's mind. No decent writer, one may suppose, would play such games—except, by accident, on himself. Yet many contemporary writers do, and some, like Stanley Elkin, do it on principle, preferring comic surprise to energetic discovery and looking for fictive energy not in character and action but in power of the writer's performance or in poetic language. It is true that the freedom to follow wherever language may lead can sometimes result in the ambush of unexpected insights; and it is true, too, that Stanley Elkin no more tells conscious lies in his fiction than did John Bunyan. Nevertheless, it requires a very special talent to succeed in Elkin's way, and one may wonder if the race is worth the candle. The writer who boasts, "I can make a lady pick up a coffee cup anytime I please" may be amusing, even spell-binding, like a circus performer, but he is not, in one of the available ways, serious. Worse, the strong likelihood is that his work will be, in one important way, boring.

Discussion

1. What, according to Gardner, are some of the characteristics of moral fiction? Notice that he doesn't necessarily appreciate fiction in which a good character is pitted against a bad character (paragraph 7). Does this mean that many of the Christian romances published by religious publishing houses are immoral? Apply Gardner's criteria to books you know and try to come up with a list of books that are moral and a list that are immoral.
2. In paragraph 3, Gardner notes instances in which people have imitated literary characters. Are there other instances of such imitation that you can think of? Is it necessarily bad to imitate a character in a novel or film?
3. If a writer can make anything happen in a novel, what is wrong with his doing so? Do Gardner's comments in the last two paragraphs of this selection suggest that science fiction is immoral?
4. Gardner states that "morality by compulsion is a fool's morality." Is this true? Does it take into account humanity's tendency toward sin? How does Proverbs 22:6 respond to the concept?
5. In a following essay, Nancy M. Tischler provides a view of morality and art different from Gardner's. Compare and contrast the two views. In an essay of argumentation you might posit one as more meritorious than the other.

Novelist and Believer

Flannery O'Connor

> *In this essay, the Roman Catholic novelist Flannery O'Connor enters the debate as to what constitutes Christian literature. Does this quality inhere in the writer's vision, in the work itself, or in the perception of the audience? Here O'Connor explains how her belief shapes her writing as she crafts her stories for an audience comprised primarily of unbelievers.*

Being a novelist and not a philosopher or theologian, I shall have to enter this discussion at a much lower level and proceed along a much narrower course than that held up to us here as desirable. It has been suggested that for the purposes of this symposium [at Sweetbriar College, Virginia, in March 1963], we conceive religion broadly as an expression of man's ultimate concern rather than identify it with institutional Judaism or Christianity or with "going to church."

I see the utility of this. It's an attempt to enlarge your ideas of what religion is and of how the religious need may be expressed in the art of our time; but there is always the danger that in trying to enlarge the ideas of students, we will evaporate them instead, and I think nothing in this world lends itself to quick vaporization so much as the religious concern.

As a novelist, the major part of my task is to make everything, even an ultimate concern, as solid, as concrete, as specific as possible. The novelist begins his work where human knowledge begins—with the senses; he works through the limitations of matter, and unless he is writing fantasy, he has to stay within the concrete possibilities of his culture. He is bound by his particular past and by those institutions and traditions that this past has left to his society. The Judaeo-Christian tradition has formed us in the west; we are bound to it by ties which may often be invisible, but which are there nevertheless. It has formed the shape of our secularism; it has formed even the shape of modern atheism. For my part, I shall have to remain well within the Judaeo-Christian tradition. I shall have to speak, without apology, of the Church, even when the Church is absent; of Christ, even when Christ is not recognized.

If one spoke as a scientist, I believe it would be possible to disregard large parts of the personality and speak simply as a scientist, but when one speaks as a novelist, he must speak as he writes—with the whole personality. Many contend that the job of the novelist is to show us how man feels, and they say that this is an operation in which his own commitments intrude not at all. The novelist, we are told, is looking for a symbol to express feeling, and whether he be Jew or Christian or Buddhist or whatever makes no difference to the aptness of the symbol. Pain is pain, joy is joy, love is love, and these human emotions are stronger than any mere religious belief; they are what they are and the novelist shows them as they are. This is all well and good so far as it goes, but it just does not go as far as the novel goes. Great fiction involves the whole range of human judgment; it is not simply an imitation of feeling. The good novelist not only finds a symbol for feeling, he finds a symbol and a way of lodging it which tells the intelligent reader whether this feeling is adequate or inadequate, whether it is moral or immoral, whether it is good or evil. And his theology, even in its most remote reaches, will have a direct bearing on this.

It makes a great difference to the look of a novel whether its author believes that the world came late into being and continues to come by a creative act of God, or whether he believes that the world and ourselves are the product of a cosmic accident. It makes a great difference to his novel whether he believes that we are created in God's image, or whether he believes we create God in our own. It makes a great difference whether he believes that our wills are free, or bound like those of the other animals.

St. Augustine wrote that the things of the world pour forth from God in a double way: intellectually into the minds of the angels and physically into the world of things. To the person who believes this—as the western world did up until a few centuries ago—this physical, sensible world is good because it proceeds from a divine source. The artist usually knows this by instinct; his senses, which are used to penetrating the concrete, tell him so. When Conrad said that his aim as an artist was to render the highest possible justice to the visible universe, he was speaking with the novelist's surest instinct. The artist penetrates the concrete world in order to find at its depths the image of its source, the image of ultimate reality. This in no way hinders his perception of evil but rather sharpens it, for only when the natural world is seen as good does evil become intelligible as a destructive force and a necessary result of our freedom.

For the last few centuries we have lived in a world which has been increasingly convinced that the reaches of reality end very close to the surface, that there is no ultimate divine source, that the things of the world do not pour forth from God in a double way, or at all. For nearly two centuries the popular spirit of each succeeding generation has tended more and more to the view that the mysteries of life will eventually fall before the mind of man. Many modern novelists have been more concerned with the processes of consciousness than with the objective world outside the mind. In twentieth-century fiction it increasingly happens that a meaningless, absurd world impinges upon the sacred consciousness of author or character; author and character seldom now go out to explore and penetrate a world in which the sacred is reflected.

Nevertheless, the novelist always has to create a world and a believable one. The virtues of art, like the virtues of faith, are such that they reach beyond the limitations of the intellect, beyond any mere theory that a writer may entertain. If the novelist is doing what as an artist he is bound to do, he will inevitably suggest that image of ultimate reality as it can be glimpsed in some aspect of the human situation. In this sense, art reveals, and the theologian has learned that he can't ignore it. In many universities, you will find departments of theology vigorously courting departments of English. The theologian is interested specifically in the modern novel because there he sees reflected the man of our time, the unbeliever, who is nevertheless grappling in a desperate and usually honest way with intense problems of the spirit.

We live in an unbelieving age but one which is markedly and lopsidedly spiritual. There is one type of modern man who recognizes spirit in himself whom he can adore as Creator and Lord; consequently he has become his own ultimate concern. He says with Swinburne, "Glory to man in the highest, for he is the master of things," or with Steinbeck, "In the end was the word and the word was with men." For him, man has his own natural spirit of courage and dignity and pride and must consider it a point of honor to be satisfied with this.

There is another type of modern man who recognizes a divine being not himself, but who does not believe that this being can be known anagogically or defined dogmatically or received sacramentally. Spirit and matter are separated for him. Man wanders about, caught in a maze of guilt he can't identify, trying to reach a God he can't approach, a God powerless to approach him.

And there is another type of modern man who can neither believe nor contain himself in unbelief and who searches desperately, feeling about in all experience for the lost God.

At its best our age is an age of searchers and discoverers, and at its worst, an age that has domesticated despair and learned to live with it happily. The fiction which celebrates this last state will be the least likely to transcend its limitations, for when the religious need is banished successfully, it usually atrophies, even in the novelist. The sense of mystery vanishes. A kind of reverse evolution takes place, and the whole range of feeling is dulled.

The searchers are another matter. Pascal wrote in his notebook, "If I had not known you, I would not have found you." These unbelieving searchers have their effect even upon those of us who do believe. We begin to examine our own religious notions, to sound them for genuineness, to purify them in the heat of our unbelieving neighbor's anguish. What Christian novelist could compare his concern to Camus'? We have to look in much of the fiction of our time for a kind of sub-religion which expresses its ultimate concern in images that have not yet broken through to show any recognition of a God who has revealed himself. As great as much of this fiction is, as much as it reveals a wholehearted effort to find the only true ultimate concern, as much as in many cases it represents religious values of a high order, I do not believe that it can adequately represent in fiction the central religious experience. That, after all, concerns a relationship with a supreme being recognized through faith. It is the experience of an encounter, of a kind of knowledge which affects the believer's every action. It is Pascal's experience after his conversion and not before.

What I say here would be much more in line with the spirit of our times if I could speak to you about the experience of such novelists as Hemingway and Kafka and Gide and Camus, but all my own experience has been that of the writer who believes, again in Pascal's words, in the "God of Abraham, Isaac, and Jacob and not of the philosophers and scholars." This is an unlimited God and one who has revealed himself specifically. It is one who became man and rose from the dead. It is one who confounds the senses and the sensibilities, one known early on as a stumbling block. There is no way to gloss over this specification or to make it more acceptable to modern thought. This God is the object of ultimate concern and he has a name.

The problem of the novelist who wishes to write about a man's encounter with this God is how he shall make the experience—which is both natural and supernatural—understandable, and credible, to his reader. In any age this would be a problem, but in our own, it is a well-nigh insurmountable one. Today's audience is one in which religious feeling has become, if not atrophied, at least vaporous and sentimental. When Emerson decided, in 1832, that he could no longer celebrate the Lord's Supper unless the bread and wine were removed, an important step in the vaporization of religion in America was taken, and the spirit of that step has continued apace. When the physical fact is separated from the spiritual reality, the dissolution of belief is eventually inevitable.

The novelist doesn't write to express himself, he doesn't write simply to render a vision he believes true, rather he renders his vision so that it can be transferred, as nearly whole as possible, to his reader. You can safely ignore the reader's taste, but you can't ignore his nature, you can't ignore his limited patience. Your problem is going to be difficult in direct proportion as your beliefs depart from his.

When I write a novel in which the central action is a baptism, I am very well aware that for a majority of my readers, baptism is a meaningless rite, and so in my novel I have to see that this baptism carries enough awe and mystery to jar the reader into some kind of emotional recognition of its significance. To this end I have to bend the whole novel—its language, its structure, its action. I have to make the reader feel, in his bones if nowhere else, that something is going on here that counts. Distortion in this case is an instrument; exaggeration has a purpose, and the whole structure of the story or novel has been made what it is because of belief. This is not the kind of distortion that destroys; it is the kind that reveals, or should reveal.

Students often have the idea that the process at work here is one which hinders honesty. They think that inevitably the writer, instead of seeing what is, will see only what he believes. It is perfectly possible, of course, that this will happen. Ever since there have been such things as novels, the world has been flooded with bad fiction for which the religious impulse has been responsible. The sorry religious novel comes about when the writer supposes that because of his belief, he is somehow dispensed from the obligation to penetrate concrete reality. He will think that the eyes of the Church or of the Bible or of his particular theology have already done the seeing for him, and that his business is to rearrange this essential vision into satisfying patterns, getting himself as little dirty in the process as possible. His feeling about this may have been made more definite by one of those Manichean-type theologies which sees the natural world as unworthy of penetration. But the real novelist, the one with an instinct for what he is about, knows that he cannot approach the infinite directly, that he must penetrate the natural human world as it is. The more sacramental his theology, the more encouragement he will get from it to do just that.

The supernatural is an embarrassment today even to many of the churches. The naturalistic bias has so well saturated our society that the reader doesn't realize that he has to shift his sights to read fiction which treats of an encounter with God. Let me leave the novelist and talk for a moment about his reader.

This reader has first to get rid of a purely sociological point of view. In the thirties we passed through a period in American letters when social criticism and social realism were considered by many to be the most important aspects of fiction. We still suffer with a hangover from that period. I launched a character, Hazel Motes, whose presiding passion was to rid himself of a conviction that Jesus had redeemed him. Southern degeneracy never entered my head, but Hazel said "I seen" and "I taken" and he was from East Tennessee, and so the general reader's explanation for him was that he must represent some social problem peculiar to that part of the benighted South.

Ten years, however, have made some difference in our attitude toward fiction. The sociological tendency has abated in that particular form and survived in another just as bad. This is the notion that the fiction writer is after the typical. I don't know how many letters I have received telling me that the South is not at all the way I depict it; some tell me that Protestantism in the South is not at all the way I portray it, that a Southern Protestant would never be concerned, as Hazel Motes is, with penitential practices. Of course, as a novelist I've never wanted to characterize the typical South or typical Protestantism. The South and the religion found there are extremely fluid and offer enough variety to give the novelist the widest range of possibilities imaginable, for the novelist is bound by the reasonable possibilities, not the probabilities, of his culture.

There is an even worse bias than these two, and that is the clinical bias, the prejudice that sees everything strange as a case study in the abnormal. Freud brought to light many truths, but his psychology is not an adequate instrument for understanding the religious encounter or the fiction that describes it. Any psychological or cultural or economic determination may be useful up to a point; indeed, such facts can't be ignored, but the novelist will be interested in them only as he is able to go through them to give us a sense of something beyond them. The more we learn about ourselves, the deeper into the unknown we push the frontiers of fiction.

I have observed that most of the best religious fiction of our time is most shocking precisely to those readers who claim to have an intense interest in finding more "spiritual purpose"—as they like to put it—in modern novels than they can at present detect in them. Today's reader, if he believes in grace at all, sees it as something which can be separated from nature and served to him raw as Instant Uplift. This reader's favorite word is compassion. I don't wish to defame the word. There is a better sense in which it can be used but seldom is—the sense of being in travail with and for creation in its subjection to vanity. This is a sense which implies a recognition of sin; this is a suffering-with, but one which blunts no edges and makes no excuses. When infused into novels, it is often forbidding. Our age doesn't go for it.

I have said a great deal about the religious sense that the modern audience lacks, and by way of objection to this, you may point out to me that there is a real return of intellectuals in our time to an interest in and a respect for religion. I believe that this is true. What this interest in religion will result in for the future remains to be seen. It may, together with the new spirit of ecumenism that we see everywhere around us, herald a new religious age, or it may simply be that religion will suffer the ultimate degradation and become, for a little time, fashionable. Whatever it means for the future, I don't believe that our present society is one whose basic beliefs are religious, except in the South. In any case, you can't have effective allegory in times when people are swept this way and that by momentary convictions, because everyone will read it differently. You can't indicate moral values when morality changes with what is being done, because there is no accepted basis of judgment. And you cannot show the operation of grace when grace is cut off from nature or when the very possibility of grace is denied, because no one will have the least idea of what you are about.

The serious writer has always taken the flaw in human nature for his starting point, usually the flaw in an otherwise admirable character. Drama usually bases itself on the bedrock of original sin, whether the writer thinks in theological terms or not. Then, too, any character in a serious novel is supposed to carry a burden of meaning larger than himself. The novelist doesn't write about people in a vacuum; he writes about people in a world where something is obviously lacking, where there is the general mystery of incompleteness and the particular tragedy of our own times to be demonstrated, and the novelist tries to give you, within the form of the book, a total experience of human nature at any time. For this reason the greatest dramas naturally involve the salvation or loss of the soul. Where there is no belief in the soul, there is very little drama. The Christian novelist is distinguished from his pagan colleagues by recognizing sin as sin. According to his heritage he sees it not as sickness or an accident of environment, but as a responsible choice of offense against God which involves his eternal future. Either one is serious about salvation or one is not. And it is well to realize that the maximum amount of seriousness admits the maximum amount of comedy. Only if we are secure in our beliefs can we see the comical side of the universe. One reason a great deal of our contemporary fiction is humorless is because so many of these writers are relativists and have to be continually justifying the actions of their characters on a sliding scale of values.

Our salvation is a drama played out with the devil, a devil who is not simply generalized evil, but an evil intelligence determined on its own supremacy. I think that if writers with a religious view of the world excel these days in the depiction of evil, it is because they have to make its nature unmistakable to their particular audience.

The novelist and the believer, when they are not the same man, yet have many traits in common—a distrust of the abstract, a respect for boundaries, a desire to penetrate the surface of reality and to find in each thing the spirit which makes it itself and holds the world together. But I don't believe that we shall have great religious fiction until we have again that happy combination of believing artist and believing society. Until that time, the novelist will have to do the best he can in travail with the world he has. He may find in the end that instead of reflecting the image at the heart of things, he has only reflected our broken condition and, through it, the face of the devil we are possessed by. This is a modest achievement, but perhaps a necessary one.

Discussion

1. O'Connor asserts that what a novelist believes has a great impact on the fictional world she creates. What should the fictional world created by a Christian writer be like?

2. Mystery assumes a high priority in O'Connor's thought, but it is a term that perhaps few of us use in the sense that she does. To try to increase your awareness of her use of the term, list what you see as the most powerful mysteries of human existence.

3. What would Gardner think of O'Connor's advocacy of distortion to produce mystery?

4. Referring to all types of literature, O'Connor writes that "drama usually bases itself on the bedrock of original sin, whether the writer thinks in theological terms or not." Can you think of examples of books by non-Christians in which this seems to be the case? Speculate on why this might be true.

5. Contrast the qualities of that fiction that O'Connor believes is good fiction and that fiction that she calls "sorry religious fiction."

The Christian Reader

Nancy M. Tischler

> *The matter of what makes a book good is more complicated for the Christian than for the non-Christian. As Nancy M. Tischler, a professor of English at Pennsylvania State University, points out in this essay, the Christian needs to make judgments about the implied values as well as about the aesthetics of a work of literature. The question she considers here is whether there is a way to define what Christian literature is.*

The Need for Christian Evaluation

Read any good books lately? This time-honored conversation-starter leads to a discussion of the latest novel on the coffee table. It can even lead to an aesthetic or philosophical debate over values.

But behind this simple question is an implied premise—that we know how to identify a good book. For the usual reader or critic, this is a matter of aesthetic judgment. In a well-written book, certain accumulated standards in such areas as language, characterization, point of view, and probability, are presupposed. (In actuality, even in an age of "rules criticism" such as the eighteenth century there has been precious little agreement on such standards in particular cases, so we can expect even less in our libertarian era.)

For the Christian reader or critic, "good" involves more than an aesthetic judgment. It is an ethical and religious term, implying standards of another sort. To most of us, standards for goodness are even less clearly perceived than those for beauty. This perhaps accounts for the increasing array of criticism in which Christians analyze literature without evaluating it. Although we eagerly identify Christ figures or discuss religious imagery, we hesitate to posit a standard for good (moral or beautiful) literature.

On the other hand, we are often quite clear about what is bad: it is the book that is poorly conceived and clumsily written, thematically debasing, shallow, and false. Most books written in any age are not art. They may be propaganda, uplifting or downgrading tracts; they may serve a moral or spiritual function; but they are not art. Few works of Christian literature have enough beauty or intellectual content to be judged in the same category with the real touchstones of Christian literature: *The Divine Comedy, Pilgrim's Progress, Paradise Lost, Ash Wednesday.* These pieces all have a grandeur in scope, a precision in expression, a reality in detail, a psychological truth, and an enduring appeal. The writers love words and form. They are craftsmen as well as impressive thinkers, who know how to transform individual experience into objects of beauty that communicate to man regardless of differences in country or period. Thus, we must first establish that a work is art; then we can explore the next question—is it Christian?

Issues in the Christian's Assessment of Literature

Is there a formula for Christian literature? One might be tempted to generalize about characteristics that must be present, such as: God must be a part of the story as an active force; man must be presented in a balanced, serious, and responsible way; actions must be seen to have significance and consequences; there can be no dishonest endings to reward the innocent and punish the guilty; the style must call attention to the idea rather than to the artist; the plot must reflect a universe with order and meaning. But such rules begin to sound suspiciously constricting. They ominously echo those precise regulations of the medieval church that perverted so much of art for so many years—the significance of colors, the proper subject matter, and the appropriate expression, composition, and presentation were all carefully dictated by the clergy. Even in the Renaissance we are repelled by orthodoxy's infringement on the artist: putting loincloths on Michelangelo's glorious nudes and whitewashing the rainbow colors of the cathedrals. And the eighteenth century with its precise criticism seems equally unenlightened.

While the Protestant may be somewhat less likely than the medieval or modern Catholic to restrict the artist in a programmed manner (except perhaps in his response to pornography), he is likely to have a deep-seated suspicion of beauty and a proclivity toward iconoclasm. Like the Old Testament Jew, he is distrustful of the graven image. Our capacity to create—to be makers—is but a dim reflection of that ultimate Creator's genius; yet it tempts man to feel pride and to worship. The image of God looks at the products of his own creativity and worships both the golden calf he forms and the hands that formed it. Thus, we see that the golden calf is neither better nor worse than the cherubim of the temple; both are lifeless matter formed by man and surprisingly capable of eliciting a response in man. Yet one was created for the glorification of man and the other for the greater glory of God.

The difference lies not only in the motivating force behind the artist (which is always difficult to discern) but also in the response of the viewer. Do we marvel at the beauty of the work, at the genius of the artist, or at the magnificence of the God who gave man such capabilities? The Hebrew, living under the law, revered that beauty which pointed toward God—the temple, the paean of faith, the poetry of vision. But the Christian, inheritor of pagan as well as Hebrew traditions, has found his path more complex. Paul tells us we are obliged to walk with the Spirit as free men. This liberty has proven a blessing and a burden to the artist.

Although there was little temptation to use pagan narrative forms in the early centuries of the Church—the narratives of the apostles (except for John's) were simple catalogues of events with minimal stylistic interference—the early Christians did assimilate pagan architecture and art. In addition, Paul knew how to unite history with imagery for maximum effect.

After the theatres were condemned and closed, pagan drama moved over into the Church; and the medieval Christian writers drew heavily on such poets as Virgil for their technical inspiration. Gradually, as Christians grew willing to agree that fiction is not untruth, they incorporated this form into their culture as well. Thus, though the early Christian would have frowned on the frivolous and decadent forms of pagan prose, fiction, drama, and poetry, later Christians gradually learned to use these art forms as tools for their faith. The medieval mystery plays, the poetry of Dante, the narrative of Bunyan's Pilgrim all owe clear debts to pagan ancestors.

That early reluctance to embrace pagan beauty has reversed itself in the twentieth century. The Christian increasingly looks at the art world as territory to be colonized. Scholars are busily discovering the religious implications in Vonnegut's latest novel, or the ritual structure of Albee's plays. It reminds one of the days when Christians strove to find redeeming elements in Virgil so they could be justified in reading and copying him.

The growing zeal for religious content has resulted in (or perhaps resulted from) a growing tendency among artists to play with religious themes and ideas. It is natural that art would return to such central concerns of man. Art and religion both center on man's deepest needs: for truth and beauty and meaning. Serious artists in the contemporary world frequently explore the nature of man, of innocence, of guilt, of freedom, of love, of death, and of God. The critic-scholars often see their obligation to help us understand our artists, and perhaps even to evaluate them.

Reading from a Christian Perspective

This brings us back to our original problem: When the Christian reader or critic explores a novel, poem, or play, how does he judge? Does he analyze the ideas, hold them up against standards of orthodoxy (his, or the artist's, or some church's), and then evaluate the work as good or bad according to its "correctness"? Does he have in mind a model of the good play, novel, or poem? Does he believe there is such a thing as "Christian" literature?

Most critics refuse to deal with this final question. Certainly a novel cannot be Christian any more than a golden calf can be pagan. It is the artist and the viewer who must bear the brunt of such judgment, not the work itself. Some works are more likely to provide orthodox responses than others. For example, Robert Penn Warren's *All the King's Men* provides rich materials for contemplating the Fall and the nature of man; the novel carries the reader along a path of thought that most Christians would approve. But this novel is more often read as a statement about the nature of American politics. The pagan reader can enjoy the social commentary and the romatic adventure, skipping hastily over the theological sections. Graham Greene's *The Power and the Glory* makes a very powerful statement about God and his priests in a most effective form. But again many readers enjoy the novel for its degrading portayal of the whiskey priest who fathered an illegitimate child, missing the central point altogether.

We do not posit an ideal novel, poem, or play, because we cannot. We can cite touchstones of Christian expression (Milton's or Dante's) that grew out of those ages and those men and those audiences that once in a great while come together to produce greatness, but more than that we cannot do. Like Aristotle, who could tell us only what his favorite tragedy looked like, not what all good tragedy must be, most of us can point out novels or plays we have liked or disliked but cannot say what novels or plays must be. We can be analytic and descriptive, but not proscriptive and prescriptive.

Art is, after all, an exploration often beyond the limits of rational thought. It is frequently wiser than the artist; under the inspiration of the Muses or the Holy Spirit, he may have recorded more than he knew. Man cannot limit art without destroying it. Even in an individual artist this is obvious. *War and Peace,* growing out of the troubled, confused mind of Tolstoy, is aesthetically superior to the clear, doctrinaire products of his conversion to Christianity. The Communist world has found that its neat rules destroy art and breed rebellion. Ireland has found its artists leave when it seeks to legislate their art. We who have freedom in Christ are obliged to remember that this responsible freedom must extend to the writer and reader as well.

Not all writers respond responsibly to their freedom. Milton commented on the license that so often replaces liberty. The plethora of pornography today is evidence that man is all too eager to sell his soul and his pen for a price. The chaotic content and form of so much modern literature shows man's willingness to reflect his meaningless world rather than to strive for meaning and order. The delight in depravity and sniggering at morality should not surprise those of us accustomed to viewing man as fallen. We live, after all, east of Eden, where the world, man, and his art are all fallen and in need of redemption.

Even Christian writers lapse from time to time, substituting license for their liberty. In their day, all our heroes of Christian art have had their critics who pointed with horror to the feet of clay. The Church was shocked at Dante's divine poetry; the orthodox were appalled by Milton's view of creation and temptation, not to mention his defense of divorce; and many moderns doubt Eliot's sincerity and artistry. We have no examples of perfect Christian artists, but then we have only one example of the perfect Christian. We should know better than to expect perfection. We should know better than to expect we shall ever see an artist who can satisfy Christians for his orthodoxy and critics for his excellence.

Finding Pieces of the Truth

I am therefore inclined to accept Milton's view that we must learn to piece together bits of perfection. Truth, he said, is like the body of Osiris, fragmented and scattered. Our job is to collect, to judge, and to select those pieces that truly belong to God. Thus we must learn to make use of those scattered insights that the artist captures and communicates.

Regardless of Solzhenitsyn's religious stance, we can gain from his understanding of the nature of evil. He need not call man "fallen" to show that he is. Nor need he call those occasional flashes of beauty in human nature the "image of God." Those moments of heroism, of generosity, of personal integrity, and of compassion in the cancer ward or prison camp portray man transcending his hellish surroundings. They make mockery of Pavlovian psychology and Marxian materialism.

Faulkner, in *The Sound and the Fury*, as he portrays the simple faith of Dilsey, who so willingly bears another's burdens, also reflects something of the true experience of the Christian. The ageless black heroine takes the idiot offspring of the white "aristocrats" to her black church, where she staunchly faces the furious congregation. Her love for Benjy has nothing to do with race, class, sex, or mentality. But this does not mean Faulkner's whole book is built on the Christian world-view. I would reject his central vision that life is a tale told by an idiot, full of sound and fury, signifying nothing. One the contrary, I am convinced that we are part of a great plan and that each human life signifies a great deal.

But this is what I mean by our need to take bits and pieces out of our reading to enrich our life and our faith. God can speak to us through secular literature in a manner parallel to his speaking in sacred literature. A phrase, an idea, or a situation will suddenly catch our attention and magically illumine our lives. A really good novel or poem or play—by either a Christian or a non-Christian writer—generally includes a host of such moments.

We might wish for a day like Dante's when the creative imagination was aflame with Christian doctrine; but even in Dante's day, Boccaccio and Chaucer were inspired by other materials. We are indeed lucky that the twentieth century has given us such Christian literary giants as Eliot and Auden, whom we should appreciate without growing uncritical in our love. God obviously intends us to find random flowers among the briars, testing us by our choices here as elsewhere in life. Literature allows us to experience people and situations out of our ken, to enlarge our ideas as well as our experience. It is as full of temptations as the life it mirrors; it is as full of vitality and peril as Adam and the Garden he inhabited. And we are as free as Adam was to choose which fruits we select to eat. A free man now, as then, is judged by his strength in the face of temptation.

Trusting the majesty and power of God, we need fear no words or ideas. We can devote the whole man to living the Christian life, using the mind to understand what is written, the eye and the heart to appreciate it emotionally and aesthetically. We should also bring to the analysis and appreciation of culture our wonder, responding to art as a mystery and a miracle, testimony to God's creative power. The Christian's response to art is parallel to his response to nature, joy in the created world, and worship of the Creator reflected in it.

Discussion

1. In paragraph 5, Tischler suggests some possible characteristics of Christian literature only to reject them as a formula. Do you agree with her that they are too limiting? What tactic does she employ to convince us that they are overly restrictive? Later in the essay, Tischler writes that "a novel cannot be Christian any more than a golden calf can be pagan," suggesting that how the reader interprets the literature is as important as what is written on the page. Does this mean that each individual can decide whether a work is Christian or not? What criteria would you use to decide?

2. If there are "pieces of truth" in all literature, are there any books that Christians should not read?

3. How might Gardner or O'Connor respond to the fact that Tischler avoids defining moral or Christian literature?

On Evil in Art

Thomas Howard

Christians often struggle with the issue of whether to read books or view movies that might be "bad"—that present evil too realistically. For this reason, at various points in history they have avoided novels (or plays or movies) altogether. Since most of us wouldn't find that option appealing, we have to attempt what Thomas Howard, a professor of English, attempts here. We need to find ways of judging an author's intention when we encounter evil subject matter in a work of art.

The Problem of Portraying Evil in Art

On the recommendation of a friend I went to see the film *The Devils*. It is about an outbreak of supposed demon possession in a convent in Loudun, France, in the seventeenth century. Before the depicted situation gets sorted out, everyone has been embroiled in political intrigue, carnal chaos, emotional havoc, inquisition, cruelty, and the most bizarre forms of voluptuous decadence imaginable.

The makers of this film chose to handle their subject matter as vividly as they could. The opening scene whisks one straight into a perfumed moral bog, with Louis XIV participating in a dionysian frolic in front of a bored and elegant Mazarin. From then until he leaves the theater, the viewer is up to his neck in blood, incense, silk, tinsel, grapes, powder, wine, and flesh.

The film exhibits rather vividly a matter that is worth our attention. It is a matter we encounter in one form and another again and again in our own epoch. It has to do with the *Zeitgeist*, and with public imagination, and eventually, with the whole aesthetic question.

309

Perhaps what I am referring to ought to be cast as a question: Does there come a point at which the artistic portrayal of evil crosses a certain line and itself begins to participate in the very evil it is portraying?

All the red flags are up and aflutter as soon as anyone embarks on a line of thought like this. Censorship! Tyranny! The Index! Didacticism! Inquisition! Prudery! Victoria! Mrs. Grundy! But perhaps if we back off a bit and look at what is entailed, it will not appear so outrageous.

We would have to back all the way off to the question of what art *is* if we were really to get the discussion on a firm footing, but what with Aristotle and the Renaissance Florentines and Elizabethans and Goethe and Shelley and a thousand others, we would never get to the matter at hand. It may be enough here to say that art, whatever else it does, represents the effort of the human imagination to get hold of its experience of life by giving some concrete *shape* to it all. That shape may appear in stone or syntax or oils or melody, but the whole enterprise of poetry and sculpture and drama (and hence cinema) does bespeak that effort.

Parenthetically, the question of entertainment might arise here. Isn't all this appeal to heady aesthetic doctrine likely to dignify and elevate something that isn't half so weighty? What about mere enjoyment? What about the books that have been written and the plays that have been produced simply to divert people for a couple of hours? Let's not read Armageddon in every playroom scuffle, or the Beatific Vision in wallpaper.

It is not easy to find the border between "art" and "entertainment," if indeed there is one. By its very nature, art aims at furnishing pleasure, and we are entertained by pleasure. But the word *entertainment* with its suggestion of diversion and lightness doesn't serve very well when we speak of Dante or Vermeer, say, since the pleasure we get from what these artists have done seems to partake rather of sublimity than of mere diversion. Perhaps entertainment is a subdivision of pleasure—or a low rung on the ladder whose top reaches to Paradise.

It is a fact, of course, that a great deal of what we call "great art" came into being for rather utilitarian reasons—a rich man's commission, a new cantata for next Sunday, a play for the Globe theater; and on that level it is hard to untangle the occasional from the sublime. What happens is that an occasional piece may turn out to be sublime because the man who made it is a genius. His sonnet about the Piedmont massacre or the death of the Countess, unabashedly occasional, somehow participates in the sublime because he has a great and noble imagination. On the other hand, we can get planning committees together and decide to have a breathtaking spectacle and hire all the necessary professionals and work out all the logistics and blow all the trumpets—and succeed only in bringing forth appalling bathos (viz. Radio City Music Hall Christmas and Easter productions, or the cinematic biblical extravaganzas that started with *The Ten Commandments*).

Let us say, then, that authentic art emerges from a noble imagination whatever the occasion is that has asked for it. And, further, that if a noble imagination is at work, authentic art appears, whether the subject matter happens to be "high" or "low." It is not very difficult, on the one hand, to see how great feats of courage, skill, or strength (as in Beowulf, Achilles, Hercules) can give rise to noble treatment. By the same token, the long-ings, perplexities, or doubts that beset the human mind have been fruitful sources of high utterance (for Shelley, Browning, and Wordsworth, for example). Or the soul's experience of God often furnishes the matter for genuine poetry (Donne, Herbert, Eliot). These are easy enough to cite in connection with a theory of good art.

But what about evil—real evil—as subject matter? How do we work this in?

Dante, for instance, writes about hell, which is as low as you can get. And he writes explicitly and at great length. Here are all the damned, pictured vividly, with discussions of what it was that landed them there and of what their particular torment is. There are explicit notations of sin—lechery, gluttony, wrath, avarice, sloth, and so on.

Or take Shakespeare. What, after all, is *Macbeth* about? Foul murder. We watch Lady Macbeth turning herself into a monster. Or what about Chaucer? One of his most mature poems, the *Troilus and Criseyda*, is about illicit love. Then there is one of the most towering figures in all of English poetry—Milton's Satan.

It will be obvious here that a distinction needs to be made between "good and evil" on the one hand, and "high and low" on the other. Clearly, great evil can furnish "high" subject matter (as in Dante and Milton). The *Inferno* and Satan are "low" only on some cosmic hierarchical account-ing. They are "high" in the sense that they embody the biggest issues conceivable by the human imagination.

Similarly, really "low" stuff can afford the matter for genuine art. Take Fielding, with his tumble of hilarious but scurrilous situations in eigh-teenth-century England (or, for that matter, Faulkner's wholly serious handling of American decadence).

What seems to emerge from this line of observation is that it is entirely the *treatment* that decides the worth (and hence the goodness or badness) of a piece of art. There can be good art about bad things, and bad art about good things (a discussion of this last would embarrass us all, alas).

Preserving Aesthetic Distance and Privacy

Which brings us back to the question about *The Devils*. It is, to use the favorite word of blurbs and critics now, "frank." Isn't that a point in its

favor? It treats demonism (or bogus demonism—that is never really decided), and all; the carnality and terror and horror that follow in its wake,
colorfully and explicitly. What's wrong with this? Can't we be bold? Can't
we call a spade a spade? Haven't we done well to shake off our nineteenth-
century humbug and timorousness (and by this time, we all know we can
be talking about only one possible topic—sex)?

No. We have not done well. In its frenetic disavowal of sexual reticence, the twentieth century has torn the veil and blundered into the
Holy of Holies, as it were—and you can't do that with impunity. It is in
the nature of the case that the Ark be secluded: you can't use it for a
sawhorse. It is in the nature of the case that the shewbread be reserved—David didn't eat it for lunch every day. And by the same token,
it is in the nature of the case that human sexuality be shrouded. It is not
a public matter. (Someone will bring up the *Canticles* here: that is a
great poem of carnal love; perhaps it is not a *public* poem?) Not only is
nothing gained by the louder, shriller, more frequent and explicit discussion and portrayal of sexuality, but there is every reason to suppose
that something is being lost—something good, along with the humbug
and prudery.

And this is not necessarily to take a huggermugger or sanctimonious view of sexuality. Anyone who misses the fun—even the
funny—in sex is missing part of it. But, like a tiresome three-year-old's
pun, the human cloys when it is insisted upon too loud and long.

But sex isn't really the center of the matter. The guilt of *The Devils*
(and of a hundred novels, plays, revues, and films one could trot out) is
broader than that. It is that it fails to preserve *distance*. It not only
points to the stew. It stirs it. It jumps in.

To isolate and articulate the difference between Dante's handling of
hell and this film's handling of Loudun is difficult. Perhaps it has to do
with a leer. If anything is leering from Dante's pit, it is leering at the
poet as well as the reader, whereas you get the uneasy feeling in *The
Devils* that not only Louis XIV leers at you from the screen but the
filmmaker does as well.

We cannot say, of course, that *all* filmmakers (and novelists and
poets) whose work fails because of this failure of distance are leering.
That would be to pass a dangerous judgment on a great many people.
Perhaps there is a prior fault in the era that the artists, because they
live and work in the era, can escape only with difficulty. The fault
would have something to do with the erosion in the modern world of
such categories as absolute truth, and glory, and the holy, and thence of
such responses as awe, humility, and reticence.

Finally, one has the unhappy feeling that in a great deal of contemporary art, literature, and cinema, inadequate imaginations are at-

tempting very high summits. Scriptwriters, directors, producers, agents, and the rest, whose interest must be, above all, commercial, are addressing themselves quite blithely to imponderables that would give pause to the most sublime imaginations of history. The result is a proliferation of peepshows in Vanity Fair.

Discussion

1. Can the subject matter of a work of fiction ever do what Howard suggests in paragraph 4; that is, can fiction become evil by portraying evil? What do you think he means later when he talks about a work of art leering at its subject matter? Do you agree with him that the works of Dante and Shakespeare don't leer at the evil they portray?

2. Howard asserts that art "represents the effort of the human imagination to get hold of its experience of life by giving some concrete *shape* to it all." What do you think he means by this? Can you think of a story or novel that provides a good example of what you think he means here?

3. The question raised by the essay—can evil be the subject of good art?—can also be reversed: Can good art ever be evil? As you attempt to think of examples, try to establish criteria for deciding when good can become evil.

Frater Ave Atque Vale

Elva McAllaster

> Sometimes our effort to locate theme and meaning in literature is rewarded by a quick insight, a fleeting and surprising insight into reality. Perhaps it is like spotting a rare bird before it darts off into the air. The widely-published poet Elva McAllaster treats the transience of earthly things, and mortal visions, in the following poem, dedicated to "E. D. Z., too transiently my student."

He can't be true. A bird
Does not exist with such
Flame-neon brilliant feathers.

He moves, looks, turns,
Attacks from clustered seeds
As though he were a bird.

Be careful. Sudden motion might
Make any brilliant illusion
Take to its wings for good.

Wings. Are they wings?
Is he some newer Tolkien thing,
Some nightmare's full antithesis?

Flick-flick. Flick-flick.
True scarlet wings ascend
And almost leave a burn

Imprinted on the gravel.
Yes. I did watch him
On the sandy earth. Right there.

Discussion

1. The poem's title may be translated "Brother Hail and Farewell." How does it shape the meaning of the poem?

2. A modern poem usually begins in a picture of physical reality, and then opens insights for the reader. What physically happens in this poem? Where does McAllaster open the poem to the reader's imagination?

3. A good poet captures experiences for the reader. In the words of Robert Frost, "For me the initial delight is in the surprise of remembering something I didn't know I knew" ("The Figure a Poem Makes"). Have you had an experience that you can identify with this poem? How does the epigraph guide the meaning of the poem?

Letter to a Christian Artist

H. R. Rookmaaker

> *H. R. Rookmaaker, the well-known Dutch philosopher of art, celebrated both physical sensation and the divine revelation of God as bases for appreciating beauty in art. "We live in a wonderful world," he once wrote, "a world that discloses itself to us through our senses, but is at the same time far more than what our senses alone can reveal." Clearly and forcefully, Rookmaaker turns our understanding toward the revelation of God in the creative arts. The following letter addresses the place of the creative arts in the Christian life generally, a place which literature also takes.*

Diemen, The Netherlands
August 23, 1966

Your letter reached me yesterday after its trans-Atlantic voyage, and I propose to answer you directly. Your request touches on a problem I have been thinking about for a long time. Maybe what follows can be of help to you. I'd like to approach the matter in a schematic way, pointing out some principles.

Your questions concern your wish to paint—that is, to work as an artist—as a Christian. It really is remarkable that you decided to do this when you were just converted. Many times new Christians just drop their artistic careers because they think painting and art today are incompatible with being a real Christian. I'm glad you made this decision and hope to help you by suggesting the following principles for Christian artists:

1. If God has given us *talents* we may use them creatively—or rather, we *must* use them creatively. A Christian artist is not different from, say, a Christian teacher, minister, scholar, merchant, housewife, or anybody else who has been called by the Lord to specific work in line with his or her talents. There are no specific rules for artists, nor do

they have specific exemptions to the norms of good conduct God laid down for man. An artist is simply a person whose God-given talents ask him to follow the specific vocation of art. There may be circumstances when love towards God would forbid certain artistic activities or make them impossible, but the present moment in history does not ask for such a sacrifice. Quite the contrary. We—the Christian world and the world at large—desperately need artists.

2. To be God's child means to be offered *freedom*—the Christian freedom Christ himself and Paul in his letters say much about. This freedom is most important for anybody who wants to do artistic work. Without freedom there is no creativity, without freedom no originality, without freedom no art, without freedom even no Christianity. This freedom can exist only if it is based on love towards God and our neighbors, and if we become new men through the finished work of Christ and the Holy Spirit is given to us. Without this base, freedom may easily mean being free from God and consequently free to indulge all the cravings of the sinful heart of unredeemed man. (For more on this matter of freedom, see Paul's letter to the Galatians.)

Christian freedom is different from humanistic freedom, the freedom man gives himself to build a world after his own devising (as was tried by the Enlightenment and the humanist development after that time in the Western world). Humanistic freedom leads to all kinds of problems, as our Western world is now learning from experience. Freedom in the biblical sense is in no way negative—shun this, don't do that, you must leave that alone, keep away from this. Christian freedom has nothing to do with a set of rules by which you must bind yourself; indeed, such rules may easily be pseudo-Christian. Freedom is the necessary basis for creativity, for creativity is impossible when there is timidity, when you allow yourself to be bound by narrow rules. Do not think the modern art world is free—but we will turn to that later.

Freedom is positive. It means being free from tradition, from the feeling that everything you do has to be original, from certain fixed rules said to be necessary in art—but also from the thought that to be creative you must break all kinds of rules and standards.

Freedom means also that there are no prescriptions for subject matter. There is no need for a Christian to illustrate biblical stories or biblical truth, though he may of course choose to do that. An artist has the right to choose a subject that he thinks worthwhile. But nonrepresentational art provides no more freedom than the most involved allegorical or storytelling art.

Freedom includes the right to choose your own style, to be free from tradition but also from modernity, from fashion, from today and tomorrow as well as from yesterday. Yet there is no need to slap the contemporary in the face, as some streams of art nowadays deem necessary. Christian freedom also is freedom from the sinful lust for money, from seeking man's praise, from the search for celebrity. It is the freedom to help a neighbor out and give him something to delight in.

3. There are *norms for art* that are a part of God's creation. Without them art would be an empty name without sense. To say a person has been given a feeling for art and beauty (everybody has, to a certain extent), that he has been granted a strong subjective sense of artistic rightness, is but another way to say that he has been given an understanding of certain norms God laid down in his creation, the world in which we live. We call this *taste*, a feeling for design and color, the ability to grasp the inner harmony of a complex of forms and colors, the understanding of the inner relationship among elements of the subject matter, the ability to recognize the indefinable dividing lines between poor and good art, between worn-out symbols and fresh ways of saying things that are important to man.

These norms do not stand in the way when we want to live in Christian freedom; they are a part of our world and our nature. Only when man revolts and does not want to be a creature, when he wants to be God and not man, does he feel bound by these norms. For those who love the Lord and rejoice in his good and beautiful creation, these norms provide the opportunity to live in freedom and to create. As one cannot act and live free as a woman if one is not a woman and has not the possibilities of a woman, so the norms for beauty and art are at the same time the opportunities to see beauty and create art.

4. When God created—and in that way made the perception of beauty and the human creation of art possible—he gave art (or any artistic endeavor) a place in this world in which we live; and that world he called good. (I added artistic endeavor because we have to think not only of the rarefied museum type of art called Art with a capital *A* today, but also of all other types, including ceramics, dance music, pictures used in Sunday schools, and so on. We shall come back to this.) Art is here because God meant it to be here.

So art has its own task and meaning. There is no need to try to justify one's artistic activity by making works with a moralistic message, even if one is free to emphasize moral values. Nor is there any need to think one has to serve as a critic of culture, or always provide eye-openers to the nonartists, or teach, or evangelize, or do whatever other lofty things one can think of. Art has done its task when it provides the neighbor with things of beauty, a joy forever. Art has direct ties with life, living, joy, the depth of our being human, just by being art, and therefore it needs no external justification. That is so because God, who created the possibility of art and who laid beauty in his creation, is the God of the living and wants man to live. God is the God of life, the Life-giver. The Bible is full of this.

Art is not autonomous. "Art for art's sake" was an invention of the last century to loosen the ties between art and morality; that is, to give art the freedom to depict all kinds of sins as if they were not sinful, but simply human. The human understanding of depravity, of morality, of good and bad was thereby undermined or erased. The results we are seeing today, in our century. The meaning of art is its being art; but it is not autonomous, and it has thousands of ties with human life and thought. When artists cease to consider the world in its manifold forms outside the artistic domain, their art withers into nothingness, because it no longer has anything to say.

Much abstract art today is art, yes; but it has little meaning because it is *only* art. All its ties with reality have been cut. This applies as much to a ceramic product as to a painting. Art has its own meaning and needs no excuse. But it loses its meaning if it does not want to be anything but art and therefore cuts its ties with life and reality, just as scholarly work loses its importance and interest if learning is sought for its own sake. Art and science become aestheticism and scholasticism if made autonomous. They become meaningless idols.

The artist's work can have meaning for the society God put him in if he does not go to live in the ivory tower, or try to play the prophet or priest, or—turning in the other direction—in false modesty consider himself only a craftsman. He has to make art while thinking of his neighbors in love, helping them, and using his talents in their behalf.

5. Most art today expresses a spirit, *the spirit of our age*, which is not Christian. In some ways it is post-Christian, in others anti-Christian, in still others humanistic. Here and there are Christian artists who try to do their work in a godly spirit. But often their brethren leave them alone, distrusting their creativeness or doubting that they are Christians. False art theories that have pervaded the Christian world—the artist as an asocial being, a nonconformist in the wrong sense, a dangerous prophet, an abnormal being who lives in an alien world—are often responsible for this attitude. But some Christian artists themselves hold these false views and look down with contempt at their fellow-Christians. Anyway, there is a lot of confusion.

That the art of the world at large is also in a deep crisis does not make things easier. We live in a society where there is a break manifest between the mass of men and the elite, and another break between the natural sciences and technical realities on one side and religion (most of the time rather mystical) of a completely subjectivistic and irrationalistic type on the other. We who live in this world cannot act as if these deep problems did not exist.

There is *no real Christian tradition* in the arts today to turn to. If an artist wants to work as a Christian and do something that he can stand for and bear responsibility for, he has to start with the freedom based in a true faith in the living God of Scripture. He has to make art that is relevant to our day. Therefore, he has to understand our day. And, in order to gain from all that is good and fine today and yet avoid being caught by the spirit of our age and its false art principles, he must study modern art in all its different aspects deeply and widely. He must try to analyze the language modern artists use, their syntax and grammar, in order to be able to hear correctly the message they profess to speak. To analyze, understand, and criticize lovingly, loving man but hating sin, in order to avoid their mistakes but gain from their achievements—that is the Christian artist's task. A new Christian tradition, as a fruit of faith, can grow only if artists who understand their work and task, their world and its problems, really set to work.

6. But what has the Christian artist to offer the world? He has *a freedom to do something*, not just the freedom for freedom's sake. What should he aim at? Let's be careful not to lay down new rules. There are no biblical laws that art must be realistic or symbolic or sentimental, or must seek only idealized beauty.

The artist as a Christian is free, but not with a purposeless freedom. He is free in order to praise God and love his neighbors.

These are basic laws. What do they mean in practice? May I refer, this time without comment, to Philippians 4:8—"Finally, brethren, whatsoever things are true, whatsoever things are honest, whatsoever things are just, whatsoever things are pure, whatsoever things are lovely, whatsoever things are of good report; if there be any virtue, and if there be any praise, think on these things." Here we read what a Christian standing in freedom as a new man, in God's strength and with the help of the Holy Spirit, must search for. This also applies to the Christian as an artist. It is up to him to work, to pray, and to study, in order that he may realize as much as he possibly can of these truly human and life-promoting principles.

In the Lord,
H. R. Rookmaaker

Discussion

1. Central to Rookmaaker's artistic theory, as it is in this letter, is the nature of Christian freedom. What does it mean to be "free in Christ"? Or, to be free as an artist? What restrictions does Rook-

maaker place upon freedom in order to be genuinely free? In *The Great Divorce* C. S. Lewis makes a distinction between slavery and obedience, between insistence upon individual rights and acknowledging the rights of others. Does this pattern also apply to making art?

2. Compare Rookmaaker's idea of artistic freedom with that of John Steinbeck in the selection from his *Travels with Charley* in the following chapter. What limitations does Steinbeck, a non-Christian, accept and for what reasons?

3. Rookmaaker argues that "art is not autonomous." Apply his principle here to the world of contemporary rock music.

4. Rookmaaker observes that "there is no real Christian tradition in the arts today to turn to." But since the date of his essay (1966), a number of Christian authors have gained wide eminence: C. S. Lewis, J. R. R. Tolkien, Larry Woiwode, Walter Wangerin, Jr., Luci Shaw, and many others. Are they creating a new tradition for us? If you have read any of their works, try to generalize about what typifies them.

Writing Assignments for Chapter 12

1. Write a dialogue between Plato and one of the other writers in this chapter. You may wish to have them discuss a particular short story or novel as a means of focusing their arguments.

2. John Gardner suggests that not "even the worst bad art should be outlawed, since morality by compulsion is a fool's morality." Write a letter to your local school board arguing for or against the removal of a given story from the school's curriculum. You may wish to refer to some of Flannery O'Connor's statements as you craft your letter.

3. The question of whether morality can be legislated extends beyond the discussion of art and literature. Write an essay that explains how laws can or cannot compel morality. Be sure to use biblical criteria in defining your answer to this question.

4. Write an essay in which you devise your own criteria for judging whether a work of literature can be called Christian. Use the ideas of the other writers in this chapter to form a context for your ideas.

5. Write a letter to your high school teacher in which you argue one of the following points: 1) that a new story that you've read really presents an exciting Christian vision of the world; 2) that a story you were prevented from reading in high school really is worth reading; or 3) that high school students should be prevented from reading a specific story that you did read in high school.

13

Using Language

The right thing in speaking really is that we should be satisfied
not to annoy our hearers, without trying to delight them; we
ought in fairness to fight our cause with no help beyond the
bare facts.

—Aristotle, *Rhetoric*

How did He come except that "the Word was made flesh, and
dwelt among us"? It is as when we speak. In order that what
we are thinking may reach the mind of the listener through the
fleshly ears, that which we have in mind is expressed in words
and is called speech. But our thought is not transformed into
sounds; it remains entire in itself and assumes the form of
words by means of which it may reach the ears without
suffering any deterioration in itself. In the same way the Word
of God was made flesh without change that He might dwell
among us.

—Saint Augustine, *On Christian
Doctrine*

Men living in democratic countries, then, are apt to entertain
unsettled ideas, and they require loose expressions to convey
them. As they never know whether the idea they express today
will be appropriate to the new position they may occupy
tomorrow, they naturally acquire a liking for abstract terms. An
abstract term is like a box with a false bottom; you may put in
what ideas you please, and take them out again without being
observed.

—Alexis de Tocqueville, *Democracy
in America*

Men of few words are the best men.
> —William Shakespeare, *Henry V*

Language is simply alive, like an organism. We all tell each
other this, in fact, when we speak of living languages, and I
think we mean something more than an abstract metaphor. We
mean alive. Words are the cells of language, moving the great
body, on legs.
> —Lewis Thomas, *Lives of a Cell*

W
hat's the good word?" "Have you heard the latest word on the
situation in Lebanon?" "Put in a word for me, will you?" We use the
word *word* to mean many things; in these short sentences, we have
already used it to mean "hello," "news," "recommendation," and "unit
of meaning." We don't think twice about using it in different ways, nor
should we; part of the wonder of language is its flexibility. But we *do*
need to pay close attention to implications of our language, for ultimately our language says who we are.

Imagine a world stripped of words. A barren and a cold place indeed. Although some words we wouldn't mind doing without, others
we would cling to with all our power. On the one hand, we might gladly
dispense with even a fraction of the words that advertisers bombard us
with day by day, those noises that career unheeded through our hearing. We might be willing to do without "This bill is overdue." On the
other hand, how we treasure words of endearment, words of joy, words
of faith.

Human language, in all its spiritual and linguistic complexity, remains a glorious gift, one unique to humanity. We hardly dare imagine
living without it, for such a disappearance would wipe clean our book-
shelves, rob us of Scripture, erase the joy of conversation, and ultimately reduce us to something less than human.

In a sense all Christians should be linguists. If we believe that Jesus
is the Word, and that his message of redemption was revealed in language for our sakes, we must take our words seriously. His revelation as
the Word makes all language more sacred than it otherwise would be,
for it is through language that we come to understand much of his
character.

Moreover, as several of the essays in this chapter suggest, our use of
language has cultural ramifications. We do not talk or write in a vacuum; rather, we do so in society. Consequently, we need to govern our
speech with the same kind of integrity with which we govern our other
activities. We must remember that the Lord loves justice, and that, as
Isaiah proclaims, he hates robbery and wrong. But to really under-

stand how our language affects others we need to understand how it works. By using words well we can avoid harm and turn language to good, enjoying the full glory of this gift.

This should make us consider our relationship with words. Again and again the prophets speak the word of God, urging their listeners to make it their word. Obedience is put in terms of response to God's word; Psalm 119:16 is typical in its pledge of obedience: "I will not forget thy word." Moses also makes this clear. "This is what the LORD has commanded," he writes. "When a man vows a vow to the LORD, or swears an oath to bind himself by a pledge, he shall not break his word; he shall do according to all that proceeds out of his mouth" (Num. 30:1–2). We should consider our pledge of faith in God such a pledge— one that entails obedience, that requires us to make our words fit with his Word.

We must also undertake such a venture mindful of James's warning that "the tongue is a fire . . . an unrighteous world among our members, staining the whole body, setting on fire the cycle of nature, and set on fire by hell" (James 3:6). Words can be used for blessing or for cursing, for building up or for tearing down. This chapter will explore ways of using words with care.

The Living Word
The Bible in Translation

> In the beginning was the Word, and the Word was with God, and the Word was God.
>
> [John 1:1, RSV]

One of the important parts of the preceding text is the identification of the version as the Revised Standard Version (RSV). We translate the Word of God into words we understand. In the original Greek the passage would be a mystery to most of us. In Korean, Chinese, or Arabic the words would be meaningless. In this effort to make the Word of God, the Bible, clear to humans using different languages, translators constantly update and refine the language.

Interesting questions arise. Surely not all Christians are called to learn the original languages of biblical transcription—Hebrew, Aramaic, and Greek. But does translation ever reach the point where the language becomes so relative to one language group that the original meaning and force are lost? And how does a translator relate biblical concepts to a culture that has absolutely no understanding of the Old Testament sacrifice or the New Testament crucifixion? Some of us have difficulty understanding Saint Paul's complex terms such as "propitiation" or "expiation." How can these terms be made clear to a people who have no inherent concept of guilt or justification? In his book *Peace Child* Don Richardson tells precisely this story of how he tried to make such terms meaningful to the primitive Sawi tribe from the jungles of New Guinea.

Then, too, questions arise within the biblical text. For example, how does the translator render the name of God? According to the Hebrew tradition, God revealed his personal name Yahweh (the tetragrammaton YHWH) to Moses at the time of the exodus. Should this name be used for all Old Testament references? The Anchor and Jerusalem Bibles do so. But during the sixth century B.C. the name used for God became *Adonai*, commonly translated "my Lord." Another name used for God is *Elohim*, commonly translated "God." Which one is correct?

325

Recognizing on the one hand that Bible translators attempt to make the Word of God meaningful to one people in one place at one time, and on the other hand that there is a danger of making the Word of God simply relative to these people so that the clear Word itself becomes obscured, contrast the following biblical translations. The selections are the same: Isaiah 63:16–64:4 from the Old Testament, Mark 8:36–38 from the New Testament Gospels, and 1 John 5:9–13 from the New Testament Epistles.

King James Version (1611)

The first English translation of the Bible from the original Hebrew and Greek was made by William Tyndale; his effort met with such severe opposition that he was publicly burned at the stake in October 1536. Despite the tragic consequences of Tyndale's work, a half dozen other translators brought out English versions during the rest of the century, resulting finally in King James's commissioned version, a work which was decreed the "Authorized Version" of all English-speaking people.

Doubtless thou *art* our father, though Abraham be ignorant of us, and Israel acknowledge us not: thou, O LORD, *art* our father, our redeemer; thy name *is* from everlasting.

O LORD, why hast thou made us to err from thy ways, *and* hardened our heart from thy fear? Return for thy servants' sake, the tribes of thine inheritance.

The people of thy holiness have possessed *it* but a little while: our adversaries have trodden down thy sanctuary.

We are *thine:* thou never barest rule over them; they were not called by thy name.

Oh that thou wouldest rend the heavens, that thou wouldest come down, that the mountains might flow down at thy presence,

As *when* the melting fire burneth, the fire causeth the waters to boil, to make thy name known to thine adversaries, *that* the nations may tremble at thy presence!

When thou didst terrible things *which* we looked not for, thou camest down, the mountains flowed down at thy presence.

For since the beginning of the world *men* have not heard, nor perceived by the ear, neither hath the eye seen, O God, beside thee, *what* he hath prepared for him that waiteth for him. [Isa. 63:16–64:4]

For what shall it profit a man, if he shall gain the whole world, and lose his own soul?

Or what shall a man give in exchange for his soul?

Whosoever therefore shall be ashamed of me and of my words in this adulterous and sinful generation; of him also shall the Son of man be ashamed, when he cometh in the glory of his Father with the holy angels. [Mark 8:36–38]

If we receive the witness of men, the witness of God is greater: for this is the witness of God which he hath testified of his Son.

He that believeth on the Son of God hath the witness in himself. He that believeth not God hath made him a liar; because he believeth not the record that God gave of his Son.

And this is the record, that God hath given to us eternal life, and this life is in his Son.

He that hath the Son hath life; *and* he that hath not the Son of God hath not life.

These things have I written unto you that believe on the name of the Son of God; that ye may know that ye have eternal life, and that ye may believe on the name of the Son of God. [1 John 5:9–13]

Revised Standard Version (1952)

The King James Version endured for many years, and has been loved by many for a certain majestic power in its prose. It still remains for many people the sole English version. Yet by the middle of the nineteenth century two important changes had occurred. First, archaeologists found original biblical manuscripts that predated those used for the King James Version. Second, the English language had changed considerably. Thus the Church of England called for a new version, but this version actually appeared in two forms which recognized a variation in language—the Revised English Version in 1881–85 and the American Standard Version, using American preferences, in 1901. With archaeological and linguistic methods still changing rapidly, the Revised Standard Version appeared, a version which enjoys international appreciation.

For thou art our Father,
 though Abraham does not know us
 and Israel does not acknowledge us;
thou, O LORD, art our Father,
 our Redeemer from of old is thy name.
O LORD, why dost thou make us err from thy ways
 and harden our heart, so that we fear thee not?
Return for the sake of thy servants,
 the tribes of thy heritage.
Thy holy people possessed thy sanctuary a little while;
 our adversaries have trodden it down.

We have become like those over whom thou hast never ruled,
  like those who are not called by thy name.

  O that thou wouldst rend
  the heavens and come down,
  that the mountains might quake
    at thy presence—
as when fire kindles brushwood
  and the fire causes water to boil—
to make thy name known to thy adversaries,
  and that the nations might tremble at thy presence!
When thou didst terrible things which we looked not for,
  thou camest down, the mountains quaked at thy presence.
From of old no one has heard
  or perceived by the ear,
no eye has seen a God besides thee,
  who works for those who wait for him. [Isa. 63:16–64:4]

"For what does it profit a man, to gain the whole world and forfeit his life? For what can a man give in return for his life? For whoever is ashamed of me and of my words in this adulterous and sinful generation, of him will the Son of man also be ashamed, when he comes in the glory of his Father with the holy angels." [Mark 8:36–38]

If we receive the testimony of men, the testimony of God is greater; for this is the testimony of God that he has borne witness to his Son. He who believes in the Son of God has the testimony in himself. He who does not believe God has made him a liar, because he has not believed in the testimony that God has borne to his Son. And this is the testimony, that God gave us eternal life, and this life is in his Son. He who has the Son has life; he who has not the Son of God has not life.

  I write this to you who believe in the name of the Son of God, that you may know that you have eternal life. [1 John 5:9–13]

The Living Bible (1971)

Translations attempt a close fidelity to the literal meaning of the original languages. A paraphrase focuses more upon the language of today, attempting to put the original meanings into common expressions which today's readers can easily comprehend. Quite often, therefore, the challenge to the translator is to simplify complex terms in the original, making the Bible easier to understand.

Surely you are still our Father! Even if Abraham and Jacob would disown us, still you would be our Father, our Redeemer from ages past. O

Lord, why have you hardened our hearts and made us sin and turn against you? Return and help us, for we who belong to you need you so. How briefly we possessed Jerusalem! And now our enemies have destroyed her. O God, why do you treat us as though we weren't your people, as though we were a heathen nation that never called you "Lord"?

Oh, that you would burst forth from the skies and come down! How the mountains would quake in your presence! The consuming fire of your glory would burn down the forests and boil the oceans dry. The nations would tremble before you; then your enemies would learn the reason for your fame! So it was before when you came down, for you did awesome things beyond our highest expectations, and how the mountains quaked! For since the world began no one has seen or heard of such a God as ours, who works for those who wait for him! [Isa. 63:16–64:4]

"And how does a man benefit if he gains the whole world and loses his soul in the process? For is anything worth more than his soul? And anyone who is ashamed of me and my message in these days of unbelief and sin, I, the Messiah, will be ashamed of him when I return in the glory of my Father, with the holy angels." [Mark 8:36–38]

We believe men who witness in our courts, and so surely we can believe whatever God declares. And God declares that Jesus is his Son. All who believe this know in their hearts that it is true. If anyone doesn't believe this, he is actually calling God a liar, because he doesn't believe what God has said about his Son.

And what is it that God has said? That he has given us eternal life, and that this life is in his Son. So whoever has God's Son has life; whoever does not have his Son, does not have life.

I have written this to you who believe in the Son of God so that you may know you have eternal life. [1 John 5:9–13]

New International Version (1978)

In 1967 the New York Bible Society began work on a new translation guided by these goals: "It would be an accurate translation and one that would have clarity and literary quality. . . ." The translators pursued these goals, "united in their commitment to the authority and infallibility of the Bible as God's Word in written form." The concern of these translators was to capture the style of different biblical authors; to render faithfully and accurately the meanings, to be sure, but also to achieve something of the distinct personality of Paul, or Luke, or Isaiah as authors. Finally, their effort was to render the original meanings, capture the personality of the authors, but to do this in language that is meaningful to today's reader.

But you are our Father,
>though Abraham does not know us
>or Israel acknowledge us;
you, O LORD, are our Father,
>our Redeemer from of old is your name.
Why, O LORD, do you make us
>>wander from your ways
>and harden our hearts so we do not revere you?
Return for the sake of your servants,
>the tribes that are your inheritance.
For a little while your people possessed your holy place,
>but now our enemies have trampled down your sanctuary.
We are yours from of old;
>but you have not ruled over them,
>they have not been called by your name.

>Oh, that you would rend the
>heavens and come down,
>that the mountains would tremble
>before you!
As when fire sets twigs ablaze
>and causes water to boil,
come down to make your name known to your enemies
>and cause the nations to quake before you!
For when you did awesome things that we did not expect,
>you came down, and the mountains trembled before you.
Since ancient times no one has heard,
>no ear has perceived,
no eye has seen any God besides you,
>who acts on behalf of those who wait for him. [Isa. 63:16–64:4]

"What good is it for a man to gain the whole world, yet forfeit his soul? Or what can a man give in exchange for his soul? If anyone is ashamed of me and my words in this adulterous and sinful generation, the Son of Man will be ashamed of him when he comes in his Father's glory with the holy angels." [Mark 8:36–38]

We accept man's testimony, but God's testimony is greater because it is the testimony of God, which he has given about his Son. Anyone who believes in the Son of God has this testimony in his heart. Anyone who does not believe God has made him out to be a liar, because he has not believed the testimony God has given about his Son. And this is the testimony: God has given us eternal life, and this life is in his Son. He who has the Son has life; he who does not have the Son of God does not have life.

I write these things to you who believe in the name of the Son of God so that you may know that you have eternal life. [1 John 5:9–13]

An Inclusive Language Lectionary, Readings for Year B (1984)

A lectionary is a series of biblical passages arranged as "lessons" or "readings" during the course of the church year. The lessons are appropriate to the season, Advent through Pentecost. Believing that "all persons are equally loved, judged, and accepted by God," the Division of Education and Ministry of the National Council of the Churches of Christ has prepared lectionaries which are nondiscriminatory in language of gender. The Revised Standard Version is the basis of the text, but references to gender are changed: "The text [is] revised only in those places where male-biased or otherwise inappropriately exclusive language could be modified to reflect an inclusiveness of all persons." In the text, bracketed material indicates additions to the Revised Standard Version. A full explanation of changes is provided in the introduction and appendixes to the lectionary.

> For you, O God, are our Father [*and Mother*],
>   though Abraham [*and Sarah*] do not know us
>   and Israel does not acknowledge us;
> you, O SOVEREIGN ONE, are our Father [*and Mother*],
>   our Redeemer from of old is your name.
> O SOVEREIGN ONE, why do you make us err from your
>   ways
>   and harden our heart, so that we do not fear you?
> Return for the sake of your servants,
>   the tribes of your heritage.
> Your holy people possessed your sanctuary a little while;
>   our adversaries have trodden it down.
> We have become like those over whom you have never
>   ruled,
>   like those who are not called by your name.
> O that you would rend the heavens and come down,
>   that the mountains might quake at your presence—
> as when fire kindles brushwood
>   and the fire causes water to boil—
> to make your name known to your adversaries,
>   and that the nations might tremble at your presence!
> When you did terrible things which we looked not for,
>   you came down, the mountains quaked at your presence.
> From of old no one has heard
>   or perceived by the ear,
> no eye has seen a God besides you,
>   who works for those who wait for God. [Isa. 63:16–64:4]

"For what is one profited, if one gains the whole world and forfeits one's life? For what shall one give in return for one's life? For whoever is ashamed of me and of my words in this adulterous and sinful generation, of that one will the Human One also be ashamed, when the Human One comes in the glory of God with the holy angels." [Mark 8:36–38]

If we receive human testimony, the testimony of God is greater; for this is the testimony of God that God has borne witness to God's own Child. Those who believe in the Child of God have the testimony within themselves. Those who do not believe God have made God a liar, by not believing in the testimony that God has borne to God's own Child. And this is the testimony, that God gave us eternal life, and this life is in God's Child. Whoever has that Child has life; whoever does not have the Child of God does not have life.

I write this to you who believe in the name of the Child of God, that you may know that you have eternal life. [1 John 5:9–13]

Discussion

1. What version of the Bible did you grow up with? Which of the five preceding versions do you prefer now? How do you account for your preferences?
2. Can the effort to make the Bible *relevant* to today's reader also make the Bible *relative* to today's reader? Is there a danger of the Word being lost in the words we use? Can you find examples of this in the passages quoted above? What should be the chief aims of a Bible translator?
3. As an exercise to appreciate the difficulties of Bible translation, select a passage that you particularly like and paraphrase it in your own words.
4. What qualities should a good translation have?

A Vital Language

Henry Zylstra

While many complain about the low quality of the language of American culture, few offer standards for its improvement. Henry Zylstra is one who does. A literary critic who until his death in 1956 wrote widely in Reformed and evangelical publications, Zylstra here treats two issues that he valued highly and wrote about often: language and the Christian life. In this essay we can see his endeavor, in the words of one biographer, "to make all things subservient to the mind of Christ."

The plea for a more vital language in our preaching and apology arises from time to time among us. It is a plea which is ignored by some as a matter of no consequence, feared by some, too, as a threat to orthodoxy, and welcomed by others as an important and legitimate concern.

Those who ignore the call for vitality in the diction, language, or style of our spoken and written word are, it seems to me, making a mistake. What they have at the back of their minds is probably something like this: the important thing is the truth, the whole truth, and nothing but the truth. That, they feel, is the main thing, and they go on to imply that the form in which that truth is uttered is neither here nor there really. The content, the idea, the substance is what matters. To talk about the language of such content, the style of such substance, seems to them like talking about the paper on which a king's message is written.

All the same, such separation of truth from statement, of content from form, of idea from style, is a false and fatal separation. The form is essential to the meaning, to the understanding of it, and to the communication of it. The thing we have to say is inert, dead, and incommunicable until it becomes significant, gets its *sign*, assumes form. The truth, thought of as mere matter, is, if it be without form, like the chaos of Genesis. It is void.

Some have called language the dress in which thought is garbed. The figure is mechanical, and it does not go far enough. Language is not so much the dress as the incarnation of the thought. The word is truth become flesh. Language is the body of the idea, and it is only in the body that we can become aware of it. When this body of the language fits the soul of the thought, it is characteristically expressive of that soul. This is what Buffon over-stated when he said, "The style is the man."

We sometimes say that the apparel oft proclaims the man. This is so, but we should go further, still following Shakespeare. "Your face, my thane," said Lady Macbeth, "is as a book Where men may read strange matters." Or again: "False face must hide what the false heart doth know." The body, the face, tells more than the dress. Appearances are not superficial. And language, as Wordsworth hinted, is the countenance of science.

It is this integrity, this wholeness of message and medium, that puts those in the wrong who ignore the plea for vital language in our speaking and writing. In a good preacher or apologist, a person, that is, with a firm faith, with convictions really felt, with thought that is disciplined in its discriminations, the style is a telling index to the man. He must be defined man, at one with himself and in command of his thought and life, an individuality, in short, and unique, therefore. He must be a significant man. Such a man's language, such a man's style, reveals the soul of him, the spirit of him, his self.

John Milton, for example, was such a man. He had conviction. He had philosophy. He had disciplined his thinking. He was learned. After the University, he went home to his father's house to master the classics he had missed at Cambridge. He had languages: ancient and modern. He had a passion for excellence, born in part from his Puritan sense of working always under "the great task-master's eye." He had, too, a consciousness of calling, an ideal for the work he was to do, and a will for the demanding effort of preparing himself for it. Those are good qualifications for vital language. Well, someone remarked of John Milton, that almost any line of his verse would be as good an identification as his signature at the bank.

So organic is the relationship of language and thought, of language and character, even. This is what Milton had to say of it himself:

> . . . I was confirmed in this opinion, that he who would not be frustrate of his hope to write well hereafter in laudable things ought himself to be a true poem, a composition and pattern of the best and hònourablest

things; not presuming to sing high praises . . . unless he have in himself the experience and practise of all that which is praiseworthy.

It is the common testimony of all those who best understand the wholeness of *logos*, the integrity of thought and word. Hear Goethe: "Altogether the style of a writer is a faithful representative of his mind; therefore if a man wish to write a clear style, let him first be clear in his thoughts; and if he would write a noble style, let him first possess a noble soul." Or hear John Newman, author of *Lead, Kindly Light*, and of moving sermons and books one after another. A man, he says

writes passionately because he feels keenly, forcibly because he conceives vividly; he sees too clearly to be vague; . . . he can analyze his subject, and therefore he is rich; he embraces it as a whole and in its parts and therefore he is consistent; he has a firm hold of it, and therefore he is luminous. . . . He always has the right word for the right idea, and never a word too much. . . .

So it is. The moment we write a sentence or voice a statement we identify ourselves. Our speech betrays us. This is all very humbling for us men of ordinary talent, but genius must be our mentor in this. Since we are human, there is something of the artist in us all. Any sermon, speech, or piece of writing which goes to affirming the faith is in some sort a work of art. Somerset Maugham states it forcefully: "Every production of an artist should be an expression of an adventure of his soul. This is a counsel of perfection, and in an imperfect world a certain indulgence should be allowed . . . but this surely is the aim he should keep before him."

If we cannot have genius, if we do not have it, we can at least try for one of its earmarks: Genuineness. Thomas Carlyle, who was a great man for vitality, and was often preaching it, always traced the dynamism of it back to what he called the Real, the Genuine. Now it may do no good to go around telling people to be real, to be genuine, but those of us who have a Christian profession to make, in speech, sermon, article, or whatever, ought perhaps to begin there. It is as helpful a statement as any that can be made in this matter that if we are real our language will be vital, and that if we are not real our language will betray the lack.

Always this genuineness—shall I call it honesty?—lies at the basis of vital apology and witness. We all know when our language is least adequate. It is when we manufacture a sentiment instead of saying a truth. Think of the tritenesses and banalities, the threadbare phrases and stock diction, of our public courtesies. It is all so hollow. Language is at its worst in forced effort, in servile work, in fabricated products. The yawning editor who must get out his thousand words by noon, whether the news be susceptible to comment or not, whether he be ready for interpreting it or not—it is he who will abuse the language. His piece may be fairly convincing, and the unwary may be taken in. If they were not, none of the staff-written, formula-ridden copy, advertising and editorial both, of the big-time slick magazines would be read. But his piece is false.

There is in the jaded editorial, the puffed advertisement, the canned jacket-blurb, the mercenary ghost-writer's piece, and the cranked-out sermon of an old hand at extempore preaching—there is in all these what Carlyle would have called Sham, Puffery, Quackery, and Falsehood. The product may have a certain polish, a practised skill, a rhythmical cadence, and a reasonably good facsimile of style. But the thing remains, for want of genuineness, a No-Thing, a piece of *Ersatz*. The soul is out of it. This is what John Burroughs, the American naturalist, had in mind when he lumped the Sunday sermon with the newspaper editorial as "generally pieces of machine work, as if you turned the crank and the discourse came out."

If this be following the right line, that genuineness is the key to vitality in our Christian profession, then we shall have to take pains to be real, to achieve, so far as may be, a kind of self-integrity. We can lodge our message only if we believe. We cannot lodge it, flesh our sword in it, make it telling, if we say only what we ought to believe. This is the humbling and the denuding thing in the plea for a more vital language. This requires humble, prayerful, and determined searching. For it is a peril of orthodoxy of any kind—political, economic, D.A.R., Stalinist, Catholic, or Reformed—that the official is substituted for the real conviction, that propaganda is substituted for witness. The style of propaganda, the diction of party-manifestoes, the "line" of the dictator, however embellished and ornamented, remains lifeless and artificial. The soul of the free self is out of them. The faith believed, the conviction felt, and the truth acknowledged—these sustain orthodoxy, and from such self-integrity and honesty a vital profession is born.

Such genuineness most emphatically requires humility and requires prayer. Something akin to inspiration is needed, and inspiration, which is the breath of the Spirit, is—let us admit it—not a thing achieved, but a gift given. We Protestants do not make enough of religious exercises. We cannot come in from a week of calls, committees, affairs, and business, look at the church calendar, find the question and answer of the Catechism that is due for Sunday, proceed to the pulpit, and make something of it. We need the spiritual nurture of prayer, reading, reflection, and leisure. We teachers, speakers, and writers, too, wasting our substance in riotously confusing duty, must sit and think. "We must lie like the spider," said Sir Walter Raleigh, "until we have material to continue our web."

Being real, being genuine, with a view to being vital in our Christian profession, requires caliber, too, and it requires education. If genius has the least difficulty being dynamic in its affirmation, this is partly because genius has original force and creative reach. One cannot look for a living language from an imitative mind; such a mind tries but remains always at the mercy, in some part, of convention, custom, and habit. There is no earned awareness there to penetrate tradition and sustain it.

And education. Education, including even pedestrian learning, is indispensable to a genuineness that can last. We all know it, and we all say in one way or another that "words are grown so false, we are loathe to prove reason with them." But to learn what words once meant involves prodigious labor in many kinds, and to know what words now mean involves almost as much. We dare not blink at this fact or we shall be leaning upon words after awhile behind which there is no truth.

We have our treasure, we know, in earthen vessels. But that does not give us leave to do poor work. The plea for a more vital language in our spoken and written word is in order. We shall have to try for the genuine article. Ruskin is right: "So long as words are uttered but in faithfulness, so long the art of language goes on exalting itself; but the moment it is shaped and chiselled on external principles, it . . . perishes. . . . No noble or right style was ever yet founded but out of a sincere heart."

Discussion

1. In paragraph 3, Zylstra uses language that suggests that writing is analogous to Creation. Write an impromptu paragraph in which you describe your process of writing; try to list everything you do and think as you set forth upon a writing assignment. Does your process seem similar to or different from the act that Zylstra describes?

2. Why is language as the dress of thought an inadequate description of the concept? To get at this, try to write as many sentences as you can that refer to language in terms of dress, for example, "She *disguised* her ideas." "That answer doesn't *fit*." See also the essay "Metaphors We Live By" in this chapter.

3. Do you agree with the statement that "appearances are not superficial"? Does this apply to all aspects of life?

4. What does Zylstra mean by *genius* and what is its connection to genuineness?

5. What is the difference between propaganda and witness? Try to find some writing from a Christian publication that fits Zylstra's use of the word *propaganda* here.

6. In his conclusion, Zylstra refers to 2 Corinthians. Read the whole passage, 4:6–12, and speculate on what it implies for writing in a vital language.

Pure Poppycock

Kathryn Lindskoog

> *Kathryn Lindskoog, a free-lance writer living in California, has published many articles and several books. Recently she stepped back into the classroom to teach writing. Her impressions of some contemporary guides for good writing follow.*

It all started when I began the new year wrong. On January 1, 1983, I was unwillingly coerced into watching the evening news on CBS in Los Angeles. Fortunately, I had pen and paper handy, and here are three of the astounding statements I heard.

1. "At the Rose Parade today there was only elbow room." (Only?)

2. "At Venice Beach on New Year's Day some people went into the water where only penguins fear to tread." (I always assumed that penguins were more cowardly than angels, but not in cold water.)

3. "You say, 'What is the weather going to be like in Los Angeles tomorrow?' It will improve! Of course, it was excellent today. But if it gets even better, we'll have too many people at the broadcasts of the parade and game." (The parade and game, broadcasts and all, would not occur again for a full year; in the meantime I puzzle about what it means to have too many people at broadcasts.)

No wonder that our nation's melting pot is full of mental mush. Young people today grow up listening to television announcers who sound as if they cleared their sinuses with cocaine before going on the air.

Shortly after the new year began I ventured where not only penguins fear to tread—into the freshman composition classroom of my local college, to rejoin the fray on the side of clear thinking and good writing. I had been out of the fight for 20 years, like Rip Van Winkle. I opened the bright-covered, highpriced English textbooks expectantly and got the shock of my life.

"There are varying degrees of bilinguals," someone intoned cryptically in the model outline for a model research paper. I flipped a few pages to see how such a model research paper would conclude. "If the oral phase of learning a language can be mastered before a child starts school, the other interrelated phases (reading and writing) should follow with relative ease." If a child learns to talk before he enters school, he will probably learn to read and write in school?

I flipped a few more pages and found direct instruction about how to write such a research paper:

> To put it another way more bluntly, it is not enough to demonstrate that you have read; you must in turn have something to say about what you have read, and you must be able to say that "something" at least clearly, and hopefully even gracefully.

This is not satire; I checked.

> Here is a suggested thesis for a research paper:

> The current fear of human's [sic] being displaced by machines, or what alarmists term the "automation hysteria," seems to be based on insubstantial reports.

To me that thesis seems to be based on insubstantial comprehension of both apostrophe use and alarmist rhetoric. I decided to skip the section on research papers.

The next section was on writing about literature. Students were warned:

> Passages from the work should be liberally quoted to support your paper's interpretation of it. Above all, never assume that any reading of a work, no matter how unsupported or farfetched, will do.

I don't even assume that any reading of that sentence will do. Ever.

"Write a 'third bear' story on the style of your favorite author," the book suggests to students. Ignorant about what "third bear" stories are, I checked the previous pages and learned that the editor was referring to "The Three Bears," which he seems to have confused with something else. (I know of an excellent book called *The Third Peacock*.)

The writer concluded this section with what he may have meant as a flourish:

> Saying that Hemingway's male characters suffer from *machismo* is a little like an anthropology student opining that humans are bipedal. Both remarks are undoubtedly true, but they are neither original nor

insightful. You should, therefore, check out the prevailing critical opinions on a writer before attempting to rashly dogmatize on your own.

I have not yet checked out the prevailing critical opinion on this writer, but I bet I could rashly dogmatize on my own anyway.

As their inadvertant contribution to the ongoing problems that freshmen have with quotation marks gone to seed, the editors included this:

> In modern existentialist terms, you are what you do; so change what you do and you change what you are. After all, isn't "growing up" a matter of adopting views and roles consistent with your concept of being "a man" or "a woman" of the kind you would like to be?

My answer is no, it isn't. I wouldn't be "a man" or "a woman" for anything. Those cute quotation marks serve as a broad wink and a poke in the ribs.

"That prose literature has unity is easily seen by examining almost any book or magazine article." Come again?

> Very often, when skilled students read a book, they underline certain passages. This is a good technique—if the proper sections are selected. The single sentence that should be underlined is the thesis or purpose statement of the book, its generative sentence.

Are students supposed to laugh or cry over the price they paid for this book that tells them they should underline just one sentence in every book? Perhaps what they should underline in this one is the pricemark; it serves as a kind of purpose statement.

> In the beginning was the *logos*, says the Bible—the idea, the plan, caught in a flash as if in a single word. Find your *logos*, and you are ready to round out your essay and set it spinning.

Somehow this new exegesis of a key New Testament passage makes me into a blasphemous unbeliever right off. But how does one find one's *logos?* The author explains.

> The *about-ness* puts an argumentative edge on the subject. When you have something to say *about* cats, you have found your underlying idea.

The spinning of this particular essay about how to form and spin an essay makes me queasy. Some poor students still don't know how to hone their *logos* with *about-ness.*

Well, perhaps Harcourt Brace has been having a bad decade since it started publishing *Readings for Writers*. With some confidence I turned to *Macmillan Handbook of English*, which is over forty years old and hence one of my peers. But it has been spruced up. It was all right until I got to page seven.

> Precision and clarity are the primary requirements of effective writing, and weaknesses here are most vulnerable to attack from casual readers and instructors.

This means, I take it, do as we say, not as we do. It's these casual readers and instructors who are always out to get you.

> *The evidence is convincing that recognized expository writers use precise, uninflated Anglo-Saxon—not multisyllabic—words in their essays.*

Hmph.

All goes well again until page ten. "No doubt you have experienced the sense of dismay with which ideas tumble out of your head when someone mentions topics like abortion. . . ." Frankly, when ideas tumble out of my head they don't seem dismayed at all. They are glad to get loose. I am the one who is dismayed, and the thing that dismays me is a grossly misplaced modifier on the printed page of an English book.

> Modern English, however, is an uninflected language, that is, the position of the word in the sentence determines meaning, function, and so forth.

I don't know what "and so forth" means here, but I do know that this is a run-on sentence, otherwise known as a comma splice.

> We know *sail* is the verb in the following sentence because it comes after the subject and before the object: "They sailed to Sicily."

Nice try, but there is no object in "They sailed to Sicily." Maybe no one will notice.

> It is of course quite possible for communication to function, as it were, on a single plane without degrees of structural emphasis.

How many degrees does structural emphasis usually have?

Maybe that's what I long for—for communication to function as it were.

Not that I'm an impractical idealist or a mossback intellectual snob. Sometimes I dream of angling my way into teams that write new improved *Math* textbooks for college students. I think I could write math textbooks with as little precision as some of the present English textbooks have. The results might seem innovative or liberating to people who don't care about math. And a decline in the dependability and accuracy of math instruction might make our English instruction look better.

In the long run, though, I think the low quality of English textbooks is bound to come to the attention of high-quality publishers ready to fill our need. In ten years we will probably have excellent texts again. We'll import them from Japan.

Discussion

1. Part of the fun of knowing how to use language well is finding the mistakes of others—particularly of English teachers. Try to discover several ungraceful sentences in this or another English book, but be prepared to explain what's wrong with them.
2. If finding mistakes is fun, finding sparkling prose should be more fun. Search the magazines in your college library to find a paragraph of exciting writing. Be prepared to explain what its strengths are.

Profanity and Realism

John Steinbeck

John Steinbeck's The Grapes of Wrath, *published in 1939, has the dubious distinction of being one of the most frequently censored novels in American history. Undeniably a literary masterpiece, the work has nonetheless met wide resistance for its political and social implications, but more particularly for its profanity. In Steinbeck's view, he was faithfully and accurately depicting a tough, downtrodden people. If they spoke profanely, he believed he should record that accurately. His artistic point of view was set forth in a letter written January 3, 1939, to his friend and editor Pascal Covici:*

> I went over the mss and made some changes. I made what I could. There are some I cannot make. When the tone or overtone of the normal speech requires a word, it is going in no matter what the audience thinks. This book wasn't written for delicate ladies. If they read it at all they're messing in something not their business. I've never changed a word to fit the prejudices of a group and I never will.[1]

Many years later Steinbeck, accompanied by his poodle named Charley, undertook a tour of the United States in a pickup-camper that he named Rocinante. Once again, Steinbeck confronted a group of people he wanted to record in his book Travels with Charley, *but this time their language was so obscene that he didn't want to record it for the reader. It was not the commonplace profanity which marked the language of a certain socio-economic class of people, but a harsh and obscene language, full of hatred.*

1. John Steinbeck, *A Life in Letters*, ed. Elaine Steinbeck and Robert Wallsten (New York: Viking, 1975), p. 175.

Steinbeck had traveled to New Orleans during the integration of formerly all-white schools by black students who were ushered to classes by federal marshals. Along the route so-called cheerleaders led the crowd in shouting obscenities at the black students. Struggling with the problem of how to convey the reality without using the language that sickened him, Steinbeck wrote the following note to his agent Elizabeth Otis:

What started out as a simple piece of truth now wears all the clothing of sensationalism and has lost every vestige of its purity. It doesn't feel clean to me any more. The only value of the passage lay in its shock value. Now it has become that book with the dirty words and by a magical turnabout the dirty words are no longer the cheerleaders' but mine. When I get the galleys I shall see what I want to do. I know that by simple suggestion I can make them much uglier without saying them. (A Life in Letters 734)

Following is the scene as it finally appeared in Travels with Charley, *revised by Steinbeck from overt use of obscenity to what he called "simple suggestion."*

While I was still in Texas, late in 1960, the incident most reported and pictured in the newspapers was the matriculation of a couple of tiny Negro children in a New Orleans school. Behind these small dark mites were the law's majesty and the law's power to enforce—both the scales and the sword were allied with the infants—while against them were three hundred years of fear and anger and terror of change in a changing world. I had seen photographs in the papers every day and motion pictures on the television screen. What made the newsmen love the story was a group of stout middle-aged women who, by some curious definition of the word "mother," gathered every day to scream invectives at children. Further, a small group of them had become so expert that they were known as the Cheerleaders, and a crowd gathered every day to enjoy and to applaud their performance.

This strange drama seemed so improbable that I felt I had to see it. It had the same draw as a five-legged calf or a two-headed foetus at a sideshow, a distortion of normal life we have always found so interesting that we will pay to see it, perhaps to prove to ourselves that we have the proper number of legs or heads. In the New Orleans show, I felt all the amusement of the improbable abnormal, but also a kind of horror that it could be so.

At this time the winter which had been following my track ever since I left home suddenly struck with a black norther. It brought ice and freezing sleet and sheeted the highways with dark ice. I gathered Charley from the good doctor. He looked half his age and felt wonderful, and to prove it he ran and jumped and rolled and laughed and gave little yips of pure joy. It felt very good to have him with me again, sitting up right in the seat beside me, peering ahead at the unrolling road, or curling up to sleep with his head in my lap and his silly ears available for fondling. That dog can sleep through any amount of judicious caresses.

Now we stopped dawdling and laid our wheels to the road and went. We could not go fast because of the ice, but we drove relentlessly, hardly glancing at the passing of Texas beside us. And Texas was achingly endless—Sweetwater and Balinger and Austin. We bypassed Houston. We stopped for gasoline and coffee and slabs of pie. Charley had his meals and his walks in gas stations. Night did not stop us, and when my eyes ached and burned from peering too long and my shoulders were side hills of pain, I pulled into a turnout and crawled like a mole into my bed, only to see the highway writhe along behind my closed lids. No more than two hours could I sleep, and then out into the bitter cold night and on and on. Water beside the road was frozen solid, and people moved about with shawls and sweaters wrapped around their ears.

Other times I have come to Beaumont dripping with sweat and lusting for ice and air-conditioning. Now Beaumont with all its glare of neon signs was what they called froze up. I went through Beaumont at night, or rather in the dark well after midnight. The blue-fingered man who filled my gas tank looked in at Charley and said, "Hey, it's a dog! I thought you had a nigger in there." And he laughed delightedly. It was the first of many repetitions. At least twenty times I heard it— "Thought you had a nigger in there." It was an unusual joke—always fresh—and never Negro or even Nigra, always Nigger or rather Niggah. That word seemed terribly important, a kind of safety word to cling to lest some structure collapse.

And then I was in Louisiana, with Lake Charles away to the side in the dark, but my lights glittered on ice and glinted on diamond frost, and those people who forever trudge the roads at night were mounded over with cloth against the cold. I dogged it on through La Fayette and Morgan City and came in the early dawn to Houma, which is pronounced Homer and is in my memory one of the pleasantest places in the world. There lives my old friend Doctor St. Martin, a gentle, learned man, a Cajun who has lifted babies and cured colic among the shell-heap Cajuns for miles around. I guess he knows more about Cajuns than anyone living, but I remembered with longing other gifts of Doctor St. Martin. He makes the best and most subtle martini in the world by a process approximating magic. The only part of his formula I know is that he uses distilled water for his ice and distills it himself to be sure. I have eaten black duck at his table—two St. Martin martinis and a brace of black duck with a burgundy delivered from the bottle as a baby might be delivered, and this in a darkened house where the shades have been closed at dawn and the cool night air preserved. At that table with its silver soft and dull, shining as pewter, I remember the raised glass of the grape's holy blood, the stem caressed by the doctor's strong artist fingers, and even now I can hear the sweet little health and welcome in the singing language of Acadia which once was French and now is itself. This picture filled my frosty windshield, and if there had been traffic would have made me a dangerous driver. But it was pale yellow frozen dawn in Houma and I knew that if I stopped to pay my respects, my will and my determination would drift away on the particular lotus St. Martin purveys and we would be speaking of timeless matters when the evening came, and another evening. And so I only bowed in the direction of my friend and scudded on toward New Orleans, for I wanted to catch a show of the Cheerleaders.

Even I know better than to drive a car near trouble, particularly Rocinante, with New York license plates. Only yesterday a reporter had been beaten and his camera smashed, for even convinced voters are reluctant to have their moment of history recorded and preserved.

So, well on the edge of town I drove into a parking lot. The attendant came to my window. "Man, oh man, I thought you had a nigger in there. Man, oh man, it's a dog. I see the big old black face and I think it's a big old nigger."

"His face is blue-gray when he's clean," I said coldly.

"Well I see some blue-gray niggers and they wasn't clean. New York, eh?"

It seemed to me a chill like the morning air came into his voice. "Just driving through," I said. "I want to park for a couple of hours. Think you can get me a taxi?"

"Tell you what I bet. I bet you're going to see the Cheerleaders."

"That's right."

"Well, I hope you're not one of those trouble-makers or reporters."

"I just want to see it."

"Man, oh man, you going to see something. Ain't those Cheerleaders something? Man, oh man, you never heard nothing like it when they get going."

I locked Charley in Rocinante's house after giving the attendant a tour of the premises, a drink of whisky, and a dollar. "Be kind of careful about opening the door when I'm away," I said. "Charley takes his job pretty seriously. You might lose a hand." This was an outrageous lie, of course, but the man said, "Yes, sir. You don't catch me fooling around with no strange dog."

The taxi driver, a sallow, yellowish man, shriveled like a chickpea with the cold, said, "I wouldn't take you more than a couple of blocks near. I don't go to have my cab wrecked."

"Is it that bad?"

"It ain't is it. It's can it get. And it can get that bad."

"When do they get going?"

He looked at his watch. "Except it's cold, they been coming in since dawn. It's quarter to. You get along and you won't miss nothing except it's cold."

I had camouflaged myself in an old blue jacket and my British navy cap on the supposition that in a seaport no one ever looks at a sailor any more than a waiter is inspected in a restaurant. In his natural haunts a sailor has no face and certainly no plans beyond getting drunk and maybe in jail for fighting. At least that's the general feeling about sailors. I've tested it. The most that happens is a kindly voice of authority saying, "Why don't you go back to your ship, sailor? You wouldn't want to sit in the tank and miss your tide, now would you, sailor?" And the speaker wouldn't recognize you five minutes later. And the Lion and Unicorn on my cap made me even more anonymous. But I must warn anyone testing my theory, never try it away from a shipping port.

"Where you from?" the driver asked with a complete lack of interest.

"Liverpool."

"Limey, huh? Well, you'll be all right. It's the goddamn New York Jews cause all the trouble."

I found myself with a British inflection and by no means one of Liverpool. "Jews—what? How do they cause trouble?"

"Why, hell, mister. We know how to take care of this. Everybody's happy and getting along fine. Why, I *like* niggers. And them goddamn New York Jews come in and stir the niggers up. They just stay in New York there wouldn't be no trouble. Ought to take them out."

"You mean lynch them?"

"I don't mean nothing else, mister."

He let me out and I started to walk away. "Don't try to get too close, mister," he called after me. "Just you enjoy it but don't mix in."

"Thanks," I said, and killed the "awfully" that came to my tongue.

As I walked toward the school I was in a stream of people all white and all going in my direction. They walked intently like people going to a fire after it has been burning for some time. They beat their hands against their hips or hugged them under coats, and many men had scarves under their hats and covering their ears.

Across the street from the school the police had set up wooden barriers to keep the crowd back, and they paraded back and forth, ignoring the jokes called to them. The front of the school was deserted but along the curb United States marshals were spaced, not in uniform but wearing armbands to identify them. Their guns bulged decently under their coats but their eyes darted about nervously, inspecting faces. It seemed to me that they inspected me to see if I was a regular, and then abandoned me as unimportant.

It was apparent where the Cheerleaders were, because people shoved forward to try to get near them. They had a favored place at the barricade directly across from the school entrance, and in that area a concentration of police stamped their feet and slapped their hands together in unaccustomed gloves.

Suddenly I was pushed violently and a cry went up: "Here she comes. Let her through. . . . Come on, move back. Let her through. Where you been? You're late for school. Where you been, Nellie?"

The name was not Nellie. I forget what it was. But she shoved through the dense crowd quite near enough to me so that I could see her coat of imitation fleece and her gold earrings. She was not tall, but her body was ample and full-busted. I judge she was about fifty. She was heavily powdered, which made the line of her double chin look very dark.

She wore a ferocious smile and pushed her way through the milling people, holding a fistful of clippings high in her hand to keep them from being crushed. Since it was her left hand I looked particularly for a wedding ring, and saw that there was none. I slipped in behind her to get carried along by her wave, but the crush was dense and I was given a warning too. "Watch it, sailor. Everybody wants to hear."

Nellie was received with shouts of greeting. I don't know how many Cheerleaders there were. There was no fixed line between the Cheerleaders and the crowd behind them. What I could see was that a group was passing newspaper clippings back and forth and reading them aloud with little squeals of delight.

Now the crowd grew restless, as an audience does when the clock goes past curtain time. Men all around me looked at their watches. I looked at mine. It was three minutes to nine.

The show opened on time. Sound of sirens. Motorcycle cops. Then two big black cars filled with big men in blond felt hats pulled up in front of the school. The crowd seemed to hold its breath. Four big marshals got out of each car and from somewhere in the automobiles they extracted the littlest Negro girl you ever saw, dressed in shining starchy white, with new white shoes on feet so little they were almost round. Her face and little legs were very black against the white.

The big marshals stood her on the curb and a jangle of jeering shrieks went up from behind the barricades. The little girl did not look at the howling crowd but from the side the whites of her eyes showed like those of a frightened fawn. The men turned her around like a doll, and then the strange procession moved up the broad walk toward the school, and the child was even more a mite because the men were so big. Then the girl made a curious hop, and I think I know what it was. I think in her whole life she had not gone ten steps without skipping, but now in the middle of her first skip the weight bore her down and her little round feet took measured, reluctant steps between the tall guards. Slowly they climbed the steps and entered the school.

The papers had printed that the jibes and jeers were cruel and sometimes obscene, and so they were, but this was not the big show. The crowd was waiting for the white man who dared to bring his white child to school. And here he came along the guarded walk, a tall man dressed in light gray, leading his frightened child by the hand. His body was tensed as a strong leaf spring drawn to the breaking strain; his face was grave and gray, and his eyes were on the ground immediately ahead of him. The muscles of his cheeks stood out from clenched jaws, a man afraid who by his will held his fears in check as a great rider directs a panicked horse.

A shrill, grating voice rang out. The yelling was not in chorus. Each took a turn and at the end of each the crowd broke into howls and roars and whistles of applause. This is what they had come to see and hear.

No newspaper had printed the words these women shouted. It was indicated that they were indelicate, some even said obscene. On television the sound track was made to blur or had crowd noises cut in to cover. But now I heard the words, bestial and filthy and degenerate. In a long and unprotected life I have seen and heard the vomitings of demoniac humans before. Why then did these screams fill me with a shocked and sickened sorrow?

The words written down are dirty, carefully and selectedly filthy. But there was something far worse here than dirt, a kind of frightening witches' Sabbath. Here was no spontaneous cry of anger, of insane rage.

Perhaps that is what made me sick with weary nausea. Here was no principle good or bad, no direction. These blowzy women with their little hats and their clippings hungered for attention. They wanted to be admired. They simpered in happy, almost innocent triumph when they were applauded. Theirs was the demented cruelty of egocentric children, and somehow this made their insensate beastliness much more heartbreaking. These were not mothers, not even women. They were crazy actors playing to a crazy audience.

The crowd behind the barrier roared and cheered and pounded one another with joy. The nervous strolling police watched for any break over the barrier. Their lips were tight but a few of them smiled and quickly unsmiled. Across the street the U.S. marshals stood unmoving. The gray-clothed man's legs had speeded for a second but he reined them down with his will and walked up the school pavement.

The crowd quieted and the next cheer lady had her turn. Her voice was the bellow of a bull, a deep and powerful shout with flat edges like a circus barker's voice. There is no need to set down her words. The pattern was the same; only the rhythm and tonal quality were different. Anyone who has been near the theater would know that these speeches were not spontaneous. They were tried and memorized and carefully rehearsed. This was theater. I watched the intent faces of the listening crowd and they were the faces of an audience. When there was applause, it was for a performer.

My body churned with weary nausea, but I could not let an illness blind me after I had come so far to look and to hear. And suddenly I knew something was wrong and distorted and out of drawing. I knew New Orleans, I have over the years had many friends there, thoughtful, gentle people, with a tradition of kindness and courtesy. I remembered Lyle Saxon, a huge man of soft laughter. How many days I have spent with Roark Bradford, who took Louisiana sounds and sights and created God and the Green Pastures to which He leadeth us. I looked in the crowd for such faces of such people and they were not there. I've seen this kind bellow for blood at a prize fight, have orgasms when a man is gored in the bull ring, stare with vicarious lust at a highway accident, stand patiently in line for the privilege of watching any pain or any agony. But where were the others—the ones who would be proud they were of a species with the gray man—the ones whose arms would ache to gather up the small, scared black mite?

I don't know where they were. Perhaps they felt as helpless as I did, but they left New Orleans misrepresented to the world. The crowd, no doubt, rushed home to see themselves on television, and what they saw went out all over the world, unchallenged by the other things I know are there.

Discussion

1. Compare Steinbeck's 1939 letter to Covici to his February 1962 letter to Otis. What is his position regarding profanity and what limits has he placed upon it?
2. How has Steinbeck handled the Cheerleaders' obscenity with "simple suggestion"? Has this made the scene more or less effective than if he had printed the actual words?
3. What are the limits for a Christian writer in representing reality accurately? Doesn't the Christian writer have a biblical responsibility to "tell the truth"? But the writer is also responsible for every word he utters. How can such a writer make use of Steinbeck's technique of "simple suggestion"?
4. Steinbeck's prose achieves power from what his critics call "telling detail." Can you find examples of his use of such detail in this passage? What is the significance, for example, of his looking closely to see if Nellie wears a wedding ring on her left hand?
5. Have you experienced racial discrimination? When? The Cheerleaders did not want change to occur; when did you last struggle against a need to change? Or, how have you worked to change things? How would an outsider describe your hometown? Perhaps you could write an account of what Steinbeck saw as experienced by the black child.
6. Steinbeck does a splendid job of giving us his personal response to an experience; choose a memorable episode (bitter or joyous) in your own life and report the experience along with your responses to it.

Jordan [II]

George Herbert

> The poems of the seventeenth-century poet George Herbert are often termed "metaphysical" because of the language they employ. The term comes from Samuel Johnson's charge that in the poems of Herbert and like poets, "the most heterogeneous ideas are yoked by violence together." Johnson's complaint was that the poets seemed to ransack "nature and art" to find metaphors for their poems; in short, that their poems were filled with inappropriate language. The charge is one that Herbert would have taken seriously had he lived to hear it, for he took the selection of words seriously. In fact, Herbert destroyed all the secular poetry he wrote, leaving only religious poems for the literary record. The frequent theme of his writing is the maintenance of the Christian's relationship with Christ; here, he explores the difficulty of finding the right language to address God in poetry.

When first my lines of heavenly joyes made mention,
Such was their lustre, they did so excell,
That I sought out quaint words, and trimme invention,
My thoughts began to burnish, sprout, and swell,
Curling with metaphors a plaine intention,
Decking the sence, as if it were to sell.

Thousands of notions in my braine did runne,
Offring their service, if I were not sped:
I often blotted what I had begunne.
This was not quick enough, and that was dead.
Nothing could seeme too rich to clothe the sunne,
Much lesse those joyes, which trample on his head.

As flames doe worke and wind, when they ascend:
So did I weave my self into the sense.
But while I bustled, I might heare a friend
Whisper, how wide is all this long pretence;
There is in Love a sweetnes ready penn'd:
Coppy out onely that, and save expence.

Discussion

1. What, according to Herbert, was wrong with his early attempts
   at religious poetry? Explain the relationship of the first three
   lines of the poem to the fourth line. What connotations do the
   words *burnish, sprout,* and *swell* have?
2. Try to list several metaphors that describe God or an attribute of
   God but that somehow seem inappropriate. Can you identify
   what's wrong with them?
3. What do the sixth line and the last line suggest about Herbert's
   view of the purpose of poetry? Do you agree?
4. In a magazine or book, try to find a poem that illustrates what
   Herbert calls for in the last stanza of the poem.

Metaphors We Live By

George Lakoff and Mark Johnson

We all use metaphors. We tell each other that "life is a
bowl of cherries" or that "our love is like a red, red
rose." Yet, according to the authors of this essay, we
use metaphors in many more ways than these poetic
examples would suggest. George Lakoff and Mark
Johnson argue that metaphor pervades our language
and, consequently, that the metaphors that we use may
both reflect and shape our values. The fact that we talk
about argument in terms of war, or time in terms of
money, influences the way that we interact with other
people. Indeed, as the title of their book suggests,
metaphor is something we live by.

Concepts We Live By

Metaphor is for most people a device of the poetic imagination and
the rhetorical flourish—a matter of extraordinary rather than ordinary language. Moreover, metaphor is typically viewed as characteristic of language alone, a matter of words rather than thought or
action. For this reason, most people think they can get along perfectly
well without metaphor. We have found, on the contrary, that metaphor
is pervasive in everyday life, not just in language but in thought and
action. Our ordinary conceptual system, in terms of which we both
think and act, is fundamentally metaphorical in nature.

The concepts that govern our thought are not just matters of the
intellect. They also govern our everyday functioning, down to the most
mundane details. Our concepts structure what we perceive, how we
get around in the world, and how we relate to other people. Our conceptual system thus plays a central role in defining our everyday realities. If we are right in suggesting that our conceptual system is largely

metaphorical, then the way we think, what we experience, and what we do every day is very much a matter of metaphor.

But our conceptual system is not something we are normally aware of. In most of the little things we do every day, we simply think and act more or less automatically along certain lines. Just what these lines are is by no means obvious. One way to find out is by looking at language. Since communication is based on the same conceptual system that we use in thinking and acting, language is an important source of evidence for what that system is like.

Primarily on the basis of linguistic evidence, we have found that most of our ordinary conceptual system is metaphorical in nature. And we have found a way to begin to identify in detail just what the metaphors are that structure how we perceive, how we think, and what we do.

To give some idea of what it could mean for a concept to be metaphorical and for such a concept to structure an everyday activity, let us start with the concept ARGUMENT and the conceptual metaphor ARGUMENT IS WAR. This metaphor is reflected in our everyday language by a wide variety of expressions:

ARGUMENT IS WAR

Your claims are *indefensible*.

He *attacked every weak point* in my argument.

His criticisms were *right on target*.

I *demolished* his argument.

I've never *won* an argument with him.

You disagree? Okay, *shoot!*

If you use that *strategy*, he'll *wipe you out*.

He *shot down* all of my arguments.

It is important to see that we don't just *talk* about arguments in terms of war. We can actually win or lose arguments. We see the person we are arguing with as an opponent. We attack his positions and we defend our own. We gain and lose ground. We plan and use strategies. If we find a position indefensible, we can abandon it and take a new line of attack. Many of the things we *do* in arguing are partially structured by the concept of war. Though there is no physical battle, there is a verbal battle, and the structure of an argument—attack, defense, counterattack, etc.—reflects this. It is in this sense that the ARGUMENT IS WAR metaphor is one that we live by in this culture; it structures the actions we perform in arguing.

Try to imagine a culture where arguments are not viewed in terms of war, where no one wins or loses, where there is no sense of attacking or defending, gaining or losing ground. Imagine a culture where an argument is viewed as a dance, the participants are seen as performers, and the goal is to perform in a balanced and aesthetically pleasing way. In such a culture, people would view arguments differently, experience them differently, carry them out differently, and talk about them differently. But *we* would probably not view them as arguing at all: they would simply be doing something different. It would seem strange even to call what they were doing "arguing." Perhaps the most neutral way of describing this difference between their culture and ours would be to say that we have a discourse form structured in terms of battle and they have one structured in terms of dance.

This is an example of what it means for a metaphorical concept, namely, ARGUMENT IS WAR, to structure (at least in part) what we do and how we understand what we are doing when we argue. *The essence of metaphor is understanding and experiencing one kind of thing in terms of another.* It is not that arguments are a subspecies of war. Arguments and wars are different kinds of things—verbal discourse and armed conflict—and the actions performed are different kinds of actions. But ARGUMENT is partially structured, understood, performed, and talked about in terms of WAR. The concept is metaphorically structured, the activity is metaphorically structured, and, consequently, the language is metaphorically structured.

Moreover, this is the *ordinary* way of having an argument and talking about one. The normal way for us to talk about attacking a position is to use the words "attack a position." Our conventional ways of talking about arguments presuppose a metaphor we are hardly ever conscious of. The metaphor is not merely in the words we use—it is in our very concept of an argument. The language of argument is not poetic, fanciful, or rhetorical; it is literal. We talk about arguments that way because we conceive of them that way—and we act according to the way we conceive of things.

The most important claim we have made so far is that metaphor is not just a matter of language, that is, of mere words. We shall argue that, on the contrary, human *thought processes* are largely metaphorical. This is what we mean when we say that the human conceptual system is metaphorically structured and defined. Metaphors as linguistic expressions are possible precisely because there are metaphors in a person's conceptual system. Therefore, whenever in this book we speak of metaphors, such as ARGUMENT IS WAR, it should be understood that *metaphor* means *metaphorical concept*.

The Systematicity of Metaphorical Concepts

Arguments usually follow patterns; that is, there are certain things we typically do and do not do in arguing. The fact that we in part conceptualize arguments in terms of battle systematically influences the shape arguments take and the way we talk about what we do in arguing. Because the metaphorical concept is systematic, the language we use to talk about that aspect of the concept is systematic.

We saw in the ARGUMENT IS WAR metaphor that expressions from the vocabulary of war, e.g., *attack a position, indefensible, strategy, new line of attack, win, gain ground*, etc., form a systematic way of talking about the battling aspects of arguing. It is no accident that these expressions mean what they mean when we use them to talk about arguments. A portion of the conceptual network of battle partially characterizes the concept of an argument, and the language follows suit. Since metaphorical expressions in our language are tied to metaphorical concepts in a systematic way, we can use metaphorical linguistic expressions to study the nature of metaphorical concepts and to gain an understanding of the metaphorical nature of our activities.

To get an idea of how metaphorical expressions in everyday language can give us insight into the metaphorical nature of the concepts that structure our everyday activities, let us consider the metaphorical concept TIME IS MONEY as it is reflected in contemporary English.

TIME IS MONEY

You're *wasting* my time.

This gadget will *save* you hours.

I don't *have* the time to *give* you.

How do you *spend* your time these days?

That flat tire *cost* me an hour.

I've *invested* a lot of time in her.

I don't *have enough* time to *spare* for that.

You're *running out* of time.

You need to *budget* your time.

Put aside some time for ping pong.

Is that *worth your while?*

Do you *have* much time *left?*

He's living on *borrowed* time.

You don't *use* your time *profitably.*

I *lost* a lot of time when I got sick.

Thank you for your time.

Time in our culture is a valuable commodity. It is a limited resource that we use to accomplish our goals. Because of the way that the concept of work has developed in modern Western culture, where work is typically associated with the time it takes and time is precisely quantified, it has become customary to pay people by the hour, week, or year. In our culture TIME IS MONEY in many ways: telephone message units, hourly wages, hotel room rates, yearly budgets, interest on loans, and paying your debt to society by "serving time." These practices are relatively new in the history of the human race, and by no means do they exist in all cultures. They have arisen in modern industrialized societies and structure our basic everyday activities in a very profound way. Corresponding to the fact that we *act* as if time is a valuable commodity—a limited resource, even money—we *conceive of* time that way. Thus we understand and experience time as the kind of thing that can be spent, wasted, budgeted, invested wisely or poorly, saved, or squandered.

TIME IS MONEY, TIME IS A LIMITED RESOURCE, and TIME IS A VALUABLE COMMODITY are all metaphorical concepts. They are metaphorical since we are using our everyday experiences with money, limited resources, and valuable commodities to conceptualize time. This isn't a necessary way for human beings to conceptualize time; it is tied to our culture. There are cultures where time is none of these things.

The metaphorical concepts TIME IS MONEY, TIME IS A RE-SOURCE, and TIME IS A VALUABLE COMMODITY form a single system based on subcategorization, since in our society money is a limited resource and limited resources are valuable commodities. These subcategorization relationships characterize entailment relationships between the metaphors. TIME IS MONEY entails that TIME IS A LIMITED RESOURCE, which entails that TIME IS A VALUABLE COMMODITY.

We are adopting the practice of using the most specific metaphorical concept, in this case TIME IS MONEY, to characterize the entire system. Of the expressions listed under the TIME IS MONEY metaphor, some refer specifically to money *(spend, invest, budget, profitably, cost)*, others to limited resources *(use, use up, have enough of, run out of)*, and still others to valuable commodities *(have, give, lose, thank you for)*. This is an example of the way in which metaphorical entailments can characterize a coherent system of metaphorical concepts and a corresponding coherent system of metaphorical expressions for those concepts.

Metaphorical Systematicity: Highlighting and Hiding

The very systematicity that allows us to comprehend one aspect of a concept in terms of another (e.g., comprehending an aspect of arguing in terms of battle) will necessarily hide other aspects of the concept. In allowing us to focus on one aspect of a concept (e.g., the battling aspects of arguing), a metaphorical concept can keep us from focusing on other aspects of the concept that are inconsistent with that metaphor. For example, in the midst of a heated argument, when we are intent on attacking our opponent's position and defending our own, we may lose sight of the cooperative aspects of arguing. Someone who is arguing with you can be viewed as giving you his time, a valuable commodity, in an effort at mutual understanding. But when we are preoccupied with the battle aspects, we often lose sight of the cooperative aspects.

A far more subtle case of how a metaphorical concept can hide an aspect of our experience can be seen in what Michael Reddy has called the "conduit metaphor." Reddy observes that our language about language is structured roughly by the following complex metaphor:

IDEAS (or MEANINGS) ARE OBJECTS.

LINGUISTIC EXPRESSIONS ARE CONTAINERS.

COMMUNICATION IS SENDING.

The speaker puts ideas (objects) into words (containers) and sends them (along a conduit) to a hearer who takes the idea/objects out of the word/containers. Reddy documents this with more than a hundred types of expressions in English, which he estimates account for at least 70 percent of the expressions we use for talking about language. Here are some examples:

The CONDUIT Metaphor

It's hard to *get* that idea *across to* him.

I *gave* you that idea.

Your reasons *came through* to us.

It's difficult to *put* my ideas *into* words.

When you *have* a good idea, try to *capture* it immediately *in* words.

Try to *pack* more thought *into* fewer words.

You can't simply *stuff* ideas *into* a sentence any old way.

The meaning is right there *in* the words.

Don't *force* your meanings *into* the wrong words.

His words *carry* little meaning.

The introduction *has* a great deal of thought *content.*

Your words seem *hollow.*

The sentence is *without* meaning.

The idea is *buried in* terribly dense paragraphs.

In examples like these it is far more difficult to see that there is anything hidden by the metaphor or even to see that there is a metaphor here at all. This is so much the conventional way of thinking about language that it is sometimes hard to imagine that it might not fit reality. But if we look at what the CONDUIT metaphor entails, we can see some of the ways in which it masks aspects of the communicative process.

First, the LINGUISTIC EXPRESSIONS ARE CONTAINERS FOR MEANINGS aspect of the CONDUIT metaphor entails that words and sentences have meanings in themselves, independent of any context or speaker. The MEANINGS ARE OBJECTS part of the metaphor, for example, entails that meanings have an existence independent of people and contexts. The part of the metaphor that says LINGUISTIC EXPRESSIONS ARE CONTAINERS FOR MEANING entails that words (and sentences) have meanings, again independent of contexts and speakers. These metaphors are appropriate in many situations—those where context differences don't matter and where all the participants in the conversation understand the sentences in the same way. These two entailments are exemplified by sentences like

The meaning is *right there in* the words,

which, according to the CONDUIT metaphor, can correctly be said of any sentence. But there are many cases where context does matter. Here is a celebrated one recorded in actual conversation by Pamela Downing:

Please sit in the apple-juice seat.

In isolation this sentence has no meaning at all, since the expression "apple-juice seat" is not a conventional way of referring to any kind of object. But the sentence makes perfect sense in the context in which it was uttered. An overnight guest came down to breakfast. There were four place settings, three with orange juice and one with apple juice. It was clear what the apple-juice seat was. And even the next morning, when there was no apple juice, it was still clear which seat was the apple-juice seat.

In addition to sentences that have no meaning without context, there are cases where a single sentence will mean different things to different people. Consider:

We need new alternative sources of energy.

This means something very different to the president of Mobil Oil from what it means to the president of Friends of the Earth. The meaning is not right there in the sentence—it matters a lot who is saying or listening to the sentence and what his social and political attitudes are. The CONDUIT metaphor does not fit cases where context is required to determine whether the sentence has any meaning at all and, if so, what meaning it has.

These examples show that the metaphorical concepts we have looked at provide us with a partial understanding of what communication, argument, and time are and that, in doing this, they hide other aspects of these concepts. It is important to see that the metaphorical structuring involved here is partial, not total. If it were total, one concept would actually *be* the other, not merely be understood in terms of it. For example, time isn't really money. If you *spend your time* trying to do something and it doesn't work, you can't get your time back. There are no time banks. I can *give you a lot of time*, but you can't give me back the same time, though you can *give me back the same amount of time*. And so on. Thus, part of a metaphorical concept does not and cannot fit.

On the other hand, metaphorical concepts can be extended beyond the range of ordinary literal ways of thinking and talking into the range of what is called figurative, poetic, colorful, or fanciful thought and language. Thus, if ideas are objects, we can *dress them up in fancy clothes, juggle them, line them up nice and neat*, etc. So when we say that a concept is structured by a metaphor, we mean that it is partially structured and that it can be extended in some ways but not others.

Orientational Metaphors

So far we have examined what we will call *structural metaphors*, cases where one concept is metaphorically structured in terms of another. But there is another kind of metaphorical concept, one that does not structure one concept in terms of another but instead organizes a whole system of concepts with respect to one another. We will call these *orientational metaphors*, since most of them have to do with spatial orientation; up-down, in-out, front-back, on-off, deep-shallow, central-peripheral. These spatial orientations arise from the fact that we have bodies of the sort we have and that they function as they do in our physical environment. Orientational metaphors give a concept a spatial orientation; for example, HAPPY IS UP. The fact that the concept HAPPY is oriented UP leads to English expressions like "I'm feeling *up* today."

Such metaphorical orientations are not arbitrary. They have a basis in our physical and cultural experience. Though the polar oppositions up-down, in-out, etc., are physical in nature, the orientational metaphors based on them can vary from culture to culture. For example, in some cultures the future is in front of us, whereas in others it is in back. We will be looking at up-down spatialization metaphors, which have been studied intensively by William Nagy, as an illustration. In each case, we will give a brief hint about how each metaphorical concept might have arisen from our physical and cultural experience. These accounts are meant to be suggestive and plausible, not definite.

HAPPY IS UP; SAD IS DOWN
I'm feeling *up*. That *boosted* my spirits. My spirits *rose*. You're in *high* spirits. Thinking about her always gives me a *lift*. I'm feeling *down*. I'm *depressed*. He's really *low* these days. I *fell* into a depression. My spirits *sank*.

Physical basis: Drooping posture typically goes along with sadness and depression, erect posture with a positive emotional state.

CONSCIOUS IS UP; UNCONSCIOUS IS DOWN
Get *up*. Wake *up*. I'm *up* already. He *arises* early in the morning. He *fell* asleep. He *dropped* off to sleep. He's *under* hypnosis. He *sank* into a coma.

Physical basis: Humans and most other mammals sleep lying down and stand up when they awaken.

HEALTH AND LIFE ARE UP; SICKNESS AND DEATH ARE DOWN
He's at the *peak* of health. Lazarus *rose* from the dead. He's in *top* shape. As to his health, he's way *up* there. He *fell* ill. He's *sinking* fast. He came *down* with the flu. His health is *declining*. He *dropped* dead.

Physical basis: Serious illness forces us to lie down physically. When you're dead, you are physically down.

HAVING CONTROL or FORCE IS UP; BEING SUBJECT TO CONTROL or FORCE IS DOWN
I have control *over* her. I am *on top of* the situation. He's in a *superior* position. He's at the *height* of his power. He's in the *high* command. He's in the *upper* echelon. His power *rose*. He ranks *above* me in strength. He is *under* my control. He *fell* from power. His power is on the *decline*. He is my social *inferior*. He is *low man* on the totem pole.

Physical basis: Physical size typically correlates with physical strength, and the victor in a fight is typically on top.

MORE IS UP; LESS IS DOWN
The number of books printed each year keeps going *up*. His draft number is *high*. My income *rose* last year. The amount of artistic activity in this state has gone *down* in the past year. The number of errors he made is incredibly *low*. His income *fell* last year. He is *underage*. If you're too hot, turn the heat *down*.

Physical basis: If you add more of a substance or of physical objects to a container or pile, the level goes up.

FORESEEABLE FUTURE EVENTS ARE UP (and AHEAD)
All *up*coming events are listed in the paper. What's coming *up* this week? I'm afraid of what's *up ahead* of us. What's *up*?

Physical basis: Normally our eyes look in the direction in which we typically move (ahead, forward). As an object approaches a person (or the person approaches the object), the object appears larger. Since the ground is perceived as being fixed, the top of the object appears to be moving upward in the person's field of vision.

HIGH STATUS IS UP; LOW STATUS IS DOWN

He has a *lofty* position. She'll *rise* to the *top*. He's at the *peak* of his career. He's *climbing* the ladder. He has little *upward* mobility. He's at the *bottom* of the social hierarchy. She *fell* in status.

Social and physical basis: Status is correlated with (social) power and (physical) power is UP.

GOOD IS UP; BAD IS DOWN

Things are looking *up*. We hit a *peak* last year, but it's been *downhill* ever since. Things are at an all-time *low*. He does *high*-quality work.

Physical basis for personal well-being: Happiness, health, life, and control—the things that principally characterize what is good for a person—are all UP.

VIRTUE IS UP; DEPRAVITY IS DOWN

He is *high*-handed. She has *high* standards. She is *upright*. She is an *upstanding* citizen. That was a *low* trick. Don't be *underhanded*. I wouldn't *stoop* to that. That would be *beneath* me. He *fell* into the *abyss* of depravity. That was a *low-down* thing to do.

Physical and social basis: GOOD IS UP for a person (physical basis), together with a metaphor that we will discuss below, SOCIETY IS A PERSON (in the version where you are *not* identifying with your society). To be virtuous is to act in accordance with the standards set by the society/person to maintain its well-being. VIRTUE IS UP because virtuous actions correlate with social well-being from the society/person's point of view. Since socially based metaphors are part of the culture, it's the society/person's point of view that counts.

RATIONAL IS UP; EMOTIONAL IS DOWN

The discussion *fell to the emotional* level, but I *raised* it back *up to the rational* plane. We put our *feelings* aside and had a *high-level intellectual* discussion of the matter. He couldn't *rise above* his *emotions*.

Physical and cultural basis: In our culture people view themselves as being in control over animals, plants, and their physical environment, and it is their unique ability to reason that places human beings above other animals and gives them this control. CONTROL IS UP thus provides a basis for MAN IS UP and therefore for RATIONAL IS UP.

Discussion

1. Consider the implications of talking about argument as dance. Replace the italicized words in the "argument is war" example with dance terms.
2. The article implies that there may be cultural or ethical ramifications of our use of metaphor. Is that true for the metaphorical concept "time is money"? What implications does this concept hold for stewardship? Does it mean, for example, that Christians should tithe their time as well as their money?
3. Lakoff and Johnson argue against the validity of the concept that "linguistic expressions are containers for meaning," urging instead that context often determines meaning. Try to write a sentence that will be meaningful only in its context or that will mean different things in different contexts.
4. If a given sentence or piece of writing can mean different things to different people, does that mean that the reader always brings the meaning to what is read? In other words, can a reader make a sentence mean whatever the reader wants it to mean?
5. Sportscasters use a wide variety of metaphors in announcing the scores of various games. Listen to a broadcast and try to categorize and analyze the metaphors used in a given situation.
6. A metaphorical concept that social critics often associate with racism is that which suggests that "white is good and black is bad." Do you think that this concept leads to racism? If so, what could we do as a culture to alter this view?

Have You Committed Verbicide Today?

D. G. Kehl

> *Language, as D. G. Kehl explains in his essay, is sometimes used to obscure and confuse meanings. We can be seduced by a word, be hooked by a phrase, be led astray by a sentence. How often does this happen in Christianity? According to Kehl, who is a professor of English at Arizona State University, "Christianity seems to be choking in fuzz, fluff, and flummery."*

Advertising sells a lot more than cars, cookies and computers," a recent Advertising Council Ad states. It also sells culture, colleges, candidates, and churches. The rhetoric of ad men transforms standard brands into graven images for profit. Moreover, in the area of religion, politics, and charities, as well as business, there is a growing trend to sell an image instead of a fact, person, or project.

This image-vying and image-buying is, according to Wright Morris, "a 'religious' rite in the sense that it involves idols behind altars . . ." (*A Bill of Rites, A Bill of Wrongs, A Bill of Goods*, New American Library, 1968, p. 135). These "idols of the marketplace," to borrow Francis Bacon's phrase, are hawked in a liturgical lingo. However, this religious doublespeak has another side; while Madison Avenue uses religious ideas and language, churchmen have adopted the techniques and language of Madison Avenue.

A typical use of religion in advertising is the ad for Italian slacks called "Jesus Jeans," which displays a girl in tight-fitting shorts branded *he who loves me, follows me.* Biblical echoes in other recent ads are Michelob's *Do unto others*, Johnnie Walker's *Honor Thyself*, and Seagram's *Stop loving thy neighbor's—Get thine own.* Yardley of London asks *Can a woman live by detergents alone?* and Rolf's of Amity Leather Products offers a wallet *For your daily bread* or a beatific, *Welcome to the fold.* Such ads are designed to transfer positive associations to products that otherwise might have no appeal.

If the advertiser, sometimes verging on sacrilege, borrows language from the churchman, placing idols behind altars, the churchman, sometimes verging on desacralization, borrows jargon and technique from the advertiser, placing altars behind idols. We hear such phrases as Things go better with Christ; Jesus is the Real Thing; You've got a lot to live and Jesus has a lot to give; Relief is just a prayer away; Try Him—you'll like Him; and Give the Master Charge of your life. Such expressions bring to mind Paul's warnings about those who corrupt the Scriptures, as well as those who peddle religion for gain.

A Committee on Public Doublespeak, established by the National Council of Teachers of English, has been studying semantic distortion by public officials, political candidates and commentators, advertisers, and all who use the mass media. The fact that religious doublespeak has not been examined is perhaps due to the false notion that those who disseminate the word of truth have no problems with truth of the word. But, as C. S. Lewis's Screwtape reminds us, nowhere is temptation so successful as on the very steps of the altar. "We have contrived that their very language should be all smudge and blur," Screwtape says (*Screwtape Proposes a Toast*, Macmillan, 1961, p. 172).

Lewis recognized that the smudge and blur begins first in the heart and mind and then transfers to speech. Similarly, George Orwell says doublethink is both a cause and an effect of doublespeak: "To know and not to know, to be conscious of complete truthfulness, while telling carefully constructed lies, to hold simultaneously two opinions which canceled out, knowing them to be contradictory and believing in both of them, to use logic against logic, to repudiate morality while laying claim to it . . ." (*Nineteen Eighty-Four*, Harcourt, 1949, p. 163).

Doublethink and doublespeak have roots in the sinful nature of man. Montaigne wrote over three centuries ago that "We are, I know not how, double in ourselves, so that what we believe we disbelieve, and we cannot rid ourselves of what we condemn."

It is human nature that produces Orwellian doublethink, which, in turn, produces doublespeak, leading often to doubledealing (that is, hypocritical, cunning deception; veiled duplicity of action), and finally even to doublecross (flagrant misrepresentation and treachery). The children of men "Speak lies each with his neighbor," the psalmist wrote, "with false lips and double heart they speak." Or as the Book of Common Prayer puts it, men "do but flatter with their lips, and dissemble with their double heart."

Basic to doublespeak is incongruity between what is said and what really is, between word and referent. Doublespeak is characterized by incongruity between what language is supposed to do—communicate—and what doublespeak does—obscure. It is the incongruity between the specific referent and the ambiguity, abstraction, or inaccuracy of words. It is the incongruity between what should be said and what is left unsaid or slanted to cloak essential but unpleasant facts.

Incongruity between the medium and the message has no place in communication of Christian truth. The verbal medium must conform to the message, never vice-versa. In a Christian context at least, the medium is *not* the message; rather the Christian message is itself also the medium: the Word is both subject and object. Effective Christian communication is possible when words and their referents are united through the instrumentality of the Holy Spirit. "We speak not in words which man's wisdom teacheth, combining spiritual things with spiritual words" (I Cor. 2:13, NAS).

A common variety of religious doublespeak might be called rhetorical overkill, which in its milder forms is inane verbosity and in its more severe forms is tasteless bombast. "A fool's voice is known by a multitude of words," Solomon wrote (Eccl. 5:3). We often hear expressions such as free gift, God incarnate in the flesh, self image of yourself, unmerited favor, real reality, ascend up to heaven, and essentials necessary to Christian growth. Such tautology results from ignorance of language or a lack of faith in the power of the Word.

In *Studies in Words* (Cambridge, 1967, p. 7), C. S. Lewis discussed several forms of "verbicide" that men commit "because they want to snatch a word as a party banner, to appropriate its 'selling quality.'" One of the commonest of those cited by Lewis is inflation: "Those who taught us to say *awfully* for 'very', *tremendous* for 'great', *sadism* for 'cruelty', and *unthinkable* for 'undesirable' were verbicides." Because of the use of adjectives such as awful and wonderful to describe commonplace things, these words have lost their impact when used to describe the sacred; their original meaning has been lost or vitiated through inflation. Makers of Gillette Blue Blades have experienced this similar problem: because of the use of inflated language in past advertising, they have no words left to meaningfully describe improvements in their product. "What can we do?" a company executive asks. "Say, 'This time we *really* mean it'?"

Christendom seems to be choking in fuzz, fluff, and flummery—epitomized by the ubiquitous slogan, "Have a nice eternity." This pseudo-statement illustrates what might be called rhetorical underkill or blunderkill. The incongruity between noun and modifier renders the phrase oxymoronic—with due emphasis on the second syllable.

Linguistic puffery in a religious context has brought about the lie that is not quite a lie and the truth that is not quite the truth. A church ad states, "Your friendly neighborhood church is just a few short miles off the freeway, just a few short minutes from practically anywhere in the Valley." Ours, you see, is an age of relativity, even in linear and chronological measurement—although our friendly neighborhood pastor probably preaches absolutes in the pulpit. Think of it. The miles to church are not restricted to 1,609.35 meters each, and Ptolemy's minute can be shortened as one drives there. A religious breakthrough has come. If Madison Avenue can advertise a large pint, a big, big gallon, and a full quart, why can't the churches advertise short miles, short minutes, a full Gospel, and a full salvation, as well as an eternity that's gonna last a long, long, time?

Another form of religious doublespeak is the use of euphemism. Some euphemisms, of course, serve a legitimate purpose in situations where tact, taste, and courtesy are required. Used responsibly, they can be the soft words that turn away wrath. But when they cloak essential truth, when language belies reality, when manipulation and exploitation are the motive, they become pernicious words in sheep's clothing or the whitewash on sepulchres full of corruption. By use of euphemism some preachers avoid a clean exposition of sin, a central and essential doctrine in Christian teaching. "Whatever became of sin?" Karl Menninger asked in his recent book. A myriad of euphemisms have replaced and obscured it; sin becomes a faux pas, a peccadillo, a lapse, a slip, a breach, a misdeed, or an impropriety. One does not sin; one is simply being human.

In T. S. Eliot's *The Cocktail Party*, Celia Coplestone, in a session with her psychiatrist, describes her guilt:

> "I had always been taught to disbelieve in sin.
> Oh, I don't mean that it was ever mentioned.
> But anything wrong, from our point of view,
> Was either bad form, or was psychological. . : .
> But when everything's bad form or mental kinks,
> You either become bad form, and cease to care,
> Or else, if you care, you must be kinky.
> (*Complete Poems and Plays 1909–1950*, Harcourt, 1971, p. 361).

An age in which sin is bad form is a doublespeaking age in which the power to define a word can be the power to shape ideas and control minds. G. K. Chesterton, in his essay "On Evil Euphemisms," aptly characterizes our time: "Everything is to be called something that it is not. . . . Everything is to be recommended to the public by some sort of synonym which is really a pseudonym. It is a talent that goes with the time of electioneering and advertisement and newspaper headlines; but whatever else such a time may be, it certainly is not specially a time of truth" (*Essays, Stories, and Poems*, I. M. Dent and Sons, 1935, pp. 208–9).

Still another form of religious doublespeak is the use of jargon. The use of esoteric, theological terms inappropriate to audience and occasion is the stock-in-trade of the religious doublespeaker who says thaumaturgy rather than working of miracles, viable Weltanschauung rather than sensible world-view, and relevant Kerygma rather than effective proclamation of the Gospel. This person lives in a pastorium; interacts with and gets input and feedback from his prayer-cell circle of the Committed in a Christian Life Center; has dialogue in Christian constructs; opts for viable alternatives to implement, and Outreach Explosion to the unchurched. The Apostle Paul warned the Ephesian believers, "Let no man deceive you with vain [or empty] words" (Eph. 5:6), and Peter warned believers of those who would make merchandise of them with false words (II Pet. 2:3).

A first cousin of this type of doublespeak is what might be called "purr words"—highly general, abstract language that is long on impression and short on repression, designed to sell rather than to tell. These words and expressions have such vague associations and referents that no clear meaning is conveyed or even intended—for example, the American Way of Life, a meaningful religious experience, distinctively Christian, and the word religious itself.

Another form of religious doublespeak consists of what Ralph Ellison has called "church-house rhetoric"—that is, hackneyed language, prefabricated pietisms, sanctimonious stereotypes. One who uses pious platitudes not only speaks mechanically, but also reveals the quality of his thinking and devotion. If the blessings of God are new every morning, why is the language of testimony and prayer threadbare and stale? It is certainly not the clarity of some expressions that have led to their overuse; consider: the battlements of heaven (Is the Holy City under siege?) or a journey to far-flung corners of the globe (to be accomplished, I suppose, by throwing caution to the four winds). We must be aware not only of what we mean to say but also of what we say without meaning to. Consider this common expression: May God add his blessing to the reading of the Word. The implication is that man has blessed the Word by reading it and Almighty will add a little something.

Although some words lose their value to communicate through hackneyed stereotypes, others do the same thing through a hip rhetoric slanted to accomodate a particular audience. Such expressions as Groove with God; Let Jesus turn you on; get high on Jesus, and take the ultimate trip with the Big Man upstairs fall dangerously short of any biblical referent. Paul's advice to Timothy to "shun profane and vain babblings: for they will increase into more ungodliness" (II Tim. 2:16) is appropriate warning to anyone who is guilty of this form of doublespeak.

One of the most subtle forms of current religious doublespeak is the use of what Theodore Roosevelt called weasel words. These are words that have been emptied of their meaning, like eggs sucked empty by a weasel. As Mario Pei points out, the term "can be legitimately extended to cover any word of which the semantics are deliberately changed or obscured to achieve a specific purpose" (*Words in Sheep's Clothing*, Hawthorne, 1969, p. 2). For example, Neo-Orthodox theologians often use Christian terms while denying their historical basis in fact, which in effect empties the word of meaning. This is true of their use of the terms virgin birth, revelation, and resurrection. With respect to the last Charles Ryrie has noted that "Barthians say that the accounts of the resurrection in the Bible are not the ground of our faith in the resurrection; nevertheless, they are an important element in the witness to revelation of the resurrection, and this revelation is the ground of our faith. Reduced to simple doubletalk this means that theoretically we would not need the Bible accounts of the resurrection in order to believe it, but admittedly they help, and actually we could not believe without them" (*Neo-Orthodoxy*, Moody Press, 1956, p. 60).

Paul warned Timothy that in the latter days men would "be full of big words," maintaining a "facade of religion but their conduct will deny its validity" (II Tim. 3:1–5, Phillips). Such is the incongruity of religious doublespeak. If doublespeak is the language of corruption issuing from the deceitfulness of the human heart, then the desideratum is a language of integrity. Amelioration of doublespeak will result from the single-mindedness of an integrated and regenerate personality. When the word of Christ dwells richly within, when the Holy Spirit combines "spiritual things with spiritual words" doublespeak will diminish.

Discussion

1. Professor Kehl accuses modern Christendom of reducing belief to popular phrases and buzzwords. To a certain extent this is indeed true. You can probably supply examples of your own to add to his. Can it also be the case, however, that certain slogans evoke a spirituality, that certain sayings provide us considerable comfort?
2. Study the lyrics of several contemporary Christian songs. Do they fall prey to what Kehl describes as doublespeak or doublethink?

3. Language, as the poet Robert Frost was fond of pointing out, is always attended by implications beyond mere words. The way the speaker says something, and the gestures accompanying the spoken words, also convey meaning. Study several advertisements to see how the accompanying pictures, the layout, and the script all contribute to the meaning of the message.

4. Kehl details the dangers in modern religious language—euphemism, jargon, hackneyed language—that serve to obscure Christian doctrine and belief. However, Kehl fails to provide positive qualities that should ideally characterize religious language. By inference from his list of negative qualities, what would you say these positive qualities are?

Writing Assignments for Chapter 13

1. Write an essay that explains or explores some of the metaphorical language of the Bible. Take an image (being washed in the blood) or a group of images (of God's nurture, of Satan's nature, of the Christian life) and devise a thesis that explains their significance or implications. Use examples of metaphorical language to support your points. Cite your references in parentheses at the end of the sentence that contains the reference; for example, if in this sentence we had just made a point about the twenty-eighth verse of chapter 1 of Genesis, we would cite that reference as we do here: (Genesis 1:28).

   Shape your writing to one of these audiences: 1) an unbelieving friend (here you would be writing a serious letter); 2) the readers of a religious magazine; 3) the readers of a tract (i.e., you'll be writing one); 4) the readers of a religion column in a newspaper; 5) readers of a journal such as *The Wittenburg Door;* 6) readers of a meditational book.

2. Love poems typically use metaphorical language. Compare the metaphors and language of Song of Solomon to those of a contemporary love song or poem. Analyze the language to see what it reveals about each writer's attitudes toward love and relationships. You may wish to write this in the form of a letter to a friend or as an article for a publication such as *Campus Life* or *Christianity Today.*

3. A few years ago in military circles, a directive was issued to "eschew obfuscation." Regardless of the directive, jargon still infiltrates all levels of writing in and out of the military. The Pentagon may be guilty of calling peace "permanent prehostility," but people in other fields are equally guilty of using infelicitous language. Pure poppycock—Kathryn Lindskoog's

name for jargon—abounds in modern publications. For this assignment, locate one such piece in a newspaper or magazine and
write a brief analysis of its use of jargon.

4. Study the prefaces and introductions of five different versions of
the Bible. Usually these will provide reasons and guidelines for
the translation. From these different statements, develop your
own theory, or rationale, for Bible translation. What guidelines
should govern translation?

5. For an essay in argumentation you might assert one translation
over several others. Remember to concede certain merits to those
you dislike, but clearly demonstrate why you consider one version superior to the others. Ample research materials are available in both popular magazines (see *Reader's Guide to Periodical
Literature*) and specialized journals (see *Index of Religious Studies*).

14

Understanding Ourselves in Relation to Society, Education, and Psychology

Experience and fact irritate us because
they do not give us knowledge. . . .
Knowledge is something quite different from experience or
from fact. . . .
                    —Lev Shestov, *Athens and Jerusalem*

You ought to thank God, perhaps. How do you know? Perhaps
God is saving you for something.
                    —Fyodor Dostoyevsky, *Crime and Punishment*

The paradox of faith is this, that the individual is higher than
the universal, that the individual . . . determines his relation to
the universal by his relation to the absolute, not his relation
to the absolute by his relation to the universal.
                    —Søren Kierkegaard, *Fear and Trembling*

Some humans leave a terrible scar on history. Some humans work a healing of those wounds. Some humans, very few, shape the course of history itself.

Those few seem to be the bright ones, the shining ones, whose meteoric blaze through a few brief pages of history lights a way for others to follow. Who are such people? Each person constructs a special list, but wouldn't all the lists include Plato, whose intellectual genius paved the road for all later philosophy? Wouldn't they include Jesus, whose life and death and resurrection shaped meaning for a word—*faith*—and the hope of life everlasting? Perhaps they would also include Augustine, Charlemagne, Aquinas, Calvin, Joan of Arc, Mother Teresa.

History seems the province of such figures. Yet we all have our histories—our triumphs and travails, our shining hours and dark nights. We are shaped by a past and are shaping a future. We are called by God to act at the present moment in such a way that it bears eternal significance. And at this moment, we are no less to ourselves and others than those figures whose names loom monumentally from the past.

Each action we commit, each commitment we act upon, is also at once an act of understanding ourselves and others. To say, "This I believe," and "Because of that, so shall I act," begins in an act of individual faith and ends . . . who knows where? Who knows what lives we touch, and in how many ways, each day?

We never think and act in a vacuum. Our convictions and actions are not in isolation. In this section, the readings explore three formative powers on our understanding of ourselves.

First, the "who we are" often begins in our perception of what others think we are. We know ourselves in part by social influences, by what others urge us and tell us to believe. This route of understanding, however, is not a one-way street. We bear an urgent responsibility to inform society of what we believe to be true and right.

Second, each of us has been shaped in our self-understanding by education. At its highest level, when it transcends the mere passing along of factual data, when it transcends necessity and approaches nobility, when it transcends rote mechanics and genuinely explores, education permits us room for self-discovery, forces us to positions, guides us in the knowledge of the way, the truth, and the light.

And, third, we are shaped in our own private histories, our own self-understanding, by psychology. It was simply too easy for Plato to tell his listeners, "Know thyself." That "self" is sometimes an incredible complex of chemical and emotional factors that we can scarcely comprehend. While many of us live quite contentedly knowing little or nothing about the functions of our psyches, others of us live a daily battle trying desperately to understand. The question, "What is God's will for me?" often becomes "Why did God make me like I am?"

Here then are three important arenas in which we test our self-understanding: in relation to society, to education, and to psychology.

But we acknowledge a subtle danger here. We acquire self-understanding by our experience in, our relation to, society, education, and psychology. But how do we understand society, education, and psychology? The world today has us placed on a bridge spanning a great divide. On one side lies a way of tradition, where belief in God and values derived from God's revelation guide our understanding. On the other side lies a world stripped of the presence of God, a world that declares that social, educational, and psychological knowledge must be humanly centered. The flow of the crowd on that bridge is decisively toward the latter brink.

Here we begin to see the significance of the different authority and value structures that guide our understanding of ourselves and the world about us. Consider just one case in point. In 1948 B. F. Skinner published a book which was to shake the worlds of psychology, education, and sociology: *Walden Two*. Here, in a fictional world focused on the commune-like Walden Two, Skinner demonstrated his belief that human behavior can be engineered. Scientific technology reigns over man. The eventual product? A perfected humanity.

The goal sounds attractive. Christians are mindful, both theologically and experientially, of a humanity that is sinful and in need of redemption. But Skinner offers an alternative. If humanity's behavior can be engineered into perfectibility, there is absolutely no need of a divine savior. Humanity can save itself. The perfected world of paradise can exist on this earth.

It is attractive indeed. No crime. No sadness. Instant gratification of desires, because we will desire only those things that can be gratified instantly. But there is a difficulty. In Christianity one recognizes the absolute authority of God, and the fact that he so loved the world that he sent his only begotten Son to assure that those who love him will not perish but have everlasting life. But in *Walden Two* the reader is left with this perplexing question. If we accept behavioral engineering, just who is it that will do the engineering? Finally, the situation redounds to one human controlling others in a world willfully stripped of the divine. This is not a new pattern, the astute reader will observe. Hitler tried much the same thing. So did Lenin, as Aleksandr Solzhenitsyn points out in his Templeton Address, reprinted in this section.

Here, then, lies the crisis point in understanding ourselves. Each of us must ask, "To whom will I give my obedience, my allegiance? Which authority will I recognize as directive for my life?"

The Empty Manger

A Christmas Story

Walter Wangerin, Jr.

> *Walter Wangerin, Jr., recently left his pastorate at the Grace Lutheran Church in the inner city of Evansville, Indiana, to devote himself full-time to writing. His effort as a writer is the same as a pastor: to bring the Word of God to bear upon the daily lives of people. He is the author of several books, including the best-selling* The Book of the Dun Cow.

*M*y daughter wept on Christmas Eve. What should I say to the heart of my daughter? How should I comfort her? What should I tell her of tears, who has learned only their strength and perturbation, but knows no words for them?

Her name is Mary, truly. She is very young.

Therefore, she didn't cry the older, bitter tears of disappointment. She hasn't experienced the desolation of adults, who try so hard but find so little of spirit in the season, who cry unsatisfied, or merely for weariness.

Neither did she weep the tears of an oversold imagination, as the big-eyed children may. It wasn't that she dreamed a present too beautiful to be real or expected my love to pay better than my purse. She's greedy for my touch, is Mary, more than for my presents; and touching—Lord! I have much of that for Mary.

Nor was she sick on Christmas Eve. That were an easier pain for a father to console.

Nor was she hungry for any physical thing.

No, she was hungry for Odessa Williams, that old black lady—for her life. That's why Mary cried. The child had come suddenly to the limits of the universe, and stood there, and had no other response for what she saw than tears, and then she wept into my breast, and I am her father. And should I be helpless before such tears? Or mute? Oh, what should I say to the heart of my daughter Mary?

This is what happened: It is the custom of our congregation to gather on the Sunday evening before Christmas—adults and youth and children, members of the choir particularly—to go out into the cold December night, and to carol the elderly. A common custom. Little elemental usually comes of it.

We bundle thick against the night wind. Our faces pinch—the white ones pink, the black ones (we are mostly black ones) pale. The kids can hardly walk for all their clothing, but run nonetheless. And then we sing a boisterous noise. Our breath puffs clouds at our lips. The old people smile through their windows and nod to the singing and close their eyes and seem to dream a little of the past. We lift our keys and jangle them to the chorus of "Jingle Bells." And sometimes, sometimes those sweetest voices among us will sing alone. Young "Dee Dee" will take a descant trip on "Silent Night" that makes the rest of us drop our eyes and wonder at so clear and crystalline a melody; and Tim Moore will set himself free, and us and all the night streets of the city, with "O Holy Night"; he will, with an almighty voice, ride to heaven on the song and then return to earth in the merest murmur, "When Christ was born, when Christ was born"—and we will find the tears freezing on our eyelashes, moved by beauty on a cold, dark, winter's sidewalk.

But these are good tears, and not the tears of my Mary.

We went, one such Sunday evening, December the twentieth, through a snowless dark, to Saint Mary's Hospital. We divided ourselves among the wards. We carried our caroling to those members who were patients there. And I, with Mary and Dee Dee and Tim Moore and a handful of the children who sang in the choir, slipped finally into Odessa Williams's room, to sing to her.

She had a curtain pulled round her bed; therefore, we had to stand right close. And though the light was dim at the bedstead, we could see the old lady's face. The sight made the children solemn and quiet, quiet. Her brown cheeks had gone to parchment, were sunken, her temples scalloped; her hair and her arms together were most thin, her nails too long, her eyes beclouded. Odessa was dying of cancer.

This was the first time that the children had met her. They gazed, and they waited to be led.

As her pastor, I had been visiting Odessa for years, first in her apartment, then in a nursing home, finally here, a long descent. But her soul belonged fiercely to Grace Church, and she had, at her distance, followed every event of the congregation. She set her jaw (when her teeth were in) to speak of that church; and she worked her gums (when they were not) busily, passionately, when she worried for its future. Because of her wasting disease, she had never appeared among the people; but that did not mean she loved them any less. Simply, they were unaware how much she did love them. Yet Odessa could communicate such a message with sudden speed and indelibly.

So the children, in dim yellow light, were circled round a stranger, were staring at a stranger, delicate, old, and dying, lying on her back.

Odessa, for her part, said nothing. She stared back at them.

"Sing," I said to the children. "What's this? Y'all gone munching on your tongues? Sing the same as you always do. Sing for Miz Williams."

And they did, that wide-eyed ring of children.

One by one they sang the carols everyone knew, though children had no keys to jangle. One by one they relaxed, and their faces melted, and I saw that my Mary's eyes went bright and sparkled—and she smiled, and she was smiling on Odessa Williams. The children gave the lady an innocent concert, as clean and light as snow.

Odessa, too, began to smile.

For that smile, for the gladness in an old lady's face, I whispered, "Dee Dee, sing 'Silent Night' once more."

Dear Dee Dee! That child, as dark as the shadows around her, stroked the very air as though it were a chime of glass. (Dee Dee, I love you!) So high she took her crystal voice, so long she held the notes, that the rest of the children unconsciously hummed and harmonized with her, and they began to sway together, and for a moment they lost themselves in the song.

Yet, Odessa found them. Odessa snared those children. Even while they still were singing, Odessa drew them to herself. And then their mouths were singing the hymn, but their eyes were fixed on her.

Odessa Williams, lying on her back, began to direct the music.

She lifted her arms and marked the beat precisely; her lank hands virtually shaped the tone of Dee Dee's descant; and her thin face frowned with a painful pleasure. She pursed her lips as though tasting something celestial and delicious, so the children thought themselves marvelous; and she let another music smoke at her nostrils. The lady took them. The lady carried them. The lady led them meek to the end of their carol and to a perfect silence; and then they stood there round her bed, astonished, each one of them the possession of Odessa Williams, restrained. And waiting.

Oh, what a power of matriarchal authority was here, keenly alive!

Nor did she disappoint them. For she began in a low and husky voice, to talk. No, Odessa preached.

"Oh, children, you my choir," she said. "Oh, choir, you my children for sure, every las' one of you. And listen me." She caught them one by

one with her barbed eyes. "Ain' no one stand in front of you for goodness, no! You the bes', babies! You the final *best*."

The children gazed at her, and the children believed her absolutely,
and my Mary, too, believed what she was hearing, heart and soul.

"Listen me," Odessa said. "When you sing, wherever you go to sing,
whoever's sittin' down in front of you when you sing—I'm there with
you. I tell you truly: I alluz been with you, I alluz will be. And how can I
say such a mackulous thing?" She lowered her voice. Her eyelids
drooped a minimal degree. "Why, 'cause we in Jesus. Babies, babies,
we be in Jesus, old ones, young ones, us and you together. Jesus keep us
in his bosom, and Jesus, no—he don't never let us go. Never. Never. Not
ever—"

So spoke Odessa in the dim long light. So said the lady with such
conviction and with such a determined love for children whom she'd
never met till now, but whom she'd followed with her heart, that these
same children rolled tears from their wide-open eyes, and they were
not ashamed.

They touched the hump of her toes beneath the hospital blankets.
Stumpy black fingers, baby affection, and smiles.

And my Mary's eyes I saw to glisten. The lady had won my daughter.
In that holy moment, so close upon the Holy Day, so brief and so lasting
at once, Mary came to love Odessa Williams completely. This is the
power of a wise love wisely expressed: it can transfigure a heart, suddenly, forever.

But even these tears, shed Sunday evening in the hospital room, are
not the tears that wanted my comforting. They are themselves a comfort. No, the tears that I had to speak to were the next my daughter
wept. Those, they came on Christmas Eve.

Three days before Christ's birthday, Odessa died.

It was a long time coming. It was quick when it came. She died that
Tuesday, the twenty-second of December. On Wednesday her body was
in the care of the undertaker. The funeral was set for 11 in the morning,
Thursday, the twenty-fourth. There was no alternative; the mortuary
would be closed both Friday and the weekend. Throughout these
arrangements—while at the same time directing preparations for
special seasonal services—I was more pastor than father, more admin-
istrator than wise.

Well, it was a frightfully busy, hectic week. This was the very crush
of the holidays, after all, and my doubled labor had just been trebled.

Not brutally, but somewhat hastily at lunch on Wednesday I told my
children that Miz Williams had died. They were eating soup. This was

not an uncommon piece of news for me to bear them: the congregation has its share of the elderly.

Mary, I barely noticed, ceased eating.

I wiped my mouth and rose from the table.

Mary stopped me briefly with a question and a statement. Staring at her soup, she said, "Is it going to snow tomorrow?"

I said, "I don't know, Mary. How would I know that?"

And she said, "I want to go to the funeral."

So: she was considering what to wear against the weather. I said, "Fine," and left.

Thursday came grey and hard and cold and windless. It gave a pewter light. It made no shadow. The sky was sullen, draining color even from the naked trees. I walked to church. How still was all the earth around me—

It is the custom of our congregation, before a funeral, to set the casket immediately in front of the chancel and then to leave it open an hour until the service itself. People move silently up the aisle for a final viewing, singly or else in small groups, strangers to me who look and think and leave again. Near the time appointed for the service they do not leave, but find seats and wait in silence. I robe ten minutes to the hour. I stand at the back of the church and greet them.

And so it was that I met my Mary at the door. In fact, she was standing outside the door when others pushed in past her.

"Mary?" I said. "Are you coming in?"

She looked at me a moment. "Dad," she whispered earnestly, as though it were a dreadful secret, "it's snowing."

It was. A light powder grew at the roots of the grasses, a darker powder filled the air. The day was too cold for flakes—just a universal sifting of powder that seemed to isolate every living thing.

"Dad," Mary repeated, gazing at me, and now it was a grievous voice, but what was I supposed to do? "It's snowing!"

"Come, Mary. We haven't much time. Come in."

My daughter and I walked down the aisle to the chancel and the casket, and she was eight years old, then, and I was robed. People sat in the pews like sparrows on telephone wires, huddled under feathers, watching dark-eyed.

Mary slowed and paused at the casket and murmured, "Oh, no."

Odessa's eyes were closed, her lips pale; her skin seemed pressed into place, and the bridge of her nose suffered glasses. Had Odessa worn glasses? Yes, she had. But these were perched on her face slightly askew, unnaturally, so that one became sadly, sadly aware of eyeglasses for the first time. What belonged to the old lady any more, and what did not?

These were my speculations.

Mary had her own. She reached out and touched Odessa's long fingers, crossed waxy at the breast. "Oh, no," she whispered. The child bent and brushed those fingers with her cheek, then suddenly stood erect again.

"Oh, no," Mary said, and she looked at me, and she did not blink, but she began to cry. "Dad," she whispered. "Miz Williams is so cold. Dad," wept Mary. "But it's snowing outside—it's snowing in Miz William's grave!" All at once Mary buried her face in my robes, and I felt the pressure of her forehead and all her grief against my chest—and I was a father again, and my own throat swallowed and my eyes burned.

"Dad," sobbed Mary. "Dad, Dad, it's Christmas *Eve!*"

These were the tears. These were the tears my daughter cried at Christmas. God in heaven, what do I say to tears like these? It is death my Mary met. It's the end of things, that things *have* an end, good things, kind and blessed things, things new and rare and precious: that love has an end; that people have an end; that Odessa Williams, the fierce old lady who seized the heart of my Mary and squeezed it and possessed it but four days ago, who was so real in dim light, waving her arms, that *she* has an end, ended, is gone, is dead.

How do I comfort these tears? What do I say to the heart of my daughter?

Jesus, Jesus, pity me. I said nothing.

I knelt down. I took Mary's streaming face between my hands. But she so pierced me with the question in her eyes that I couldn't look at her, and I gathered her to myself, and I held her tightly, I held her hard, until I'd wrung the sobbing from her body; and I released her.

I watched her go back down the aisle and turn into a pew and sit. It was a silent Mary who went. She sat by her mother, but she asked no questions any more. Why should she, sad Mary, when there were no answers given?

So, the funeral. And so, the sermon.

"But there will be no gloom for her that was in anguish." Isaiah. "The people who walked in darkness have seen a great light." Prophecy and truth. "For to us a child is born, to us a son is given"—Christmas. But what were Isaiah and prophecy and all the sustaining truths of the faith to my daughter Mary? Nothing. Odessa had been something to her, but Odessa was dead. The casket was closed. Death was something to her now, and maybe the only thing.

The weather at graveside was grey and cold and snowing. The people stood in coats and shivered.

Mary said not a word nor held her mother's hand nor looked at me. Neither was she crying any more.

It is the custom of our family to open our gifts late Christmas Eve. I wondered, that afternoon, whether we oughtn't vary custom this year for Mary's sake. *She* was still in her gloom and anguish, separated from us all by silence. There must have been a tumult of thought in her brain, but none of it showed on an eight-year-old face made severe. Oh, Mary, what joy will you have in presents, now? How frivolous the ribbons and wrappings would seem to one so thoughtful.

But that private custom of ours depended upon another custom of the congregation: we would not open the gifts until first we'd participated in the children's Christmas service at church. This service gave me the greatest hesitation, because my Mary was to be *the* Mary in it, the mother of the infant Jesus. Could she accomplish so public a thing in so private a mood?

I asked her. "Mary, do you think we should get another Mary?"

Slowly she shook her head. "No," she said. "I'm Mary."

Mary, Mary, so much Mary—but I wish you weren't sad. I wish I had a word for you. Pastor, father, old and mute. Mary, forgive me, the heart of my daughter. It is not a kind world after all. Not even the holidays can draw a veil across the truth and pretend the happiness that is not there. Mary, bold Mary—

"You are Mary," I said. "I'll be with you. It'll be all right."

We drove to church. The snow lay a loose inch on the ground. It swirled in snowdevils behind the cars ahead of us. It held the grey light of the city near the earth, though this was not nighttime, and dark. Surely, the snow had covered Odessa's grave as well, a silent seamless sheet of no warmth whatsoever.

Ah, these should have been my Mary's thoughts, not mine.

The church sanctuary was full of a yellow light and noise, transfigured utterly from the low, funereal whispers of the morning. People threw back their heads and laughed. Parents chatted. Children darted, making ready for their pageant, each at various stages of dress, caught halfway between this age's blue jeans and the shepherds' robes of two millennia ago. Children were breathless. But Mary and I moved through the contumely like sprites, unnoticed and unnoticing. I was filled with her sorrow. She seemed simply empty.

In time the actors found their proper places, and the glad pageant began.

"My soul," said Mary, both Marys before a little Elizabeth—but she said it so quietly that few could hear and my own heart yearned for her—"magnifies the Lord, and my spirit rejoices in God my Savior—"

And so: the child was surviving. But she was not rejoicing.

The angels came and giggled and sang and left.

A decree went out.

Another song was sung.

And then three moved into the chancel: Joseph and Mary and one other child to carry the manger, a wooden trough filled with old straw and a floppy doll.

The pageant proceeded, but I lost it entirely in watching my daughter.

For Mary began to frown fiercely on the manger in front of her—not at all like the proud and beaming parent she was supposed to portray. At the *manger*, she was staring, which stood in precisely the same spot where Odessa's casket had sat that morning; and one was open as the other had been, and each held the figure of a human. Mary frowned so hard at it that I thought she would break into tears again, and my mind raced over things to do when she couldn't control herself any more.

But Mary did not cry!

While shepherds kept watch over their flocks by night, my Mary played a part that no one had written into the script. The girl reached into the manger and touched the doll, thoughtfully. *What are you thinking?* Then, as though it were a decision, she took the doll out by its toes and stood up and walked down the chancel steps. *Mary, where are you going?* I folded my hands on account of her and yearned to hold her, to hide her, to protect her. But she carried the doll away into the darkened sacristy and disappeared. *Mary? Mary?* In a moment the child emerged again with nothing at all. She returned to the manger quickly, and she knelt down and she gazed upon the empty straw with her palms together like the first Mary, full of adoration. And her face—Mary, my Mary, your face was radiant then!

O Mary, how I love you!

Not quite suddenly there was in the chancel a multitude of the childish host praising God and saying, "Glory to God in the highest!" But Mary knelt unmoved among them, and her eight-year-old face was smiling, and there *was* the glistening of tears on her cheeks, but they were not unhappy, and the manger, open, empty, seemed the cause of them.

My soul magnifies the Lord! My spirit rejoices in God my Savior, for he has regarded the low estate of his handmaiden. Mary, what do you see? What do you know that your father could not say to the heart of his daughter? Mary, mother of the infant Jesus, teach me too!

She sat beside me in the car when we drove home. A sifting snow made cones below the streetlights. It blew lightly across the windshield and closed us in.

Mary said, "Dad?"

I said, "What."

She said, "Dad, Jesus wasn't in the manger. That wasn't Jesus. That was a doll." Oh, Mary: all things are struck real for you now, and there is no pretending any more. It was a doll indeed. So, death reveals realities—

She said, "Jesus, he doesn't *have* to be in a manger, does he? He goes back and forth, doesn't he? He came from heaven, and he was borned here; but when he was done he went back to heaven again, and because he came and went he can be coming and going *all* the time, right?"

"Right," I whispered. Teach me, little child. Teach me this Christmas gladness that you know.

"The manger is empty," Mary said. And then she said, "Dad, Miz Williams' box is empty, too. We don't have to worry about the snow." The next wonder my daughter whispered softly, as though peeping at presents; "It's only a doll in her box. It's like a big doll, Dad, and we put it away today. If Jesus can cross, if Jesus can go across, then Miz Williams, she crossed the same way, too, with Jesus—"

And Jesus, no—he don't ever let us go. Never.

"Dad?" said Mary, my Mary, the Mary who could ponder so much in her heart. "Why are you crying?"

Babies, babies, we be in Jesus, old ones, young ones, us and you together. Jesus keep us in his bosom, and Jesus, no—he don't never let go. Never. Never. Not ever.

"Because I've got no other words to say," I said to Mary. "I haven't had the words for some time, now."

"Dad?"

"What."

"Don't cry. I can talk for both of us."

It always was; it always will be; it was in the fullness of time when the Christ child first was born; it was in 1981 when my daughter taught me the times on Christmas Eve; it is in every celebration of Jesus' crossings back and forth; and it shall be forever—that this is the power of a wise love wisely expressed: it can transfigure the heart, suddenly, forever.

Discussion

1. In *The Orphean Passages* (San Francisco: Harper and Row, 1986), Wangerin defines faith like this: "It is a relationship with the living God—*enacted in this World*, this world of the furious swirl, in which all things flow" (11). How does the definition apply to this story?

2. Mary asks several times whether it is going to snow. What does that mean for her?
3. Contrast the father's self-understanding with that of his daughter. How do they both come to self-understanding through Odessa Williams's death?
4. Characterize the tone of the narrator in the story. How do the narrative techniques of word order and diction support the tone?

The Templeton Address: Men Have Forgotten God

Aleksandr Solzhenitsyn

Aleksandr Solzhenitsyn has been persecuted in and exiled from his Russian homeland for one reason only. He dared to tell the truth. He insisted upon telling it, with power and undeniable clarity, through years of imprisonment, through back-breaking labor camps, through his exile. As this essay makes clear, the greatest truth—the truth worth living and dying for—is the truth of God. Solzhenitsyn won the Nobel Prize for Literature in 1970, and lives today in Vermont. The Templeton Address is translated by Alexis Klimoff.

More than half a century ago, while I was still a child, I recall hearing a number of older people offer the following explanation for the great disasters that had befallen Russia: "Men have forgotten God; that's why all this has happened."

Since then I have spent well-nigh fifty years working on the history of our Revolution; in the process I have read hundreds of books, collected hundreds of personal testimonies, and have already contributed eight volumes of my own toward the effort of clearing away the rubble left by that upheaval. But if I were asked today to formulate as concisely as possible the main cause of the ruinous Revolution that swallowed up some sixty million of our people, I could not put it more accurately than to repeat: "Men have forgotten God; that's why all this has happened."

What is more, the events of the Russian Revolution can only be understood now, at the end of the century, against the background of what has since occurred in the rest of the world. What emerges here is a process of universal significance. And if I were called upon to identify briefly the principal trait of the *entire* twentieth century, here too I would be unable to find anything more precise and pithy than to repeat once again: "Men have forgotten God." The failings of human consciousness, deprived of its divine dimension, have been a determining factor in all the major crimes of this century. The first of these was World War I, and much of our present predicament can be traced back to it. That war (the memory of which seems to be fading) took place when Europe, bursting with health and abundance, fell into a rage of self-mutilation that could not but sap its strength for a century or more, and perhaps forever. The only possible explanation for this war is a mental eclipse among the leaders of Europe due to their lost awareness of a Supreme Power above them. Only a godless embitterment could have moved ostensibly Christian states to employ poison gas, a weapon so obviously beyond the limits of humanity.

The same kind of defect, the flaw of a consciousness lacking all divine dimension, was manifested after World War II when the West yielded to the satanic temptation of the nuclear umbrella. It was equivalent to saying: Let's cast off our worries, let's free the younger generation from its duties and obligations, let's make no effort to defend ourselves, to say nothing of defending others—let's stop our ears to the groans emanating from the East, and let us live instead in the pursuit of happiness. If danger should threaten us, we shall be protected by the nuclear bomb; if not, then let the world be burned in Hell for all we care. The pitifully helpless state to which the contemporary West has sunk is in large measure due to this fatal error: the belief that the defense of peace depends not on stout hearts and steadfast men, but solely on the nuclear bomb.

Only the loss of that higher intuition which comes from God could have allowed the West to accept calmly, after World War I, the protracted agony of Russia as she was being torn apart by a band of cannibals, or to accept, after World War II, the similar dismemberment of Eastern Europe. The West did not perceive that this was in fact the beginning of a lengthy process that spells disaster for the whole world; indeed the West has done a good deal to help the process along. Only once in this century did the West gather its strength—for the battle against Hitler. But the fruits of that victory have long since been lost. Faced with cannibalism, our godless age has discovered the perfect anaesthetic—trade! Such is the pathetic pinnacle of contemporary wisdom.

Today's world has reached a stage that, if it had been described to preceding centuries, would have called forth the cry: "This is the Apocalypse!"

Yet we have grown used to this kind of world; we even feel at home in it.

Dostoevsky warned that "great events could come upon us and catch us intellectually unprepared." That is precisely what has happened. And he predicted that "the world will be saved only after a visitation by the demon of evil." Whether it really will be saved we shall have to wait and see; this will depend on our conscience, on our spiritual lucidity, on our individual and combined efforts in the face of catastrophic circumstances. But it has already come to pass that the demon of evil, like a whirlwind, triumphantly circles all five continents of the earth.

We are witnesses to the devastation of the world, be it imposed or voluntarily undergone. The entire twentieth century is being sucked into the vortex of atheism and self-destruction. This plunge into the abyss has aspects that are unquestionably global, dependent neither on political systems, nor on levels of economic and cultural development, nor yet on national peculiarities. And present-day Europe, seemingly so unlike the Russia of 1913, is today on the verge of the same collapse, for all that it has been reached by a different route. Different parts of the world have followed different paths, but today they are all approaching the threshold of a common ruin.

In its past, Russia did know a time when the social ideal was not fame, or riches, or material success, but a pious way of life. Russia was then steeped in an Orthodox Christianity that remained true to the Church of the first centuries. The Orthodoxy of that time knew how to safeguard its people under the yoke of a foreign occupation that lasted more than two centuries, while at the same time fending off iniquitous blows from the swords of Western crusaders. During those centuries the Orthodox faith in our country became part of the very patterns of thought and the personality of our people, the forms of daily life, the work calendar, the priorities in every undertaking, the organization of the week and of the year. Faith was the shaping and unifying force of the nation.

But in the seventeenth century Russian Orthodoxy was gravely weakened by an internal schism. In the eighteenth, the country was shaken by Peter's forcibly imposed transformations, which favored the economy, the state, and the military at the expense of the religious spirit and national life. And along with this lopsided Petrine enlightenment, Russia felt the first whiff of secularism; its subtle poisons permeated the educated classes in the course of the nineteenth century and opened the path to Marxism. By the time of the Revolution, faith had virtually disappeared in Russian educated circles; among the uneducated, too, faith had declined.

It was Dostoevsky, once again, who drew from the French Revolution and its seething hatred of the Church the lesson that "revolution must necessarily begin with atheism." That is absolutely true. But the world had never before known a godlessness as organized, militarized, and tenaciously malevolent as that practiced by Marxism. Within the philosophical system of Marx and Lenin, and at the heart of their psychology, hatred of God is the principal driving force, more fundamental than all their political and economic pretensions. Militant atheism is not merely incidental or marginal to Communist policy; it is not a side effect, but the central pivot. To achieve its diabolical ends, Communism needs to control a population devoid of religious and national feeling, and this entails the destruction of faith and nationhood. Communists proclaim both of these objectives openly, and just as openly go about carrying them out. The degree to which the atheistic world longs to annihilate religion, the extent to which religion sticks in its throat, was demonstrated by the web of intrigue surrounding the recent attempts on the life of the Pope.

The 1920s in the USSR witnessed an uninterrupted procession of victims and martyrs among the Orthodox clergy. Two metropolitans were shot, one of whom, Veniamin of Petrograd, had been elected by the popular vote of his diocese. Patriarch Tikhon himself passed through the hands of the Cheka-GPU and then died under suspicious circumstances. Scores of archbishops and bishops perished. Tens of thousands of priests, monks, and nuns, pressured by the Chekists to renounce the word of God, were tortured, shot in cellars, sent to camps, exiled to the desolate tundra of the far north, or turned out into the streets in their old age without food or shelter. All these Christian martyrs went unswervingly to their deaths for the faith; instances of apostasy were few and far between.

For tens of millions of laymen access to the Church was blocked, and they were forbidden to bring up their children in the faith: religious parents were wrenched from their children and thrown into prison, while the children were turned from the faith by threats and lies. One could argue that the pointless destruction of Russia's rural economy in the 1930s—the so-called de-kulakization and collectivization, which brought death to 15 million peasants while making no economic sense at all—was enforced with such cruelty, first and foremost, for the purpose of destroying our national way of life and of extirpating religion from the countryside. The same policy of spiritual perversion operated throughout the brutal world of the Gulag Archipelago, where men were encouraged to survive at the cost of the lives of others. And only atheists bereft of reason could have decided upon the ultimate brutality—against the Russian land itself—that is being planned in the USSR today: The Russian north is to be flooded, the flow of the northern rivers reversed, the life of the Arctic Ocean disrupted, and the water channeled southward, toward lands already devastated by earlier, equally foolhardy "feats of Communist construction."

For a short period of time, when he needed to gather strength for the struggle against Hitler, Stalin cynically adopted a friendly posture toward the Church. This deceptive game, continued in later years by Brezhnev with the help of showcase publications and other window dressing, has unfortunately tended to be taken at face value in the West. Yet the tenacity with which hatred of religion is rooted in Communism may be judged by the example of its most liberal leader, Khrushchev: for though he undertook a number of significant steps to extend freedom, Khrushchev simultaneously rekindled the frenzied Leninist obsession with destroying religion.

But there is something they did not expect: that in a land where churches have been leveled, where a triumphant atheism has rampaged uncontrolled for two-thirds of a century, where the clergy is utterly humiliated and deprived of all independence, where what remains of the Church as an institution is tolerated only for the sake of propaganda directed at the West, where even today people are sent to labor camps for their faith and where, within the camps themselves, those who gather to pray at Easter are clapped in punishment cells— they could not suppose that beneath this Communist steamroller the Christian tradition would survive in Russia. It is true that millions of our countrymen have been corrupted and spiritually devastated by an officially imposed atheism, yet there remain many millions of believers: it is only external pressures that keep them from speaking out, but, as is always the case in times of persecution and suffering, the awareness of God in my country has attained great acuteness and profundity.

It is here that we see the dawn of hope: for no matter how formidably Communism bristles with tanks and rockets, no matter what successes it attains in seizing the planet, it is doomed never to vanquish Christianity.

The West has yet to experience a Communist invasion; religion here remains free. But the West's own historical evolution has been such that today it too is experiencing a drying up of religious consciousness. It too has witnessed racking schisms, bloody religious wars, and rancor, to say nothing of the tide of secularism that, from the late Middle Ages onward, has progressively inundated the West. This gradual sapping of strength from within is a threat to faith that is perhaps even more dangerous than any attempt to assault religion violently from without.

Imperceptibly, through decades of gradual erosion, the meaning of life in the West has ceased to be seen as anything more lofty than the "pursuit of happiness," a goal that has even been solemnly guaranteed by constitutions. The concepts of good and evil have been ridiculed for several centuries; banished from common use, they have been replaced by political or class considerations of short-lived value. It has become embarrassing to appeal to eternal concepts, embarrassing to state that evil makes its home in the individual human heart before it enters a political system. Yet it is not considered shameful to make daily concessions to an integral evil. Judging by the continuing landslide of concessions made before the eyes of our own generation alone, the West is ineluctably slipping toward the abyss. Western societies are losing more and more of their religious essence as they thoughtlessly yield up their younger generation to atheism. If a blasphemous film about Jesus is shown throughout the United States, reputedly one of the most religious countries in the world, or a major newspaper publishes a shameless caricature of the Virgin Mary, what further evidence of godlessness does one need? When external rights are completely unrestricted, why should one make an inner effort to restrain oneself from ignoble acts?

Or why should one refrain from burning hatred, whatever its basis—race, class, or ideology? Such hatred is in fact corroding many hearts today. Atheist teachers in the West are bringing up a younger generation in a spirit of hatred of their own society. Amid all the vituperation we forget that the defects of capitalism represent the basic flaws of human nature, allowed unlimited freedom together with the various human rights; we forget that under Communism (and Communism is breathing down the neck of all moderate forms of socialism, which are unstable) the identical flaws run riot in any person with the least degree of authority; while everyone else under that system does indeed attain "equality"—the equality of destitute slaves.

This eager fanning of the flames of hatred is becoming the mark of today's free world. Indeed, the broader the personal freedoms are, the higher the level of prosperity or even of abundance—the more vehement, paradoxically, does this blind hatred become. The contemporary developed West thus demonstrates by its own example that human salvation can be found neither in the profusion of material goods nor in merely making money.

This deliberately nurtured hatred then spreads to all that is alive, to life itself, to the world with its colors, sounds, and shapes, to the human body. The embittered art of the twentieth century is perishing as a result of this ugly hate, for art is fruitless without love. In the East art has collapsed because it has been knocked down and trampled upon, but in the West the fall has been voluntary, a decline into a contrived and pretentious quest where the artist, instead of attempting to reveal the divine plan, tries to put himself in the place of God.

Here again we witness the single outcome of a worldwide process, with East and West yielding the same results, and once again for the same reason: Men have forgotten God.

Confronted by the onslaught of worldwide atheism, believers are disunited and frequently bewildered. And yet the Christian (or post-Christian) world would do well to note the example of the Far East. I have recently had an opportunity to observe in Free China and in Japan how, despite their apparently less clearly defined religious concepts, and despite the same unassailable "freedom of choice" that exists in the West, both the younger generation and society as a whole have preserved their moral sensibility to a greater degree than the West has, and have been less affected by the destructive spirit of secularism.

What can one say about the lack of unity among the various religions, if Christianity has itself become so fragmented? In recent years the major Christian churches have taken steps toward reconciliation. But these measures are far too slow; the world is perishing a hundred times more quickly. No one expects the churches to merge or to revise all their doctrines, but only to present a common front against atheism. Yet even for such a purpose the steps taken are much too slow.

There does exist an organized movement for the unification of the churches, but it presents an odd picture. The World Council of Churches seems to care more for the success of revolutionary movements in the Third World, all the while remaining blind and deaf to the persecution of religion where this is carried through most consistently—in the USSR. No one can fail to see the facts; must one conclude, then, that it is deemed expedient not to see, not to get involved? But if that is the case, what remains of Christianity?

It is with profound regret that I must note here something which I cannot pass over in silence. My predecessor in the receipt of this prize last year—in the very month that the award was made—lent public support to Communist lies by his deplorable statement that he had not noticed the persecution of religion in the USSR. Before the multitude of those who have perished and who are oppressed today, may God be his judge.

It seems more and more apparent that even with the most sophisticated of political maneuvers, the noose around the neck of mankind draws tighter and more hopeless with every passing decade, and there seems to be no way out for anyone—neither nuclear, nor political, nor economic, nor ecological. That is indeed the way things appear to be.

With such global events looming over us like mountains, nay, like entire mountain ranges, it may seem incongruous and inappropriate to recall that the primary key to our being or non-being resides in each individual human heart, in the heart's preference for specific good or evil. Yet this remains true even today, and it is, in fact, the most reliable key we have. The social theories that promised so much have demonstrated their bankruptcy, leaving us at a dead end. The free people of the West could reasonably have been expected to realize that they are beset by numerous freely nurtured falsehoods, and not to allow lies to be foisted upon them so easily. All attempts to find a way out of the plight of today's world are fruitless unless we redirect our consciousness, in repentance, to the Creator of all: without this, no exit will be illumined, and we shall seek it in vain. The resources we have set aside for ourselves are too impoverished for the task. We must first recognize the horror perpetrated not by some outside force, not by class or national enemies, but within each of us individually, and within every society. This is especially true of a free and highly developed society, for here in particular we have surely brought everything upon ourselves, of our own free will. We ourselves, in our daily unthinking selfishness, are pulling tight that noose.

Let us ask ourselves: Are not the ideals of our century false? And is not our glib and fashionable terminology just as unsound, a terminology that offers superficial remedies for every difficulty? Each of them, in whatever sphere, must be subjected to a clear-eyed scrutiny while there is still time. The solution of the crisis will not be found along the well-trodden paths of conventional thinking.

Our life consists not in the pursuit of material success but in the quest for worthy spiritual growth. Our entire earthly existence is but a transitional stage in the movement toward something higher, one rung of the ladder. Material laws alone do not explain our life or give it direction. The laws of physics and physiology will never reveal the indisputable manner in which the Creator constantly, day in and day out, participates in the life of each of us, unfailingly granting us the energy of existence; when this assistance leaves us, we die. And in the life of our entire planet the Divine Spirit surely moves with no less force: this we must grasp in our dark and terrible hour.

To the ill-considered hopes of the last two centuries, which have reduced us to insignificance and brought us to the brink of nuclear and non-nuclear death, we can propose only a determined quest for the warm hand of God, which we have so rashly and self-confidently spurned. Only in this way can our eyes be opened to the errors of this unfortunate twentieth century and our hands be directed to setting them right. There is nothing else to cling to in the landslide: the combined vision of all the thinkers of the Enlightenment amounts to nothing.

Our five continents are caught in a whirlwind. But it is during trials such as these that the highest gifts of the human spirit are manifested. If we perish and lose this world, the fault will be ours alone.

Discussion

1. Some notes may be necessary to understand the full impact of Solzhenitsyn's address. He was himself a prisoner in the prison camps, seized as a "zek" or political prisoner. He was an artillery captain, decorated for bravery in World War II, when he was arrested in 1945 for criticizing Stalin in some letters to friends. He served eight years in the Soviet labor camp known as "the Gulag Archipelago," a string of camps stretching across Siberia.

   In the second paragraph of his address, Solzhenitsyn cites the figure of sixty million Russians who were killed or who died during the Soviet repression which began in 1918 under Lenin and continues today.

   Solzhenitsyn refers to "a blasphemous film about Jesus." An unconfirmed but likely candidate is *The Life of Brian* by Monty Python, which was released in the U.S. shortly before the date of his speech. Solzhenitsyn's predecessor for the Templeton Award, to whom he refers at the close of the address, was the Reverend Billy Graham, who had the year before undertaken a crusade in the Soviet Union.

2. In a foreword to *The Gulag Archipelago*, in which Solzhenitsyn details the story of the Soviet prison camps, he writes:

   This Archipelago crisscrossed and patterned that other country within which it was located, like a gigantic patchwork, cutting into its cities, hovering over its streets. Yet there were many who did not even guess at its presence and many, many others who had heard something vague. And only those who had been there knew the whole truth.

   But, as though stricken dumb on the islands of the Archipelago, they kept their silence.

   By an unexpected turn of our history, a bit of the truth, an insignificant part of the whole, was allowed out in the open. But those same hands which once screwed tight our handcuffs now hold out their palms in reconciliation: "No, don't! Don't dig up the past! Dwell on the past and you'll lose an eye."

   But the proverb goes on to say, "Forget the past and you'll lose both eyes."

Apply the proverb to "Men Have Forgotten God." Does it also apply to our own society, in our own time? Can you provide examples?

3. Solzhenitsyn is a widely acknowledged master of rhetoric. Words seem to dance from his pen; sentences flow in choreographed movements. His prose, as a result, carries both narrative authority and conviction. Analyze several paragraphs of his prose to discover how he achieves this, particularly through his structuring of clause and sentence patterns. Midway through the essay, for example, he uses a 107-word sentence—in a paragraph consisting of only two sentences. How is the sentence structured through subordinate clauses?

4. Speaking from your own experience of American culture, list ways in which "men have forgotten God."

The Liberal Arts
What and Why?

Arthur F. Holmes

> *Imagine someone confronting you, and asking you a question that you may already have asked of yourself: "What good is a liberal arts education? Of what use is it in today's world of hard, practical reality?" Arthur F. Holmes, professor of philosophy at Wheaton College, responds to such questions in the following essay.*

A typical college student sat in my office. He had come to pre-register, and beneath his hesitation I detected confusion about the purpose of his education. Should he take another literature course, or something in accounting? Why the history of philosophy or of art, or of anything else for that matter? He was majoring also in psychology, but why experimental psychology or personality theory when what he wanted was to understand people so as to communicate more effectively? What would he ever *do* with all this stuff anyway: literature, history, philosophy, experimental psychology? Whatever *use* does it have in "real life," and in particular for the Christian?

I could have taken several approaches. I could have asked, Socratic style, "What do you mean by *real* life?" And I might have led him to see that literature and history and philosophy and psychology deal with reality to a larger extent and in deeper dimensions than any collection of "how to do it" courses. I could have talked about the cultural mandate under which the first task of mankind to which God's grace has restored us as Christians is to glorify God in all our creatureliness, and therefore to understand the creation and with heart and mind to join in the cultural undertaking of the human race. I could simply have pontificated that this is a liberal arts college and he should get a liberal education. But not being sure he would understand the implications of that, I suggested instead that his was the wrong question to ask about education.

Asking the Right Question

We are reminded by those who try to buffer us against "future shock" that our present job-skills will soon be outmoded, and that the things we learn to do now will be vastly different in a few short years. Education should therefore prepare us to adapt, to think, to be creative. Whether these prophets exaggerate or not, it is also true that the "I" who in a few short years will "do something in real life" will by then be a different "I" from the "I" who now takes a course in college. My personality is not static but dynamic, growing, changing. The question to ask about education, then, is not "What can I do with all this stuff anyway?" because both I and my world are changing, but rather "What will all this stuff do to me?" This question is basic to the concept of liberal education.

When I began to teach, someone reminded me that the verb "to teach" carries a double object. Teaching is like telling: I have just told a story about a student, but I have also told you. When people ask what I teach, I sometimes say "philosophy," but sometimes (and partly to tease them) I say "students." For the question a teacher must ask about his teaching is not "What can they do with it?" but rather "What will it do to them? What sort of men and women will they become by wrestling with this material in the way I present it? And what sort of materials and methods could I develop to help them become more fully the people they are capable of being?"

Now this "whatever-can-I-do-with-all-this-stuff" question comes up in various disguises. Perhaps the most frequent is the vocational: what will history and literature and philosophy contribute to my work as a businessman, a doctor, an engineer or a minister? Liberal education contributes far more than is sometimes supposed to many vocations. Moreover, we must never underestimate the importance of work; its value in the order of creation is far greater than the value of earning a living. A man's daily work, whatever it is, should be an offering to God (Eph. 6:5–9), as well as a service to others and a means to his own personal growth and dignity. This biblical approach to work is vastly different from the aristocratic attitude of Aristotle and some of the Greeks who unduly elevated the life of the mind in contrast to more mundane tasks. But to realize this is to uncover the fallacy in a purely vocational approach to education. The human vocation is far larger than the scope of any job a person may hold because we are human persons created in God's image, to honor and serve God and men in all we do, not just in the way we earn a living.

None of us wants the kind of dehumanized brave new world that manufactures men and women to fill jobs. Our technological society has been indicted of late for making productivity the purpose of society, rather than people. Yet the same indictment could be leveled against the view that education is job training, for it too has sold out to the productivity principle by subordinating what people are to what they do. A person is not just *homo faber*, man who makes things. If he were just a worker, vocational training would suffice; but since he is more than a worker it follows that vocational training is not enough.

Vocations and jobs are made for men, not men for vocations and jobs. The question to ask about an education is *not* "What can I do with it?", but rather "What is it doing to me—as a person?" Education has to do with the making of persons, Christian education with the making of Christian persons. Since this is what God's creative and redemptive work is about—the making of persons in his own image—it follows that an education that helps make us more fully persons is especially important to Christians.

Definitions

What is liberal education that makes it larger and more enriching than vocational preparation? What do we mean by the liberal arts? A term may be defined by its extension or by its intensions. To define by extension, we identify the class of particular things to which a term refers. The term "man" extends to Tom, Dick, Harry, Mary, Jane, Sue— the whole gamut. To define by intension, we try to capture the concept involved, the underlying nature that all members of that class have in common, the essence of it.

An extensional definition of the liberal arts would refer to a set of academic disciplines. In the Middle Ages the term referred to a trivium plus a quadrivium of disciplines. The initial three concerned the art of language and were grammar, rhetoric and logic; the four (geometry, arithmetic, music and astronomy) were regarded as essentially mathematical and taught the art of reasoning and abstract thought.

So the liberal arts were a group of disciplines having to do with language and thinking, and something of the intension of the term emerges as a result. Along with these liberal arts were disciplines like theology and law, which not only equipped men to serve God and society but also provided the subject matter for their rational inquiry. Theology and science rapidly became part of the liberal arts. By the time we get to the eighteenth and nineteenth century, the extension of the liberal arts broadens and becomes synonymous with classical education, so that you are not liberally educated without Latin and Greek and classical literature, and unless you can write Latin poetry and give speeches in classical languages. For a while it included natural philosophy (science), moral philosophy (ethics and political science) and mental philosophy (logic and metaphysics), so that to this day the "Doctor of Philosophy" degree can be earned in almost any discipline. In the twentieth century, there has been a tendency to equate the liberal arts with a broad, general education that ranges across the natural sciences, the social sciences and the humanities, and religion is increasingly considered as one of the liberal arts.

Whatever the disciplines cited, extensional definitions are insufficient. They refer to the changing content of human knowledge rather than to the purpose for which one learns, so that students still ask, "*Why* do we have to learn this stuff anyway?" and "*Why* is this important?" If liberal education is equated with general education, then the liberally educated person is one who has dabbled in a promiscuous variety of things. Such a scope is insufficient either to fully motivate students or to justify itself, because it is hopelessly fragmented. It might allow the principle that all truth is God's truth wherever it is found, but it disregards the unity of truth. It does nothing to unify a man or his view of life, and it might well encourage the conclusion that life has no overall meaning at all. It simply creates a connoisseur of the fragments of life. But a jack of all trades is a master of none: he is a fragmented individual. What today we label as general education requirements do not themselves make for the unified understanding that education desires.

To see what we mean by liberal education we have to get beyond the extensional to intensional definitions and grasp the unifying essence of the thing. Cicero suggested that liberal education is the education of men for freedom, the education of free men for the exercise of their freedom rather than of slaves. Aristotle leaves the impression that education is for the wise use of one's leisure, for free men are leisured men who do not have to work but are in a position to exercise political and social leadership. In that sense liberal education becomes education for leadership, and in that spirit the early American college emphasized preparation for the leadership exercised by the professions, hence a non-professional preparation for the professions through developing a man's rational powers. More recently the stress has been on education for citizenship in a democracy. Here again the conception is of a free man and a role he must play in life beyond his remunerative work.

In all of this, the needed clue is that the liberal arts are those which are appropriate to man as man, rather than to man in his specific function as a worker or as a professional or even as a scholar. A man may be all of these things, but he is more basically man. It was Cicero who defined the liberal arts as those which are appropriate to humanity. If man is to be anything more than a half-human specialist or technician, if a man is to feel life whole and to live it whole rather than piecemeal, if he is to think for himself rather than live secondhand, the liberal arts are needed to educate the person. There is no difficulty in transferring this clue concerning liberal education to a Christian conception of man. Man is created in the image of God. We are to image God in all of our creaturely activities, our cultural existence and every phase of our humanity. To image God in the fulness of our humanity is our highest calling. A liberal education that develops our humanity therefore implements God's calling, and the creation mandate finds expression in the educational process.

In his classic nineteenth-century work, *The Idea of a University,* John Henry Newman distinguishes between liberal and useful arts. It is not a complete disjunction, for the liberal arts are also useful, and the useful arts are based on liberal arts and sciences. But the point is that some arts are more liberal than others, and some more useful to man for economic and other particular purposes than they are of value to man as such. The distinction is worth preserving. It is the distinction between intrinsic and instrumental value. Some things have little but instrumental value: a shining new coin with the head of George Washington on one side and the American eagle on the other has instrumental worth: it is good for what you can buy with it but little else. If you tell me it is of intrinsic worth and you value it for itself, I call you a miser. Other things have far more intrinsic worth as well as some instrumental value. Understanding is valued for itself. Beauty and goodness are of value in themselves. In addition to the fact that beauty may have some utilitarian function and that it pays to be good and that knowledge can be useful, in addition to their instrumental worth, is their intrinsic worth. Liberal learning concerns itself with truth and beauty and goodness, which have intrinsic worth to men considered as persons rather than as workers or in whatever function alone.

We may distinguish along these lines between literature as one of the liberal arts and journalism in which the *use* of what is written predominates; between the natural sciences as man's quest to understand nature, which is liberal learning, and the technology that does something else with it; between political science on the one hand as the attempt to understand political institutions and processes, and propaganda techniques on the other; between the science of psychology and the useful art of counseling; between theology and the work of evangelism; between philosophy as a liberal art and apologetics as one use it might have. Usefulness is no crime. But the practical uses of things we learn are limited and changeable, while the effect of learning on the person is less limited because it lasts. Liberal learning therefore takes the long-range view and concentrates on what shapes a person's understanding and values rather than on what he can use in one or two of the changing roles he might later play.

The question to ask about education is not "What can I do with it?" That is the wrong question because it concentrates on instrumental values and reduces everything to a useful art. The right question to ask is rather "What can it do to me?"

What Is Man?

Starting with this clue, what do the liberal arts contribute to the making of a man? This depends on the prior question: "What is man?" Here the Christian and the Christian college must be extremely careful. If you take a Freudian or a Marxist or a pragmatist or a behavioristic view of man, your conception of education will be geared accordingly. What then is man? Three essential aspects of our human identity are basic for Christian higher education. The list may not be exhaustive, although other aspects may well be embraced in this rubric. Nor do these three aspects correlate with a Greek or Enlightenment psychology that separates the three faculties of reason, will and emotion from each other. Faculty psychology has been outmoded by recent psychology and faulted by biblical theology, both of which require a more unified conception of personality such that the person as a whole thinks and chooses and feels and acts: thinking can proceed neither without choosing goals and assumptions nor without emotion. In the following account each of the three aspects characterizes the person as a whole and is inseparably intertwined with the others.

First, man is *a rational being.* I do not intend by this the Enlightenment conception of reason as unimpassioned and uncommitted, detached and neutral on matters of faith and value, so that from universally clear and distinct ideas we infer necessarily and demonstrably true conclusions. Something of the sort may occur in mathematics, but it is relatively localized. In other areas we are more limited: "we see through a glass darkly," and "we know in part." Yet, as Aristotle said, all men by nature desire to know, we are inquisitive, we wonder. Too often our God-given intellectual curiosity has been deadened in earlier education, or thinking has been transformed into an idle spectator sport. The first task of liberal education is to fan the spark and ignite this native inquisitiveness.

To be rational is also to be analytic. Inquisitiveness leads us to examine more and more closely what is going on. "How does this happen? What do you mean? How can this be?" Reasoning is asking what and why and how. It asks about the meaning of life and probes the mysteries of our existence. It seeks understanding. Man has to ask questions and probe analytically, he has to learn to think and to think critically for himself, because this is part of what it is to be human.

To be rational is also to see things in relationship, to organize ideas into an ordered whole, to be systematic, to work toward a unified understanding. Three educational implications follow. First, inter-disciplinary approaches to learning are important. Second, theoretical questions are unavoidable because man alone in creation is a theorizing being who extrapolates beyond the known and speculates about the unknown, formulates hypotheses for science to explore and imagines new worlds for art to create. Third, world-views must be examined and shaped, for man still strives to see things whole, however imperfectly he envisions that unity of truth which he seeks.

Bertrand Russell suggests that education has two purposes: to form the mind and to train the citizen. The Athenians, he says, concentrated on the former but the Spartans on the latter. The Spartans won but the Athenians were remembered. To form the mind, to stretch the understanding, to sharpen one's intellectual powers, to enlarge the vision, to cultivate the imagination and impart a sense of the whole—this is the task of liberal education.

If God, too, is rational and man struggles within the limitations of his creatureliness to think God's thoughts after him, then the rational life has religious significance. Like all of human existence, thinking has religious roots and proceeds from the heart; in the final analysis it is a man's religion that unifies his understanding. To the Christian in the Christian college, then, the development of rational inquiry becomes an expression of faith and hope and love addressed to God. It is part of man's response to God's self-revelation.

Intellectual development requires that we read and write. Reading is of course prerequisite to informed conversation, an art that is often sadly underdeveloped today. Writing is prerequisite to exactness of thought and expression. They accomplish what "discussion" alone can never achieve, unless it is constantly monitored and analyzed by an unusually competent teacher who forces the discussants to think and then to reshape their thoughts in more and more consistent and cogent and lucid ways. To read is to gain input, to fertilize thought, to objectify, to conceptualize, to follow an argument, to evaluate. To write is to become articulate, to express what I feel and explain why I feel as I do, to expound, to argue, to offer good reasons, to explore relationships, to have a sense of the whole, to see things in total context. To teach a person to read and to write is to teach him to think for himself, to develop more fully the possession of his God-given powers. He becomes in fact, not just in possibility, a rational being.

Second, man is *a historical being* with a past, present and future. Young people tend to turn off the past, but thereby they lose the sense of their own identity, for the present and the future are what they are in relation to the past. We have knowledge of the past only insofar as the past again becomes present and is known and understood and relived now in our minds. And the past shapes the present and future, so that we are what we are and where we are, and are heading where we are, because of the past. To understand our present and influence our future, then, we must grasp our past.

The existentialist reminds us that man is not merely a product of historical processes, stretching uniformly from the remote past into the distant future, but also an agent who transcends his past by acting to shape his future. This capacity for self-transcendence distinguishes man from the things he uses and from the rest of nature, for natural forces are not free so to act. To say that man is a historical being means that he participates in his own history, shaping his times and helping create his future. A man can transcend what he is now and act to make himself what he is not yet.

As such a historical agent, he is in the image of his Maker. God, too, transcends the purely natural processes and outcomes of the created order when he acts in history and in the affairs and lives of men. By our creative action, we image the creativity of God. Liberal education that helps people develop into free agents who participate creatively in history is therefore a sacred task. It helps a person understand his history and develop a sense of direction, it contributes to far-sighted and wise decisions, it leads to intelligent and strategic action. For in order to act intelligently we must know where we are now and where, apart from our action, we are likely going.

Two educational goals follow. One is a critical appreciation of the past. Appreciation is positive: it captures the continuity of a heritage from the past into the present. But I say "critical appreciation" because unless we see the limitations of our past we will never be motivated to transcend those limitations in shaping our future. Critical appreciation of our past will free us to see creative possibilities for the future. The other goal is therefore creative participation in the future. I say "in the future" for two reasons. One is that the present is an abstraction. As soon as I say "now" it is past: all that we really have is the past and the future, and the future glides into the past. The other reason is that by politicizing the university as the locus of revolution, the activist generation of students involved itself too deeply in the present. Involvement in the now has its values, educational and otherwise, but the "now" becomes the "then" and leaves us unprepared for the future. We must keep an eye on the historical role for which man is created, whether he fulfils that role as churchman, parent or citizen, as scientist, teacher or businessman. As a historical agent he will inevitably participate in his future, and liberal education can help him do so with intelligence and creativity.

Third, man is *a valuing being*. We make value judgments and act to realize our values. The theological foundations of the last chapter [in *The Idea of a Christian College*] brought the *value* of higher education into focus. A world-view that ties our thinking together and gives direction to what we do is not simply a theoretical system of value-neutral propositions, but a valuational orientation to life. It expresses what we hope as well as what we think; it says what we love and what we desire. If a man values the truth, he speaks it; if he values justice, he works for it; if he has hope amidst life's turmoil, his life has meaning. A man values peace and justice, love and beauty, community and solitude. He expresses his values in his arts and sciences, his political life, his social institutions, in the very history he creates. In the humanities—literature, the arts, philosophy, history—human values become explicit. The value a man places on various aspects of life comes out in the literature he writes. Read Hemingway or Tolstoi or Brecht and grapple with their views, for literature and the arts are a laboratory of life: one does not need to experiment with drugs and sex and violence in order to understand life's experiences and emotions for himself.

Values are more than feelings. By now the emotivist theory of value should be dead and can be buried, for it has been taken to pieces by philosophers who have shown beyond doubt that valuing also involves reasons that can be argued and generalized. Yet experience-oriented young people still seem to reduce values to feelings: a thing is right that you feel right about. It is "right for me." The result, as C. S. Lewis shows in his *Abolition of Man*, is a thorough relativism. For the Christian theist, values are more than feelings and they are not all relative; they have their basis in the very nature of what a man is in God's creation and so in the wisdom and the will of God. We image our Creator as valuing beings, for he, too, values: he loves, he delights, he seeks to realize the values he invested in his creation, and our values must follow from his.

Another educational goal accordingly follows, to teach values as well as facts. Somewhere in the curriculum, the student should be exposed to ethics, to aesthetics and other areas of value, and to the logical structure of value judgments. How do I make a moral judgment that is not a simple case of black or white, of obvious right or wrong? Are the consequences of an action all that matters (its instrumental value) or are some things intrinsically better than others? In a Christian college one must come to see the distinctive ingredients and bases of Christian values, and will hopefully make those values his own.

Man is at least a rational, historical and valuing being, and a liberal education is one that develops his capacity in these regards. It is perhaps significant that these three have all been associated with freedom in man. By acting rationally, Kant argued, we act free from the constraint of appetite and inclination. By historical action we are free to transcend our present condition. By valuing we reach beyond the actualities that otherwise hold us in their grip. Liberal education prepares a man for the wise exercise of the God-given freedom he can enjoy.

Perhaps other aspects should be considered as well. We have not distinguished man's religious nature, for it is the very heart of his being from which everything else stems. The religious dimension of life is lived in and through the rational life, the historical action and the values that are our own.

What of the physical and the social? If we were after a list of activities or courses that liberal education should embrace, then it would probably be important to list them separately. But we have tried to avoid extensional definitions because they lead to fragmented general education listings, in favor of the intensional definition of liberal education as having to do with what is intrinsically and distinctively human. While there are other physical and social creatures than men, man's physical and social activities are simply means whereby he exercises the rational, historical and valuational nature that marks him off from the beasts.

The physical provides a necessary but insufficient condition of all a man is and does in this life, and it should be valued and developed accordingly. But by definition, liberal education should concern itself with physical education as with other curricular areas in relationship to the goals of liberal education. That is, the primary concern will not be with physical skill or strength or stamina, but with the development of the person—his emotional balance and self-understanding, his ability to act decisively and creatively, his values. The measure of a man is neither his athletic prowess nor his lack thereof. It is other characteristics that make a man truly man. Physical training will not automatically either enhance these characteristics or detract from them, although it can contribute in either direction. Plato said that excessive emphasis on athletics without literature or philosophy produces a pretty uncivilized type with no use for reasoned conviction, whose life is one of clumsy ignorance unrelieved by grace or beauty; whereas a purely academic life without athletic training leaves a man with little backbone. He seems on the right track, but he forgets that some sports are also arts, creative and beautiful, so that the athlete may well learn to understand and appreciate aesthetic values rather than simply acquiring strength, skill, self-reliance and a team spirit. In any case the Christian college must not only value highly the body God made but also teach physical education in a humanizing and liberating way, whether the values are aesthetic or moral and social, or whether the end-product is decisive action based on carefully argued plans.

Man's social nature must be cultivated without drifting into the extremes of individualism or collectivism. The social, like the physical, is a necessary but insufficient precondition for rational, historical and valuing beings. Rational inquiry is not carried on in isolation but in dialog with other minds of the past and present: because it builds on their work, it is a social undertaking. Historical understanding and participation are both social, for a man's past and future are inevitably intertwined with the culture and the social institutions of which he is, thus far at least, a part. Our values are in large measure acquired from parents and peers and others, they are implemented in whatever social groups we belong to, and we seek to transmit them to others. Man's social nature is thus part and parcel of all the rest. To that extent at least, the goals of liberal education will include not only self-understanding, but also an understanding of other people and of social institutions and processes. This is essential in preparing men and women for participation in society, whether through marriage or through citizenship activities or through business and professional relationships.

Liberal education is an open invitation to join the human race and become more fully human. Its general goals include the ability to read and write and thereby think independently, a critical appreciation of the past and creative participation in the future, and an appreciation of lasting values coupled with the ability to make sound value judgments and live by them. Generalizations of this sort can readily be translated into objectives for different disciplines, so that the science professor will stress an understanding and appreciation of methods and concepts, and the historical development of his science and its cultural ramifications, rather than stressing technique alone or making the student into a narrow specialist. A considerable degree of specialization is of course appropriate in any major field of concentration, sufficient to prepare the student for graduate work in a highly competitive situation, but the liberal arts college has no business producing narrow specialists who see no further than their laboratory, and who have no sense of human and cultural undertaking. It would be inexcusable nowadays for a Christian college to teach science without discussing the moral and social problems it has raised. Similarly the art teacher will work toward an understanding and appreciation of the creative process, of aesthetic values and the history and social role of art, for artists like scientists can become narrowly specialized technicians.

Liberal education is an opportunity to become more fully a human person in the image of God, to see life whole rather than fragmented, to transcend the provincialism of our place in history, our geographic location or our job. Provincialism isolates us from our past, isolates us from segments of the human race; cultural provincialism isolates the American way of life from anything else; vocational provincialism limits the horizon to a certain kind of task. But liberal education is an opportunity to become whole and to see life whole rather than provincially, fragmented in one way or another. It is an opportunity to find meaning for everything I am and do. Christian liberal arts education is concerned that we do this in the light of God's self-revelation, so that we learn to think Christianly, to participate in history in thoroughly Christian ways, and to value as Christians should. I would think it worthwhile if a student, when asked what he learned in college, could reply "I learned what it is to see and think and act like the human person God made me to be."

If the person, including what he becomes in this life, has an eternal destiny, then what I become in the process of education lives forever. In that sense I can take with me some of the benefits of a liberal education, while the benefits of vocational training last only for the duration of the job for which it equips me here and now. Christian liberal arts education has an eternity in view.

Discussion

1. Implicit in Professor Holmes's essay is a distinction between education that prepares one for a job and education that prepares one for living. Is that distinction, however, artificial or unrealistic? One's job, or career, constitutes an important area of living. At what point might it dominate living?
2. In modern Christendom, Christian elementary and secondary schools have developed into a powerful force. You might consider the merits and dangers of such a Christian education. Do they prepare us to engage the world in a redemptive fashion? Do they simply shield us from the world?
3. Holmes discusses three attributes of humanity in response to his question, "What is man?" What are other essential attributes of humanity (for example, an emotional being?), and how does a Christian liberal arts education respond to these other attributes?

You're Still Failing

I. M. Cross

In the 1960s a frustrated professor of composition named Henry F. Ottinger wrote a blistering letter to his class entitled "Why the Class Failed." In those revolutionary times, Ottinger had been reading Jerry Farber's book, The Student as Nigger, and had come to believe that his students had become "authority addicts," slaves to the power of the educational system. In response, he decided to hand all classroom authority to his students, allowing them to direct their own discussions and to write papers on topics of their own choice. After a few weeks of lively work, other academic demands began to usurp the students' attention. Discussion dwindled; papers became mechanical exercises. Having given up his classroom authority, Ottinger discovered that he was incapable of regaining it.

In Ottinger's estimation, the class failed abysmally in the responsibilities handed to it. In his letter to the class, written just a few days before the final examination, he charged that his students were incapable of learning, that they were interested only in having fun, that they had failed in a rare and glorious opportunity to acquire genuine learning. The solution, he believed, was to confer an A.B. degree upon students at birth so that only those interested in learning need come to college. Some twenty years later, a professor named Irenic M. Cross, teaching at a Christian liberal arts college, wondered if his students had changed at all from those of the sixties. His judgment follows.

Since much, if not most, of what I have said this semester has failed to penetrate the shield of your egocentrism, let me make this clear at the outset. This class has been an unmitigated failure. Why? Because *you* have failed. Failed yourselves, failed your college, failed the urgent needs of this age in which, regrettably, you find yourselves—incapable of offering anything at all to it.

That, ladies and gentlemen of the class of epic yuppiedom, is a thesis statement, something else you have failed to learn, but probably the least important. A thesis, may I remind you for the thousandth time, is something you believe, something you set down as true. Remember? Probably not. I've seen precious few in your papers as you wander aimlessly about like a computer off the wire. There's a term you will recognize—a term as superficial, as transient, as most of your ideas.

Some of your papers were real winners, dredging up such moldy topics as the illegalities of college recruiting of athletes, Christians in sports, and, of course, that weary topic: the dangers or the safety (depending upon your parents' beliefs) of nuclear power. When we talked about ethics, the right and wrong of a thing, your faces fell blank. When we talked about literary analysis, writing about ideas instead of events, your eyes locked in a drugged stupor. Ideas? Where can you buy them? Right here, but you never paid your dues.

So I sit here in my office preparing a final exam for you. I wonder why. You have all failed. That is my thesis. Will the exam be proof of it? Probably not. You are the bright young generation, schooled like chimpanzees in the art of arranging ciphers and making the appropriate noises at the appropriate times. Like exam time. You will, no doubt, pass this exam. The thesis is nonetheless true. You have failed in ways you won't understand because they can't be added in a row like the bank accounts you hotly anticipate.

Here in my office are testaments to what I wanted to teach you—to have you learn. When I tried, I confronted the insuperable wall of indifference.

On one wall of my office hangs a photograph of a Vietnamese orphan. She is about four years old, blind, wearing a dress that barely covers her nakedness. The dress is more a bundle of rags strung together. A soldier holds her in his arms. He also is filthy. He wears a bush hat; his fatigues lie wetly against the sweat of his body. Behind the soldier and the girl rises the ruined hulk of an orphanage, one wing shattered by mortar fire, the jungle rising behind it like a dark mouth.

I was that soldier, but I wanted to make that girl your child.

I keep the picture because it contains one of the lessons I wanted to teach you: "The poor you have always with you." What are you going to do about it?

I'm afraid I know the answer. You'll click the doors of your BMWs in the morning, glide to your place of "work," receive admirable—in your perverted view—paychecks, and write quarterly checks to some church charity. Like the creature in Robinson's poem "Karma," you'll fish "a dime for Jesus who had died for men."

Here's one lesson you have failed, then. You have failed the needy. Failed to acquaint yourselves with servanthood. Failed to cast your lives in terms of "what can I do" instead of "what can I make."

But you protest. "I can supply jobs through the business I plan to own/take over/inherit." Great! Really great. And who are you going to hire? Other bright young yuppies like yourselves. What about those incapable of working? What about the destitute, the starving, the streetpeople? Those whom Gwendolyn Brooks calls "the noxious needy ones"? Will you sell them your products—your chromium-plated automatic five-speed doodads? Somehow, I really don't know how, you've grown with hearts of stone rather than hearts of servants.

There is another picture on my office wall. This one is of a child, by a child. Curious isn't it? "A child shall lead them." But you forget the children. You are all so perfectly *adult*. So thoroughly grown-up. You started this route with two years of preschool before kindergarten. You were lost by the second grade, when a teacher placed your wobbly little fingers that never had time to play with toys upon the keys of an Apple Computer. Is our current attitude toward children, toward the unborn and the barely born, really any wonder? Childhood is the bad thing you can't wait to grow out of. You have had no time to be children. You have killed childhood in your mad rage to be grown up. You are always in a hurry. As Thoreau said, "You start digging your graves the day you're born."

I realize that you've never heard of Thoreau, or Gwendolyn Brooks, or E. A. Robinson. You've been too busy playing computer games or reading stock market reports. I see you reading *that* journal in the coffee shop. But I'll quote them anyway in hope that some word or two will slip through a crack in your understanding and momentarily foul up the gears. It might even make you think. Horrors!

This second picture on my office wall has a scrawl of orange and green lines. If you look carefully you can make out a nose and eyes. And see, there is a mouth, laughing. Yes, it's supposed to be a picture of a girl laughing. Her hands, even if they seem to come from the top of her head, are raised in joy. The child who drew it told me that. She was three at the time. And she made some marks that are supposed to be words at the bottom of the drawing. She told me what they mean: "I love Jesus."

If your first failure is the lesson of servanthood, here is the second lesson you have failed: love.

Remember the second day of class? I'm sure you don't because you have no notes for it. That was the day I refused to let you take notes. All I saw was a sea of bowed heads, bent before the altar of facts. "Stop writing," I said. "I want to work with your minds, not my mouth." One of you smiled. A light flickered. Most of you, my perfect Doonesbury class, bent back to your pads and copied down what I had just said. No, it won't be on the final, in response to the question you inevitably ask to distinguish important from dismissible information. It won't be on the final because it isn't important. It applies to your hearts, and you don't have any. Only a hard muscle there that keeps pumping blood because you exercise it on the Nautilus three times a week, forty minutes at a stretch. Just one more routine.

Routines! Your lord is the clock. Both for the day and your lives. T. S. Eliot's character Gerontion confesses: "I have lost my passion." He was sad about it. You don't even care. Your second failure is a failure to love, to passionately involve yourselves in the needs of those who have no hope.

That's right. You need examples. "Case studies" you call them in the jargon of yuppiedom. Let me give you a few case studies.

Start on this campus. Last fall the Student Senate sponsored a Hunger Walk. Some twenty-five walkers, about .7 percent of the student body, collected six hundred dollars. Last week you had a food fight in the cafeteria involving a thousand students. I can't fathom it. The college president fined two dormitories three thousand dollars each. No sweat. It was fun. We need that in the spring. I wish he had fined you three thousand hours of volunteer work for Gleaners.

Another case study? Last fall there was a lecture on abortion and adoption. Twenty students attended. Last week a lecture on investment opportunities attracted ten times that number. You are pro-life? Whose life? Only your own, insofar as I can see.

And so, understandably, a third of the students on the campus are enrolled in some sort of business major. That's where the bucks are. The liberal arts are the departments of diminishing returns. Besides, you might risk learning something about life, instead of merely living, there.

College costs so much, you say. Big deal. Who said servanthood doesn't carry a price? Who said love is free? The strung-out hippies of the sixties spoke of "free love," only to discover there is always a price to pay. You're paying a far higher price learning how not to love.

Sure, I know your arguments. I read the newspapers, and I suffer through your papers. Indebtedness by college students rose from

$2,100 in 1975 to $7,900 in 1984. You have to get good jobs to pay that back, you say. You're only cheating yourself. In one survey, 84 percent of the students on a state university campus listed music as their first love; only 2 percent chose music as a career. Where do you go? Where you have prepared to go. Petroleum engineers in 1986 start at an average salary of $33,144; computer science majors at $26,172; liberal arts majors at $17,560. So from birth you prepare for your career. When do you prepare for life? When do you learn to love? Keep writing those quarterly checks, folks. It's the only thing you're prepared to do.

Yes, college costs a great deal. Probably too much for the kind of effect it has had on you, which is close to zero. If you came here to prepare for a career, you'd be better off at a state school. Better yet, borrow the money and start a business. Then you wouldn't have to bother with fossils like me worrying about all these nonproductive things like servanthood and love. Maybe we *should* confer an A.B. degree at birth.

If your first failure is servanthood, and your second is love, your third is thinking.

Oh, yes. You do make decisions. And aren't they difficult? Who shall I room with next year? (Never mind that it should be *whom;* some of you took notes on that and will catch it.) Whom should I vote for? What shall I wear? Which car shall I buy? Decisions. Decisions.

Robert Frost wrote in "Birches" that when he's "weary of considerations," he likes to let loose, get away for a while. Where do you get away to think? Your thinking is mental software. You suck in data and vomit it out at the press of a button called an exam.

Oh, but Professor Cross. The competition is so tough! So is life, and it takes a bit of reflection. I hope you find time for that before you start living it, because you haven't started yet. You've sheltered yourselves in your G.P.A.s and haven't dared expose yourself to thinking. That's a risk, and you're not programmed for risks.

I have this third picture on my office wall as I sit here reflecting on your failure. It is a picture of a unicorn. A student drew it for me once, tucked it inside her exam. It has one word on it: *Thanks.*

Unicorns, you see, don't exist. You, of course, knew that. But their existence is worth pondering. A TV ad, for a computer firm of course, has the slogan "What if. . . ." That's a question you don't dare ask.

You have lost your sense of wonder. You have lost the ability to dream. Robots are precisely like that—mechanical, incapable of wonder.

This, as I have pointed out relentlessly, has affected your writing. You're not bad writers; you're just so awfully safe. Like the computer you study options; never possibilities. Remember the exercise in imagery I assigned? How baffled you were. One of you handed back the sheet with only this written on it: "I can't do this." The pity is that you didn't care. Your minds can't fathom metaphor, simile, symbolism. Suggestive language to you means a dirty joke. Your minds wade in two-inch waters of data. Oh, but you arrange it nicely, all those neat, word-processed papers with Chek-Spell. Like yourselves, your papers are lifeless, skimming the safe surfaces of things. Your eyes go blank when confronted with the unknown.

This final picture on the office wall comes to my attention, for it suggests the greatest possibility man has ever dared dream. It is a poster of Aslan, the great lion of C. S. Lewis's Chronicles of Narnia. It has a line from *The Last Battle:* "The dream is ended; this is the morning."

That is your final, most horrifying failure: the possibility of a life beyond this. Not only have you lost the ability to dream; you live only for today. To pass this exam, I would want you to live only and always for the resurrection morning, to live each day in this life as if it were the dawning of eternity.

It is time now to set this imaginary exam, which you have failed so terribly, aside. You have failed question 1: Do you live in servanthood? Question 2: Do you live in love? Question 3: Do you dare dream? And question 4: Do you live each day in the possibility of eternity?

That is the exam I would like to give. But I know the responses. I can see the panic on your tanned, smooth faces. The slight rustle of your coiffed hairdos as you shake your heads.

So I will ask the rote things your rote minds can comprehend, and most of you will pass. Pass on to what, I don't have the slightest idea.

And maybe that's my failure: I have given you what you can handle, have fed you the data you so desire.

Anyway, see you at the final. See you when the dream is ended. Maybe see you in the morning. And may all your BMWs last five years or more.

Discussion

1. How would you characterize the tone of Cross's letter? One way to determine tone is to study the language a writer uses. Does the language here suggest anger? sadness?
2. Cross suggests at the end of his letter that perhaps he also failed. In what ways would you say he has?
3. How would you summarize Cross's view of life? Is he simply romantic in his dreaming?

4. Analyze the style of his letter. It may be effective, but would you use it as an example of good rhetoric? What did the writer hope to accomplish by it?

Mr. Chips Couldn't Make It Today

John J. Timmerman

> *A prolific essayist and master teacher, John J. Timmerman is well qualified to comment on life inside the classroom. Professor of English emeritus at Calvin College, Timmerman previously taught at Grundy Center Junior College (Iowa), Grand Rapids Christian High School (Michigan), and Eastern Academy High School (New Jersey). Here Timmerman notes the rise in violence and disorder in the classroom, a phenomenon that began in the 1960s but continues to the present.*

Mr. Chips, to whom James Hilton paid an eloquent if sentimental farewell in his novel *Good-bye Mr. Chips*, had in a long career as schoolmaster and Latin teacher only "slight and occasional discipline problems"; he mellowed into pleasing eccentricity, repeating old jokes with impunity year after year, and moved into legend before retirement and into myth after that. Of course, the book was published in 1934, and Chips ended his career near the close of 1918—all now lost in the dark abyss of the irrecoverable past. When I read of the tribulations of teachers today, I recall Mr. Chips, musing at eighty on a tranquil past in which his harshest disciplinary act was the assignment of a hundred lines to a student who intentionally dropped the lid of a desk in class. How would Mr. Chips, a good man and a good and gentle teacher, fare in the Latin classes, if there are any left, in the violent schools we read about in the papers?

We usually associate casualties with football players, policemen, and the armed services. I have never heard of a clergyman trounced by a parishioner, a lawyer beaten up by a client, or seldom of doctors mending each other after being lacerated by a patient. During the past year, however, over 70,000 schoolteachers have been physically attacked by their pupils; one had her hair set on fire and some have died.

Teachers in some schools suffer from battle fatigue, and many sweat fear in classrooms, corridors, and playgrounds. At the same time, many Americans, including an hysterical journalist in *The New Yorker* of May 30, 1977, are violently angry because the United States Supreme Court refused to recognize proper paddling as a form of "cruel and inhuman punishment."

What does one make of all this? In the first place, after teaching over forty years in peaceable schools, one feels like an immigrant in one's own country. The stark and dramatic contrast between many contemporary schoolrooms and my own grammar and high school days almost defies belief. In my youth the student body was markedly different. At fourteen the disaffected and the stupid left school for the factory or the farm. The underachievers were flunked and the overachievers skipped grades. We all had homework and our parents usually hovered over us until it was finished. I saw more violence on the playground than I ever did in the classroom: the school pump was in regular use for rehabilitation.

I spent half of my grammar school days in a public school and the other half in a Christian school. Discipline was uncomfortably tight in both places; the ruler, the paddle, the stinging slap were in infrequent but always in potential use. Teachers were not worried about bruising the egos of smart alecks. My third-grade teacher, a Miss Graham, was a real cracker. When I was in the seventh grade, half a dozen older boys tossed a lavishly dressed sissy in a sizable barnyard puddle. After recess the six boys were ordered to the front of the class, made to bend over, then soundly whacked. In a high school chapel, a minister given to lengthy and inexplicable pauses saw a boy laughing in the front row; he reached out and smacked him soundly in the face (you could feel it burn) and then calmly went on with his speech and pauses. If discipline was reported at home, more usually followed.

The parents, whether they supported Christian or public schools, believed in orderly classrooms and refused to tolerate disruptive behavior. The children and the administration feared the parents, who feared nobody. Today, as someone said, the administration fears the parents, the parents fear the children, and the children fear nobody. Authority was genuine. I remember no unjustified punishment and no discernible damage. We didn't always love our teachers, but we had to behave and we did learn. The idea of attacking a teacher was simply unimaginable, though we sometimes felt like it. How we felt was largely irrelevant to what we had to do: the parents, the public, and the school system made sure we did it, and because of that ordinary teachers could survive and gifted ones could make a lasting impression.

In such a lost world paddling made sense. In contemporary schools supported by a unified community with similar values it still does. I assume, of course, that the paddling is administered in the proper place, in a proper amount, by a teacher who finds it disagreeable but effective. Is there really anything in this that common sense or the Scriptures can fault? I am old-fashioned enough to believe in punishment as well as rehabilitation, and naive enough to think that the former may promote the latter. I have no sympathy with sentimentalists who weep over the hard treatment of toughs who beat up old women. I don't believe one can attribute all viciousness to insanity. I know a man whom no one considers insane who tied up my former neighbor Alice and then attached her to the back of his car and drove off dragging her over a block. My wife and I saw her bloody face and battered body. What does he deserve? A psychiatric hospital or forty stripes? He got neither.

On the other hand, to suggest paddling as a disciplinary measure in classrooms, corridors, and playgrounds which exhibit the violence portrayed in the media would be dangerous indeed. Such schools are supported by communities which are writhing under the complex burden of Pandora's box opened in the 1960s: romantic individualism; eroded or nonexistent Christian values; alcoholism and drug abuse among the young; overdue rectification of racial discrimination; parental absenteeism; permissiveness, crookedness, and sexual immorality at every level; raw violence on television and the films; widespread adherence to educational philosophies whose wisdom is alien to Christianity. It is a wonder to me that the problems are not more severe and that so much good survives in purely secular schools. It is a pity that so many teachers are in the eye of the storm, particularly when they have achieved professional competence, prestige, and pay.

The solution to these problems is far beyond my competence to find, but I should like to record a fact and offer a timid suggestion.

First the fact. For the last twenty-five years we lived across the street from the Oakdale Christian School in Grand Rapids, from which our four children were graduated. I saw this neighborhood change from white middle American to half black and half white, now becoming increasingly black. Neither the changing character of the community nor the taut pressures of the late sixties dimmed the vision or witness of this school. Instead of flight there has been adaptation, and a steady evolution into a multi-racial student body. Through love, persistent innovation, competent teaching, fairness, and faith, the initial tensions in the student body were relaxed, so that the student body is simply Oakdale Christian, supported by parents of various races devoted to sound learning and living according to the law of our Lord. This school is to us a witness to the grace of God and the loyalty of his servants. It is a good school and it is a good Christian school.

The suggestion, I fear, may strike the readers who have survived up to this point as simplistic and unpalatable. No schoolroom can function without order; the order may be loosely and creatively structured, but it must be present. The final responsibility for such order rests, I believe, on the parents. Children do not belong to the state; neither are they the final responsibility of the state. Teachers cannot be psychologists, policemen, and servants of the juvenile court as well as masters of subject matter and normally successful methods of teaching it. Persistently disruptive students should be banned from the schools until parents and society make them fit to profit from them.

Discussion

1. List the attributes of the best teacher you have ever had. Is discipline among the list of traits? Why or why not?
2. Do you agree with Timmerman that paddling is appropriate in given situations?
3. One of the problems of the schools, according to Timmerman, is romantic individualism. What do you think he means by this?
4. Does every person have a right to education? Respond to the assertion made in the last sentence of the essay.

Long-Distance Compliments (from Father to Son)

Sietze Buning

> *Education requires us to look backward as well as
> forward, to see who we have been as well as who we
> want to be. For many of us that means an examination
> of our ethnic heritage, an exploration of the culture of
> our parents and grandparents, many of whom may
> have been immigrants or lived in immigrant
> communities. Sietze Buning recreates the joys and
> foibles of one such community—the Iowa Dutch—in
> his* Purpaleanie and Other Permutations. *This poem
> presents a typical split between generations as it
> records conversations between a father in the
> community and a son who has left the community to
> make his fortune in the world.*

I.
Ja, is it really worth it
that we make the trip
for commencement?
Couldn't you just as well
graduate by yourself
and then we will celebrate
when you get home?

II.
Sorry we couldn't be there today
for your wedding.
Why didn't you get married closer by?
Congratulations anyway.
And take good care of her, Sietze,

but don't forget
she can do that pretty well for herself too.

III.
Sietze, you mean it?
You read the sermon today?
And you only a deacon yet, Sietze.
I'm prouder of you now than when you got
married and when you graduated. I'm as proud
as my father was of me when I read my first sermon.
But Sietze,
did you remember
to change your voice
for the prayer? Sietze?
Sietze, are you there?
Sietze!

IV.
Congratulations, Sietze, on your doctor's title.
What is your book called again?
Say it slow so Mother can write it down.
A Linguistic Analysis of Words Referring to Monsters—
In what was that again?
How do you spell it?
B-E-O-W-U-L-F-
—In Beowulf.
Could you please send two-three copies?
So many people want to read it,
like Aunt Alice and Aunt Lyda and Aunt Gertie
and Art and Rodney
and Dominie and all the highschool teachers
and, of course, we too.
Could you maybe send four-five?

V.
Ja, is it really worth it
that we make the trip
for your university commencement?
We didn't go to your college commencement either?
Could you just as well graduate
with your own family there
and then next month we will come
and celebrate.

VI.
You took the job at Calvin College?
Congratulations!
You'll be teaching our own Covenant children.
I know you always say you can do the Lord's work
just as well at Florida State or Western Arkansas,
helping Presbyterians be better Presbyterians,
Lutherans better Lutherans, and Catholics better Catholics.
But you've got to admit
you're always more sure of your own kind though.

VII.
Congratulations on the baby, Sietze.
Thanks for giving him my name.
Don't forget the main reason
any Christian couple gets a baby:
that the number of the saints
may be full.

VIII.
You have a Fulbright?
And your whole family
will be in Amsterdam
for a whole year?
O O O poor you!
Amsterdam
is such a worldly city.

IX.
Seitze, Klaas got elected and I got elected,
and we were wondering did you get elected?
Congratulations!
All three of us are elders
in different churches and different classes.
Sietze, see whether you can get to Synod
because if all three of us got sent
maybe they'd put our pictures
in *The Banner.*

Discussion

1. How, if at all, does the relationship of the father and son shift over
   the course of the poem?

2. Describe the values of each speaker. What seems to be important to each? Do they share values? Do they differ on any?
3. Do you think that the differences between the two speakers are typical of all generations, or do they have something to do with the family's immigrant status or rural identity? Do you feel any such lack of understanding when you attempt to explain your college experience to your parents?
4. *The Banner* is a denominational magazine of the Christian Reformed Church. What does using this as a standard imply about the father's values?

His Path Is in the Sea

Lillian V. Grissen

> *For many years, depression has been the secret sickness. It is still difficult for people to understand. Even those who understand it as an illness sometimes tend to blame the patient for being sick. Christians, moreover, often respond with platitudes instead of empathy. Here, Lillian V. Grissen, associate editor of* The Banner, *and her husband, Ray, present an unusual picture of the suffering and healing of depression.*

Like the Old Testament psalmist, I have known hell:

> Day and night I cry out before you. . . .
> My soul is full of trouble. . . .
> I am set apart with the dead . . .
>   whom you remember no more,
>   who are cut off from your care.
> You have put me in the lowest pit,
>   in the darkest depths.
> Your wrath lies heavily upon me. . . .
> Why, O Lord, do you reject me
>   and hide your face from me? . . .
> Your wrath has swept over me;
>   your terrors have destroyed me. . . .
>   (from Psalm 88)

These words racked my soul thirty years ago. I can write these words today without tears, thirty years after hospitalization for depression—a nervous breakdown, as it is sometimes called. It was the lowest and longest period in my life.

My husband had been forced to take me and our four preschool children home from Nigeria, where he had been a builder for Christian

425

Reformed World Missions. Utter disgrace—I thought. I just knew "they," our colleagues and the doctor in Lupwe, wanted to put me away.

My suspicion was confirmed when I awoke in a Christian psychiatric hospital. How ashamed I was. How bitter. How angry. I wanted to hit everyone hard, but steel mallets pounded in my head and allowed me no movement. I had to lie still.

I awoke in terror. It wasn't a nurse I saw—just a mountain of pallid white, a moldy, ghostlike apparition. Like a medieval torture press, the walls of my room squeezed my head and even my body. God, why am I here? God, where are you? God, who are you? God, *are* you?

What I had feared for many, many months, even in the months preceding the birth of our last daughter, had happened. I had prayed so hard. Everybody knows that such things don't happen to people who are right with God.

But God didn't answer me. Where was this God anyway, when I needed him? And if he didn't answer my prayers, it had to be because I was not his child. I felt guilty because I was so sad and depressed. How ungrateful could I be? Everything in the Bible seemed to damn me. I didn't know until much later that God was there all along.

I wanted to die. The dark earth in which I would be buried looked like an ermine-trimmed, black-velvet sleeping bag. But I didn't dare die. Much as I wanted oblivion, I didn't dare face judgment. Even though I believed God had rejected me, I very much believed God was there and his judgment faced me.

The thought of personally appearing before a perfect God terrified me. He had already separated himself from me on this earth. I didn't stand a chance with him. Earlier the Bible had always been the light on my path and the comfort in my down moods. Now it only condemned me.

"Put your Bible away," my doctor said. "You don't know how to use it right just now. Put it away, and just keep your hands busy. This needs time. This didn't happen overnight, and it will take some time for us to work together on it."

Time, I thought bitterly. Time! Time! Who wants time? I dreaded long, sleepless nights. Yet I dreaded morning because it would mean I would have to live another day.

Shock treatments—not painful, but scary—terrorized me. They provided a few short, precious, dreamless hours of oblivion. But the depression always returned.

I Am Depressed. So many people say, "I'm depressed," at one time or another. But being blue is certainly not the same as being depressed. When you feel blue or down, you usually have a way to cheer yourself up: shopping, calling a friend, reading a good book, and, often, recalling favorite Bible passages.

The dictionary defines depression as an emotional condition characterized by feelings of hopelessness and inadequacy. Definitions are so neat, so manageable. They are so objective, so clinical. But when *you* are depressed, it's different. Depression expresses itself differently in different people.

I can speak only about what I experienced and fought for five years and suffered intermittently for much of my adult life. For me depression was

- being too tired to move my jaws up and down to chew lettuce.
- having recurring headaches that pounded like perpetually exploding bombs.
- crying hysterically at almost anything, even at the ring of the telephone or doorbell.
- trying to read and being unable to move my eyes past the first word.
- seeing and hearing my baby cry, but being too dull to give her a bottle.
- believing my children would be better off with a mother other than me.
- knowing that any woman would be a better wife to my husband than I.
- knowing that God wanted no part of me.

My years of psychiatric care included three extended periods of hospitalization, years of intermittent shock treatments, and countless hours of therapy with a Christian psychiatrist.

And was God there? Of course he was! God was always there, but I was too muddled to realize it. God worked through people to bring me back. He used three men in particular.

My Minister. Rev. Henry De Mots (now emeritus) consoled me often. In fact, he produced the turning point. One day, while I was hopelessly caught in a convulsion of despair, he sat by me quietly, held my hand, and said, "Lillian, did you ever believe you were saved?"

"Of course," I answered bitterly (the tone of most of my talking). "You know that."

He said gently, "Well, what makes you think God ever changes his mind about those whom he has saved?"

His question made sense. It was a tiny seed of life, planted in barren earth. But a hint of hope reached my soul.

My Doctor. The late Dr. Gelmer Van Noord of Pine Rest Christian Hospital was my psychiatrist and friend. Endlessly I cried, talked, ranted, argued. Patiently he listened, loved, guided. With professional tact he extracted my ideals, aspirations, disappointments, attitudes, faults, and shortcomings. He never judged me. He introduced me to *me.* He helped me and my self to get acquainted. He helped me to see who and what I am. He taught me to accept myself, warts and all, and to appreciate myself as a woman, a God-image, totally redeemed, new in Christ and fully free.

Indeed, God was there. God had made *me*—as I was and as I am. Skillfully my doctor taught me that I didn't have to be perfect to be loved by God and others. My doctor gave me courage to make mistakes. He taught me that God's reasons are so far beyond ours that we can't begin to understand them. He showed me that depression is illness, like diabetes or tuberculosis, not something for which I was guilty. He helped me understand that I had not chosen my illness. He also showed me, however, that I could choose whether my illness would make me bitter or better.

My Husband. God used my husband too—and continues to use him as a balance to me. My husband saw, long before biblical feminism became a buzzword, how important it was for me to be a whole person, a complete woman, capable not only of being a wife and mother, living and loving, raising children, and making a home but also of learning and thinking, teaching, and developing a career.

Through these three men God changed me. He changed me completely. I have learned to say to God, with the psalmist:

> Your path led through the sea,
>   your way through the mighty waters,
>   though your footprints were not seen.
>   (Psalm 77:19)

Today. I still don't always see God's footprints. But I know they are beside or ahead of me. Now I can follow, even when I don't see. Even when I am down—which doesn't happen often—I know God is wherever I am.

Today recovery from depression often comes more quickly. I have been on mood-leveling and antidepressant medication for the past seven years. It still hurts to hear Christian leaders say too easily,

"People think if they are down, they can take a little pill to cure everything." They make it sound as though doctors should not prescribe pills for depression. That's a mistake. One of the blessings of modern research and technology is the medicine that helps depressed people function.

Today many professionals and others, including many Christians, still argue about the "myth of mental illness." But its *misery* remains, for both the suffering persons and their families.

Today I write willingly about my illness. I am grateful to the Lord for changing me and for so enriching my life. In addition, depression, mental illness, nervous breakdown—whatever you call it—has too long been a hush-hush, taboo subject. People wait too long to admit their need for help. The earlier they seek help from the right professionals, the sooner most of them will function again.

Yes, God was there. I was just too mixed up to feel or see him. I learned that I cannot always see his footsteps. For his way is in the sea.

Toward Understanding Depression

Raymond Grissen

One engine of our plane had iced up and stopped. A few minutes later a second engine of the four-engine prop plane cut out. This trouble fits in with the events of the last few days, I thought. The words of the doctor at Lupwe, Nigeria, rang in my ears, "Take your wife and children back to the States. She needs more help than we can give her here."

The attendants wrapped my summer-clad wife and children in warm blankets as we prepared for an unscheduled landing in Newfoundland. Our lives are falling apart, I thought. Four preschool children. A wife tormented with devastating fatigue, headaches, and despair that made living a chore. Farewells to friends, white and black, whom we had learned to love. Giving up building, supervising, and teaching construction to young African men—a task that challenged me. Why does God let things like this happen?

At first I thought we just needed a vacation by ourselves, away from our busy children, away from everyone. But no. Not a vacation, the doctor said. She's sick, and her sickness will go right along with you wherever you go. I was to learn, slowly, that my wife's problems were deep, that they had been coming for a long time, and that they would take much effort, help, and time to overcome.

Learning Bit by Bit. Missionaries can't come home from Africa ahead of schedule without people wondering what has happened to them. Was it a disgrace? How much could one say about tiredness and headaches and feeling despondent? Would people understand? A few did, but more didn't. Talking about it rather than hiding it became possible after I had grappled with my own feelings and had accepted that my wife wasn't *just* tired and feeling blue. She was sick. Depression is *sickness*. It needs to be treated by a doctor, a psychiatrist. For her, especially because her depression included spiritual dilemmas, a *Christian* psychiatrist was a must.

I soon learned that her illness affected and controlled our whole family. (Readers wanting to learn more about mental illness affecting

430

families should read Jack and Jo Ann Hinckley's *Breaking Points*.) Several months of hospitalization required regular, almost daily, visiting. Visits were often tense, difficult, and short. Even family and friends were not comfortable around us. I listened to much well-meant advice—about cheering her up, about remedies, about rearing children, and about many other matters—and I soon learned to listen quietly. I had to make my own decisions, alone—many of them.

At times I grew angry; at other times discouraged, lonely, or just plain sick of everything. Especially when it took months to see any progress, only to see it disappear in a setback. But I learned to allow myself my feelings, and gradually I became more open and honest about myself, her illness, its complex causes—and the long road ahead.

Hindsight, of course, is always 20/20. We both say now that, had we known, had we seen ahead of time what we learned during her illness, some—not all—of it might have been prevented. We would have sought help *earlier* not only for some of the symptoms but also for some of the problems that had surfaced earlier in varying degrees. We could have been spared some of the pain and suffering had we been able to see or been willing to admit that people have problems that can potentially cause emotional upsets, nervous breakdowns, deep despondency, and depression. No two situations, no two illnesses, are identical, but the same God cares for us all. We don't mind running to a medical doctor with our aches and pains, but somehow we scorn or fear running to a psychiatrist for hurts and pains that don't show. We're too often afraid of what others will think. My wife and I felt that way too—until it happened to us.

The Minister's Contribution. Many ministers must learn—as I learned—that depression is sickness. My wife shared a room with another patient who also had tumbled into the black pit of despair. Intending to cheer her, her minister said, "No one has ever died from this." She replied bitterly, "I know. I wish I could." Equally disastrous is the well-meant advice to a patient to lay her burdens before the Lord to find peace for her soul. Preaching at a depressed person is not a prescription that profits. Does a minister comfort with a lecture a person suffering from cancer or diabetes? Hardly. Admonition, sincere though it may be, essentially denies that depression is illness. Ministers help best when they allow the person to be ill and not merely out of tune with the Lord.

The quiet, steady, non-condemning presence of the minister also provides a comfort that cannot be voiced. I recall our minister's response when my wife hesitantly admitted that she had quit praying because God didn't listen to her anyway. "That's all right," comforted Rev. Henry De Mots, "because we are all praying for you. That's what fellow believers are for." When an agonizing question pops up, a minister's solid insight is like a rope flung to a drowning swimmer. He can bless the sick person with a tug of strength as she flounders in the murky waters of self-accusation, guilt, and hopelessness.

Family and Friends. I learned early that everybody, absolutely everybody, gets "depressed" at times. Almost everybody has a remedy too. But depression as *illness* is not easily understood and even less easily accepted. Somehow you should be able to stop feeling sorry for yourself. You should be able to snap out of it. You should trust the Lord. You should count your blessings. You have everything; what more could you want? A most important first step for family and friends is to realize that depression is *illness* and that it harshly affects a person's whole family.

On the first day of our return, our friends John and Jean stepped in. "What can we do?" they said. "Will you take the baby?" I asked. They opened their arms and hearts, caring for our daughter for two and a half years. Relatives took the other three children, and help poured in. (We learned then how to accept help, and that in turn has taught us more about the art of giving.)

Depression scares people, and often they want to show concern but don't know how. A few notes may be helpful to some readers:

- Remember the family; depression is not an illness in isolation.
- Be up-front in your queries. Depression is an illness. If you don't understand, say so. Your sincerity counts most.
- Be sparing in sending get-well cards filled with pious phrases or books with instructions on positive thinking. A depressed person may not be able to handle them. A few sincere words of your own may help more.
- Call before visiting, and don't be offended if the answer is no.
- Allow the person to be ill. Moods can vary greatly. Keep your visit short unless the person clearly indicates otherwise.
- Dare to love. If you want to do something, follow your heart. The act may boomerang, but it's better having that than having not tried at all.
- Don't give up. It's hard to make a warm, positive impression on a depressed person (she's so convinced she isn't worth it). A small

thought or kindness expressed regularly may eventually get through.

Seeking Help. Most important, don't wait too long if you suspect problems in yourself or in your family. Not until that five-year period in my life did I realize how sensitive, integrated, and complex we are.

A thermometer can measure fever. An X ray can show a broken bone. A biopsy can reveal a malignancy. But no instrument can register the degree of fatigue or the depth of despair in a person suffering from depression.

The late Dr. Gelmer Van Noord, formerly director of Pine Rest Christian Hospital in Grand Rapids, Michigan, once said to my wife, "You can have a Cadillac intellect, personality, wit, strength, and ability, but if your battery is dead, you can't go."

He was right. It's strange, though—no one likes to think that even a Cadillac needs to be serviced occasionally.

Discussion

1. Describe the persona of the opening of "His Path Is in the Sea." What is the tone? How do those elements work for the writer?
2. Respond to the doctor's decision to keep the author from reading the Bible. Was such advice wise? Isn't Scripture appropriate to all occasions?
3. Why does God allow such suffering?
4. Mrs. Grissen indicates that the dictionary definition of depression inadequately conveys the reality of the sickness. Are dictionary definitions ever complete enough? Look at a dictionary and see if you can find other definitions that are not as full as you think they should be. Next, try to suggest experiences or anecdotes that present a fuller picture of the concept you wish to define.
5. If, as Mr. Grissen suggests in "Toward Understanding Depression," you should not urge a depressed person to lay her burdens before the Lord, what should you say?

Jesus Will Give You Joy

John C. Blattner

"Rejoice always," urges Saint Paul. And yet we struggle
with this command to act out one of the fruits of the
Holy Spirit. "If we put on a joyful face when we're
crying inside, won't we be living a lie?" we ask. "Should
we rejoice when we don't have enough money for
tuition?" "Should we rejoice when we get the word that
our mother has died?" John C. Blattner, executive
director of the Center for Pastoral Renewal in Ann
Arbor, Michigan, addresses these questions by looking
closely at Scripture and at the emotions Jesus displayed
in his life.

Most of us, I think, find it difficult to picture Jesus as a genuine,
flesh-and-blood human being. All our lives we have seen Him portrayed as an austere figure in stained-glass windows and religious
paintings. In these depictions Jesus seldom smiles, much less laughs;
He never frowns unless He is exercising judgment; He is never seen
relaxing, conversing amiably with friends, greeting others with a
warm embrace. Instead He is portrayed as "holy": somewhat detached, aloof, almost other-worldly. The ethereal halo of light that
surrounds His head only adds to the effect.

It is easy to sympathize with the motives of the artists who render
these portrayals of Jesus. He is, after all, God-become-man. As such He
is unlike any other person who has ever lived; we do well not to become
overly casual about Him. It is perfectly right for us to relate to Jesus
with the utmost respect.

Even so, we should not let ourselves lose sight of His humanness.
Remember that the incarnation has two aspects. "In Him all the fullness of God was pleased to dwell," it is true, and by looking at Jesus we
see clearly what God is like. But it is also true that Jesus is fully man,
and part of the glory of the incarnation is that in Jesus we can see

humanity as it was meant to be. Actually, it is surprising to see how often the Gospels show Jesus "acting like a normal person." He displays authentic human responses to typical human situations.

For example, He rejoices at good news. When the 70 disciples reported their success in carrying out the mission Jesus had entrusted to them, Luke says that Jesus "*rejoiced* in the Holy Spirit" (Luke 10:21). How do you picture this scene? Do you see Jesus solemnly lifting His eyes toward heaven with a transported gaze, uttering a stately psalm of thanksgiving? The word Luke uses can actually be translated "jumped for joy." Try reading the passage that way: "In that same hour Jesus jumped for joy in the Holy Spirit." You may never have imagined Jesus jumping for joy, but that is what Luke says He did.

Jesus also experienced sorrow: "And when He drew near and saw the city He *wept* over it" (Luke 19:41). When a leper approached Him and asked Jesus to heal him, Mark notes that Jesus was "moved with *pity*" (Mark 1:41). When the Pharisees balked at His healing the man with the withered hand, "He looked at them with *anger, grieved* at their hardness of heart" (Mark 3:5). When He contemplated His imminent betrayal, suffering and death, John says, "He was *troubled in spirit*" (John 13:21). Joy, sorrow, compassion, anger: in any number of situations, we see the Christ who was truly man respond in a natural, authentic human manner.

Sometimes Christians have made the mistake of thinking that they should somehow rise above their emotions, like the ancient Stoics. But Christianity has never been opposed to human feelings. Our emotions were created by God; they were part of what He saw in us when He proclaimed His creation "very good." As we grow in maturity in our Christian life, we should find our emotions helping us respond properly to God's grace rather than disappearing or ceasing to influence us.

Many Christians today seem to be less in danger of becoming Stoics than of being dominated by their emotions. Our feelings, we are told, represent our true identity; they are our surest guides to self-realization and authentic behavior. Far from despising or repressing our emotions, we are encouraged to focus on them, to stir them up, to give them free reign in our lives.

We have already discussed how this distorted view of the role of emotions can cause confusion when we try to understand the fruit of the Spirit. We tend to see the list of character traits in Galatians 5:22–23 as emotions that the Holy Spirit will produce in us. Thus we find ourselves worrying about whether we *feel* loving or peaceful or joyful, rather than whether our thoughts, speech and actions are in accord with the character of Jesus.

God does not want us to be afraid of our emotions, nor does He want us to be dominated by them. Rather He wants our emotions to serve us the way they served Jesus, by becoming a natural and spontaneous part of an authentic human response to situations that confront us.

This means that we ought to experience the right emotion at the right time. Paul, writing to the Corinthians, said that love "does not rejoice at wrong, but rejoices in the right" (1 Cor. 13:6). Love *rejoices*—emotion plays a part—but it rejoices in the right way, at the right time, for the right reason. The obvious inference is that rejoicing will be out of place in some situations. As we grow to maturity as children of God, we will find our emotions becoming increasingly integrated into an *appropriate* response to a given situation.

All this theory of how our emotions should work looks good on paper, but how can we get it to happen in real life? Granted, it would be nice if we always experienced the right emotion at the right time, but how can we help what we feel? Feelings are things we either have or don't have. Some days we feel happy and other days we feel sad and we don't really know why we feel the way we do. How can we gain control over our feelings?

We need first to understand a subtle but important distinction concerning our emotions. The distinction is between *reaction* and *response*. A reaction is what happens inside us apart from our control: someone insults us and, without thinking about it or deciding to do it, we get angry. A response is what we decide to do with our reaction: ignore the insult, perhaps—or, alternatively, punch the other person in the nose.

Usually we tend to think that the reaction determines the response: I feel angry, and so I either respond in anger or I overcome the anger and remain calm; I feel afraid, and so I either run away or overcome the fear and stay put. But it can also work the other way around: our response can shape our reaction. By deciding to act calmly I begin to feel calm; by deciding to act bravely I begin to feel courageous.

It works the same way with joy; in fact, that is what Paul was talking about in 1 Corinthians 13:6. He did not say love was supposed to "feel happy" at the right and "feel unhappy" at the wrong. He talked not about our reaction but about our response: we are to "rejoice" in the right. "Rejoice" is an active verb, it is something we *do*. As we consistently rejoice in the right, we will find in time that we also come to "feel happy" in it, too. Our reaction will be shaped by our response.

Interestingly enough, we can see this principle at work most clearly in some scriptural examples having to do with sorrow. Sorrow, grief, mourning: these are responses to pain or misfortune.

They are the opposite of joy. Now many Christians, who have heard they are supposed to be "joyful," conclude that they are never supposed to be sorrowful: that grief or mourning are somehow incompatible with being a Christian. But this is not the case.

In the eleventh chapter of his Gospel, the apostle John tells the story of the raising of Lazarus. Jesus, you recall, has been summoned to Lazarus' sickbed, but by the time he arrives Lazarus has died.

"When Jesus saw her [Mary] weeping, and the Jews who came with her also weeping, He was deeply moved in spirit and troubled; and He said, 'Where have you laid him?' They said to Him, 'Lord, come and see.' Jesus wept" (John 11:33–35).

Jesus wept. We have already seen other instances in which Jesus displayed the whole gamut of human emotions, so we are not particularly surprised to see Him weep. His friend is dead; naturally He is sorrowful.

And yet . . . look back to the beginning of the story: "He said to them, 'Our friend Lazarus has fallen asleep, but I go to awaken him out of sleep.' The disciples said to Him, 'Lord, if he has fallen asleep, he will recover.' Now Jesus had spoken of His death, but they thought that He meant taking rest in sleep. Then Jesus told them plainly, 'Lazarus is dead; and for your sake I am glad I was not there, so that you may believe'" (John 11:11–15).

Long before He arrived at Bethany, long before He saw Mary and the Jews weeping, Jesus knew that Lazarus was dead. Not only that, He also knew that He was going to raise Lazarus from death. And yet He wept. Why? It seems odd to weep for a friend several days after you know of his death; it seems positively absurd to do so when you know he is going to come back to life. Why, then, did Jesus weep?

He wept because sorrow, at the human level, is an appropriate response to pain, and the death of a loved one—even when it is to be reversed—is painful. Even when death is destined to be overcome, death still represents a victory, however short-lived, for sin and the power of darkness. It still deprives us of the presence of a loved one. Mary and the Jews felt this keenly; Jesus, in spite of what He knew lay in store, felt the same pain and responded to it as they did.

I might point out, in passing, that this example is quite relevant to the way we as Christians respond to death. We often try to approach funerals as joyous occasions. After all, our Christian friends who die are destined to be raised from death just as surely as Lazarus was (not to mention, just as surely as Jesus was), and our certainty is no less real than Jesus' certainty about Lazarus.

But something is missing in this approach, and we usually sense it. For all our joy about the resurrection to come, we still experience the pain of loss and separation, and it is appropriate to respond to this pain with grief and mourning. Paul taught the Romans, "Rejoice with those who rejoice, weep with those who weep" (Rom. 12:15). That is what Jesus was doing in John 11, and it is right for us to do the same.

Just as mourning is an appropriate response to misfortune, rejoicing is an appropriate response to good fortune.

"What man of you, having a hundred sheep, if he has lost one of them, does not leave the ninety-nine in the wilderness, and go after the one which is lost, until he finds it? And when he has found it, he lays it on his shoulders, rejoicing. And when he comes home, he calls together his friends and his neighbors, saying to them, 'Rejoice with me, for I have found my sheep which was lost'" (Luke 15:4–6).

Notice again that rejoicing is an active response, not just an emotional reaction. Now when the shepherd first finds the lost sheep he probably does feel joyful. But the shepherd does not go to his friends and say, "Feel happy with me." He says, "Rejoice with me!" It is as if he were saying, "Come to my house for a party! Celebrate my good fortune with me!"

Sometimes it is right for us to respond in joy even when our reaction is totally contrary. In the book of Nehemiah we are told of the rediscovery of the law of God by the returning exiles, who have not had access to it for several generations. Upon hearing it, they realize that they have unwittingly been disobeying the law for many years and are struck with remorse for their sin: "For all the people wept when they heard the words of the law" (Neh. 8:9).

Now this may seem to us a very commendable reaction, and in many ways it was. As it happened, however, the day on which the reading of the law took place was the Feast of Tabernacles—a day on which the Israelites were supposed to celebrate and make merry.

"And Nehemiah, who was the governor, and Ezra the priest and scribe, and the Levites who taught the people said to all the people, 'This day is holy to the Lord your God; do not mourn or weep . . . Go your way, eat the fat and drink the sweet wine and send portions to him for whom nothing is prepared; for this day is holy to our Lord; and do not be grieved, for the joy of the Lord is your strength.' . . . And all the people went their way to eat and drink and to send portions and to make great rejoicing, because they had understood the words that were declared to them" (Neh. 8:9–10, 11).

Nehemiah did not merely tell the people to *feel* differently. Their rejoicing was active; it was something they *did*, making use of familiar customs of celebration.

This same principle can be of great use to us as Christians. For many years I was somewhat troubled by my own experience of Easter. I knew

Easter was the greatest and most glorious day of the year; I knew it commemorated the most stupendous event in the history of the world; I thought I should experience it as one of the most exciting and exhilarating days of the year.

It seldom was. For one reason or another, Easter always turned out to be pretty much like most other Sundays. In fact, sometimes I worked so hard at feeling exhilarated on Easter that I would become a little depressed by how ordinary I actually felt! Of course the problem was that I was focusing on my feelings, on my reaction, rather than on the proper response. I have since found that I do better to stop trying to "feel joyful" on Easter. Instead, I concentrate on celebrating it in the ways I know are appropriate—attending church, inviting friends and family for a nice meal, singing favorite resurrection hymns—and am much better able to rejoice in the resurrection and to enter into the full experience of Easter.

So far we have been discussing rejoicing as an active response which we make to particular situations. But the joy that is the fruit of the Spirit goes beyond this. This kind of joy is an abiding character trait, something that is to characterize us at all times. Paul was quite emphatic on this point:

"Rejoice in the Lord always; again I will say, Rejoice. Let all men know your forbearance. The Lord is at hand" (Phil. 4:4–5).

"Rejoice always, pray constantly, give thanks in all circumstances; for this is the will of God in Christ Jesus for you" (1 Thes. 5:16–18).

"Rejoice in your hope, be patient in tribulation, be constant in prayer" (Rom. 12:12).

James tells us that we are even to rejoice when we are undergoing difficulties: "Count it all joy, my brethren, when you meet various trials, for you know that the testing of your faith produces steadfastness" (James 1:2).

By this point we may be tempted to ask, as Nicodemus once did, "How can these things be?" What does it mean to be joyful at all times? How can we rejoice in all circumstances when we are also supposed to grieve in appropriate situations?

To begin with, the joy that is to characterize us is not something we muster up. It comes from the work of the Holy Spirit. "The kingdom of God is not meat and drink," Paul observed, "but righteousness and peace and joy *in the Holy Spirit*" (Rom. 14:17). This is, after all, what it means to say that joy is the fruit of the Spirit.

Beyond this, we can be people who always rejoice because we are people whose fundamental situation is good. We are in Christ. We are restored to fellowship with God. We are temples of the Holy Spirit. Our eternal destiny is secure and glorious, and our joy is simply an unchanging response to these unchanging truths. Paul told the Philippians to rejoice because "the Lord is at hand." He told the Romans to rejoice "in your hope." Our joy is always based on the truth. In individual situations, it is based on the truth that the particular circumstances are good; as a general characteristic, it is based on the truth that our fundamental situation is good.

This is why James can tell us to rejoice even in trials: not because the trials themselves are enjoyable, but because of what they produce in us. Besides, no matter how unpleasant our present circumstances, we can always rejoice in our unshakable hope.

I believe the Lord wants us to learn how to call upon these fundamental truths and rejoice in them. Feeling down? Rejoice, son of God! The joy of the Lord is your strength! Screaming children getting on your nerves? Rejoice, daughter of God! The Holy Spirit lives in your heart! Short of funds? Rejoice, child of God! Your reward is great in heaven!

The fruit of the Spirit is joy. As we learn to recognize the truth of our circumstances and respond to them with rejoicing, the Holy Spirit within us will be free to change us and make us into joy-filled people.

Discussion

1. Are we more than the sum of our feelings? Explain.
2. In discussing emotions, Blattner draws a distinction between reaction and response, suggesting that our response to a given situation can sometimes color our reaction. Does your experience bear this out? Doesn't this encourage us to be hypocrites?
3. Are there any emotions that Christians shouldn't display? This article emphasizes the range of emotions that Jesus felt, suggesting that his example gives us permission to respond similarly. One emotion that it doesn't treat in detail, however, is anger. When is it appropriate for us to be angry?
4. Reread the second-to-the-last paragraph. How would you respond to a person who would claim that this was a glib, superficial way of living?
5. Can we always guide and control our emotions? Or should we try? Imagine a dialogue between Mrs. Grissen, author of "His Path Is in the Sea," and Blattner on this point.

Writing Assignments for Chapter 14

1. The Templeton Address suggests ways in which "men have forgotten God." Write an essay in which you use personal history or

world history to illustrate a similar thesis. You might wish to read William Butler Yeats's "Second Coming" for a literary portrayal of a similar idea.

2. Write a letter to I. M. Cross in which you argue one of these two topics: "Yes, we have failed"; "No, we have not failed."

3. Write a letter to a hypothetical friend who is struggling with depression. In formulating your response to this person, draw on the suggestions of John C. Blattner and the Grissens.

4. Several of the essays in this section use personal experience to illustrate a thesis. Write a narrative in which you do the same. Chronicle an event that defines faith; narrate an incident that dispels a misconception; tell a story to make a point; but, whatever you do, craft your writing so that the significance of the experience is clear to the reader.

Rhetorical Index

Argument and Persuasion

Plato, *Censorship and the Nature of Art*   272

Bertrand Russell, *Why I Am Not a Christian*   76

Jay Van Andel, *No Silent Spring*   200

Allen Verhey, *The Death of Infant Doe: Jesus and the Neonates, Mark 10:13–16*   161

Exposition

Cause and Effect

Flannery O'Connor, *Novelist and Believer*   294

Philip Yancey, *In Defense of Pain*   259

Classification and Division

I. M. Cross, *You're Still Failing*   410

John Donne, *No Man Is an Island*   174

Arthur F. Holmes, *The Liberal Arts: What and Why?*   398

Virginia Stem Owens, *And the Trees Clap Their Hands*   252

Comparison, Contrast, and Analogy

Saint Augustine, *On Good and Evil*   139
Albert Einstein, *Religion and Science*   242
James C. Rettie, *But a Watch in the Night: A Scientific Fable*   205
John J. Timmerman, *Mr. Chips Couldn't Make It Today*   417
Lynn White, Jr., *The Historical Roots of Our Ecological Crisis*   192

Definition

John C. Blattner, *Jesus Will Give You Joy*   434
Thomas Howard, *On Evil in Art*   309
C. S. Lewis, *What Christians Believe*   85
Stephen V. Monsma, *Why I Ran for Congress*   116
H. R. Rookmaaker, *Letter to a Christian Artist*   316
Lewis B. Smedes, *Why Get Married?*   146
Nancy M. Tischler, *The Christian Reader*   302

Example

John Gardner, *Moral Fiction*   289
D. G. Kehl, *Have You Committed Verbicide Today?*   367
George Lakoff and Mark Johnson, *Metaphors We Live By*   355
Aldo Leopold, *The Land Ethic*   211
Kathryn Lindskoog, *Pure Poppycock*   339
The Living Word: The Bible in Translation   325
Henry Zylstra, *A Vital Language*   333

Process Analysis

Charles Darwin, *Natural Selection*   246
James W. Fowler, *Stages of Faith and Human Becoming*   96
Aleksandr Solzhenitsyn, *The Templeton Address: Men Have Forgotten God*   388
Cathy Stentzel, *A Quiet Conversion*   154

Narration

Annie Dillard, *The Fixed*   231

Lillian V. Grissen, *His Path Is in the Sea*   425

Raymond Grissen, *Toward Understanding Depression*   430

Henri J. M. Nouwen, *A Place to Stand*   177

M. Howard Rienstra, *Who Is in Control?*   109

John Steinbeck, *Profanity and Realism*   344

Walter Wangerin, Jr., *The Empty Manger: A Christmas Story*   378

Fiction

Hugh Cook, *Pisces*   218

Dorothy M. Johnson, *Scars of Honor*   121

Poetry

Matthew Arnold, *Dover Beach*   74

Sietze Buning, *Long-Distance Compliments
(from Father to Son)*   421

Emily Dickinson, *"Faith" Is a Fine Invention*   258

Emily Dickinson, *Two Ways of Looking at God*   114

George Herbert, *Jordan [II]*   353

Elva McAllaster, *Frater Ave Atque Vale*   314